T0233758

Automated Essay Scoring

Synthesis Lectures on Human Language Technologies

Editor
Graeme Hirst, *University of Toronto*

Synthesis Lectures on Human Language Technologies is edited by Graeme Hirst of the University of Toronto. The series consists of 50- to 150-page monographs on topics relating to natural language processing, computational linguistics, information retrieval, and spoken language understanding. Emphasis is on important new techniques, on new applications, and on topics that combine two or more HLT subfields.

Automated Essay Scoring
Beata Beigman Klebanov and Nitin Madnani
2021

Pretrained Transformers for Text Ranking: BERT and Beyond
Jimmy Lin, Rodrigo Nogueira, and Andrew Yates
2021

Explainable Natural Language Processing
Anders Søgaard
2021

Finite-State Text Processing
Kyle Gorman and Richard Sproat
2021

Semantic Relations Between Nominals, Second Edition
Vivi Nastase, Stan Szpakowicz, Preslav Nakov, and Diarmuid Ó Séagdha
2021

Embeddings in Natural Language Processing: Theory and Advances in Vector Representations of Meaning
Mohammad Taher Pilehvar and Jose Camacho-Collados
2020

Conversational AI: Dialogue Systems, Conversational Agents, and Chatbots
Michael McTear
2020

Natural Language Processing for Social Media, Third Edition
Anna Atefeh Farzindar and Diana Inkpen
2020

Statistical Significance Testing for Natural Language Processing
Rotem Dror, Lotem Peled, Segev Shlomov, and Roi Reichart
2020

Deep Learning Approaches to Text Production
Shashi Narayan and Claire Gardent
2020

Linguistic Fundamentals for Natural Language Processing II: 100 Essentials from
Semantics and Pragmatics
Emily M. Bender and Alex Lascarides
2019

Cross-Lingual Word Embeddings
Anders Søgaard, Ivan Vulić, Sebastian Ruder, Manaal Faruqui
2019

Bayesian Analysis in Natural Language Processing, Second Edition
Shay Cohen
2019

Argumentation Mining
Manfred Stede and Jodi Schneider
2018

Quality Estimation for Machine Translation
Lucia Specia, Carolina Scarton, and Gustavo Henrique Paetzold
2018

Natural Language Processing for Social Media, Second Edition
Atefeh Farzindar and Diana Inkpen
2017

Automatic Text Simplification
Horacio Saggion
2017

Neural Network Methods for Natural Language Processing
Yoav Goldberg
2017

Syntax-based Statistical Machine Translation
Philip Williams, Rico Sennrich, Matt Post, and Philipp Koehn
2016

Domain-Sensitive Temporal Tagging
Jannik Strötgen and Michael Gertz
2016

Linked Lexical Knowledge Bases: Foundations and Applications
Iryna Gurevych, Judith Eckle-Kohler, and Michael Matuschek
2016

Bayesian Analysis in Natural Language Processing
Shay Cohen
2016

Metaphor: A Computational Perspective
Tony Veale, Ekaterina Shutova, and Beata Beigman Klebanov
2016

Grammatical Inference for Computational Linguistics
Jeffrey Heinz, Colin de la Higuera, and Menno van Zaanen
2015

Automatic Detection of Verbal Deception
Eileen Fitzpatrick, Joan Bachenko, and Tommaso Fornaciari
2015

Natural Language Processing for Social Media
Atefeh Farzindar and Diana Inkpen
2015

Semantic Similarity from Natural Language and Ontology Analysis
Sébastien Harispe, Sylvie Ranwez, Stefan Janaqi, and Jacky Montmain
2015

Learning to Rank for Information Retrieval and Natural Language Processing, Second
Edition
Hang Li
2014

Ontology-Based Interpretation of Natural Language
Philipp Cimiano, Christina Unger, and John McCrae
2014

Automated Essay Scoring

Beata Beigman Klebanov and Nitin Madnani

ISBN: 978-3-031-01054-5   paperback
ISBN: 978-3-031-02182-4   ebook
ISBN: 978-3-031-00193-2   hardcover

DOI 10.1007/978-3-031-02182-4

A Publication in the Springer series
SYNTHESIS LECTURES ON HUMAN LANGUAGE TECHNOLOGIES

Lecture #52
Series Editor: Graeme Hirst, *University of Toronto*
Series ISSN
Print 1947-4040   Electronic 1947-4059

Automated Essay Scoring

Beata Beigman Klebanov and Nitin Madnani
Educational Testing Service

SYNTHESIS LECTURES ON HUMAN LANGUAGE TECHNOLOGIES #52

ABSTRACT

This book discusses the state of the art of automated essay scoring, its challenges and its potential. One of the earliest applications of artificial intelligence to language data (along with machine translation and speech recognition), automated essay scoring has evolved to become both a revenue-generating industry and a vast field of research, with many subfields and connections to other NLP tasks. In this book, we review the developments in this field against the backdrop of Elias Page's seminal 1966 paper titled "The Imminence of Grading Essays by Computer".

Part I establishes what automated essay scoring is about, why it exists, where the technology stands, and what are some of the main issues. In Part II, the book presents guided exercises to illustrate how one would go about building and evaluating a simple automated scoring system, while Part III offers readers a survey of the literature on different types of scoring models, the aspects of essay quality studied in prior research, and the implementation and evaluation of a scoring engine. Part IV offers a broader view of the field inclusive of some neighboring areas, and Part V closes with summary and discussion.

This book grew out of a week-long course on automated evaluation of language production at the North American Summer School for Logic, Language, and Information (NASSLLI), attended by advanced undergraduates and early-stage graduate students from a variety of disciplines. Teachers of natural language processing, in particular, will find that the book offers a useful foundation for a supplemental module on automated scoring. Professionals and students in linguistics, applied linguistics, educational technology, and other related disciplines will also find the material here useful.

KEYWORDS

automated essay scoring, automated writing evaluation, natural language processing, educational technology, artificial intelligence, AES, AWE, NLP, EdTech, AI

To my Dad, a physicist who likes a good story, and
To my Mom, a doctor who likes a well-written one,
With love,
Beata

To my family for their enduring support … and patience!
Nitin

Contents

Preface

This book grew out of a week-long course on automated evaluation of language production that we gave at the North American Summer School for Logic, Language, and Information in 2016. As anyone who has given a natural language processing (NLP) course for NASSLLI or ESSLLI knows, one generally expects early- or middle-stage graduate students from a variety of disciplines, or advanced undergraduates; some students are looking to merely familiarize themselves with a sub-field, others want to understand how things are done in the sub-field in a hands-on fashion, and still others who already have substantial computer science training want some help in understanding the current research frontier.

In an attempt to cater to all these different types of audiences, we wrote a book that can be read in different ways by different readers. In Part I, we provide an introduction addressing the first set of questions on anybody's mind when discovering a new field of endeavor—What is it about? Why does it exist? Where does it stand? What are some of the main issues? We aimed for an introduction that isn't too technical for people without much technical background, yet that would offer a reader with such background a new perspective that would not be commonly taught in a computer science, linguistics, education, or natural language processing course—a historical perspective that highlights the hopes and promise of this line of endeavor, along with long-known and more recently discovered challenges.

The paths of different readers through the book might diverge from this point on. In Part II, we address the eager newcomer who is ready to give this sub-field some more attention; we provide a guided set of exercises to illustrate how one would go about building and evaluating an automated scoring system, and the kinds of issues one is likely to encounter (Chapter 2), followed by a broader discussion of lessons learned (Chapter 3). A reader who wanted a glimpse and a taste, without having background in either computer science or linguistics, and without the intention of engaging with the research frontier in the area, might be best served by skimming Part III (Chapters 4–8) and focusing next on Part IV, in order to get a broader view of the field—inclusive of some neighboring areas—and moving to Part V for the overall summary and discussion.

If you are a reader who is already reasonably well versed in the standard machine learning material, is perhaps taking advanced undergraduate- and graduate-level courses in NLP, and is looking for a more technical orientation into the state of the field and the relevant literature—Part III is written for you. We consider different types of scoring models (Chapter 4), describe in detail the specific aspects of essay quality that have been studied in prior research—both those that cover a relatively generic construct of a good quality essay (Chapter 5) and those that were built to address more specific requirements of task or genre (Chapter 6). Chapters 7 and 8 discuss the implementation of a scoring engine and the evaluation of its performance, respectively. The subsequent Part IV, where a variety of neighboring fields are discussed briefly, might be familiar to this type of reader, and so, perhaps, are to be skimmed on the way to the summary and discussion in Part V.

This book is not intended as a stand-alone textbook that would take the reader with no knowledge of computer science, linguistics, NLP and psychometrics to the cutting edge of current research. We believe that some of the perspectives offered in this book would help teachers of courses in natural language processing who consider including automated scoring as one of the modules/exercises to supplement instruction. We also hope that teachers of courses in linguistics, applied linguistics, educational technology, and other related disciplines would find the material here useful for supplementing their instruction. The large majority of the work discussed in this book has been done on essays in English; we provide some pointers to work on automated essay scoring in other languages in Part V.

Finally, we want to say a few words on the typographical emphases we will use in the book. We will use small caps—like THIS—when an important concept is most fully explained; these locations are linked from the Definitions-in-Context section. You can track mentions of these concepts throughout the book using the index. We will use italics for local emphasis, and boldface to draw the reader's attention to an important statement or finding, as well as for tracking some chapter-level organizational elements.

Beata Beigman Klebanov and Nitin Madnani
August 2021

PART I

Introduction

CHAPTER 1

Should We Do It?
Can We Do It?

1.1   THE CASE FOR AUTOMATED SCORING OF ESSAYS

Automated essay scoring is one of the earliest practical application of natural language processing (NLP) to have been attempted, though not the earliest one. Speech recognition and machine translation came earlier—in 1952, with the Bell Labs Audrey system for speech recognition, and in 1954, with the Georgetown-IBM demonstration of machine translation. In both cases, the early systems, while able to illustrate the idea and inspire the imagination, failed to generalize sufficiently to make them practicable. The early enthusiasm, along with funding, dwindled down toward the 1970s, with a renewed interest in later decades, when the advances in computing technology allowed progressively sophisticated and data-and-space-hungry algorithms to be implemented and tested. It is only in the last few years that both machine translation and speech recognition are rapidly reaching sufficient maturity for a large-scale use, evidenced by widely used applications such as Google Translate and Siri.

The trajectory for automated scoring of essays shares some characteristics with other early NLP applications. The classic paper by Ellis Page demonstrating the possibility of scoring essays by a computer appeared in 1966 (Page, 1966), yet the technology of the time made actual implementation in a consequential scoring context costly and impractical. The technology caught up with the research before long, however, and automated scoring of essays in large-scale high-stakes contexts has been around since the late 1990s (Shermis et al., 2013).

In his 1966 paper, Page spent most of his effort not on demonstrating the technical feasibility of automated scoring of essays but considering the questions of utility and desirability of such an endeavor in the first place.[1] Indeed, the iconic status of the paper is due not only to the technical demonstration but also to the carefully built argument for automated scoring. While the specifics of his PEG scoring system may or may not be similar to what modern automated scoring systems do, his discussion is as relevant today at it was 50 years ago. Let us therefore consider the arguments in Page (1966) in some detail.

---

[1]Of the six pages in Page (1966), only one is devoted to describing the system and the results.

1.1.1   ARGUMENT FROM NEED AND POSITIVE CONSEQUENCE

> Almost everyone knows what students should do in English: preferably a daily writ-
> ing stint; at least a weekly theme. Each exercise should be carefully planned, and each
> should be returned to the student with extensive and wise comment, correction, ex-
> hortation, and encouragement, thoughtfully managed by a teacher who understands
> the student's fumbling progress from inarticulate solecism toward organized clar-
> ity. (Page, 1966)

In Page's day as today, this is generally not what is in fact happening. The described ideal would
be extremely time-consuming and laborious for the teacher. Moreover, not all teachers, especially in subject-matter classes, would know how to provide this kind of "extensive and wise"
comment that would help students improve their writing. Page contends that "English faculty
are 'appalled' at the poor English ability of incoming freshmen". Indeed, college faculty are
still unhappy about the writing skills of incoming freshmen: a recent survey of K–12 and college faculty found that "Educators reported students' general lack of preparedness for required
writing assignments. Overall results indicated that 53% and 57% of K–12 and college faculty,
respectively, reported that they disagreed that students were well-prepared for required writing assignments" (see Burstein et al., 2016, p. 126); similar conclusions are reached in Mezler
(2014).

Page's vision (below) must have sounded like magic in 1966; arguably, we aren't there today
either, but we hope to show in this book that some progress has been made:

> Just for a moment, then, imagine what the result would be if all student essays could
> be turned over to a computer, which would perform a stylistic and subject-matter
> analysis according to the general rules desired, and deliver extensive comment and
> suggestion for the student to the teacher by the first bell the next day. (Page, 1966)

1.1.2   ARGUMENT FROM FEASIBILITY I: COMPUTERS ARE SMART

> Most of the limitations people apply to computers don't really exist. You will hear
> that computers "only do what you tell them to do". This has a tinge of truth, but still
> it is a seriously misleading statement, since computers "can be told" to learn from
> their own experience and modify their own behavior. (Page, 1966)

These statements reflect early-day optimism for automation; Frank Rosenblatt's 1957 article
"The Perceptron—a perceiving and recognizing automaton" (Rosenblatt, 1957) was hailed by the
New York Times as "the embryo of an electronic computer that [the Navy] expects will be able
to walk, talk, see, write, reproduce itself and be conscious of its existence".[2]

Yet, at the time there were already demonstrations that showed that machines can do
better than the humans who taught them. A case in point is A. Samuel's program that played

---

[2]https://www.nytimes.com/1958/07/08/archives/new-navy-device-learns-by-doing-psychologist-shows
-embryo-of.html

checkers: "Enough work has been done to verify the fact that a computer can be programmed so that it will learn to play a better game of checkers than can be played by the person who wrote the program. Furthermore, it can learn to do this in a remarkably short period of time (8 or 10 hours of machine-playing time) when given only the rules of the game, a sense of direction, and a redundant and incomplete list of parameters which are thought to have something to do with the game, but whose correct signs and relative weights are unknown and unspecified. The principles of machine learning verified by these experiments are, of course, applicable to many other situations" (Samuel, 1959).

We are deeply inside the machine learning paradigm today, with more data and faster processing, shifting toward deep learning where the machine is no longer tasked with "only" optimally using pre-specified parameters (that represent those characteristics of the input that are deemed important for the target task) but with figuring out how to best represent the input in the first place, by representing and re-representing the input in a series of "layers". As we discuss in Chapters 2 and 4, effective automated scoring systems can be built using both the traditional supervised learning and the deep learning paradigms.

1.1.3 ARGUMENTS FROM FEASIBILITY II: DEFINE THE GOAL

What we have taken as our first goal is the imitation, or simulation, of groups of expert judges. How we reach this goal of successful imitation is not the central question, so long as it is reached, and so long as we can actually match or surpass the human judge in accuracy and in usefulness. In attacking the problem in this way we are clearly not doing a "master analysis" or generating measures of what the true characteristics of the essays are, as ordinarily discussed by human raters. Rather, we are content to settle for the *correlates* of these true characteristics.

To express this important distinction, we have been forced to coin two words: *trin* and *prox*. A *trin* is the in*trin*sic variable of real interest to us. For example, we may be interested in a student's "aptness of word choice", or "diction". A *prox*, on the other hand, is some variable which it is hoped will ap*prox*imate the variable of true interest. For example, the student with better diction will probably be the student who uses a less common vocabulary. At present, the computer cannot measure directly the semantic aptness of expression in context, or "diction". But it *can* discover the proportion of words not on a common word list, and this proportion may be a *prox* for the *trin* of diction. (Page, 1966) [original italics]

Page seems to do away rather quickly with trying to measure the actual thing—the set of all and only "true characteristics of essays"—or *trins*. Why is that? He explains:

Notwithstanding the wonders of the computer, we have to develop a strategy in order to tell the computer what to do. The difficult part is the development of this strategy. It is difficult because we do not really understand what the psychological components are in the judgment of essays. It is easy enough to get persons to expound authoritatively on such judgment, but the fuzziness and inutility of their thinking becomes at once evident when the effort is made to translate it into a computer program. (Page, 1966)

In essence, Page's argument is that we do not know precisely enough what human raters are doing to try to implement that. Some work on rater cognition has been done already in the early 1950s and early 1960s, for example in the context of the College Entrance Examination Board's development of the General Composition Test. Diederich et al. (1961) had 53 distinguished individuals from various academic disciplines and beyond (English, Social Science, Natural Science, Law, Writers and Editors, Business Executives) sort student essays "in order of merit", with no definition thereof, instructing readers as follows:

Use your own judgment as to what constitutes "writing ability". Do not assume that we want you to do this or that. We want you to use whatever hunches, intuitions, or preferences you normally use in deciding that one piece of writing is better than another. You need not even act as a representative of your field, since individuals in any field have varying tastes and standards. (Diederich et al., 1961)

Readers were also asked to write a brief comment on anything that they liked or disliked about the given essay, on as many essays as possible. For the study, a sample of U.S. college freshmen were asked to write essays in response to four topics as part of their homework. A total of 300 essays addressing 2 topics were chosen for the analyses, sampled so as to make sure that the full range of abilities is represented (using SAT Verbal scores to estimate ability). The researchers performed a factor analysis on the matrix of pairwise correlations among the readers, and identified groups of readers (factors) that represent five "schools of thought" about writing quality. Analyzing the comments made by readers who belong to the different "schools of thought", they identified five categories that were each prioritized by one of the groups of readers:

1. Ideas (including relevance, clarity, quantity, development, persuasiveness)

2. Form (including spelling, organization, analysis, coherence)

3. Flavor (including style, originality, quality of ideas, interest, sincerity)

4. Mechanics (including punctuation, grammar, sentence structure, phrasing)

5. Wording (including felicity of expression, comments on specific word choices, clichés)

It is based on such findings as the above that general scoring criteria have emerged (Deane, 2013) and morphed into scoring rubrics. These are explicit criteria set by, and for, human raters for evaluating essays. For example, in order to get the top score in the Issue essay-writing task on the General Record Examination,[3] one typically:

---

[3]https://www.ets.org/gre/revised_general/prepare/analytical_writing/issue/scoring_guide

- articulates a clear and insightful position on the issue in accordance with the assigned task,

- develops the position fully with compelling reasons and/or persuasive examples,

- sustains a well-focused, well-organized analysis, connecting ideas logically,

- conveys ideas fluently and precisely, using effective vocabulary and sentence variety, and

- demonstrates superior facility with the conventions of standard written English (i.e., grammar, usage and mechanics), but may have minor errors.

While these are fairly typical rubrics for a support-an-opinion-on-an-issue essay, the specifics of a scoring rubric, as well as its relative importance for the overall score, may vary depending on the specifics of the task.

In the current practice of automated scoring of standardized tests, developers of a scoring system often need to provide a *construct validity argument* in order to show that what the system is measuring is actually aligned with the *writing construct*—the actual set of writing skills that the test is supposed to measure, as set forward in the scoring rubric. We discuss the notion of validity at length in Chapter 8.

Some of the human-oriented scoring rubrics are specific enough for a reasonably direct implementation: misspellings, specific grammar or punctuation errors, the extent to which a writer varies syntactic structure across the essay's many sentences. It might be the case that the system would miss some grammar errors and declare an error where there is none, but a grammar assessment system can be built for identifying specific, observable instances of errors that a human reader such as one focused on mechanics would be likely to pick upon, as well.

For other parts of a rubric, a more complex process might be needed. First, one might need to drill down and articulate a reliable guideline for humans to assess that particular aspect of the essay. Second, ask human readers to annotate a substantial enough number of essays using the guidelines to make machine learning from those annotated essays possible. Third, come up with automatically measurable properties of essays, often called FEATURES, that would provide information relevant to that particular target aspect of essay quality. This would be a mix between what Page called a *prox* and a *trin*, in that a particular, intrinsically interesting, aspect of an essay can be identified reliably by humans, and an automated system can learn how to approximate that particular construct. Such approaches have been developed for organization, for coherence, as well as for aspects of scoring rubrics that are more task-specific, related, for example, to narrative writing or to argumentation; we will discuss some of this work in Chapters 5 and 6.

Finally, for some parts of the rubric, it is not clear exactly how to reliably translate the relevant aspect of the writing construct into annotation guidelines, and so *proxes* might be employed. For example, consider Page's argument for capturing "diction" (appropriate word choice) through word frequency—a writer who can use many different words, including rarer and often semantically nuanced ones, is likelier to make precise word choices than a writer who uses a more limited vocabulary. Another example is essay length; while length itself is not part of the scoring rubric, an argument can be made that a goal such as "develops the position fully" or "conveys ideas fluently" can hardly be achieved without actually putting more than a bare minimum of words on the page. To quote Mozart's famous reply to the Emperor Joseph II's complaint that his music has too many notes: "Exactly as many as are necessary, Your Majesty" (see Hall & Saerchinger, 1915, p. 124). Not every writer is a Mozart, but, arguably, every idea requires not-too-few-and-not-too-many words to be expressed in a way that would be perceived as compelling, persuasive, clear, and insightful. Approaches to capturing topicality or essay development through properties of vocabulary distribution, without human annotations of topicality and development, also belong to this category and will be discussed in Chapters 5 and 6.

1.1.4   ARGUMENT FROM QUALITY AND UTILITY: HIGH-QUALITY LOW-COST LARGE-SCALE SCORING

> We have begun by saying that *the basic evaluation* of overall essay quality must be human. But which human? If only one expert English teacher grades an essay, we know that the judgement would not be very dependable. We know that other judges will reach a somewhat different conclusion, and even the same judge, if he were grading again, would probably shift his evaluation. [...] On the other hand, when a group of independent experts have graded an essay, and when these grades are averaged, this average has a rapidly improving dependability. [....] What we have taken as our first goal is the imitation, or simulation, of **groups** of expert judges. (Page, 1966) [original italics, our boldface—B.B.K. and N.M.]

It might be possible to build an automated scoring system to emulate a particular human rater very precisely, but if humans tend to differ, all we will have done is learn to emulate the biases and quirks of a particular individual. Indeed, research has shown that individual raters may differ in *severity* (general tendency to assign higher or lower score) and even exhibit *bias* (tendency to give higher or lower scores to a particular group of test-takers) (Bachman et al., 1993).

Setting the target as a group of people rather than a single individual changes the picture substantially. While any two humans might disagree fairly often, human scores averaged over multiple individual raters are much more dependable. All other aspects of the writing test design being equal, T. McNamara & Lumley (1997) report increases of 14% in a dependability measure when moving from a single rater per item to two raters, and another 5% when moving from two raters per item to three. Moreover, while novice raters might be individually less reliable than expert raters, a group of novice raters who successfully passed a 30-minute training procedure modeled after the operational practice can achieve similar reliability to a group of expert raters (Attali, 2016).

In the context of automated scoring, it has been shown that human-machine true-score correlations, namely, correlations corrected using estimates of reliability of human and machine scores, can be very high—above 0.9 (Attali, 2013; Attali & Burstein, 2004). We further discuss evaluation of scoring systems in Chapters 2 and 8.

And here Page comes to one of the strongest points in defense of automated scoring:

> So it *is* possible to get reliable human judgement of essay quality [using a group of human experts—B.B.K. and N.M.] But it is extremely, prohibitively expensive and time-consuming when applied to any large-scale testing. However, getting a reliable human judgment is not too expensive for a *sample* of essays. If we can find a way to imitate, then, what the expert human judges do with this sample, and if we apply this strategy to a computer program for a huge number of other essays, we capture **high quality of judgment at low cost**. (Page, 1966) [original italics, our boldface—B.B.K. and N.M.]

Actually, it is not necessary to obtain group judgments for even a sample of essays, at least not for training the automated system.[4] An automated scoring system trained using *a single human score per essay* where raters from a large pool are *randomly* assigned to essays can achieve results that have very high agreement with an *average* human rater. Thus, using single-scored training data one can get the benefit of a score that reflects very well what a group of human raters would have agreed upon. **That is, as a single rater, an appropriately trained automated system can be substantially more reliable than a single human.** The main reason for this spectacular result is the tolerance of many machine learning methods to random noise in the training data—rater variability being one type of such noise. This dependability of the automated score is utilized, for example, in confirmatory and contributory scoring schemes, where an automated rater is used as a second rater instead of a human; we will discuss scoring schemes further in Chapter 3.

1.2   CHALLENGES TO AUTOMATED SCORING OF ESSAYS

Along with putting forward arguments in support of automated scoring, Page also addressed some anticipated objections to this idea, to which we now turn.

1.2.1   ANTICIPATED OBJECTION #1: ORIGINALITY

What about the gifted student who is off-beat and original? Won't he be overlooked by the computer? Not necessarily; not any more than he is now. The first problem is getting expert human judges to agree on which essays show desirable "originality". Assuming a reasonable amount of agreement, research (perhaps multiple-discriminant analysis) may then be conducted to discover what essay characteristics are associated with such agreement. (Page, 1966) [original italics]

---

[4]It is typical to double-score samples of essays in order to assess inter-rater reliability.

Page uses a kind of argument-by-reduction here—originality seems no less and no more subjective than the notion of essay quality itself, and so can undergo a similar kind of treatment that he proposed for the latter—use a group of experts to reliably detect original essays in a given large enough sample of essays (or perhaps even score all essays on the originality dimension, if humans can agree on more than a binary judgment), and then see what is special about them.

Under-scoring of original writing might be happening, to a certain extent, in modern automated scoring systems. Powers et al. (2001) found that use of extended metaphor and literary allusion was a successful strategy in getting an essay scoring system to under-score your paper. Addressing originality computationally is still work in progress, as of today. Some pioneering work has been done on comparing writing that is recognized as outstanding (through receiving prestigious prizes) vs writing that is "merely" good in the domain of scientific journalism (Louis & Nenkova, 2013). There is also work on trying to capture some more creative aspects of student writing, such as use of metaphor (Beigman Klebanov & Flor, 2013a; Beigman Klebanov, Leong, & Flor, 2018). Certain types of potentially original writing can be detected through the automated scoring ecosystem, though usually in order to be delegated to a human rater rather than to the automated essay scoring engine—formatting that suggests that the submitted piece of writing might be written in verse is one case in point.

Originality might be a desirable property in recreational and professional writing, as well as for some of the writing in the instructional context; it is less clear that originality is the best strategic choice when writing for a high-stakes test—even if your reader is a human. This is because original writing by its very nature runs a higher-than-usual risk of being misunderstood or misconstrued by a reader, so a cautious test-taker, especially one who is not a very confident writer, might decide to focus on making the essay clear and the argument easy to follow, rather than attempting an extended allegory that might or might not be understood or appreciated by the reader. Indeed, findings reported by Beigman Klebanov, Kaufer, et al. (2016) suggest that argumentative writing for a test, while sharing most of the rhetorical characteristics of writing for a class, seems to be somewhat more conservative as far as incorporating elements that are not typically associated with argumentative writing, such as rich descriptive detail or narration. Thus, the context of writing for a test—show that you can do it in a clear and unambiguous fashion that is easy to see, rather than show that you are a sophisticated writer and can engage a reader sensitive to nuance of thought and expression—might impact the student's choices in ways that might partially mitigate the shortcomings of a scoring system.

1.2.2   ANTICIPATED OBJECTION #2: CONTENT

> We are talking awfully casually about grading subject matter like history. Isn't this a wholly different sort of problem? (Page, 1966)

It is probably fair to say that scoring for correctness of content is a different sort of problem. A more precise statement would be that, depending on the task, correctness of content might be more or less well-defined and more or less important. If the task is such that content, or specific aspects thereof, are central to the scoring rubric, then, at a minimum, scoring features need to be built in order to capture the content aspect of interest; in other cases, a wholly different type of features and scoring models might be needed.

As an example, consider source-based writing—a common type of writing task both on tests and in high school and college. In such tasks, the writer needs to make reference to a particular set of texts in their essay. In an argument critique essay (such as the Analyze an Argument task on the GRE[5]), the student needs to critically evaluate the arguments presented in a prompt text, which is typically someone else's argument on a certain issue (e.g., in a letter to the mayor, a citizen is arguing for a change in a specific municipal policy). In a summary essay, one could be asked to summarize the main points in multiple source texts, and draw a contrast between them—this would be a fairly typical literature-review-style exercise. It is also possible that the student has to write their own essay but has to draw on specific source texts for evidence and provide explicit citations (e.g., PRAXIS source-based essay[6]).

In all of these cases, the scoring rubric makes an explicit reference to the need to incorporate material from the source text(s) into the student's essay. Still, the other parts of the rubric usually focus on aspects such as essay development, coherence, organization, vocabulary—namely, source-based essays still need to be readable and clearly laid-out extended compositions. Such cases can often be dealt with by introducing features that capture source-usage into the more general essay scoring models. We will discuss such features in Chapter 6.

In contrast, there are writing tasks that focus centrally on eliciting what students know, have learned, or can do in a *specific* subject area such as Computer Science, Biology, or Music, with the fluency of the response being secondary. For example, some spelling errors or grammar errors are acceptable as long as the desired specific information (e.g., scientific principles, trends in a graph, or particular details from a reading passage) is included in the response. In such cases, somewhat different design considerations come into play; we provide a brief survey of approaches to automated content scoring in Chapter 10.

1.2.3   ANTICIPATED OBJECTION #3: GAMING

> Won't this grading system be easy to con? Can't the shrewd student just put in the proxies which will get a good grade? (Page, 1966)

Indeed this is a possibility. Powers et al. (2001) asked students and faculty to write essays in response to GRE prompts trying to trick the automated scoring system into giving a higher-than-deserved or lower-than-deserved score. 87% of cases where participants predicted that the system would over-rate an essay were confirmed. The most successful strategy for getting a higher-than-deserved score was to repeat a good sounding few sentences many times, with slight variation. Bejar et al. (2014) showed that using unnecessarily sophisticated-sounding vocabulary could lead to a higher-than-deserved score for a fraction of low-scoring essays.

---

[5]https://www.ets.org/gre/revised_general/prepare/analytical_writing/argument/
[6]https://www.ets.org/s/praxis/pdf/5722.pdf

Generally, various GAMING strategies (or strategies for obtaining, through behavior that is irrelevant to the skill being tested, a higher score than one would have deserved for one's best good-faith effort) typically land on the system developers' "drawing board", so to speak.[7] In such cases, a solution to a particular gaming strategy is often implemented as an *advisory*, or a *filter* (Yoon et al., 2018)—a method that detects a specific type of attempted gaming behavior, such as excessive repetition, overuse of vaguely relevant generic language, inappropriate use of "fancy" words, or grammatical but non-sensical writing. Essays flagged by advisories often bypass the automated scoring pipeline and go straight to a human reader, who, presumably, will not get fooled. We will review some approaches to detecting gaming behaviors in Chapter 12.

1.2.4   ANTICIPATED OBJECTION #4: FEEDBACK

"So far, the work looks like grading, not correcting. Isn't the need much greater for correction and comment? Yes. And some corrections are a fair time away in the future. But others are practically ready now. In our recent symposium, we outlined the sort of feedback which could almost be programmed right now: John [we are told that using first names softens criticism], please correct the following misspellings: beleive, recieve. Note the *ie, ei* problem. You overuse the words *interesting, good, nice*; *then* was repeated six times. Check trite expressions. All of your sentences are of the subject-verb variety and all are declarative. Reconstruct. Check subject-verb agreement in second paragraph. You had trouble with this in your last paper. Title lacking. Do the following related assignments for tomorrow ..." (Page, 1966) [original italics]

Today a substantial amount of writing feedback, particularly about spelling and grammar, is incorporated into widely used text editors such as Microsoft Word, Google Docs, and Overleaf. Dedicated writing assistance software such as ETS's Writing Mentor®[8] (Burstein et al., 2018), ASU's Writing Pal[9] (Allen et al., 2014; Roscoe & McNamara, 2013), ETS' *Criterion*®[10] (Burstein et al., 2004), Grammarly's Writing Assistant,[11] CambridgeEnglish's Write & Improve™[12] (Yannakoudakis et al., 2018), Ginger's Essay Checker,[13] TurnItIn's Revision Assistant,[14] Vantage Learning's MY Access!,[15] Pearson's My Writing Lab Writing Practice Module and WriteToLearn™[16,17] typically go beyond grammar and spelling.[18] Such tools pro-

---

[7]In some contexts, a human rater scores the essay first and an automated system serves as a second rater; in such cases, responses flagged by the human as "non-scorable" would not even reach the automated scoring system.

[8]https://mentormywriting.org/

[9]http://www.adaptiveliteracy.com/writing-pal

[10]http://www.ets.org/criterion

[11]https://www.grammarly.com/

[12]https://writeandimprove.com/

[13]https://www.gingersoftware.com/essay-checker

[14]https://www.turnitin.com/products/revision-assistant

[15]http://www.vantagelearning.com/products/my-access-school-edition/

[16]https://www.pearsonmylabandmastering.com

[17]http://wtl.pearsonkt.com

[18]Writing Pal does not provide specific grammar and spelling feedback.

vide feedback on discourse structure (Criterion), topic development and coherence (Writing Mentor), tone (Writing Assistant (S. Rao & Tetreault, 2018)), thesis relevance (Writing Pal), sentence "spicing" through suggestions of synonyms and idioms (Ginger's Sentence Rephraser), and style and argumentation-related feedback (Revision Assistant).

Can we then put a green check-mark against Page's agenda for automated feedback, which "may magnify and disseminate the best human capacities to criticize, evaluate, and correct"? Alas, not yet; research on effectiveness of automated feedback on writing is inconclusive. In Chapter 9, we will briefly look at some studies that focus on feedback and discuss evaluation of feedback systems.

1.3   SUMMARY

In a classic paper from 1966, Ellis Page envisioned automated writing evaluation that would alleviate a teacher's burden and increase effective practice opportunity for students by providing accurate and timely assessment of student writing. Page argued for near-term feasibility of such a system using easy-to-compute approximations of elements of the writing construct, and provided a discussion of the design of such a system, as well as of its anticipated merits and limitations.

Page's thoughtful discussion can serve as a guide to making sense of much of the subsequent work around building automated essay scoring systems. Questions such as—Who exactly are we trying to replicate? How do we navigate the space of a subjective human endeavor? What kinds of writing tasks and writing strategies would be easier or harder to deal with for an automated scoring system? How can a system be built and used to reap the most benefits from automation yet to maintain strong validity for the specific use case?—underlie the automated scoring research agenda. In this introduction, we provided forward pointers to many of the chapters in this book, to show how the specific research discussed in the relevant chapter fits in the bigger picture of the automated essay scoring enterprise. Granted, Page has not anticipated all the issues (and so we pointed to many but not all chapters!). For example, issues that come up when a system needs to provide accurate and timely scores for *millions* of essays written in response to many different essay questions by a large variety of test-taker populations—namely, scalability and stability—only became apparent when such applications were in fact attempted (see Chapter 7). In addition, and having in mind a reader of this manuscript who learns best by doing, we included a guided exercise in building an automated scoring system (Chapter 2), which, we hope, will help the reader better appreciate the subsequent discussion.

PART II

Getting Hands-On

CHAPTER 2

Building an Automated Essay Scoring System

2.1 INTRODUCTION

In this chapter, we will take you, the reader, through the exercise of building and evaluating an automated essay scoring system on real data. Our goal is illustrative rather than definitive: we plan to use this hands-on exercise as an opportunity to highlight issues that must be considered when building automated essay scoring systems rather than to build the best possible automated essay scoring system using state-of-the-art techniques.

2.2 SETTING UP

Automatically assigning scores to essays is most commonly treated as a SUPERVISED LEARNING problem where we are given some training data (essays) with reference scores assigned by human raters and the goal is to learn a predictive model that can assign scores to previously unseen essays. Although there are other possible ways to approach this problem (see Chapter 4), we focus on the supervised machine learning formulation in this chapter.

In this section, we describe the various components that we will use for this hands-on machine learning exercise.

2.2.1 DATA

Over the years, a number of automated essay scoring datasets have been available to the community. The ETS Corpus of Non-Native Written English contains 12,100 English essays written by TOEFL®test-takers who self-identified as non-native English speakers.[1] Specifically, the dataset contains 1,100 English essays for each of the 11 native languages sampled from 8 different topics along with a score level (low/medium/high) assigned to each essay. This dataset is often referred to as the TOEFL11 dataset. Another popular dataset is the CLC FCE dataset which contains over 1,244 human-scored English essays written by Cambridge FCE (First Certificate in English) test-takers. For each essay, the dataset also includes annotations of grammatical errors as well as test-taker demographics in additional to the essay score.[2] Finally, the MERLIN corpus (Boyd et al., 2014) contains 2,286 human-scored English essays written by

---

[1]https://catalog.ldc.upenn.edu/LDC2014T06
[2]https://ilexir.co.uk/datasets/index.html

learners of Czech, Italian, and German that were taken from written examinations and eventually human-rated for various CEFR levels.[3]

For this chapter, however, we use data from the Automated Student Assessment Prize (ASAP) competition.[4] This competition was organized by the Hewlett Foundation in 2012 to foster the development of state-of-the-art approaches to automated essay scoring. The competition included a total of 8 writing tasks that were administered to students in grades 7–10 in the U.S. The responses to each task were scored by two human raters on a scale from 1 to 6. Each task was different, e.g., some required the students to use additional source material in their responses and some did not. We use 2 out of the 8 tasks for our exercise. Figure 2.1 shows the prompts for these two tasks which ask the students to write persuasive essays regarding two different topics.

Figure 2.2 shows the distribution of human scores for the Task 1 training set. Looking at this distribution, we see that all of the six score points on the scale are represented and that the distribution looks approximately normal. The first observation is important, since having a reasonable number of instances for each score point on the scale is essential to learn an accurate model from the data. The second observation also makes for a good heuristic to quickly check that things look as expected, since, in a large enough sample, most students are likely to be average writers. If the distribution looks significantly different from a normal distribution or indicates that there might not be sufficient examples for one or more score points, collecting more data might be a good course of action.

The ASAP competition organizers provided a training dataset, a validation dataset, and the final, held-out test dataset for download. However, the human scores for the validation and the held-out datasets were not shared with the participants or made publicly available. Since we need human scores for training as well as for evaluation, we will use *only* the training dataset for our exercise. We split it into three parts—one for training the model, one for development, and one for held-out evaluation. This type of three-way split is a standard exercise in machine learning experiments to ensure that the model training process does not overfit the data used for evaluation.

2.2.2   MODEL AND FEATURES

We plan to use a traditional feature-based machine learning system for the scoring system we will build in this exercise. While it is possible to use supervised deep learning methods to learn a model that can *directly* take raw essays as inputs—bypassing the need to explicitly represent an essay using specific features—and produce scores as outputs, doing so will not provide the same opportunities for useful discussions that we hope to spur as part of this hands-on exercise.

Specifically, we will use *linear regression* as the model underlying our scoring system. Our choice is motivated by the following: (a) Linear regression (or one of its variants) is the

---

[3]https://www.merlin-platform.eu/C_mcorpus.php1
[4]https://www.kaggle.com/c/asap-aes/

More and more people use computers, but not everyone agrees that this benefits society. Those who support advances in technology believe that computers have a positive effect on people. They teach hand–eye coordination, give people the ability to learn about faraway places and people, and even allow people to talk online with other people. Others have different ideas. Some experts are concerned that people are spending too much time on their computers and less time exercising, enjoying nature, and interacting with family and friends.

Write a letter to your local newspaper in which you state your opinion on the effects computers have on people. Persuade the readers to agree with you.

(a)

"All of us can think of a book that we hope none of our children or any other children have taken off the shelf. But if I have the right to remove that book from the shelf—that work I abhor—then you also have exactly the same right and so does everyone else. And then we have no books left on the shelf for any of us." —Katherine Paterson, author

Write a persuasive essay to a newspaper reflecting your views on censorship in libraries. Do you believe that certain materials, such as books, music, movies, magazines, etc., should be removed from the shelves if they are found offensive? Support your position with convincing arguments from your own experience, observations, and/or reading.

(b)

Figure 2.1: The prompts for the two writing tasks from the ASAP dataset chosen for our hands-on exercise: (a) Task 1 and (b) Task 2.

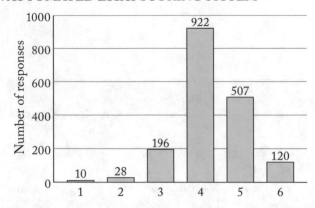

Figure 2.2: The distribution of the scores assigned by the human raters to the essays in the training set for Task 1.

model of choice for currently operational, state-of-the-art automated scoring systems (Burstein, Tetreault, & Madnani, 2013; Zechner et al., 2009), and (b) Since the actual model does not have a *huge* impact on the didactic goal of the exercise, we choose to use a more interpretable model for ease of illustration. That said, we will compare the performance of linear regression to another model toward the end of our exercise.

A linear regression model assumes that the human score (also known as the "dependent" variable) is a weighted linear combination of the numerical feature values (the "independent" variables). In our case, the weights (or "model parameters") are computed via "least squares" estimation—minimizing the squared error between the human score and the model prediction. For more details on linear regression, we refer the reader to Chapter 4, as well as to Freedman (2009).

In order to decide on the features to use for an automated essay scoring model, the most informative source is always the SCORING RUBRIC for the writing task that is to be scored. A rubric refers to a scoring guide that is used by human raters to evaluate the quality of test-takers' constructed responses, i.e., the essays. A rubric has three essential components: evaluative criteria, quality definitions, and a scoring strategy (Popham, 1997).

- **Evaluative criteria** are the aspects of the responses that should be paid attention to in order to assign them a score; examples might include: the organization of the essays (e.g., discourse structure), its mechanics (e.g., spelling), and word choice (e.g., vocabulary) among other things.

- **Quality definitions** describe how specifically to use the evaluative criteria to judge a particular response. For example, the rubric might say that a response must have no spelling errors in order to earn a perfect score on the mechanics criterion. In order to be useful, a rubric must provide quality definitions for each criterion and each score point. For example, if the writing task is to be scored on a four-point scale, the rubric must say how each criterion should be judged for each score point.

- A **scoring strategy** might be either holistic or trait-based. For a holistic scoring strategy, human raters must take into account all of the evaluative criteria but produce a single, final score for the response. For trait scoring, human raters must produce separate scores for different response traits (usually overlapping with the list of evaluative criteria) that may or may not also be aggregated into a single score.

From examining the scoring rubric for Task 1,[5] we see the following.

1. Responses to this task were scored holistically by two different human raters on a scale from 1 to 6.
2. The evaluative criteria for this task are "elaboration", "organization", "fluency", and "audience awareness".
3. The quality definitions are shown in Figure 2.3. While this list of definitions is a helpful guideline, it cannot possibly be exhaustive, i.e., it is not possible to perfectly describe every possible response from a specific score-point.
4. The scoring rubric explicitly says that errors in spelling, punctuation, grammar, and usage are not to be considered by the human raters when scoring responses.

Based on this information, we propose the following simple features that either directly or indirectly address one of the evaluative criteria in the scoring rubric and that can be computed using publicly available resources. Before computing the features, we use a tokenizer to split each essay into sentences and each sentence into words and symbols called "tokens". For example, a sentence such as "*I will be going to the market, he told her*". will be tokenized as "*I will be going to the market, he told her*". The tokenizer also separates contractions into separate tokens, e.g., "*I'm going*" is tokenized as "*I 'm going*".[6]

Elaboration

- WORDS: the number of tokens in the essay.
- LOGWORDS: the base-10 log of the number of tokens in the essay. Taking the log can smooth skewed distributions and make features work better with a linear model.
- TYPES: the number of unique lowercased non-punctuation tokens in the essay.
- LOGTYPES: the base-10 log of the number of unique lowercased non-punctuation tokens in the essay.
- AVG_WLEN: the average length of the lowercased non-punctuation tokens used in the essay.

---

[5]The complete scoring rubric can be found at https://github.com/desilinguist/aes-book-hands-on/blob/master/data/rubrics/task1.pdf.

[6]We used the **segtok** tokenizer available at https://github.com/fnl/segtok.

Score Point 1: An undeveloped response that may take a position but offers no more than very minimal support.

Typical elements:
- Contains few or vague details.
- Is awkward and fragmented.
- May be difficult to read and understand.
- May show no awareness of audience.

Score Point 2: An under-developed response that may or may not take a position.

Typical elements:
- Contains only general reasons with unelaborated and/or list-like details.
- Shows little or no evidence of organization.
- May be awkward and confused or simplistic.
- May show little awareness of audience.

Score Point 3: A minimally developed response that may take a position, but with inadequate support and details.

Typical elements:
- Has reasons with minimal elaboration and more general than specific details.
- Shows some organization.
- May be awkward in parts with few transitions.
- Shows some awareness of audience.

Score Point 4: A somewhat-developed response that takes a position and provides adequate support.

Typical elements:
- Has adequately elaborated reasons with a mix of general and specific details.
- Shows satisfactory organization.
- May be somewhat fluent with some transitional language.
- Shows adequate awareness of audience.

Score Point 5: A developed response that takes a clear position and provides reasonably persuasive support.

Typical elements:
- Has moderately well-elaborated reasons with mostly specific details.
- Exhibits generally strong organization.
- May be moderately fluent with transitional language throughout.
- May show a consistent awareness of audience.

Score Point 6: A well-developed response that takes a clear and thoughtful position and provides persuasive support.

Typical elements:
- Has fully elaborated reasons with specific details.
- Exhibits strong organization.
- Is fluent and uses sophisticated transitional language.
- May show a heightened awareness of audience.

Figure 2.3: The quality definitions from the Task 1 scoring rubric.

- `SD_WLEN`: the standard deviation of the length of the lowercased non-punctuation tokens used in the essay.
- `AVG_WFREQ`: the average frequency of the lowercased non-punctuation tokens used in the essay across all English books indexed by Google Books.[7]
- `SD_WFREQ`: the standard deviation of the frequency of the lowercased non-punctuation tokens used in the essay.

Organization

- `%QUESTION`: the proportion of tokens in the essay that are question marks.
- `%EXCLAM`: the proportion of tokens in the essay that are exclamation marks.
- `%CC`: the proportion of tokens in the essay that are coordinating conjunctions.[8]
- `%CD`: the proportion of tokens in the essay that are numbers.
- `%DT`: the proportion of tokens in the essay that are determiners ("a", "an", "the").
- `%FUNC`: the proportion of non-punctuation tokens in the essay that are "function" words, i.e., words that usually do not carry a lot of semantic content but indicate grammatical relationships (e.g., "of", "for", "the", etc.).[9]
- `%IN`: the proportion of tokens in the essay that are prepositions.
- `%JJ`: the proportion of tokens in the essay that are adjectives.
- `%MD`: the proportion of tokens in the essay that are modals ("could", "would", etc.).
- `%NN`: the proportion of tokens in the essay that are nouns.
- `%PRP`: the proportion of tokens in the essay that are pronouns.
- `%RB`: the proportion of tokens in the essay that are adverbs.
- `%VB`: the proportion of tokens in the essay that are verbs.

Fluency

- `%MISSPELLED`: the proportion of non-punctuation tokens in the essay that are misspelled. Although the rubric explicitly says that misspellings should not be considered for scoring, we reason this feature might still be useful since a large proportion of misspellings might actually be "difficult to read and understand", per the rubric.[10]
- `%REPEATED`: the proportion of lowercased non-punctuation, non-function-word tokens in the essay that are repeated at least five times.
- `MEAN_LM`: a numerical value indicating, on average, how often the essay contains word combinations that are observed in a very large collection of well-formed English newspaper text. We measure this using a trigram language model trained on the English

---

[7]We produced a list of counts of words in Google Books from the raw count data available at `http://storage.googleapis.com/books/ngrams/books/datasetsv2.html`.

[8]We used ZPar (Y. Zhang & Clark, 2011) to compute parts-of-speech tags where needed.

[9]We use NLTK's English stopwords corpus.

[10]We used the MySpell American English dictionary to flag misspellings that can be downloaded from `https://cgit.freedesktop.org/libreoffice/dictionaries/tree/en`.

Gigaword corpus.[11] More precisely, we compute the average log probability of each tokenized essay sentence and then divide by the number of sentences. Less negative values indicate "more fluent" essays.

- IS_NATIVE: A numerical feature with value 1 indicating that the person writing the essay is a native English speaker and value 0 indicating that they are not, based on the student's self-report included in the metadata.[12]

Notes:

- For this exercise, the organization features are rather simple and only capture the distributions of parts-of-speech. This category often also includes features that capture coherent sequencing of ideas. We will discuss some such features in Chapter 5.

- We do not have any features that address the audience awareness evaluative criterion. This means that our automated scoring system is not able to internally represent the same set of information that a human rater may use when scoring a response. Such a situation is referred to as "construct under-representation", where the term CONSTRUCT refers to the set of respondent skills that a test is designed to measure. The idea of a construct is important in automated essay scoring for many reasons and we return to it in Chapters 3 and 8.

2.2.3   EVALUATION METRICS

The following metrics are commonly employed when evaluating automated essay scoring systems.

1. **Pearson's Correlation Coefficient** (r), or PEARSON'S r, is a statistical measure of the strength of a linear relationship between paired data, i.e., given a sample containing data from two variables, it indicates how strong the linear relationship between them is. By design, $-1 \leq r \leq 1$; positive values of r denote positive correlation between the two variables, negative values denote negative correlation, and a value of 0 denotes no correlation. The closer the value is to 1 or -1, the stronger the correlation. It is important to note that in a given sample, the actual absolute values of the two variables do not matter as much as whether the trends in the two variables are similar, e.g., if variable A increases as variable B does, they have a positive linear correlation. Figure 2.4 shows images illustrating various types of linear correlations that may occur between the human scores and machine (automatic) scores in some hypothetical sample of essays. In general, correlation tells us more about whether there is a linear relationship between essay scores than whether the score assigned to each individual essay is correct or not. In addition to Pearson, the **Spearman's**

---

[11] English Gigaword Corpus (4th Edition), LDC Catalog No. LDC2009T13.

[12] We will discuss this feature in more detail later in the chapter. For now, we simply assume that it is available for us to use in the model.

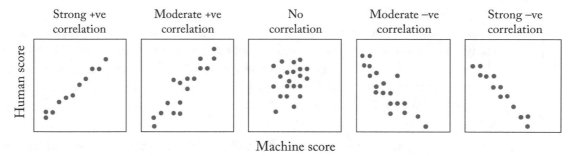

Figure 2.4: Images illustrating various types of linear relationships between the human score and the machine score. The values of the Pearson correlation coefficient will be closer to $+1$ and -1 for the strong "+ve" (short for "positive") and "-ve" (short for negative) cases, respectively, compared to the moderate cases. The Pearson value for the no-correlation image will be close to 0.

Rank Correlation Coefficient (ρ), or SPEARMAN's ρ may also be used to evaluate essay scoring systems. While Pearson's correlation examines linear relationships between two variables, Spearman's correlation examines monotonic relationships based on the rankings of the two variables.

2. **Cohen's Kappa** (κ), or COHEN's κ, is a measure of agreement where two raters (e.g., an automated system and a human) are rating items, such as essays, on a scale. It measures the agreement between the two raters *beyond* what is expected due to chance. By design, $-1 \leq \kappa \leq 1$. Positive values denote agreement beyond what is expected by chance, negative values denote less agreement than what is expected by chance (e.g., potential systematic disagreements), and a value of 0 denotes *no* agreement beyond chance. For automated essay scoring evaluations, a weighted version of κ is more commonly used since the scoring scale tends to be ordinal rather than nominal. For WEIGHTED κ, human and automated scores that are closer together are weighted higher than those that are farther part. For example, when computing **quadratically weighted kappa** κ_q, a difference of 1 point between the human score and the automated score would be weighted more than a difference of 2 points. More precisely, if we denote human raters as **H** and the automated system as **M** (for "machine"), the quadratic weight corresponding to a human score of H_i and a machine score of M_j is computed as follows:

$$w(H_i, M_j) = 1 - \frac{(M_j - H_i)^2}{(H_{\max} - H_{\min})^2},$$

where $H_{\min}$ and $H_{\max}$ are the ends of the scoring scale. So, for a 3-point scale, for example, the quadratic weight corresponding to a human score of 1 and an automated score of

2 (a difference of 1) is $1 - (1/4) = 0.75$ whereas the quadratic weight corresponding to a human score of 1 and an automated score of 3 (a difference of 2) is $1 - (4/4) = 0$. Essentially, weighted κ assigns partial credit to all disagreements *except* the maximum possible disagreement whereas unweighted kappa only assigns credit to exact agreement. Figure 2.5 shows how to compute unweighted and quadratically-weighted kappa for a hypothetical sample of 100 essays that are scored by both a human rater and an automated system on a scale from 1 to 3.

The above formulation of quadratically weighted kappa requires scores to be rounded which means that some useful information is being lost. Haberman (2019) proposed an alternative formulation for quadratically weighted kappa that allows computing it directly for continuous scores:

$$\kappa_q = \frac{2 * Cov(M, H)}{Var(H) + Var(M) + (\bar{M} - \bar{H})^2},$$

where $\bar{H}$ is the mean of the human scores, $\bar{M}$ is the mean of the machine scores, $Var(H)$ is the variance of the human scores, $Var(M)$ is the variance of the machine scores, and $Cov(M, H)$ is the co-variance of the human and machine scores. Note that, in this specific case, the variances and co-variance should use N as the denominator and not $N - 1$, as is usually the case.

3. **Mean Squared Error** (MSE) is the average of the squared differences between the predicted machine scores and the human scores over the whole set of essays being scored. This is different from the previous two metrics in that it is actually a measure of disagreement rather than agreement, i.e., *lower* values of MSE indicate a better-performing automated scoring system. Related metrics include Root Mean Squared Error (RMSE) which is defined as the square root of the MSE and R^2 which is defined as $1 - \dfrac{\text{MSE}}{Var(H)}$.

4. **Exact Agreement** & **Adjacent Agreement** are defined as the proportion of essays whose predicted scores either agree *exactly* with the corresponding human scores or are within one score point of the corresponding human scores, respectively.

5. **Precision, Recall, and F_1 score** are measures that can be used to evaluate automated essay scoring by treating it as a classification problem. These metrics were originally developed in the context of information retrieval where the task is to find a document of interest from a collection of documents. For classification problems, PRECISION is defined as the proportion of items that were correctly classified as belonging to the class of interest—say, a given score point on the scale. Mathematically, this equals proportion of true positives out of all (true and false) positives. Similarly, RECALL is defined as the proportion of all items that truly belong to the class of interest that were actually classified as such—namely, the proportion of true positives out of all true positives and false negatives. Finally, F_1 SCORE

	M: 1	M: 2	M: 3	Total
H: 1	10	5	4	19
H: 2	7	33	4	44
H: 3	3	12	22	37
Total	20	50	30	100

(a) Observed counts

	M: 1	M: 2	M: 3
H: 1	0.19 * 20 = 3.8	0.19 * 50 = 9.5	0.19 * 30 = 5.7
H: 2	0.44 * 20 = 8.8	22	13.2
H: 3	0.37 * 20 = 7.4	18.5	11.1

(b) Expected counts

	M: 1	M: 2	M: 3
H: 1	1	0	0
H: 2	0	1	0
H: 3	0	0	1

(c) Weights—none

	M: 1	M: 2	M: 3
H: 1	1	0.75	0
H: 2	0.75	1	0.75
H: 3	0	0.75	1

(d) Weights—quadratic

Unweighted kappa

Overall agreement by chance = 3.8 + 22 + 11.1 = 36.9/100 = 0.369

Overall observed agreement   = 10 + 33 + 22   = 65/100   = 0.65

kappa = (observed − chance)/(1 − chance) = (0.65 − 0.369(1 − 0.369) = 0.445

Quadratically weighted kappa

Overall weighted agreement by chance

= (3.8 * 1) + (9.5 * 0.75) + (8.8 * 0.75) + (22 * 1) + (13.2 * 0.75) + (18.5 * 0.75) + (11.1 * 1)

= 74.4/100 = 0.744

Overall weighted observed agreement

= (10 * 1) + (5 * 0.75) + (7 * 0.75) + (33 * 1) + (4 * 0.75) + (12 * 0.75) + (22 * 1)

= 86/100 = 0.86

QWK = (observed − chance)/(1 − chance) = (0.86 - 0.744)/(1 − 0.744) = 0.453

Figure 2.5: Computing unweighted and quadratically weighted Cohen's kappa for a hypothetical automated essay scoring example applied to a sample of 100 essays scored by both a human rater (**H**) and an automated system (**M**). Quadratically weighted kappa weights smaller score differences more than larger ones (see matrix labeled `Weights - quadratic` in figure). Unweighted kappa can also be considered a special case of weighted kappa with the identity weight matrix (labeled `Weights - none` in figure). Note that this figure is simply to help explain the idea of weighted agreement; we actually use the Haberman (2019) version of quadratically weighed kappa as our metric since it can directly operate on continuous scores.

is defined as the harmonic mean of precision and recall, $\frac{2 \times \text{Precision} \times \text{Recall}}{\text{Precision} + \text{Recall}}$. To use these metrics for evaluating how an automated essay scoring system is performing across all score points, one can compute the values for each score and then take their average. Two well-known types of averaged measures are: macro-average (compute P/R/F for each score point separately and then average) or micro-average (accumulate the true and false positives and negatives over each score point and then compute P/R/F). Another way to think about the micro-averaged measures is that the P/R/F are effectively weighted by the number of essays for each score point.

For our hands-on exercise, we will primarily use Pearson's correlation (r) and the Haberman (2019) version of quadratically weighted kappa that we denote as κ_q.

2.2.4   SOFTWARE

We use **RSMTool** (Madnani, Loukina, von Davier, et al., 2017) to train and evaluate our automated essay scoring system. RSMTool[13] is an open-source Python package that can automate multiple stages in the automated essay scoring pipeline. It outputs a comprehensive, customizable HTML report containing several kinds of evaluations including the metrics defined above.[14]

The report is easy to follow and quite useful for a hands-on exercise like ours. We will discuss RSMTool in more detail in Chapter 8 when we discuss methods and tools for more comprehensive evaluations of automated scoring. For now, we treat it simply as a tool that can train our linear regression model with the given set of features on the training data and generate an evaluation report of that same model on our test data.

2.3   BUILDING THE SYSTEM

In this section, we will use RSMTool v8.1.2 to build an automated essay scoring system for Task 1 on the training set, evaluate it on the development set, and then examine the salient sections of the evaluation report.

There are some additional practical details worth mentioning before we start building the system:

1. Feature values can be *standardized* using the z-transform $[z = (x - \mu)/\sigma]$ before being fed into the model since that might make the feature weights easier to interpret. STANDARD-IZATION of features may also be necessary in order for other machine learning algorithms (not linear regression) to work as expected. By default, RSMTool standardizes each feature by subtracting the training set mean and dividing by the training set standard deviation, though this option can be turned off.

---

[13]https://github.com/EducationalTestingService/rsmtool

[14]RSMTool computes a wide range of metrics to make it easy for the system developer to pick the ones that are most appropriate for their application and their users.

2. The scores predicted by the automated scoring system can be *rescaled* to have the same mean and standard deviation as the human score distribution over the training set. RESCALING can improve the κ_q values by making the distribution of the predicted scores similar to that of the human scores and by improving the likelihood that all points on the score scale are covered. For example, if human raters assigned the top score to 5% of the essays in the training set but the machine only assigns the top score to 2% of the essays in the development set, rescaling will artificially modify the scores to address this mismatch in score distribution. However, by artificially rescaling the distribution, the error in the predictions can increase significantly. For this reason, RSMTool provides the option to rescale predicted scores but disables it by default.

3. Since regression outputs can take *any* possible value, the scores predicted by the automated scoring system require trimming or TRUNCATION to respect the desired scoring scale. RSMTool truncates the predicted scores to the range $[\text{score}_{min} - \epsilon, \text{score}_{max} + \epsilon]$, where score_{min} and score_{max} are the lowest and highest points on the score scale and ϵ is a tolerance value used to pad the truncation range. RSMTool truncates scores by default with $\epsilon = 0.49998$[15] but allows users to specify a different value, if needed.

We structure this section as a collection of experiments—each experiment proposing a set of features to use for the automated scoring system, running that feature set through the RSMTool pipeline, analyzing the impact on various RSMTool metrics, and concluding with a discussion as to whether or not the experiment was well-motivated. For each experiment, we will train our model on the training set and evaluate on the *development* set. Once we are satisfied that our experiment has yielded the best possible model and no further experiments are necessary, we will then evaluate that final model on the held-out evaluation set. All of the files necessary to replicate the experiments can be found in our GitHub repository.[16] This repository also contains documentation for the overall directory structure, for the installation of RSMTool, and for running each experiment.

2.3.1   EXPERIMENT 0: USE ALL FEATURES

As our baseline experiment—which we will also use as an introduction to running RSMTool and examining its output report—we simply include all of our proposed features into our scoring model. To run this experiment, we first create the following RSMTool configuration file (`config.json`):

This configuration file relies on CSV files containing features for both the training and development set for Task 1. Each CSV file contains the feature columns previously described,

---

[15]Therefore, scores predicted by our model will be truncated to the range $[0.50002, 6.49998]$. This approach is better than simply clipping them to $[1, 6]$ since it retains the scores as real-valued—which are more informative than discrete-valued scores—and ensures that they fall within the desired range even if subsequently rounded. For example, 0.50002 will round up to 1 and 6.49998 will round down to 6.

[16]https://github.com/EducationalTestingService/aes-book-hands-on

a column containing a unique identifier for each essay, and the `score` and `score2` columns containing the scores assigned by two human raters to each essay. The paths to the two CSV files are specified as relative paths based on the directory structure.

To run this experiment, we simply run the following command in the terminal:

This will run RSMTool and produce the final report in the `report` sub-directory under the current directory. This report is available at the following: `https://bit.ly/aes-book-exp00 -report`.

The report is quite comprehensive and contains many analyses that are all described in the RSMTool documentation.[17] Below we highlight some salient parts of the report and include some screenshots of the corresponding plots and tables from the report for clarity in Figures 2.6 and 2.7. Not *every* analysis listed below is shown in the figures; we indicate the corresponding figure numbers next to the ones that are. Readers are encouraged to refer the full report at `https://bit.ly/aes-book-exp00-report` for the other analyses.

1. **Feature-level analyses**. RSMTool includes several useful analyses at the feature level such as:

   - What do the feature value distributions look like after standardization? [2.6(a)]
   - Are there some significant outliers in the values for any feature? [2.6(b)]
   - If we remove the effects of all other features, how much is each individual feature correlated with the score?
   - How inter-correlated are the various features? [2.6(c)]

   These analyses are contained in the sections of the report labeled *Overall descriptive feature statistics* and *Feature Distributions and Inter-feature Correlations*.

2. **Model-level analyses**. The next set of useful analyses computed by RSMTool are at the level of the scoring model learned on the training data:

   - What are the coefficients that the regression model learns for each of the features? [2.7(a)]
   - Are these coefficients statistically significantly different from 0, i.e., is the model confident that the feature *actually* contributes to the prediction of the human score? [2.7(a)]
   - What are the relative contributions of each of the features (interpretable only if all coefficients are positive)?

   These analyses are contained in the section of the report labeled *Model*.

3. **Prediction-level analyses**. The next set of analyses provided by RSMTool pertain to the predicted scores produced by the learned model for the evaluation set. It is important to note that these analyses are conducted on the evaluation set rather than the training set:

---

[17]`https://rsmtool.readthedocs.io`

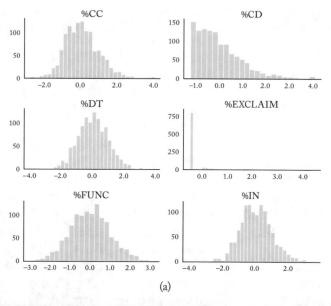

(a)

	1%	5%	25%	50%	75%	95%	99%	IQR	Mild Outliers	Extreme Outliers
%CC	0.010	0.019	0.028	0.036	0.044	0.059	0.074	0.016	24	1
%CD	0.000	0.000	0.006	0.013	0.022	0.040	0.055	0.015	34	3
%DT	0.034	0.046	0.062	0.073	0.085	0.102	0.116	0.023	13	0
%EXCLAIM	0.000	0.000	0.000	0.000	0.002	0.011	0.020	0.002	62	71
%FUNC	0.418	0.444	0.481	0.507	0.533	0.574	0.599	0.052	8	0
%IN	0.059	0.075	0.091	0.102	0.114	0.133	0.149	0.023	16	1

(b)

	sc1	%CC	%CD	%DT	%EXCLAIM	%FUNC	%IN
sc1	1.000	−0.104	0.170	0.084	0.157	−0.108	−0.072
%CC	−0.104	1.000	−0.103	−0.135	−0.071	0.107	−0.069
%CD	1.170	−0.103	1.000	−0.019	0.103	−0.063	−0.065
%DT	0.084	−0.135	−0.019	1.000	−0.052	0.131	0.093
%EXCLAIM	0.157	−0.071	0.103	−0.052	1.000	−0.034	−0.098
%FUNC	−0.108	0.107	−0.063	0.131	−0.034	1.000	0.119
%IN	−0.072	−0.069	−0.065	0.093	−0.098	0.119	1.000

(c)

Figure 2.6: Snippets of the RSMTool report from our experiment: (a) feature histograms, (b) feature distributions, and (c) inter-feature correlations for the first six features. IQR denotes the inter-quartile range—a measure of spread equal to the difference between the 75th and 25th percentiles of the values. Mild outliers lie between $[1.5, 3) * IQR$ away from the nearest quartile and extreme outliers lie $\geq 3 * IQR$ away from the nearest quartile. Numbers in red indicate correlations below 0.1 and greater than .7.

	Coef	Std Err	t	P > |t|	[0.025	0.975]
const	4.2569	0.010	436.831	0.000	4.238	4.276
WORDS	−0.3280	0.081	−4.073	0.000	−0.486	−0.170
LOGWORDS	0.5167	0.104	4.963	0.000	0.312	0.721
TYPES	−0.1244	0.097	−1.279	0.201	−0.315	0.066
LOG_TYPES	0.2872	0.114	2.517	0.012	0.063	0.511
%FUNC	0.0495	0.019	2.619	0.009	0.012	0.087
%QUESTION	−0.0063	0.011	−0.580	0.562	−0.028	0.015
%EXCLAIM	0.0187	0.010	1.790	0.074	−0.002	0.039
AVG_WLEN	0.0913	0.022	4.151	0.000	0.048	0.135
SD_WLEN	−0.0053	0.017	−0.307	0.759	−0.039	0.028
AVG_WFREQ	0.0181	0.034	0.538	0.591	−0.048	0.084
SD_WFREQ	0.0149	0.027	0.563	0.574	−0.037	0.067
%CC	−0.0004	0.012	−0.034	0.973	−0.023	0.022
%CD	0.0034	0.012	0.278	0.781	−0.021	0.027
%DT	0.0287	0.013	2.192	0.029	0.003	0.054
%IN	−0.0248	0.012	−2.097	0.036	−0.048	−0.002
%JJ	−0.0114	0.013	−0.872	0.383	−0.037	0.014
%MD	0.0075	0.012	0.633	0.527	−0.016	0.031
%NN	0.0031	0.021	0.150	0.881	−0.038	0.044
%PRP	−0.0013	0.018	−0.069	0.945	−0.037	0.035
%RB	−0.0084	0.014	−0.616	0.538	−0.035	0.018
%VB	−0.0034	0.015	−0.232	0.817	−0.032	0.025
%MISSPELLED	−0.0200	0.019	−1.078	0.281	−0.056	0.016
%REPEATED	0.0186	0.018	1.047	0.295	−0.016	0.054
LM	−0.0230	0.014	−1.590	0.112	−0.051	0.005
IS_NATIVE	0.4989	0.013	38.118	0.000	0.473	0.525

	N	corr	wtkappa	R2	kappa	exact_agr	adj_agr	RMSE
raw	300	0.930	0.920	0.860	0.751	0.000	99.000	0.351
raw_trim	300	0.930	0.920	0.860	0.751	0.000	99.000	0.351
raw_trim_round	300	0.913	0.888	0.818	0.751	84.000	100.000	0.400
scale	300	0.930	0.928	0.864	0.755	0.000	99.000	0.346
scale_trim	300	0.930	0.928	0.864	0.755	0.000	99.000	0.346
scale_trim_round	300	0.908	0.896	0.818	0.755	84.000	100.000	0.400

Figure 2.7: Snippets of the RSMTool report from our experiment showing the model coefficients on top and agreement metrics as computed over the evaluation set predictions on the bottom. The corr column contains r values and the wtkappa column contains κ_q values.

- How different are the actual distributions of the predicted scores and the human scores?
- How well do the predictions of our model agree with the human scores on the evaluation set? RSMTool computes several metrics for six different variants of the predicted scores—(a) the raw scores (`raw`), (b) the raw scores trimmed to the score scale as described above (`raw_trim`), (c) the raw scores first trimmed and then rounded to integers (`raw_trim_round`), (d) the rescaled scores (`scale`, (e) the rescaled scores trimmed to the score scale (`scale_trim`), and (f) the rescaled scores first trimmed and then rounded to integers (`scale_trim_round`). In the table, *corr* refers to *r* values, *kappa* refers to Cohen's unweighted kappa values with scores always rounded irrespective of the variant, and *wtkappa* refers to κ_q values with rounded scores treated as a special case of continuous scores. For our hands-on experiments below, we will use the `raw_trim` variants of *r* and κ_q as our evaluation metrics. [2.7(b)]
- How does the human-system agreement compare to human-human agreement (assuming we have scores from a second human rater)?

These analyses are contained in the section of the report labeled *Evaluation results*.

The analyses we just described will be the ones we will use to evaluate all of our subsequent experiments.

2.3.2   EXPERIMENT 1: FEATURE FAIRNESS

From the results of our baseline experiment—which uses *all* of the proposed features—we see that the `IS_NATIVE` feature seems to be highly predictive ($r = .813$ with human score[18]). Note, however, that this feature is not based on the essay text at all but rather a metadata feature self-reported by a test taker.

While it is reasonable that people with extensive exposure to English since early childhood would be more proficient writers of English, it is *not* fair to presume that non-native speakers cannot attain high proficiency as well. Given the strong positive weight that this feature gets assigned by the linear regression model, using this feature amounts to *punishing* non-native speakers *without* examining their essay text at all. Therefore, this feature is not a fair feature and should be removed from the model.[19] To do so, we simply remove `IS_NATIVE` from the `features` field in the RSMTool configuration file and re-run the same command as before. The report for this experiment is available at: `https://bit.ly/aes-book-exp01-report`. Although we see that the agreement of the model predictions with the human scores decreases after removing the feature (e.g., $r = .930$ before vs. $r = .843$ after), making this change is necessary in order to ensure a fair automated scoring model.

---

[18]Not visible in Figure 2.6; see full report at `https://bit.ly/aes-book-exp00-report`.

[19]This feature is *construct-irrelevant*; it does not measure the skills that the English proficiency test purports to measure. We will discuss construct-relevance in Chapter 8.

This brings us to our first lesson.

Lesson 2.1   Make sure your features are fair. Features should be based on the essay text and not on extraneous information about the test-taker.

Disclaimer: Note that the IS_NATIVE feature for our dataset is not populated with *real* self-reported values. We created the values to illustrate our point about fairness.

2.3.3   EXPERIMENT 2: FEATURE COLLINEARITY

For Experiment 1, we obtained $r = .843$ and $\kappa_q = .812$ (both raw_trim). If we examine the inter-feature correlations in that report, we see that the TYPES feature is correlated with the LOGTYPES feature with $r = .970$ *and* that these two features are equally correlated with the human score ($r = .754$ and $r = .770$, respectively). We also observe a similar situation with the WORDS and LOGWORDS pair of features. Based on these observations, we hypothesize that the same information is being introduced in the model via multiple features, resulting in MULTI-COLLINEARITY. To test our hypothesis, we remove the WORDS and TYPES features but retain their logarithmic counterparts and re-run RSMTool.

After removing TYPES and WORDS and re-running RSMTool, we obtain $r = .842$ and $\kappa_q = .811$ indicating that our hypothesis was correct, since the removal of these features had no impact on the agreement metrics. The report for this experiment is available at: https://bit.ly/aes-book-exp02-report.

Lesson 2.2   Do not unnecessarily complicate your model. You should avoid *multi-collinearity* among features, i.e., introducing the same information into the model via multiple features.

Note that the caveat about model complexity is certainly not unique to automated scoring models. It is well-known in both the statistics and machine learning literature as a way to reduce overfitting and improve the generalization of the learned model to new, unseen data. For example, the use of adjusted R^2 as a less biased estimator of model fit in statistical modeling and the principle of minimum description length in computational learning theory are both variations on the same idea. Although we manually remove collinear features in this experiment for illustrative purposes, one could also use regularized regression models such as Ridge (Hoerl & Kennard, 1970), Lasso (Tibshirani, 1996), and Elastic Net (Zou & Hastie, 2005) to reduce overfitting. We will discuss such models in more detail in Chapter 4.

2.3.4   EXPERIMENT 3: ADDITIONAL EVIDENCE FOR FEATURE CONTRIBUTIONS

If we examine the partial correlations plot from the previous experiment wherein we removed the TYPES and WORDS features (see section *Marginal and Partial Correlations* in https://bit.ly/aes-book-exp02-report), we see that many of the features actually have very low correlations with the human score once you control for the other features. As additional evidence, we also examine the table with the learned model coefficients—specifically, column P>|t| that indicates the probability that the particular coefficient is not statistically significantly different from 0. From this table, we see that the values of P>|t| for many of the features indicate their contributions to the model may not be statistically significant.

Based on this additional *empirical* evidence, removing the features from the scoring model seems like a reasonable course of action. However, there may be other types of evidence that are important. For example, if a feature is directly related to an evaluative criterion laid out in the scoring rubric, an argument could be made for keeping it in the model. We return to this discussion later in Chapter 3.

For now, we consider only the empirical evidence and exclude all of the features where the values for P>|t| are greater than 0.1. This removes the following features from the model: %CC, %CD, %DT, %EXCLAM, %JJ, %MD, %NN, %PRP, %QUESTION, %RB, %REPEATED, %VB, AVG_WORDFREQ, LM, SD_WFREQ, and SD_WLEN. Interestingly, we find that after we remove this first set of features, the %IN feature also ends up with a value of P>|t| greater than 0.1 and, therefore, we remove it too.

Re-running RSMTool without all the features we removed (as described above) yields $r = .837$ and $\kappa_q = .804$ confirming our hypothesis yet again. The report for this experiment is available at: https://bit.ly/aes-book-exp03-report.

Lesson 2.3   To assess the usefulness of a feature, consider additional empirical evidence beyond feature weights. Such evidence may include statistical significance of feature contributions and partial correlations of each feature with human scores after controlling for the other features.

2.3.5   EXPERIMENT 4: FEATURE TRANSFORMATIONS

If we look at the correlations of the remaining features with the human score in the report from the previous experiment (see the section *Inter-feature correlations* in https://bit.ly/aes-book-exp03-report), we notice that two of our features are negatively correlated with the human score: $r = -.108$ for %FUNC and $r = -.180$ for %MISSPELLED.

A negative correlation is expected for the %MISSPELLED feature since it counts occurrences of a phenomenon that has a negative impact on the final score. Nonetheless, it is usually recommended for all the features in the model to be positively correlated with the human score. Doing so it makes it easier to interpret the linear model, especially when it comes to comparing the relative contributions of the various features to the automatically assigned score.

To achieve this, we take advantage of RSMTool's ability to transform features before using them for analyses. To do so, we create a CSV file with three columns: feature, sign, and transform. The feature column contains the feature name. The sign column contains either 1 or −1 depending on whether we want to use the feature as is or negated. The transform column contains the name of a mathematical transformation we might also want to apply to the feature, e.g., taking the square root (`sqrt`), taking the inverse (`inv`), etc. For our current experiment, we simply want to negate some of the features, so our `features.csv` file looks like this:

```
feature,sign,transform
\%FUNC,-1,raw
\%MISSPELLED,-1,raw
AVG_WLEN,1,raw
LOGTYPES,1,raw
LOGWORDS,1,raw
```

This tells RSMTool to negate the values for the `%FUNC` and `%MISSPELLED` features before using them for any analyses but not to apply any other transformations. To use this file, we modify the experiment configuration file such that the `features` field contains the path to this CSV file rather than a list of features as it has done so far.

After re-running RSMTool with the modified configuration file, we see that the correlations for the two features we negated now have a positive sign as we wanted. The report for this experiment is available at: `https://bit.ly/aes-book-exp04-report`.

Lesson 2.4   Transform features to enhance interpretability or performance. Negative transformation can help understand the relative contributions of features in the model. In fact, the `LOGTYPES` and `LOGWORDS` features can be seen as logarithmic transforms that enhance the quality of the original `WORDS` and `TYPES` features.

2.3.6   EXPERIMENT 5: NEGATIVE FEATURE CONTRIBUTIONS

Looking at the section entitled *Standardized and Relative Regression Coefficients (Betas)* from the last experiment's report (`https://bit.ly/aes-book-exp04-report`), we see that the relative contribution of the `%FUNC` feature is −.064. This particular feature is positively correlated with the human score but it gets a negative weight in the model. In other words, this feature might penalize a test-taker for doing the right thing. Given the relatively small magnitude of the contribution, it's probably better to remove the feature from the model entirely.

After removing the `%FUNC` feature from model and re-running RSMTool, we see that the all remaining features now have positive relative contributions to the model and that the values of the agreement metrics are also not adversely impacted—$r = .840$ (`raw`) and $\kappa_q = .805$. The report for this experiment is available at: `https://bit.ly/aes-book-exp05-report`.

Lesson 2.5   Check that the model makes reasonable use of features. For example, in a linear model, a feature that is positively correlated with the human score but has a negative weight might present an interpretability problem.

Feature	Standardized	Relative
%MISSPELLED	0.047	0.050
AVG_WLEN	0.134	0.142
LOGTYPES	0.320	0.339
LOGWORDS	0.444	0.469

Here are the same values, shown graphically.

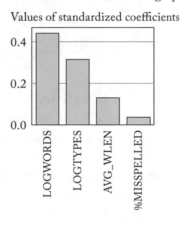

Figure 2.8: Standardized and relative contributions for features in the final model shown in both tabular as well as graphical form.

Note that another potential solution to avoid negative contributions for features that are positively correlated with human score would be to use a model such as non-negative least squares (NNLS) regression (Lawson & Hanson, 1981).

At this point, we can deem model development to be complete as we have a reasonable set of features that all make significant positive contributions to the model to obtain pretty good agreement with the human scores on our development set. The final set of features and their learned coefficients is shown in Figure 2.8.

When we introduced the %MISSPELLED feature, we hypothesized that even though the Task 1 rubric contained explicit instructions for the human raters to not penalize grammar or spelling errors, some errors may be egregious enough to make the response "difficult to read and understand". The inclusion of this feature in the final scoring model for Task 1 appears to confirm our hypothesis.

Table 2.1: The distributions of human scores for responses in the Task 1 development and evaluation sets

Score	Dev	Test
1	1.00%	0.00%
2	3.00%	0.35%
3	12.00%	11.46%
4	46.00%	54.12%
5	30.33%	26.74%
6	7.67%	7.29%

2.3.7   EXPERIMENT 6: TEST ON HELD-OUT DATA

Once model development is complete and we are reasonably confident that we have a final model, the model must be evaluated on unseen or held-out data that was not used in the development process.

To do so, we modify the configuration file such that the `test_file` field points to the CSV file containing the evaluation set (`test.csv`) instead of the file containing the development set (`dev.csv`) as it was done for all the experiments so far.

Running this experiment on the held-out evaluation set yields the following values for the agreement metrics: $r = .729$ and $\kappa_q = .691$. The report for this experiment is available at: `https://bit.ly/aes-book-exp06-report`.

These values are lower than the values we obtained on the development set. The reason is that the development set and the evaluation set have different distributions of human scores. Table 2.1 shows the percentage of essays in each set with each of the six score points.

In this particular case, since we had a relatively small data set, a random split produced different score distributions for the development and evaluation sets. For a much larger set, this may not be an issue. However, the distributions could differ due to other systemic reasons as well. For example, it is not uncommon for training (and development) data to be sampled from an initial pilot administration of the test; the score distributions for such data can vary significantly when the test is actually administered to the real population.

Lesson 2.6   Always evaluate the final model on held-out data that is not used for development. It is essential to test whether the results obtained from the model during the development process are stable and generalize relatively well to unseen data.

2.3.8   EXPERIMENT 7: CROSS-TASK EVALUATION

In this experiment, we attempt to examine whether we can score unseen responses from a *different* task (Task 2) with our final learned model for Task 1. Theoretically, this should be possible as the model we have learned is designed to score English writing proficiency; we would expect it to assign a reasonable score to a response, no matter what prompt or task it was written to.

To test this, we modify the experiment configuration file such that the `test_file` field contains the path to the Task 2 evaluation set CSV file. After running RSMTool with this modification, we observe the following:

1. The `raw` correlation for the cross-task experiment is slightly higher than for the within-task experiment ($r = .758$ vs. $r = .729$).
2. The `raw_trim` quadratically-weighted kappa for the cross-task experiment is substantially worse than for the within-task experiment ($\kappa_q = .501$ vs. $\kappa_q = .691$).

The report for this experiment is available at: `https://bit.ly/aes-book-exp07 -report`.

The primary reason for such a drastic drop in κ_q is the large discrepancy in the human score distributions between the two tasks. Figure 2.9 illustrates this: since the machine has learned from Task 1 responses, its predictions for Task 2 responses also follow a similar distribution. However, human raters assign a lot more 3s and a lot fewer 5s in Task 2 which leads to a mismatch between the machine and the human scores for those 2 score points. The large discrepancy in the human score distributions likely stems from the fact that not only were the two tasks administered to different populations (Task 1 to Grade 8 students, Task 2 to Grade 10 students) but also that the rubrics for the two tasks have somewhat different evaluative criteria (Both tasks include "Organization" but only Task 2 includes "Ideas & Content" as well as "Style").

Recall that r tells us more about linear relationships between human and machine scores and κ_q measures whether each individual essay score from the machine agrees with the human score or not. In the cross-task setting, we observe that the relative merits of the essays can still be estimated fairly well (similar r value) but the alignment to the specific human score distribution is incorrect (much lower κ_q value).

Lesson 2.7   The training and the test data must have matching target populations. Large discrepancies between r and κ_q can result if the score distributions shift between the training and test data due to unmatched populations.

2.3.9   EXPERIMENT 8: TASK-SPECIFIC MODELS

In the previous experiment, we showed that using a model trained on Task 1 was not appropriate for scoring responses written to Task 2 due to the difference in target populations and scoring

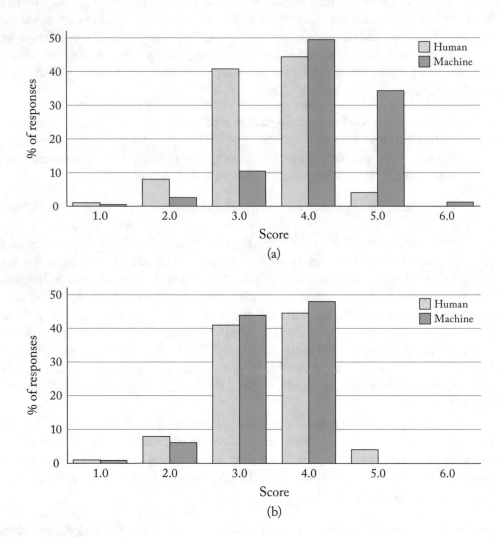

Figure 2.9: Differences between the machine score distributions for the evaluation set in the (a) cross-task experiment (§2.3.8) and the (b) within-task experiment (§2.3.9). The human score distributions are obviously identical in both figures.

Table 2.2: Relative contributions of features to models trained on Task 1 training set (**Model 1**) and on Task 2 training set (**Model 2**)

Feature	Model 1	Model 2
LOGWORDS	.469	.333
LOGTYPES	.339	.312
AVG_WLEN	.142	.189
%MISSPELLED	.050	.166

rubrics. In this experiment, we will train a new specific model for Task 2 using its training set and see how the learned task-specific model compares to the previously learned cross-task model.

To learn a task-specific model, we simply modify the experiment configuration file such that the `train_file` field points to the training set CSV file for Task 2. After re-running this experiment, we observe the following.

1. Both agreement metrics are now higher than they were in the cross-task setting ($r = .767$ and $\kappa_q = .744$) indicating that the task-specific model with matched target populations between the training and test sets performs much better.
2. The relative contributions of the features in the task-specific model are different from those in the cross-task model (see Table 2.2). From this comparison, we can infer that, according to the two models, making spelling errors is likely more detrimental to scores for Task 2 than for Task 1. Similarly, demonstrating the use of more sophisticated vocabulary might be more important in Task 2 than in Task 1.

The report for this experiment is available at: `https://bit.ly/aes-book-exp08 -report`.

Lesson 2.8   Model comparison can help understand differences and similarities in how humans rate essays. In our experiment, model comparison showed that human raters may weight things differently between tasks and/or populations but it also showed that the positive traits do generalize—it is *generally* better to write with fewer spelling errors, more sophisticated vocabulary, and more elaboration for the younger and older populations and for both tasks.

2.3.10   EXPERIMENTS 9a AND 9b: MORE RELIABLE HUMAN RATINGS

According to Page (1966), it is better for an automated scoring system to try to use the *average* of multiple human-assigned scores rather than a single human-assigned score in order to compensate for the unreliability that might be associated with a single rater. This unreliability may impact both the training as well as the evaluation process.[20]

To examine how this might impact our specific example, we make use of the second human score that is available in the ASAP dataset (the column named `score2` in both `train.csv` and `test.csv`). We first take the average of the two human scores and store the results in a new column named `average_score`. Next, we modify the experiment configuration file to change the fields `train_label_column` and `test_label_column` to point to this new column rather than the `score` column as they have done so far. Finally, we also remove the `second_human_score_column` field from the configuration file as we are now using the second human score to compute the average.[21]

Running this experiment yields the following values for our agreement metrics: $r = .796$ and $\kappa_q = .776$. Compare these to the values we obtained from Experiment 6 (§2.3.7): $r = .729$ and $\kappa_q = .691$. We see that with more reliable human scores, the system can be made more accurate and a clearer picture of the system's performance can be obtained.

Next, let us run another version of this experiment where we train on the same single score as before and only use the averaged score for evaluation. To do so, the only change we need to make is to revert the value of the `train_label_column` field back to `"score"`. This version of the experiment yields $r = .795$ and $\kappa_q = .776$. Therefore, the machine is able to learn from a single human score in a way that is robust to any noise in the label. This is a powerful demonstration that the machine is able to cull the benefit of *collective* wisdom from seeing only a *single* human score for each essay during learning.

The reports for these experiments are available at: `https://bit.ly/aes-book-exp09a-report` and `https://bit.ly/aes-book-exp09b-report`, respectively.

Lesson 2.9   Collect multiple human ratings for the essays in your evaluation set, if possible. Although it may still be possible for automated systems to learn robustly from a single human score for each essay, having multiple human scores in the evaluation set provides a truer picture of the system's capabilities.

We observe the same findings for Task 2 and leave it to the reader to confirm our findings as an exercise.

---

[20]For most large-scale tests in operation, it is *not* the case that the same human rater scores all of the essays but rather each essay is assigned to a single human rater chosen from a pool of raters. Each essay still has a *single* human score assigned to it in the end, even though the rater that assigned that score might be different for different essays. Since all raters receive the same training and are re-calibrated at regular intervals, this setup is more practical and does not raise any serious issues of rater bias.

[21]Removing this column will remove the section called *Consistency* from the report. We do not examine this section in this chapter but more details can be found in the RSMTool documentation.

2.3.11   EXPERIMENT 10: A MORE SOPHISTICATED LEARNER

Earlier in the chapter, we motivated the use of linear regression as the learner for our hands-on experiments as being more useful for the purposes of illustration. However, it would still be interesting to compare its performance with that of another, more sophisticated machine learning algorithm.

To achieve this, we take the experiment configuration file from Experiment 6 (§2.3.7) and modify the `model` field from `LinearRegression` to `MLPRegressor`. This will tell RSMTool to use the Multi-layer Perceptron (MLP) regression algorithm from scikit-learn (Pedregosa et al., 2011). This algorithm uses a single hidden layer of 100 nodes with an adaptable learning rate. This *MLP1* network (a feed-forward network with a single hidden layer) is a powerful learning algorithm and can be taught to approximate any function under the right conditions (Hornik, 1991).[22]

Running this experiment yields the following values for our agreement metrics: $r = .729$ and $\kappa_q = .693$. Compare these to the values we obtained from Experiment 6 (§2.3.7): $r = .729$ and $\kappa_q = .691$. The report for this experiment is available at: `https://bit.ly/aes-book-exp10-report`.

We see that MLP1 performs marginally better than linear regression. However, the cost of this increased performance is a reduction in algorithmic transparency, i.e., understanding what the model exactly learns and the contribution of each feature to the score for a given essay. On the other hand, a linear regression model is intrinsically interpretable and can readily provide the answers to such questions. Therefore, picking the machine learning algorithm that maximizes agreement with human scores may not always be the right choice especially in high-stakes scenarios where explaining model behavior can be critical. In fact, a more transparent model might also be used to provide some feedback to the test-taker regarding their performance, e.g., in the form of a detailed score report.

Recent work has shown that deeper neural networks with more modern architectures can perform even better on the tasks from the ASAP dataset (F. Dong et al., 2017; Taghipour & Ng, 2016). However, such models are even less intrinsically interpretable than MLP1. We discuss neural approaches to automated essay scoring in much more detail in Chapter 4.

Lesson 2.10   The machine learning model with the highest agreement values is not always the best choice. Although more sophisticated machine learning algorithms may be able to attain higher agreement with human scores, they may do so at the cost of transparency and this trade-off may be unacceptable when the automated score is part of a high-stakes decision.

---

[22]RSMTool searches for the best possible value of the following MLP1 hyper-parameters via 3-fold cross-validation on the training set: (a) the activation function for the hidden layer (possible values: [`logistic`, `tanh`, `relu`]), (b) the L2-regularization parameter α (possible values: [.0001, .001, .01, .1, 1]), and (c) the initial learning rate (possible values: [.001, .01, .1]). The `learning_rate` & the `max_iter` hyper-parameters are set to `invscaling` and 500, respectively. All other hyper-parameters use their default scikit-learn values.

We refer the interested reader to Lipton (2016) and Molnar (2019) who provide a more thorough treatment of interpretability of machine learning models.

2.4   CONCLUSIONS

In this chapter, we explored in a hands-on fashion the process of building a simple automated scoring system on real data in order to highlight and discuss practical issues that can have a significant impact on such systems. Note that many of the lessons we discussed in this chapter can apply to any type of machine learning system, not just automated essay scoring systems. In the next chapter, we will discuss general guidelines that pertain more specifically to developing automated scoring systems.

CHAPTER 3

From Lessons to Guidelines

3.1   INTRODUCTION

In this chapter, we attempt to consolidate the "lessons" from the previous chapter into more general, non-technical guidelines for developers of automated essay scoring systems. These guidelines are all based on the recognition of the fact that building an automated scoring system—in the end—is not solely an NLP enterprise. While NLP and machine learning techniques form a core part of automated essay scoring systems, there are several other non-NLP considerations that need to be taken into account when designing and developing such techniques. It is important to remember the perspectives of the other "stakeholders"—whom we identify below—when making decisions during the NLP component development, and not simply focus on having the most accurate, or fastest automated scoring systems. While it is admirable to take advantage of the recent availability of relevant data and develop novel and more sophisticated NLP techniques to advance the field, it is also necessary to take a step back and ensure that the NLP advances are also aligned with the interests of other stakeholders. Much of the material below is derived from a previous paper published by one of the authors (Madnani & Cahill, 2018).

3.2   PERSPECTIVES ON AUTOMATED SCORING

In this section, we describe the various entities who are likely to be affected by automated scoring systems, and their corresponding perspectives on the use of automated scoring. All of these entities have a stake in making sure that the automated scoring system performs in line with their own expectations and, therefore, we henceforth refer to them as "stakeholders".

- **Score Users: Individuals**. The people to whom any test or assessment is administered (test-takers) are important stakeholders since any decisions made about the scoring of the assessment affect them directly. This is particularly true in cases where the assessment is likely to have a significant impact on the test-takers' futures, e.g., by contributing to a decision about whether to admit them into a college or graduate school, or a decision whether to grant them a license to engage in a professional activity such as teaching. If an automated scoring system is being employed to score their responses to such critically positioned assessments, test-takers want to ensure that such a system measures the same set of characteristics and skills as a well-trained human scorer[1] and that such measurements are calculated accurately based on their responses. In addition, the test-takers also place emphasis on receiving their scores quickly and on a *score report* providing useful information on why they received the particular scores that they did and what, if anything, they can do to improve their scores if they decide to retake the assessment.

- **Score Users: Institutions**. Another important consumer of test scores are institutions who use the test scores to make decisions. For example, universities may use test scores to make placement decisions; immigration authorities may use test scores to make visa decisions; school districts and states may use test scores to make funding and policy decisions. Such institutions want to ensure that the scores from the test are valid and reliable and that any automated scoring component does not introduce any biases toward any particular subgroup of test-takers.

- **Teachers**. Teachers in classrooms are also likely to be affected by the decision to use automated scoring systems. It is important to them as stakeholders that scores from automated systems are not used inappropriately. For example, if the assessment—and the automated scoring system—are only designed to measure the students' writing proficiency, the scores assigned by the system should not be used for a different purpose, e.g., to assess the teacher's teaching abilities. Teachers are also impacted if automated systems are used directly in the classroom, e.g., to provide feedback to students in the context of *formative* assessments (informal assessments conducted by teachers in the classroom to improve how students learn). For such cases, the teachers want to ensure that the feedback provided by the system is reasonably accurate, does not lead the students astray from the actual learning goal, and encourages engagement with the material being taught.

- **Subject-matter Experts**. Subject-matter experts, also known as assessment developers, write the questions that are included in the assessments. In addition, they also assemble specific questions into assessments while taking into account that the chosen questions should cover a wide range of skills that are to be measured by the assessment (the construct) and that different questions try to measure complementary aspects of such skills. As part of the assessment design, they also create the scoring rubric—a document we already discussed in detail in Chapter 2. Rubrics tend to be complex and subjective, particularly for assessments that contain relatively open-ended writing or content-based questions. Such experts would like to ensure that any automated scoring system deployed to score the assessments they have designed pays attention to the

---

[1]Per our discussion of Page (1966) in Chapter 1, an automated system cannot really "read" the response in the same way that a human ("trins") can but it can use features that are reasonable approximations ("proxes") for factors that human scorers consider in their evaluation.

scoring rubric and that only construct-relevant information is used by the system during the scoring process. For example, assume that the length of a response to a question designed to measure the test-taker's writing proficiency correlates very highly with its score. However, if response length is not explicitly a part of the scoring rubric for said question, this may constitute grounds to reject length as a feature in the automated scoring system (Bejar, 2017).

- **Business Units**. It takes significant resources to develop, administer, and score well-designed assessments. Therefore, the institutions undertaking this process are more likely to be educational technology companies with dedicated staff for assessment development, psychometric analysis, and natural language processing. Therefore, there is a business aspect to educational assessments in addition to research. For example, business units at such companies might consist of people who try to procure state and federal contracts for developing and scoring K–12 assessments. When it comes to automated scoring systems, such units place emphasis on more practical business aspects of system development, such as building systems that are fast (e.g., with a short turnaround time between the submission of the response and the production of the score), cost-effective to deploy and maintain in an operational setting, and have little to no measurable impact on the effectiveness of the assessment.

- **NLP Researchers & Developers**. NLP researchers and developers tend to have a different perspective when it comes to building automated scoring systems. The automated scoring system should perform accurately, where accuracy is generally defined as agreement with human scores. Second, the system should not only build on top of state-of-the-art ideas and tools from the field but, if possible, should also advance the field forward by sharing and disseminating tools, lessons, and ideas at conferences and workshops. Another important consideration is the modularity of the system that not only allows replacement of NLP components (e.g., taggers and parsers) with newer and better-performing versions but also allows new scoring features to be seamlessly incorporated into the system. Finally, the system should be easy to maintain and well-documented, allowing new developers and researchers to use it without a lot of effort.

See Lotteridge & Hoefer (2020) for a similar discussion of stakeholder contexts for automated scoring.

Since each set of stakeholders is trying to optimize the automated scoring system for a different set of criteria, it is only natural that many of the above perspectives can be at odds with each other. Next, we specifically outline the conflicts between the perspectives of the **NLP researchers** and the other four sets of stakeholders.

(a) **vs. Business Units**. Business units might sometimes place a greater emphasis on getting systems to market faster and with a limited investment depending on the budget available. However, in order to build a system that has a reasonably high agreement with human scores and is more likely to generalize to new and unexpected responses in the field, NLP researchers might require additional time as well as investment. For example, annotation of additional responses may be required for use as training data, or an existing research technique from the literature may need to be adapted for the domain before deployment.

(b) **vs. Score Users**. As described above, one of the most important considerations for test-takers is a reasonably clear explanation of why they received the particular scores that they did. The NLP researchers optimizing for agreement with human scores might lean toward using more sophisticated machine learning models such as support vector machines (SVMs) with nonlinear kernels and deep neural networks. However, as we discussed in Chapter 2, doing so might sacrifice interpretability, or at the very least, require significant efforts to retain it. Ensuring that there are no biases in automated scores—important also for institutions using test scores to make decisions—is a topic that, until recently, has seen little discussion in the NLP literature. This is partly driven by a lack of demographic data available in publicly available datasets, as well as perhaps a focus on empirical accuracy.

(c) **vs. Subject-matter Experts**. Subject-matter experts or assessment developers want to ensure that all the hard work that has been done on their end to develop a valid (actually measuring what it is supposed to measure) and reliable assessment (scores are comparable across repeated administrations of the assessment) is not undone by an automated scoring system that is using features that are either unrelated or only partially related to the skill that is purportedly being measured.[2] It is difficult for NLP researchers to convert the salient aspects of a complicated—and subjective—document like the scoring rubric into features that are reasonably efficient to compute. Although the conversion can be aided by asking human scorers how they mentally translate the rubric into specific scoring decisions, humans are not as interpretable as one might think (Lipton, 2016).

(d) **vs. Teachers**. To make sure that automated scoring systems behave as expected if deployed for in-classroom use, NLP researchers usually like to conduct research studies with such systems in real classrooms in order to collect useful data, e.g., written responses, student behavior, and indicators of engagement which can then be used to improve the system further (Burstein et al., 2016; Burstein & Sabatini, 2016; Madnani, Burstein, et al., 2016). However, teachers want to ensure that such systems are sufficiently nuanced—and not too primitive—to handle interactions with students and do not lead to students being distracted instead of learning. Furthermore, it takes time to build up a level of trust between the teachers and NLP researchers as a system is being fine-tuned and developed especially since frequent user-testing is usually needed as part of the system development process.

It is evident from the above discussion that trying to cater to everyone is akin to solving a difficult constraint satisfaction problem. For example, if NLP researchers want to build a more

---

[2]See Chapter 6 for a detailed discussion on tailoring automated scoring systems to the specifics of the writing task.

interpretable automated scoring system that can provide more useful feedback to test-takers, it requires investing more money and time which might need to be negotiated with the business units. Or, if subject-matter experts design an assessment with more intricate, open-ended questions in order to accurately assess the required set of skills, the corresponding automated scoring system would likely require more time and resources to build and potentially be less transparent and/or less accurate.

As another example, NLP researchers may find through ablation studies that certain computationally complex features are contributing little to the overall accuracy of the model. They may choose to simplify the processing pipeline and resulting models by excluding those features, at a small cost to overall accuracy (on some held-out evaluation data). For example, recall Experiment 3 from the previous chapter (§2.3.4) where we removed features from the model based only on empirical evidence. However, if such features are measuring important aspects of the construct, removing them weakens the alignment of the system with the construct, since now the system omits measuring an important aspect of what is being measured by humans, as defined in the scoring rubric. This is very important for both subject-matter experts (who will assume that any automated system is at least trying to measure the same thing that humans are) and business units (who require a valid assessment).

Next, we attempt to provide guidelines for multi-perspective and collaborative development of automated essay scoring systems. Instead of simply providing a list of guidelines and best practices, we provide three relevant case studies and provide contextualized recommendations and suggestions.

3.3 CASE STUDIES

In this section, we describe three hypothetical case studies involving automated scoring systems. We focus on some of the stakeholder interactions that we believe are critical for successful deployment of automated scoring systems and provide guidelines and best practices. Note that many of our suggestions are adapted from the best practices that are already recommended by research practitioners in the educational measurement community (Ramineni & Williamson, 2013; Williamson et al., 2012).

3.3.1 ADDING AUTOMATED SCORING TO AN EXISTING ASSESSMENT

The decision to add automated scoring to an existing assessment can be initiated by the business units as a potential cost-saving measure or to increase test reliability. It can also be initiated by the NLP researchers who believe they have developed a system that can accurately score a particular type of written response. In either case, a number of considerations need to be taken into account before automated scoring can be added to an existing assessment.

If a business unit wants to add automated scoring for an existing assessment, they should typically first approach the NLP researchers to estimate the effort involved in developing automated scoring capabilities for the specific question types contained in the assessment (e.g., essays that measure writing quality or free-text responses that measure knowledge of some content area). NLP researchers will assess the feasibility of automated scoring for the requested item types. At this point, it is critical to engage the subject-matter experts in order to fully understand the construct being measured, the scoring rubric and any supplemental scoring guidelines, as well as to get access to any training materials used to train human scorers. Without engaging the subject-matter experts it is all too easy to make assumptions about the assessment based on observations made from a limited amount of scored data. This can lead to automated scoring systems that measure the construct inaccurately or in a limited fashion, that handle aberrant responses incorrectly, and that could ultimately lead to unfairly scored assessments yielding significant consequences for the test-takers.

If NLP researchers initiate the request to add automated scoring to an assessment, they should have already connected with the subject-matter experts to ensure that they have built a system that adequately measures the correct construct. It is important that they also consider other aspects of the assessment and communicate with all relevant stakeholders. For example, if an assessment has a low number of test-takers each year, then the amount of data available to monitor[3] the automated system may be too low. If the number of responses available for monitoring is low, then the risks are that a sample small enough for the monitoring to be cost effective will not provide statistically meaningful monitoring metrics. Conversely, a sample large enough to provide statistically meaningful metrics would effectively offset any potential cost-savings obtained from automated scoring. This consideration would be very important to the business units who have to fund both the setup costs of integrating automated scoring into an existing assessment, as well as the ongoing maintenance costs.

Another important consideration here is the nature of the automated score that is desired. The most common type of score that an automated system can provide is a single numeric score for a given written response. This HOLISTIC SCORE generally represents some overall measure, e.g., the overall writing quality for a given essay. The system producing the holistic score usually still measures multiple aspects of the writing (e.g., grammar, syntax, style) but only *produces* a single score as the output. In contrast, an automated scoring system may produce *multiple* scores, each representing a different writing trait. For example, a scoring system for argumentative writing may produce three different *trait scores*—one for *conventions* (grammar, spelling, etc.), one for *organization* (discourse structure, topic development, etc.), and one for *content* (accuracy of facts, conceptual understanding, etc.). Just like the holistic score, it is likely that the system internally computes each TRAIT SCORE as a combination of multiple underlying aspects of the writing. In trait-based scenarios, it may also happen that the scores for different traits are highly correlated with each other (Y.-W. Lee et al., 2008; Somasundaran et al., 2018). Besides the type of score, the context of its usage is also important. For example, is the automated score

---

[3]Monitoring is an important aspect of high-stakes automated scoring systems, wherein a random sample of the responses scored by the automated system are also scored by an expert human scorer to ensure that the system is performing as expected.

going to be the sole score for the assessment? If so, aberrant response detection and monitoring become even more critical. Or perhaps the automated score will be used in conjunction with a *second* score provided by a human rater? If so, will this be a CONTRIBUTORY SCORE (final score is a combination of both the automated score and the human score) or a CONFIRMATORY SCORE (final score is the human score unless the difference between it and the automated score is greater than some threshold requiring human adjudication)?

Finally, for any automated scoring system that is proposed, NLP researchers need to take into account ethical considerations regarding fairness and validity and evaluate the system on dimensions other than just the agreement with human scores. For example, it is critical to evaluate whether the system is biased toward certain sub-populations of test-takers. Aggregated metrics of agreement with human scores (such as Pearson correlation or Cohen's kappa) will not be able to capture such biases or fairness issues. We discuss real-world evaluation of automated scoring systems in much more detail in Chapter 8.

3.3.2   CREATING A NEW ASSESSMENT THAT INCLUDES AUTOMATED SCORING

This particular scenario offers many more opportunities for a collaborative and multi-perspective development process to be adopted right from the start as compared to the previous case study. As a business unit puts together the plans for a new assessment, automated scoring is often a desired component (usually for cost-saving and faster score reporting). It is important at this juncture for the subject-matter experts and the NLP researchers to collaborate in order to understand the types of questions that will be included in the new assessment, and which ones might actually be suitable for being scored automatically. It is important for the NLP researchers to understand the specific constructs being targeted by the new assessment and advise the subject-matter experts where construct-irrelevant differences might impact automated scoring.

For example, a question might use a passage about a young student with a name that is not likely to be familiar to the population of students taking the test. This means that the test-takers may guess the gender of this student, resulting in a range of pronouns appearing in the sample responses from which automated scoring models might be built. This unnecessarily "dilutes" the vocabulary of the response pool with irrelevant variation. On the other hand, giving the hypothetical student a name that has a widely acknowledged gender associated with it will help limit this kind of variation without any impact on the construct coverage or validity of the question.

At the same time, while subject-matter experts are developing the questions, it is important for the NLP researchers to assess the feasibility of automated scoring for the question types being considered for automated scoring. If a question would require NLP techniques that are in very early stages of research or have not yet been fully tested, this information needs to be shared as quickly as possible with the business units so that they can build contingency plans into their budgets and timetables.

Finally, this scenario also warrants careful consideration of score type and usage as well as a comprehensive fairness and validity evaluation since both of those are relevant whether automated scoring is being deployed for an entirely new assessment or for an existing one.

3.3.3   INCLUDING AUTOMATED SCORING IN A CLASSROOM SETTING

It is crucial that NLP researchers engage with both teachers as well as students when developing tools to be deployed in an authentic classroom setting, e.g., tools that can provide feedback on students' writing or content knowledge. An NLP researcher designing and implementing a classroom tool in isolation is not likely to be successful, no matter the accuracy or novelty of the underlying NLP techniques. Before developing any tools, the NLP researchers need to fully understand the problem they are trying to solve by engaging teachers to find out how NLP technology can be integrated in a supportive fashion to their teaching curricula. Ideally, classroom tools should be built in an iterative fashion, by learning what features or techniques improve student engagement and learning and which ones do not. An example study that evaluates the effect of a new tool in an authentic classroom setting has many non-trivial (and non-NLP-specific) components:

- Identify a representative sample of schools/classes/students for the study.
- Conduct surveys of teachers and control groups.
- Conduct teacher training.
- Analyze teachers' daily/weekly logs.
- Conduct classroom observations.
- Conduct pre- and post-study evaluations.
- Analyze tool usage logs.

This requires a lot of time and effort both from the teachers as well as the NLP researchers, but at the end of the day is more likely to lead to truly useful tools that can have a positive impact on the classroom learning process and improve students' understanding of the material being taught by the teacher.

3.4   SUMMARY

Our goal in this chapter is to bring attention to the inherent complexity of automated essay scoring, given the large number of stakeholders, often with different priorities. We take the position that in order to build fair and accurate automated scoring systems—especially for use in high-stakes assessments where the consequences of being unfair and inaccurate can be severe for the test-takers—NLP researchers must incorporate the perspectives of other stakeholders into the research and development process and avoid working in a bubble surrounded only by scored data and machine learning algorithms.

3.5   LOOKING AHEAD

This chapter marks the conclusion of Part 1 which was focused on providing an introduction to and context around the idea of automated essay scoring. In the next part of the book, we take a much more detailed and technical look inside automated essay scoring systems. Specifically, in Chapter 4, we examine the specific machine learning algorithms and approaches that have been used in the literature to build automated essay scoring systems. In Chapters 5 and 6, we discuss the development of features that have been used in the literature to capture important aspects of essay quality as defined by scoring rubrics and other considerations—Chapter 5 focuses on more general features whereas Chapter 6 focuses on genre—and task-specific features. In Chapter 7, we discuss architectural considerations for building automated essay scoring systems, i.e., how the system may be architected in order to support robust, low-latency, and high-throughput scoring demands. Finally, in Chapter 8, we try to convey to the readers what additional evidence—beyond simple agreement metrics—needs to be collected to conduct a thorough evaluation of automated essay scoring systems before they are considered ready to be deployed in the real world.

PART III

A Deep Dive: Models, Features, Architecture, and Evaluation

CHAPTER 4

Models

4.1 INTRODUCTION

In our hands-on exercises for building an automated essay scoring system in Chapter 2, we chose linear regression as the machine learning model. In this chapter, we examine the internals of this model in much more detail while also taking a more detailed look at a variety of *other* machine learning approaches that have been used for automated essay scoring, including distributional semantics and deep neural networks.

4.2 LINEAR REGRESSION

The first machine-learned model for automated scoring was proposed by Page (1966). For "Project Essay Grade"—as it was termed in the paper—276 essays written by high school students from grades 8–12 were manually assigned holistic scores by four different English teachers. The final score for the essay was taken to be the sum of the four scores. Next, Page and his colleagues at the University of Connecticut extracted features (or "proxes", as he termed them) from the essays. These features were then used to train a linear regression model (run on an IBM 7040 mainframe computer!) to predict the final human scores for the essays.

Let's look at linear regression in a bit more detail. A LINEAR REGRESSION model assumes that the *dependent variable* (the outcome variable we are trying to predict, e.g., the essay score) is linear in the inputs, also known as *independent variables* (another name for features). That is,

$$y = w_0 + w_1 x_1 + w_2 x_2 + \ldots + w_m x_m, \tag{4.1}$$

where y is the dependent variable, the x_i are our m numeric independent variables or feature values, and the w_i are the corresponding FEATURE WEIGHTS, i.e., the multiplicative parameters that control how much impact any independent variable has on the dependent variable. Estimating these weights from data constitutes the *training process* for a linear regression model, making it one of the first supervised machine learning techniques. The most common estimation algorithm is **ordinary least squares** (OLS) wherein the chosen weight values are those that minimize the residual sum of squares, i.e.,

$$\text{RSS} = \sum_{i=1}^{N} (y_i^2 - \hat{y}_i^2), \tag{4.2}$$

where N is the number of examples in the training data, y is the true value of the dependent variable for each example, and $\hat{y} = w_0 + \sum_{j=1}^{m} w_j x_j$ is the corresponding prediction from the model. Since the least-squares loss function is convex and differentiable, a unique closed-form solution for the weight vector can always be computed.

Although linear regression models largely predate the era of computational statistics and machine learning, they are still quite popular today and for good reasons. Their simplicity often yields an adequate and interpretable way of examining the relationship between the features and the dependent variable. In fact, in certain scenarios, they may even outperform more sophisticated nonlinear models (Loukina et al., 2018). When it comes to automated essay scoring, the most attractive aspect of linear regression is the interpretability it offers. For any given essay, being able to explain why a particular score was produced, in terms of the features and their weights, is extremely useful, especially in high-stakes scenarios, i.e., where the score might be used to make consequential decisions about the test-taker.

Of course, linear regression models may also become uninterpretable in certain situations, for example, with a very large number of features or if the features are heavily engineered (Lipton, 2016). One way to improve interpretability with a large number of features is to use methods like **best-subset regression** or **stepwise regression** that allow selecting a smaller subset of features exhibiting the strongest effects when it comes to explaining the variance in the dependent variable. Another way to improve interpretability is via **feature aggregation**: combining multiple, related independent variables into one single independent variable. For example, one could combine all of the features pertaining to grammar & usage (counts of different types of grammatical errors, a language model score indicating fluency, etc.) into a single `grammar` feature and use the combined feature instead of the individual features in the regression model. One can then easily interpret the learned model weights which would be fewer in number and "dedicated" to a specific aspect of essay quality.

Another problem with linear regression models is their tendency to overfit the training data which means that they may not always generalize to new data very well. For automated scoring systems, low generalizability can lead to less accurate scores for previously unseen responses once a system is deployed. One way to improve generalizability is to employ REGULARIZATION either by shrinking the feature weights or by setting some of them to zero. Regularization reduces how powerful the model can be but the sacrifice yields reduced variance on unseen data, making the model more likely to generalize. With regularization techniques, a **penalty term** is added to the regression loss function; this term imposes additional constraints on the feature weights which, in turn, limit model complexity and reduce overfitting.

The first type of regularization is **L_2-regularization** where the penalty term is expressed in terms of the L_2 norm of the feature weights, imposing a constraint on the size of the weights. The new penalized loss function is then:

$$\sum_{i=1}^{N}(y_i^2 - \hat{y}_i^2) + \alpha\|w\|_2 \tag{4.3}$$

which can also be written as:

$$\sum_{i=1}^{N}(y_i^2 - \hat{y}_i^2) + \alpha \sum_{j=1}^{m} w_j^2. \tag{4.4}$$

The weight values are then computed by minimizing this penalized loss function and α is the complexity parameter that controls the strength of the penalty. The larger the value of α, the more the weights shrink toward 0 and toward each other. L_2-regularized regression models are also known as RIDGE REGRESSION models. Dronen et al. (2015) use ridge regression models to build a large-scale automatic scoring system for English essays (written to ASAP writing tasks), while Rupp et al. (2019) use them to score English essays written by German and Swiss high-school students to measure English writing skills at secondary levels.

The second type of regularization is L_1-**regularization** where the penalty term is expressed in terms of the L_1-norm of the feature weights. The penalized loss function then becomes:

$$\sum_{i=1}^{N}(y_i^2 - \hat{y}_i^2) + \alpha \|w\|_1 \tag{4.5}$$

which can also be written as:

$$\sum_{i=1}^{N}(y_i^2 - \hat{y}_i^2) + \alpha \sum_{j=1}^{m} |w_j|. \tag{4.6}$$

This type of penalty term essentially shifts each weight by a constant factor α, truncating at 0, i.e., if the weight for a feature was w_i, its L_1-regularized version would be $\max(0, w_i - \alpha)$. Therefore, some of the feature weights might be set to zero which is another way of reducing model overfitting. L_1-regularized regression models are also known as LASSO regression models. Loukina et al. (2015) use lasso regression models for automatically scoring spoken responses.

A more recently proposed type of regularization technique includes both L_1 and L_2 penalty terms:

$$\sum_{i=1}^{N}(y_i^2 - \hat{y}_i^2) + \alpha \sum_{j=1}^{m} (\lambda w_j^2 + (1 - \lambda)|w_j|). \tag{4.7}$$

This "hybrid" penalty term is able to find a compromise between selecting features like in lasso regression and shrinking together the coefficients of correlated features like in ridge regression and can prove to be quite effective at improving model generalizability (Zou & Hastie, 2005). Methods employing this form of penalty are known as ELASTIC-NET regression methods. Somasundaran et al. (2016) use elastic-net regression models to automatically score persuasive and narrative essays, while Beigman Klebanov, Burstein, et al. (2016) use them to measure the extent to which an essay expresses the writer's utility value from studying a STEM subject.

Recall from Chapter 2 that sometimes a feature that is expected to make a positive contribution to the score ends up with a negative weight. A variant of least-squares regression is

non-negative least squares regression (NNLS) that prevents feature weights from becoming negative (Lawson & Hanson, 1981). Note that this requires all of the features to be transformed such that they are indeed expected to positively correlate with the score. For example, if one of the features is counting the preposition errors in the essay, it should be multiplied by -1. NNLS is used in the e-Rater® automated essay scoring system (Attali & Burstein, 2006).

4.3   LATENT SEMANTIC ANALYSIS

A different approach to automated essay scoring was proposed by T. K. Landauer et al. (1998) who employed a technique called **Latent Semantic Analysis** (LSA). LSA is a statistical technique that can represent words in a given text (or even entire passages) as points in a high-dimensional, semantically motivated vector space. Essentially, by aggregating over all the contexts in which words appear in a large collection of texts, it is possible to construct a system of equations whose solution can determine the similarity of meaning of words and passages to each other. LSA requires a large corpus of documents over which the system of equations is formulated and then solved.

LSA works as follows: first, a **term-document matrix** C is created with each element c_{ij} containing the count of word i in document j. A transformation is then applied to the term-document matrix to weight each word's document-specific frequency with a measure of its frequency across the whole corpus of documents (this can be said to represent how "important" the word is in the overall corpus). Although the commonly used tfidf transformation can be used, T. K. Landauer et al. (1998) recommend using the log-entropy transformation which is computed as follows:

$$w_i \;=\; 1 + \sum_j \frac{p_{ij} \log p_{ij}}{\log n} \tag{4.8}$$

$$m_{ij} \;=\; w_i \log(c_{ij} + 1), \tag{4.9}$$

where c_{ij} is the frequency of word i in document j from the original term-document matrix, $p_{ij} = \frac{c_{ij}}{\sum_k c_{ik}}$, w_i is the global weight of word i, n is the total number of documents in the collection, and m_{ij} is the transformed value in the new term-document matrix M.

Once the transformed term-document matrix M has been created, the next step is to apply **singular value decomposition** (SVD)—a well-known matrix factorization technique from linear algebra—to this matrix. The singular value decomposition of any m x n matrix M is a factorization of the form $U \Sigma V^T$, where U is an m x m square matrix, Σ is an m x n diagonal matrix, and V is an n x n square matrix. The diagonal entries $\sigma_i = \Sigma_{ii}$ are known as the **singular values** of M. If we delete some of the singular values from the diagonal matrix Σ and multiply all three matrices, what we get back is an approximation to the original matrix. Therefore, by controlling the number of singular values, we can essentially reconstruct a version of the original matrix projected onto a lower-dimensional space that we refer to as the **LSA space**. An important question is how to choose the dimensionality of the LSA space. In the authors' words, "*it is this dimensionality reduction step, the combining of surface information into a deeper abstraction, that captures the mutual implications of words and passages. Thus, an important component of applying the technique is finding the optimal dimensionality for the final representation*". Evangelopoulos et al. (2012) provide some practical recommendations on how to pick this dimensionality value. Once this value has been chosen, the computed factor matrices with the chosen dimensionality can then be used to project new documents into the LSA space.

So, how is LSA used for automated essay scoring? The authors propose multiple different ways to apply LSA to this task.

- **Method 1**. An LSA space is first created from the essays to be scored and from all of the instructional texts that the students were assigned to read before writing the essay. A small set of students' essays were then manually assigned holistic scores by human raters. This set of essays was then projected into the LSA space. To assign the score to any new essay, it was first projected into the LSA space and then a cosine similarity is computed between its LSA vector and the LSA vectors of all the pre-scored essays. The score for the new essay is then computed as a similarity-weighted average.
- **Method 2**. The LSA space is constructed as in Method 1. The teacher or the test developer writes a reference essay which is projected into the LSA space. Any new essay to be scored is first projected into the LSA space and its score is simply its cosine similarity with the reference essay.
- **Method 3**. The LSA space is constructed as in Method 1. Cosine similarity is then computed between each sentence of the instructional text and each sentence of the essay to be scored. The final score is then computed by finding the maximum cosine for each instructional text sentence among the essay sentences, and then combining these cosine values.
- **Method 4**. This method is very similar to Method 3 except that the cosine similarities are computed between the essay sentences and a *subset* of the sentences from the instructional text, specifically those that a teacher or test-developer deems as important.

The authors evaluated the above methods on several example tests with doubly scored responses and found that the automatic scores produced were as well correlated with human scores as the human scores were correlated with each other.

It is also possible to use LSA-derived semantic similarities as feature values in a traditional linear regression model for automated scoring. For example, Jorge-Botana et al. (2015) extracted features to capture discourse coherence at various levels using LSA models and used them in a linear regression model trained to score summaries written by undergraduate psychology students.

Other dimensionality reduction techniques such as probabilistic Latent Semantic Analysis (pLSA) (Hofmann, 2001) and Latent Dirichlet Allocation (LDA) (Blei et al., 2003) have also been leveraged for automated essay scoring. Kakkonen et al. (2008) provide a thorough empirical comparison of LSA, pLSA, and LDA techniques for scoring.

4.4   OTHER NON-NEURAL MODELS

Over the years, several other supervised learning models have been used for automated essay scoring. For example, Zesch, Wojatzki, & Scholten-Akoun (2015) use length, lexical, syntactic, coherence, and other types of features with support vector machines (SVMs) (Cortes & Vapnik, 1995) to automatically score German and English essays. Beigman Klebanov, Burstein, et al. (2017) use random forest regressors (Breiman, 2001) to score science essays to predict utility value scores—scores that indicate whether the essay writer has explained how the recently learned STEM material can be useful and relevant beyond the immediate academic context, for other tasks or other aspects of his or her life.

Ensembles combine predictions from multiple, different underlying machine learning models in order to produce a final prediction. A simple example of an ENSEMBLE is a voting classifier employed with an odd number of classifiers—it produces the most common prediction as the final prediction. Ensembles are fairly popular in machine learning and can yield better results than any of the underlying models especially if said models are sufficiently diverse and capture different aspects of the problem. Larkey (1998) provides one of the earliest examples of ensemble models being applied to automated essay scoring. They use a **stacked ensemble** (Wolpert, 1992) that works as follows: first, Naïve Bayes, and k-Nearest Neighbor classifiers are trained on data consisting of essays with manually assigned scores. The predictions from these models are then added as features to a linear regression model that also uses other essay-based attributes—such as number of words, number of sentences, average word and sentence lengths, among others—as features. The authors show that the ensemble model yields scores that are very well correlated with human scores.

Another way to think about the automated essay scoring problem is as a **ranking** problem rather than a regression or a classification problem, i.e., given a set of essays, rank them based on their quality of writing such that an essay with better writing quality is ranked higher than other essays. Essentially, the goal is to learn a ranking function which outputs a score for each essay in the set from which a global ordering of the essays can then be constructed. The advantage of the ranking approach is that it explicitly takes into account the ordinal nature of the automated scoring task. Yannakoudakis et al. (2011) propose a ranking formulation of the task by utilizing **rank preference support vector machines** (Joachims, 2002). They train the proposed rank SVM to maximize the number of correctly ranked pairs of essays created from the training data and its manually assigned scores. The model uses features derived from the essay text such as lexical n-grams, part-of-speech n-grams, syntactic rules extracted from constituency parses, essay length, rate of grammatical errors, etc. They evaluate their model on essays written by English-language learners for the high-stakes First Certificate in English (FCE) examination using Pearson's and

Spearman's correlations and find that rank SVMs perform better than support vector regressors. H. Chen & He (2013) propose another ranking formulation for automated essay scoring that directly incorporates the agreement between the system and the human raters into the loss function for the model rather than relying on the number of correctly ranked pairs.

Finally, Cozma et al. (2018) use **string kernels** for automated scoring. String kernels are functions that can efficiently compute similarity between pairs of strings without requiring the strings to be of the same length. The general advantage of kernel functions is that they can compute the similarity value without explicitly needing to transform the underlying data points into a feature vector. By combining machine learning algorithms like SVM that natively support kernel functions with string kernels, such algorithms are then able to work with strings directly. The authors use an **intersection kernel** that computes the similarity based on how many character n-grams the two essays share for various values of n from 1 to 15. These similarity feature values are then incorporated into a support vector regressor which is trained to maximize agreement with manually assigned scores. The authors evaluate their model on the ASAP writing tasks and report strong results in terms of quadratically weighted kappa (κ_q) in both the within-task and the cross-task settings.

4.5   NEURAL NETWORKS

Like any other NLP application, automated essay scoring has also benefited from the modern neural network technique known as *deep learning*. In this section, we first briefly explain how neural techniques, including deep learning, work in the context of supervised learning. Note that this is *not* meant to serve as a comprehensive introduction but simply to convey the basic underlying idea. A(n) (artificial) NEURAL NETWORK is a machine learning technique inspired by how biological organisms might learn from input stimuli. Such a network contains basic units of computation called **neurons** or **nodes** that are connected to each other via weights. If two nodes A and B are connected to each other via weight w, then the output of neuron A is multiplied by w before being fed into B. Furthermore, if multiple nodes $A_1, A_2, \ldots, A_n$ are connected to B, then, in the simplest case, the output of that node is simply the sum of its weighted inputs, i.e., $B = \sum_{i=1}^{N} w_i A_i$. Such a network of neurons computes its final output by propagating the computed values from the input stimulus to the final node(s) in the network. Learning can then be effected by modifying the weights that connect the various nodes.

For supervised learning, specifically, the basic idea is as follows: take each input in the training set (usually represented as a vector), propagate it through the network to get its predicted output, compute the error (or loss) between the network's prediction and the expected label for the input, and propagate an adjustment to the weights backward through the network to reduce this error. The same adjustment in weights can then be carried out for all of the other instances in the training set. The update process is then repeated, potentially going over the training set multiple times—each iteration though the set termed an **epoch**. To ensure that the network is not simply memorizing the training set, one may also compute the error over a

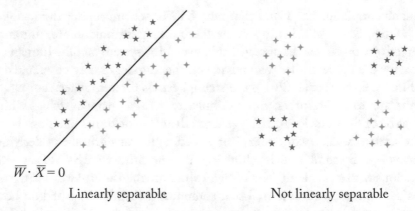

$\overline{W} \cdot \overline{X} = 0$

Linearly separable   Not linearly separable

Figure 4.1: Illustrating linearly separable vs. inseparable scenarios. Figure reproduced from Aggarwal (2018).

held-out *validation set* and stop the training process once this error starts increasing, indicating overfitting.

The simplest and earliest neural network is called the **perceptron** and it only had a single *layer* of input nodes connected to a single output node (Rosenblatt, 1958). Being a single-layer network, the perceptron was limited by its architecture and could only learn linear functions of its inputs (Minsky & Papert, 1969); it has been used primarily for a subset of binary classification problems where the two classes are *linearly separable*, e.g., as shown in Figure 4.1.

Rumelhart et al. (1986) proposed **multi-layer networks** that used multiple *hidden* layers of nodes between the input layer and the output layer; this multi-layer architecture was combined with the use of **nonlinear activation functions** at the hidden layer nodes that took the weighed linear combination of the node's inputs and passed it through a nonlinearity such as a sigmoid function or hyperbolic tangent function before passing it on to the next node. These modifications significantly increased the representational power of the resulting network, making it more useful for more complex machine learning problems, including those that are not linearly-separable. This increase in power, however, also required a more sophisticated training algorithm called **backpropagation**, a more generalized version of the training process that we described above. Multi-layer neural networks required both significantly larger amounts of data as well as significantly larger amounts of computational power for the training process to converge to a reasonable solution. Therefore, such networks were not really widely used to solve practical machine learning problems. This changed in the aughts when very large computer vision datasets became available (Deng et al., 2009) and graphical processing units (GPUs) started to be leveraged for training such networks (Bergstra et al., 2010).

We re-iterate to the reader that the above paragraphs are only meant to convey the general idea of how neural networks operate and learn; for example, we omit discussion of details such as how the weight adjustments are actually computed, whether the weights are adjusted after *each* training example or after all (or a batch) of the examples in the training set, how to set or tune the rate at which the adjustments are applied during the learning process, among many others. We believe that this level of detail is not necessary for following the current discussion and we refer the interested reader to neural network textbooks (Aggarwal, 2018; Goldberg, 2017).

4.5.1   DEEP LEARNING

Traditional multi-layer networks, as we have described them so far, usually consider the individual elements of the input vector to be largely independent of each other. During the 1980s and 1990s, research into multi-layer neural networks produced new ideas and architectures that tried to challenge this assumption. Two salient examples of such architectures include the following.

1. **Convolutional Neural Networks**. A convolutional neural network (CNN) is specifically designed to work with inputs with a grid-like spatial arrangement and strong localized dependencies, e.g., images where adjacent pixels generally share similar color values (Le-Cun et al., 1989). A CNN is designed to address the fact that elements of its inputs are not, in fact, independent. The main mathematical operation underlying a CNN is **convolution**—which essentially computes the dot-product between a "grid" of weights and a correspondingly-sized "grid" of regions in the input. CNNs may employ the convolution operation in multiple hidden layers. Although CNNs are usually used with image or video inputs, they have also been applied to text input since even text inputs exhibit some localized dependencies between adjacent words and the convolution operation can pick up on those dependencies. One way to think about convolution as applied to text is to consider it similar to n-gram extraction; it cannot capture long-range dependencies but can capture local contextual information.

2. **Recurrent Neural Networks**. For sequential input such as text, it is important to take into account the ordering of the elements (words) since that can have a major impact on the output. For example, the sentence "dog bites man" is semantically very different from "man bites dog". A recurrent neural network (RNN) can take sequential input and produce sequential output; it does so by employing a **time-layered** architecture—there is a one-to-one correspondence between the layers in the network and the position in the sequence (also referred to as the **time step**). These layers share their weights and essentially "recur in time", hence the term "recurrent" (Williams & Zipser, 1989). RNNs have been used extensively for NLP applications such as language modeling, machine translation, and text classification.

    The recurrence property bestows upon RNNs a sort of "memory" as weight updates accumulate over time. However, the update is multiplicative and successive multiplication of fractional weights tends to be unstable. This renders the RNN memory only good for "short-term" or short sequences of text. An improved variant of RNN is the **Long Short-**

Term Memory (LSTM) network which modifies the network architecture to allow the memory to work effectively over much longer sequences and, thereby, capturing long-range dependencies in the text more effectively (Hochreiter & Schmidhuber, 1997).

Both RNNs and CNNs often use a large number of hidden layers for more effective learning resulting in what are termed as DEEP LEARNING networks.[1] One motivating factor for such an architecture is that deeper networks might be able to learn in a hierarchical fashion, e.g., the first few layers of a CNN trained for facial recognition might learn how to recognize pixels, the next few might learn to recognize edges, the next few might learn to recognize combination of edges such as parts of faces, and the final layers might learn to recognize entire faces.

The same wider availability of large amounts of data and of GPU computation in the early aughts, combined with the novel CNN & RNN architectures, served to enable the **deep learning revolution**. For example, in 2012, a CNN-based system beat almost all of the other entries in an object recognition shared task by a margin of more than 10 percentage points (Krizhevsky et al., 2012). Around the same time, CNN and RNN architectures also showed significant improvements in the task of automatic speech recognition (Graves et al., 2013; Sainath et al., 2013).

4.5.2   INTERLUDE: WORD EMBEDDINGS

Before we discuss the details of deep learning techniques for automated essay scoring, we would like to introduce a crucial concept—that of WORD EMBEDDINGS. Like other neural networks, deep learning networks also accept a vector of numbers as input. For NLP applications, one way to convert the textual input into numbers is to project each word into a fixed dimensional vector space, yielding a dense vector representation for the word. Although one can use traditional n-gram or LSA-like models to compute such embedded representations, the more common approach in deep learning is to use neural networks to *learn* such embeddings from large amounts of text (Devlin et al., 2019; Mikolov, Sutskever, et al., 2013; Pennington et al., 2014; Peters et al., 2018). This is done by constructing artificial tasks to predict words or sentences in the text given other words or sentences around them as context. Although the prediction tasks themselves are formulated as supervised learning tasks, no actual supervision is required since the "labels" are simply words or sentences in the text itself.

Embeddings are usually **pre-trained**, i.e., extracted separately from the essay scoring task on large corpora of unrelated text. Such pre-trained embeddings have been shown to be more useful by themselves and also as initial inputs to deep learning networks used in other NLP tasks. An alternative to using pre-trained embeddings is to randomly initialize the embedding layer and then learn its parameters as part of the training process for the NLP task, just like the parameters of any other layer in the network. Of course, one can do both—use pre-trained embeddings but still adjust the parameters as part of the training process.

---

[1]The idea of a deep network is not exclusive to CNNs and/or RNNs; even traditional multi-layer networks can be deep.

4.5.3 DEEP LEARNING FOR AUTOMATED ESSAY SCORING

Given the success of deep learning techniques in other NLP tasks, it is only natural for them to have been applied to the task of automated essay scoring.

Early Approaches

The earliest deep learning approaches simply treated essay scoring like any other NLP task with a sequence of words as input and a numerical prediction as the final output and explored what CNNs and RNNs could achieve when applied to this problem.

One of the first applications of neural networks to essay scoring was carried out by Alikaniotis et al. (2016). The authors first modify a neural embedding model to incorporate the essay score in order to produce what they called **score-specific word embeddings**. This representation not only captures information pertaining to the word itself but also whether the word is likely to be a useful predictor of the essay score or not. The authors then derive a vector representation of each essay using these specialized embeddings that are then fed to an LSTM layer. The output of this LSTM layer essentially produces a vector representation of the entire essay. The final layer of the network is a simple linear layer which computes the essay score using the essay-level representation from the LSTM as its input. The mean squared error between the predicted score and the human score for the essay is used as the training loss function, i.e., the weights (parameters) of all the layers in the network are continually adjusted during the training process via backpropagation so as to drive the value of this loss function to zero. Once the network is trained, new essays can be run through the network to produce score predictions. The authors use the ASAP dataset that we described in Chapter 2 to evaluate their approach.[2] Their results show that their specialized embeddings combined with the LSTM-network outperforms both traditional machine learning models such as support vector machines as well as the same LSTM-network paired with "vanilla" word embeddings (embeddings without the score-specific modification).

Another influential paper from 2016 also uses an RNN-based model for essay scoring (Taghipour & Ng, 2016) with three differences compared to Alikaniotis et al. (2016)— see Figure 4.2. First, the authors choose to learn their own embeddings rather than using any pre-trained embeddings. Next, they include a convolution layer before the LSTM layer—the motivation being that the convolution layer can pick some local dependencies, similar to n-grams if we were explicitly extracting features. Finally, rather than using a simple linear layer after the LSTM layer to predict the score, they first add a **mean-over-time** layer. The mean-over-time layer averages over multiple representations in the LSTM layer instead of only using the representation at the last time step. Given that a single LSTM layer is used, the entire essay is treated as one extra-long sequence of words which can be hard to model. By averaging over multiple time steps, the mean-over-time layer can produce a much more informative essay-

---

[2]The authors combine all of the essays in the dataset across all tasks and use 80% of the data for training and the remaining 20% for evaluation.

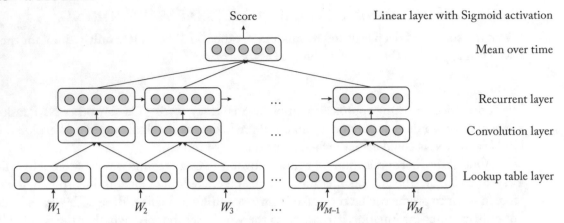

Figure 4.2: An illustration of the CNN–LSTM architecture reproduced from Taghipour & Ng (2016).

level representation which, when sent to the final linear layer, can yield more accurate score predictions. To evaluate their approach, the authors train separate models for each of the eight tasks in the ASAP competition dataset. They observe that their model outperforms the winning (non-neural) entry into the competition as well as other reasonably strong neural baselines, as measured by quadratically weighted kappa (κ_q) averaged across all eight tasks. This approach to automated essay scoring is quite popular and has also been applied to scoring essays written in Swedish (Lilja, 2018) as well as in Norwegian (Berggren et al., 2019).

The two studies we have discussed so far treated the essay as a single sequence over words. F. Dong & Zhang (2016) proposed a hierarchical model with two convolutional layers in their network, in effect modeling the essay as a sequence of sentences, which are, in turn, treated as sequences of words: the first convolutional layer learns sentence-level representations and the second downstream layer learns essay-level representations. Although they do not compare their results to the two previous studies, they find that their model does perform better than a support vector regressor and the winning entry from the ASAP competition when compared using averaged κ_q across the eight writing tasks. The authors also conduct cross-task evaluations—training the model on one ASAP task and evaluating its performance on a second, different ASAP task—and find that their model also performs significantly better compared to a previous approach that explicitly added features to allow the model to adapt to a new task. This improvement provides limited support to the hypothesis that the hierarchical CNN model is able to learn abstract, task-independent feature representations automatically.

F. Dong et al. (2017) followed up the previous study with a more principled comparison of CNN and LSTM layers when applied to automated essay scoring. They use two main dimensions along which to vary the architectures. The first is whether the essay was being modeled directly as a sequence of words (with the network using only a single LSTM layer) or whether there is a notion of hierarchy in the model (essays → sentences → words; with the network using two distinct layers in the network, i.e., CNN–CNN, LSTM–LSTM, or LSTM–CNN). The second dimension of comparison pertains to how the multiple internal representations from the CNN or the LSTM layers can be combined—or **pooled**—into more informative representations. One possible combination, as already discussed, is via a mean-over-time layer that simply averages all of the internal representations in the previous layer. The authors also use **attention pooling** which can be thought of as computing a weighted average of the representations with some words and sentences being weighted higher—or attended to more—than others. The final layer of the all the networks is the simple linear layer that produces the predicted score. The results confirm empirically that a hierarchical network with a CNN for representing sentences, an LSTM for representing essays, and attention pooling performs better than all other models.

F. Dong & Zhang (2016) showed that a hierarchical CNN model trained on one ASAP task might learn some abstract features that can help it score essays written to a different, unseen ASAP task. Jin et al. (2018) conduct more comprehensive experiments on **task-independent essay scoring**, with the goal of scoring essays for a new "target" task without explicitly training the network to do so. To achieve this, they use a two-stage solution—the first stage is a generic essay scoring model, trained on other tasks, that produces scores for essays from the target task. These essays along with their *predicted* scores are then used as pseudo-training examples to train the second stage—a deep neural network with three different parallel tiers containing multiple LSTMs each. The first tier uses pre-trained word embeddings as the input to learn semantic representations for the sentences and the essays using the hierarchical LSTM arrangement, much like previous studies. The second and third tiers, however, rely on embeddings for the part-of-speech tags and syntactic labels (from a constituency parse) assigned to the essay text to learn the hierarchical representations. The authors state that these separate semantic, part-of-speech, and syntactic sub-networks capture diverse feature representations, somewhat at odds with the idea that deep neural networks do not need to engineer explicit feature representations. In any case, the results show that the authors' approach does yield improvements over models from the previously discussed studies as measured by averaged κ_q across the eight tasks, despite the fact that the neural network has learned only from predicted pseudo-scores and not true human scores.

Incorporating Specific Aspects of Essay Quality

So far, we have discussed approaches that mostly treated the essays as sequences of sentences and tokens and used neural networks to learn a mapping between these sequences and scores. How does one induce such systems to pay attention to certain specific aspects of writing quality that the scoring rubric considers important? In the traditional machine learning setting, this is done by building features that capture, to the extent feasible, such aspects of the scoring rubric; how does one do it in the context of a neural network? One could **enrich the text representation** with more sophisticated derivatives of the raw text, adjust the network architecture accordingly (usually by adding more layers for deeper processing and integration of the different representations), and, thus, let the network utilize the additional information when predicting essay scores; notice that this comes quite close to feature engineering, as one does need to come up with the new representations and with the appropriate adjustment of the network architecture. Another option is to train a network to learn **multiple tasks**, that is, to learn to predict not only the holistic score but also *another* score that might help focus the network's attention on those aspects of the essay that are relevant to both overall score and the specific, important aspect of under consideration. These two options are often used together for more effective solutions. We will exemplify such solutions in the context of making the network attend specifically to the use of *certain source material* in an essay and to the essay's *coherence*, both important dimensions of overall essay quality. The goal here is not to conduct an in-depth review of approaches that capture coherence or source use; these will be addressed in Chapters 5 and 6, respectively.

Some writing tasks require the writer to incorporate additional information into the essay, e.g., via related articles, lectures, and videos. When scoring such source-based essays, it is important to recognize the references in the essays to these external sources and, more importantly, analyze them for whether these references incorporate the information in the right manner. For example, if the task requires the writer to summarize all of the linked sources, then the system must ensure that information from all sources is accurately represented in the essay. This type of writing task is usually employed to measure argumentative writing skills, specifically, whether the writer makes appropriate use of relevant evidence. H. Zhang & Litman (2018) describe an approach that exemplifies the representation enrichment paradigm in this context. They develop a deep learning approach to score essays by building on top of the hierarchical CNN–LSTM model originally proposed by F. Dong et al. (2017). Specifically, they replace the attention pooling layer for the LSTM with a **more sophisticated pooling layer that takes as input not just the representations for the essay sentences but also the sentences from for the external source article**. This layer allows for a different kind of weighted average to be computed over the sentence representations: sentences from the essay that are mentioned in the articles but not mentioned in other essays are weighted higher, rewarding the essay for a uniquely composed and accurate reference to the source article. The authors add another LSTM layer after this pooling layer to compute the essay-level representation, which is then fed into a linear layer to compute the final essay score.

The system of Mesgar & Strube (2018) takes the enriched representation approach for capturing discourse coherence. They incorporate a very local notion of coherence into a neural network. Their network first uses pre-trained embeddings to convert the words in an essay to their vector representations. These representations are then fed into an LSTM to obtain representations at the level of sentences. Next, the authors then **compute representations of adjacent sentence pairs** in the essay by averaging the two sentences' representations. The next layer in the network is one that computes similarities between sentence pairs to capture a somewhat limited and local notion of textual coherence. For example, if sentences 1 and 2 in an essay have high semantic similarity but sentences 2 and 3 are not very similar, it might indicate loss of coherence or increased semantic drift. The final layer in the network is a CNN layer that takes the output of the sentence pair similarity layer and outputs a "coherence vector", representing the patterns of semantic change in the essay.

Continuing with the enriched representation paradigm, Tay et al. (2018) attempt to overcome the local nature of the captured coherence in the previous study by **comparing non-adjacent sentences** separated by a configurable hyper-parameter called the "relevance width", and skipping the other sentences in between. They incorporate specific layers in their network to model these comparisons which outputs a vector of coherence features. The authors produce a score from the network itself by combining the coherence vector with the previously described mean-over-time pooled representations and then feeding the combination to a linear layer. The authors obtain competitive results on the ASAP dataset compared to previous studies.

Nadeem et al. (2019) attempt to incorporate discourse coherence by modifying the neural network architecture and by training on auxiliary tasks. In terms of the architecture, they take the hierarchical LSTM network that we discussed in §4.5.3 and modify it to be **bi-directional** in nature. Specifically, for each word, they compute a **look-back** and **look-ahead** from the first LSTM in the network. The final representation of an essay word is then created by concatenating the output of the LSTM, the look-back context vector, and the look-ahead context vector. This contextually-enhanced word representation is then used to create a sentence representation which feeds into the second LSTM and then the essay-level representation is computed. The notion of cross-sentence dependencies, as modeled by the look-back and look-ahead context vectors, is what makes this network architecture "discourse-aware". In terms of the training process, the authors first "pre-train" their network on **auxiliary tasks** before the actual training with essays and scores. The authors use two auxiliary tasks that should help the system capture important aspects of a smooth sentence-to-sentence transition: natural language inference (given a pair of sentences, predict the relationship as neutral, contradictory, or entailment) and discourse marker prediction (given a pair of sentences, predict the discourse marker, e.g., however, that links them).

Farag et al. (2018) also add a specialized architecture to capture coherence and explicitly train the network to predict both a holistic score and a coherence score. Per the usual practice, they use pre-trained word embeddings for the essay words and then use an LSTM layer to obtain sentence-level representations. At this point, they compute **representations for "cliques", or windows containing multiple consecutive essay sentences**, by applying a convolutional operation. Next, a score is predicted for each clique: 0 if it is incoherent or 1 if it is coherent via a linear layer followed by a sigmoid layer to convert them into probabilities. To train the network, the authors create synthetic training data from the ASAP essays: they create multiple permutations of each essay by shuffling its sentences and using these permutations as additional instances in the training and test data. Gold-standard scores are also computed for these instances: windows with permuted sentences get a clique score of 0 and windows containing the sentences in the original order get a clique score of 1. The network is then trained to minimize the negative log likelihood of the gold-standard scores given its predicted clique scores. For any new essay, a single coherence score is then computed as the average of the predicted clique scores. To obtain a writing quality score for the essay, the authors combine their network with the network proposed by Taghipour & Ng (2016) with the word embeddings shared between both the networks. The **joint training process** is designed to allow the two networks to learn from each other: prediction errors in *both* the essay quality score as well as the essay coherence score are backpropagated in order to update not only the two networks' individual layers but also the **shared word embeddings**.

A related line of work is building a system to score an essay on **multiple traits**, e.g., conventions vs. organization. In this formulation of the scoring task, multiple scores are produced, one for each trait, rather than a single holistic score representing overall quality. Mathias & Bhattacharyya (2020) propose an approach to predict trait scores for the ASAP writing tasks.[3] Specifically, they take the hierarchical CNN-LSTM network proposed by F. Dong et al. (2017) and apply it without modification to predict trait scores for the 8 ASAP writing tasks. They compare to a non-neural baseline with explicit feature representations and find that the deep learning approach produces significantly better κ_q values for all traits across all tasks.

Hewing Closer to the Task

In this section, we describe deep learning approaches that try to incorporate more real-world aspects of the automated essay scoring task.

To ensure that a machine learning application exhibits good performance, one important factor is that the parameters of the learning algorithm be chosen based on the metric that is actually used to evaluate the algorithm in the end. For automated essay scoring systems, κ_q is the metric that is most often used to evaluate performance. However, the neural approaches we have discussed so far do not use κ_q to choose the final values of the various network parameters. The reasons for this is that κ_q is not **differentiable** which is a requirement of the backpropagation training process: it must be possible to compute a first-order derivative (specifically, the **gradient**) for the error or loss function in order to use it to compute the adjustments to the network parameters. Given the non-differentiable nature of κ_q, it is impossible to employ it in the usual neural network training process. Y. Wang et al. (2018) propose to train a neural automated essay scoring system using a technique called **reinforcement learning**. Broadly speaking, it operates by defining a set of actions that can be taken by the algorithm with the objective of maximizing some notion of overall reward. The authors employ this technique in combination with an LSTM-based essay scoring network by casting a version of κ_q as the reward function and using the reward values to compute an adjustment that is then applied to the LSTM network

---

[3] Although trait scores are not part of the original ASAP dataset, they have been produced as part of previously published research (Mathias & Bhattacharyya, 2018).

parameters. Classification of the essay into the various score points constitutes the set of possible actions. The authors compare their results to some reasonable neural and non-neural baselines and find that the reinforced learner performs significantly better when evaluated on the eight ASAP writing tasks. Results are not directly compared to other results from the literature but a comparison shows that the authors' approach is not competitive.

A crucial factor for any supervised machine learning application is that the labels in the training data are not biased in any fashion. For an application like automated essay scoring, one source of bias can be the human raters themselves. Factors such as inconsistent application of the scoring rubric and rater fatigue can cause the scores assigned by human raters to be systematically biased (Kassim, 2011; Saal et al., 1980). If there is a systematic bias in the training scores, then any model trained on it is also likely to exhibit a bias in its predictions (Amorim et al., 2018). Given that automated scoring is often used in high-stakes educational contexts, a biased predictor of scores is likely to cause serious harm to certain test-taker populations. It is important to conduct a thorough evaluation of automated scoring systems beyond simple agreement measures such as correlation or kappa. We describe such types of evaluations in detail in Chapter 8. An alternative solution for dealing with bias in the scores is to explicitly mitigate its impact during the training process. The field of educational measurement has developed explicit models based on **item response theory (IRT)** to produce unbiased estimates of scores. Traditional IRT models usually predict the probability of a test-taker receiving a particular score for a question based on unobserved factors such as test-taker ability and question difficulty. However, such models can also be used to predict the probability of a rater assigning a particular score to a response based on various unobserved rater characteristics. Uto & Okano (2020) combine one such rater-effect IRT model (Uto & Ueno, 2018) with the hierarchical CNN-LSTM network from Taghipour & Ng (2016) in order to mitigate the ill-effects of biased scores during the training process. To do so, they first separately estimate the rater-effect IRT model from the training data and use it produce unbiased IRT estimates of essay scores in the training data. The neural network is then separately trained to predict these unbiased estimates rather than the original (biased) essay scores. At inference time, the network first produces an IRT estimate which is then converted back to the essay score. To evaluate their approach, the authors used Task 5 from the ASAP dataset. Since rater identities are not released as part of the original ASAP data, the authors recruited 38 native English speakers to re-grade the ASAP data, with 4 raters being assigned to each of the 1,805 essays written to that specific task. They found that their IRT-enhanced neural model consistently produced better κ_q values compared to their non-IRT counterparts, indicating that the proposed model is more robust to rater bias.

4.5.4   DISCUSSION

Deep learning techniques have indisputably had a significant impact on automated essay scoring and advanced the state of the art, at least in terms of agreement with human scores. However, it is also important to discuss some of the challenges associated with these techniques.

The complexity of deep neural networks makes it very difficult to understand exactly how they work and why a given response might have been assigned a specific score; they are essentially black boxes. Explaining such models via **post-hoc interpretations**—interpretations that can explain the models' predictions without taking into account the explicit mechanisms by which the models work (Lipton, 2016)—is definitely a very active area of research (Koh & Liang, 2017; Lundberg & Lee, 2017; Ribeiro et al., 2016, 2018). However, the work has not yet progressed to a stage where such models can be deployed with confidence in high-stakes contexts (Rudin, 2019; Slack et al., 2020). Furthermore, most deep learning approaches do not try to account for the scoring rubric of the writing task under consideration. This is in contrast to traditional machine learning approaches where features can be developed specifically to address various parts of the rubric.

A much-touted advantage of deep learning techniques, expressed as a motivation in almost every paper on the topic, is their non-reliance on explicit feature engineering, a staple of traditional, non-neural supervised machine learning pipelines. While it is true that deep neural networks can help produce end-to-end systems—producing the desired output (a score) *directly* from the raw text (an essay)—finding just the right architecture for such a network with the right set of hyper-parameters for each of the layers (and, indeed, the training algorithm) can be **more of an art than a science**, not unlike finding just the right set of features for a non-neural approach. Although deep learning techniques do provide the tools to build *an* end-to-end system easily, building a well-performing and robust system still requires domain as well as technical expertise. This is clearly evident from the set of approaches we have discussed in this chapter.

Many such well-performing and robust deep-learning-based systems have been proposed in the last few years and have produced impressive results on many NLP tasks. However, such systems generally have dozens to hundreds of layers and billions of parameters. To train such complex systems on the very large amount of data that is needed requires extremely powerful computational resources (hundreds or thousands of GPUs) running at full capacity for hundreds of hours at a stretch. This translates into **significant cost**: both financial (the cost of the hardware and the cloud infrastructure) as well as environmental (the carbon footprint from the energy needed to keep said hardware running). Recent studies have shown that these costs are extremely high, resulting in a negative impact not only on the field (only the biggest companies can afford to build such systems) but also on the planet (Strubell et al., 2019). In fact, for automated essay scoring specifically, Mayfield & Black (2020) show that modern deep learning techniques, despite the higher technical overhead and cost, produce results that are often no better than traditional, non-neural techniques.

CHAPTER 5

Generic Features

5.1   INTRODUCTION

In this chapter, we will review automatically computable characteristics (features) of essays that have been proposed for automated essay scoring. To help organize the discussion, let us consider the kinds of characteristics one might be looking for. The first target for such an inquiry is the **scoring rubric** , since features are meant to capture certain aspects of the rubric. As mentioned in Chapter 1, rubrics for different tasks differ somewhat; we have given an example of a rubric for defend-a-position-on-an-issue task. Let us consider the requirements again, this time paying particular attention to the general aspects rather than those pertaining to the persuasive task more specifically. In the list below, we use square brackets to mark parts of the rubric that address the [general] aspects of essay quality and italicize the *task-specific* ones:

- *articulates a clear and insightful position on the issue* [*in accordance with the assigned task*]

- [develops] *the position fully with compelling reasons and/or persuasive examples*

- [sustains a well-focused, well-organized] *analysis*, [connecting ideas logically]

- [conveys ideas fluently and precisely, using effective vocabulary and sentence variety]

- [demonstrates superior facility with the conventions of standard written English (i.e., grammar, usage and mechanics)]

The last three requirements are quite general—thus, whatever the task you are responding to, you should not be producing a randomly ordered soup of sentences (*organization*), should be using varied and nuanced expression (*vocabulary*) and standard English grammar and spelling (*conventions*).

The first two requirements have both genre-specific and more general parts. The notion of writing in accordance with the task means both adherence to genre conventions (e.g., narrative vs. persuasive writing are different; we will take these up in the next chapter) and relevance to the prompt—if the prompt (in any genre!) about music education, there should be some discussion of music education; we will call the latter *topicality*. The general notion of *development*—of a position, a narrative, or something else—is the part that could somewhat simplistically be captured by length, though it targets something like detailing in a non-repetitive kind of way, so that ideas are elaborated rather than re-stated or merely hinted at.

Aside from a rubric-based classification of features, one could consider a classification based on the levels of **linguistic structures** addressed by the feature. For example, conventions typically deal with word-level, phrase-level, and sentence-level matters—spelling, capitalization, punctuation, subject—verb agreement, missing articles, misplaced possessives, etc. In contrast, organization and development pertain to the level of *discourse*—sequencing of material beyond a single sentence. Yet, all of these—conventions, organization, development—could perhaps be considered matters of form rather than content. Topicality and vocabulary address the author's choices of content to be managed and organized into these forms—what words and meanings are going to support the presentation of the author's ideas.

Yet another perspective on classifying features is an **empirical** one—if there is a certain small number of **underlying dimensions of variation** in essay quality that are measured by a possibly large set of specific features, techniques like factor analysis can help put features into groups that are relatively independent of one another in terms of accounting for variation in scores. Attali (2007) takes this approach using essays from a standardized test of English as a foreign language, and observes that a three-factor model over a set of nine features puts the organization and development features into the first factor, vocabulary-related features into a second one, and features capturing errors in grammar, usage, and mechanics into a third factor; note that topicality was not explicitly modeled in the feature set used for that study.

Attali & Powers (2008) performed factor analysis on essay data from 4, 6, 8, 10, and 12 graders in the United States over a set of 7 features. They found that three-factor models for grades 8, 10, and 12 all assigned essay length and style to the first factor; grammar, usage, and mechanics features to the second factor; and vocabulary features to the third, which corresponds very well with the findings in Attali (2007) on a very different dataset—observing that essay length is a common proxy for development. When topicality features were added to the model, they tended to form a fourth factor, alongside vocabulary, conventions, and discourse (Attali, 2011).

While it is clear that no single pattern of feature classification will fit all circumstances, it seems that the classification into discourse-level features (organization and development), conventions, and content (vocabulary and topicality) features is a reasonable one, on grounds that it is related to the scoring rubric, to linguistic structures, and to empirical properties of feature distribution in essays. We will therefore adopt this classification for the current discussion.

While discussing systems that implement various features, we will cite evaluation results, in terms of measures such as κ, κ_q, r, and F_1. Definitions of the measures can be found in Chapter 2, Section 2.2.3 that starts on page 24.[1]

---

[1]We use κ_q for both the discrete and the continuous version of the index introduced in Chapter 2; please refer to the specific paper being reviewed for details.

5.2   DISCOURSE-LEVEL FEATURES

Discourse-level features capture properties of essay structure that make it different from a randomly sequenced set of individually well-formed sentences. Such properties have do to with essay ORGANIZATION—structures related to paragraphing, as well as overall beginning-middle-end, or introduction-body-conclusion structures; essay DEVELOPMENT—extent and forms of elaboration of ideas; COHERENCE—whether the essay makes sense as a whole and has a good flow from piece to piece, which is often separated from cohesion—the actual linguistic tools used to provide the connections between elements of text that underlie its coherence. Mathias et al. (2018) show that these discourse-level structural properties—organization, coherence—are not only matters of a reader's perception but of actual physical movements of the reader's eyes through the text. Poorly organized and low coherence texts have more fixation points scattered throughout the text and have longer durations of fixations, while well-organized and coherent ones have highly dense fixations for only certain parts of the texts. Indeed, Mathias et al. (2018) showed that gaze features can predict essay organization and essay coherence scores to a certain extent ($k_q = 0.394$ and $k_q = 0.285$, respectively). We now turn to reviewing various proposals for capturing these constructs for the purpose of automated scoring of essays.

5.2.1   ESSAY ORGANIZATION

Burstein et al. (2003) present a system for classifying sentences in an essay using the following organizational categories: title, introductory material, thesis, main idea, supporting idea, conclusion, and irrelevant. Sentence-level annotations were obtained from two raters, who showed a strong inter-annotator agreement of $\kappa > 0.8$ for each category.

To automatically classify sentences into these categories, Burstein et al. (2003) use a decision tree algorithm with boosting (C5.0) over the following set of features: (a) the rhetorical status of the sentence (nucleus or satellite) and the rhetorical relation with its parent node (such as elaboration or background), as assigned by the discourse parser from Marcu (2000) that implements elements of the Rhetorical Structure Theory W. C. Mann & Thompson (1988); (b) lexical and structural indicators that mark certain discourse roles (Burstein et al., 1998), such as the use of *first* as an adverbial conjunct, which indicates a new argument, or the use of *such as*, which indicates a detailing, as part of developing an argument; (c) category-specific lexica, such as *opinion* and *feel* as indicators for a thesis statement, or *in conclusion* as an indicator of the conclusion category; (d) grammatical features relevant for tracking discourse elements, such as subordinating and complement clauses, auxiliary verbs, sentence-final punctuation; and (e) position features that locate the sentence within the essay and the paragraph. Using 1,179 essays from 6 prompts as a training set and a set of 283 essays from the same prompts as evaluation data, the system achieved F_1 scores between 0.30 and 0.89 for the different categories, with the category of *introductory materials* being the hardest to recognize and *supporting ideas* the easiest. The authors show that performance can be improved by using a voting mechanism between the decision-tree based system, a rule-based system that uses only positional information (the first sentence in an essay is classified as introductory, the rest of the sentences in the first paragraph are classified as thesis, etc.), and a system that estimates a category-level trigram language model to gauge likely sequences; the voting system produced improved results (F_1 scores between 0.57 and 0.91).

To derive a feature for automated scoring, Attali & Burstein (2006) compute an overall essay organization score by summing up the counts of thesis, main points, supporting ideas, and conclusion elements in the essay, where consecutive sentences with the same organizational category are treated as one element. Catering more specifically to the five-paragraph essay format that is common on examinations in the U.S. education system, the scoring system counts only up to three main points, and counts supporting ideas elements only if they immediately follow a main point element. An optimally organized essay would have a thesis and a conclusion, and three main points with supporting ideas—the total of eight elements. The score is thus the actual count minus 8, to quantify the number of missing elements. Attali & Burstein (2006) show that the feature has moderately strong and consistent correlations with essay scores across a variety of datasets ($r = 0.51$–0.67), and has a standardized weight of $\beta = 0.21$–0.35 in linear regression models, making it the highest-weighted feature out of nine that also cover conventions, topicality, vocabulary, and essay development.

5.2.2   ESSAY DEVELOPMENT

The extent of essay development is sometimes captured through **essay length**, based on the observation that additional elaboration of ideas generally requires additional textual real estate. Note that count features such as essay length in words often undergo a power transformation such as a square root or a logarithm; as a result, the impact of adding a few more words to a short essay is larger than that of adding a few more words to an already long essay (see Haberman (2004) for a discussion). Essay-length-based features are often a strong baseline in terms of correlations with essay scores, especially when scoring timed essays where the rate of production of written language could differentiate between the more confident and fluent writers who also tend to get higher essay quality scores and those for whom putting words on the page is more effortful and who also tend to produce under-developed compositions when writing under a time limit.

A more nuanced approach is to combine organization and development by requiring that a discourse element (typically, a sequence of one or more sentences) be recognized as one of the target organizational units in order to be counted as part of development. Thus, Attali & Burstein (2006) describe a feature that is computed as an **average length, in words, of a discourse element** in the essay, where target discourse elements are introduction, thesis, a sequence of main points and supporting ideas, and conclusion (in the context of persuasive writing).

Another method for capturing development is comparing the **rate of introduction of new words** vs. repetition of the same ones, often measured as TYPE-TOKEN RATIO—the number of different words, also often called word *types*, to overall number of words, often called word *tokens* (Attali & Burstein, 2006). This ratio is higher when more varied vocabulary is used instead of repeating the same words over and over again. One potential issue with this measurement is that the mean frequency of tokens increases with vocabulary size (see Figure 1.1 in Baayen (2001)), so the measure is not length-invariant. Another measurement for gauging the extent of repetition is Simpson's index (Simpson, 1949) that considers the probability that two randomly selected tokens from an essay belong to the same type (Haberman, 2004); Baayen (2001) shows, however, that the issue of the relationship with vocabulary size might not be solved completely by that measure, either (see Figure 1.17 in Baayen (2001)). A related line of work where the focus is on detection of a stylistic deficiency—words with excessive repetition in an essay—is presented in Burstein & Wolska (2003); the system's performance is dominated by count and ratio features capturing the pattern of occurrence of the target word in an essay or paragraph, and this is perhaps the reason that this feature falls with other essay development features in factor analysis (Attali, 2011).

Beigman Klebanov & Flor (2013b) study the essay's vocabulary from the point of view of **word associations**. They define a word association profile of a text as the distribution of the values of PMI (Church & Hanks, 1990)—POINT-WISE MUTUAL INFORMATION—for all pairs of content words in the essay, where the accounting is done in type-based rather than token-based fashion. PMI(x,y) is defined as $log_2 \frac{P(x,y)}{P(x)P(y)}$, and thus quantifies the extent to which x and y actually appear together relatively to what one would expect by chance; Beigman Klebanov & Flor (2013b) define "appear together" as "appear in the same document", though other definitions can also be used. Word pairs with strong topical relationship tend to have high PMI values (e.g., *music/play* or *car/wheel*). Using a number of corpora, the authors show that the distribution of pairwise PMIs is normal-like with a heavy right tail, namely, there are more highly associated pairs than a normal distribution would predict. In the essay scoring context specifically, for essays written by college graduates for a standardized test for graduate school admission, the authors show that higher scoring essays tend to have higher proportions of both highly associated (PMI>2.5) and disassociated (PMI<0) pairs than lower scoring essays. Beigman Klebanov & Flor (2013b) hypothesized that this pattern would be consistent with better essays having both better topic development (hence more highly related pairs) and more creative use of language, which manifests in a higher proportion of word pairs that do not actually tend to appear together. The authors show that a feature that quantifies the proportion of word pairs in a moderately high range of PMI (between 2.33 and 3.67) is correlated with essay scores, and provides statistically significant improvement in automated essay scores when added to a competitive baseline.

Somasundaran et al. (2016) describe a **graph-based method** for tracking essay development. Initially, each sentence is represented by a set of nodes, each node corresponding to an eligible word token in the sentence. All words longer than three letters are eligible. Nodes belonging to adjacent sentences are connected with an edge. Next, all nodes corresponding to the same word token are collapsed into a single node representing the word type, which gives words repeated in multiple sentences many more neighbors in the graph than words that occur only once. Last, multiple links between two nodes are collapsed into a single weighted link.

The authors derive a number of features from the graph: (a) features based on degrees of nodes: proportion of nodes with degree 1, 2, 3; degrees of the two most connected nodes; median degree; the share of the edges connected to the most connected node out of the total number of edges (graph concentration); and (b) features based on top three and median PageRank (Brin & Page, 1998) values in raw, negative log transformed, and graph-size normalized versions. The authors show that adding these features to a competitive essay scoring baseline using the Elastic Net machine learner (Zou & Hastie, 2005) results in a significant improvement in the correlations with human scores—both for holistic scores for persuasive writing and specifically for development trait scores for narrative writing, further corroborating the supposition that the features capture aspects of essay development rather than of organization or conventions—the two other traits where the evaluation showed no significant gains as a result of adding the graph features. Analysis of specific features shows that high PageRank scores generally correspond to lower scoring essays, which could be due to larger graph size or to more distributed, rather than concentrated, link structure; indeed, the graph concentration feature is likewise negatively correlated with scores. The authors show that these features have significant partial correlation with scores controlling for essay length. O'Rourke et al. (2011) present another approach to tracking sentence-by-sentence development by measuring flow as the ratio of the sum of semantic distances between all consecutive pairs of sentences over the sum of all pairs of sentence irrespective of order, thereby capturing the extent of divergence from a random order of sentences; this measure shows a significant correlation with essay scores.

5.2.3 COHERENCE

Approaches to measuring coherence try to capture the extent to which the essay is talking about the same or related entities and the extent to which the word meanings marshaled to support the flow of ideas are reasonably related and well-sequenced. We describe both types of approaches below, starting with the entity-based one.

Entity-Grid-Based Models of Coherence

Burstein et al. (2010) describe an application of the **entity-based model of local coherence** from Barzilay & Lapata (2008) to essay data. Two annotators rated coherence quality based on "how easily they could read an essay without stumbling on a coherence barrier (i.e., a confusing sentence)". Essays were rated on a three-point scale: low coherence, somewhat coherent, and high coherence. Following an inter-annotator agreement analysis, the scale was collapsed by combining the two bottom categories into a binary classification of essays into high coherence or low coherence, with $\kappa = 0.677$. 800 essays from different test-taker populations were rated for coherence. Across three different datasets, the class distribution is quite skewed, with low-coherence essays constituting 14–25% of the data.

Barzilay and Lapata's model is inspired by the Centering Theory (Grosz et al., 1995) and other entity-based theories of discourse such as Prince (1981) and Ariel (1988), as well as by an earlier finding that a high proportion of Rough Shift transitions (a Centering theory construct corresponding to frequent shifts in the focal entity from sentence to sentence) among all sentence-to-sentence transitions can detect incoherence in student essays (Miltsakaki & Kukich, 2000). In Barzilay and Lapata's model, entities (referred to by nouns and pronouns) are represented by their roles in each sentence in a text. An entity grid that assigns each entity a role in each sentence (one of <Subject, Object, Other, Not Mentioned>) is constructed for each text, and proportions of various sentence-to-sentence entity role transitions are calculated, such as subject-to-object (as for Anne in "Anne likes Tom. Tom likes Anne."), object-to-subject (as for Tom in the previous example), etc. Entities can be detected more or less precisely—using an auxiliary system that would resolve co-reference by connecting different words that realize the same entity, like "Mother...she...", or not; entities at various degrees of discourse salience (modeled through frequency of mention) can be traced separately or together; mention tracing can be done using syntactic roles as described above, or collapsed to just a binary mention/non-mention distinction. Barzilay and Lapata explore various models for a number of tasks focused on assessment of automated text sequencing models, in contexts such as natural language generation and extractive summarization.

Burstein et al. (2010) investigate a number of models, similar to Barzilay and Lapata, as well as additional features specifically adapted for dealing with learner texts. Features based on an entity grid and other features are used as input to a decision-tree machine learning model (Quinlan, 1993). A version that includes salience and syntactic roles but without coreference is used as one of the baselines in Burstein et al. (2010); it consistently shows relatively low recall for low coherence essays (<0.35). The authors show that improvement in recall and often in precision as well can be achieved by augmenting the entity grid features with information about grammar, usage, and mechanics errors, by calculating variation in expressions used to refer to the same entity, for all entities and for non-topical nouns such as *approach, aspect, challenge*; in some cases, spell-correcting an essay also helped. The best configurations achieved F scores of 0.66–0.70 on the low-coherence class for essays written by adults and about 0.50 for essays written by middle- and high-school children; overall F scores were >0.85 for all sets of essays, due to excellent performance on high-coherence data.

Burstein, Tetreault, & Chodorow (2013) work with a larger dataset drawn from five different testing programs annotated using the same guidelines as Burstein et al. (2010); the authors investigate a number of additional features to capture coherence, such as features based on the **rhetorical structure tree** as output of a discourse parser (Marcu, 2000) and a feature called **maxLSA** that captures re-introduction of topics—maximum sentence pair Latent Semantic Analysis similarity associated with pairs that were separated by more than five intervening sentences in the essay. The authors showed that different combinations of coherence features performed best on data from different testing programs: Entity grid features, grammar error features, and type-token ratio features were included in four out of five best models each; features based on rhetorical structure were present in every best model; maxLSA participated in two best models. Burstein, Tetreault, & Chodorow (2013) show that human-annotated coherence correlates with holistic essay scores at $r = 0.46$–0.58 for the different datasets.

A number of **variants and extensions of the entity grid model** have been proposed in the literature; since they were not evaluated on essay data, it is hard to judge their relative merits for analyzing essays. Elsner & Charniak (2008) proposed additionally classifying noun phrases into those mentioning discourse-new entities (first mention) vs. discourse-old ones, as well as a pronoun coreference model. Elsner & Charniak (2011) proposed extending the grid with nouns that do not head a noun phrase (like "Bush" in "a Bush spokesman"), as well as adding entity-specific features such as discourse prominence, named entity type and coreference to distinguish between important and unimportant entities. Z. Lin et al. (2011) extended the entity grid with an additional matrix that tracks discourse roles, which is a combination of discourse relation, such as comparison, elaboration, contrast, and the argument span the mention is in. For example, in "Highland Valley has already started operating and Cananea is expected to do so soon", there is a Comparison relation between the first argument "Highland... operating" and the second argument "Cananea ... soon", hence the term "Cananea" will be tagged with a discourse role Comparison_Arg2. Guinaudeau & Strube (2013) proposed using an entity graph instead of a grid, where an initial bipartite graph is constructed of sentences and entities, where a connection between a sentence and an entity is established when the sentence mentions and entity, and it is weighted by the syntactic role of the entity in the sentence. Then a sentence graph is induced where two sentences are connected if they share at least one entity, and the weight on the connection corresponds to the number of shared entities and their roles in the sentence. Yin et al. (2019) transform the sentence-entity graph into a graph neural network (Scarselli et al., 2008) and augment it with an explicit model of a paragraph. Tien Nguyen & Joty (2017) present a convolutional neural network that operates over distributed representations of entity transitions in the entity grid, including also some of Elsner and Charniak's entity-specific features.

Lexical-Semantics-Based Models of Coherence

The second strand of coherence models focus on tracing development of ideas through usage of words with similar or related meanings, rather than of the underlying set of entities mentioned in the essay. For example, while the pair of sentences "This car has a slight wheel balancing problem. The driver should be careful when making u-turns." do not have any shared entities (the car, the wheels, or the problem are not explicitly mentioned in the second sentence), the relatively smooth flow from the first sentence to the next is achieved by talking about something related to cars and wheels (driver, u-turns) and can be seen as **developing a theme** that has to do with driving cars. The entity-based and meaning-based approaches sometimes coincide, for example, when the same word is used to refer to the same entity, thus creating a continuity in both entities and meanings. For example, entity-based coherence of "This boy is misbehaving. This boy is full of mischief." is based on the fact that the same entity is in the subject position in the two sentences; the fact that the word "boy" is repeated between the sentences also creates a meaning-based connection. It is possible to relate the two types of models even further using the notion of *bridging references*—expressions that establish an unused discourse entity which is, however, related to the already mentioned entities. In the car example above, the driver in the second sentence is not any driver but the driver of the car from the first sentence—in fact, one could argue that up until very recently (and perhaps still so in the common usage), the car implies the existence of somebody who would drive it, and in this sense the explicit mention of such a driver is not much news at all.

Yannakoudakis & Briscoe (2012) explore modeling of discourse coherence in 200–400 word texts written by English language learners for the First Certificate in English (FCE) exam, extracted from the Cambridge Learner Corpus;[2] 1,238 texts were used in the study. The essays have operational holistic scores in the 1–40 range. The authors implemented a variety of coherence models, including an entity grid model, additional discourse-management models such as pronominal coreference, detection of discourse-new vs. discourse-old noun phrases, and models based on **assessing semantic similarity between adjacent segments** of text. The authors evaluated the coherence models for their ability to improve performance of a state-of-the-art automated essay scoring system that does not use coherence features; the focus is thus on an extrinsic evaluation of these features (whether they can support scoring) rather than an intrinsic one (whether they detect differences in coherence).

The baseline automated scoring system (Yannakoudakis et al., 2011) is an SVM ranking model that uses mostly collocational and grammatical features, as well as essay length: lexical n-grams, POS n-grams, features based on syntactic parse trees, an estimate of error rate (word trigrams that are not observed in the background language model that is built using high-scoring learner texts, among others), and essay length. This model does not include coherence features; it performs at $r = 0.651$ in the cross-validation setting. The addition of four coherence feature sets yields small improvements: (a) IBM-model-POS–a model inspired by Soricut & Marcu (2006) where local coherence was modeled by the likelihood of observing words in sentence s_{i+1} conditioned on those in s_i; the IBM-model-POS represents sentences as sequences of POS tags instead of lexical sequences. The baseline augmented with this model scored $r = 0.661$. (b) The LOWBOW model from Lebanon et al. (2007) where a set of word frequency histograms obtained over different segments of text is used to model coherence; adding this model yields $r = 0.663$. (c) Average, minimum, and maximum word length were used as additional features, reasoning that "many cohesive words are longer than average, especially for the closed-class functional component of English vocabulary"; adding these features yields $r = 0.667$. We note that average word length is often conceptualized as vocabulary/lexical complexity feature rather than a coherence/organization feature; in the 3-factor analysis presented in Attali (2007), average word length tends to load most strongly on the factor dominated by vocabulary; indeed, Yannakoudakis & Briscoe (2012) note that these features could also capture lexical complexity. (d) Finally, a technique called Incremental Semantic Analysis (ISA) (Baroni

---

[2]https://ilexir.co.uk/datasets/index.html

et al., 2007) is used to produce a coherence score as follows. ISA is an incremental version of Random Indexing (Karlgren & Sahlgren, 2001), where a representation, or signature, of a word t in a semantic space is initialized randomly and then updated (thus building a *history* for t), upon encountering t with context word c using a weighted combination of the signature and the history of c. The coherence feature is the **average similarity in the semantic space between two adjacent sentences in an essay**. Adding the ISA coherence feature to the baseline system results in $r = 0.675$. The authors evaluate baseline+ISA on a test-set of essays from a different administration year, resulting in a significant improvement from $r = 0.741$ to $r = 0.749$.

Mesgar & Strube (2018) also work in an extrinsic evaluation scenario; similarly to Yannakoudakis & Briscoe (2012) they build models that are theorized to capture coherence of a text and evaluate them for their contribution to holistic scoring of essays, over a strong baseline model that does not include coherence information. The authors proposed **a neural architecture where the model explicitly captures the semantic element that is most responsible for the semantic similarity between adjacent sentences**, and includes a model for capturing essay-level dynamic of these semantic elements, to identity **patterns of good flow vs. semantic drift**, for example.

Mesgar & Strube (2018) evaluate their system on the data from the Automated Student Assessment Prize (ASAP) competition, using Enhanced AI Scoring Engine (EASE) (Phandi et al., 2015) as the baseline. The baseline system uses Bayesian Linear Ridge Regression over linguistic features—frequency-based features that count characters, words, commas, etc.; overlap with the prompt words; word- and POS-n-grams-based features. The baseline system performs at $k_q = 0.702$ on average across the 8 prompts in the ASAP dataset; the system augmented with the coherence model significantly improves the score, performing at $k_q = 0.728$. The authors examine performance by prompt, and observe that the biggest improvement over a version of the baseline system that is trained in a similar neural framework as the current system is obtained for the two narrative writing prompts, where coherent sequencing of events might be especially important.

A number of approaches to incorporating coherence into a neural network for automated scoring have been proposed that achieve results around $k_q = 0.76$ on the ASAP dataset (Farag et al., 2018; Tay et al., 2018); however, it has not been conclusively demonstrated that these improve over the neural network system of Taghipour & Ng (2016) that does not explicitly attend to coherence. These neural architectures were reviewed in more detail in Chapter 4.

Additional coherence models have been proposed in the computational linguistics literature but have not yet been evaluated for essay scoring purposes. We review a number of such models below; a comprehensive survey of models for measuring discourse coherence is outside of the focus of this book.

Louis & Nenkova (2012) proposed modeling coherence as having a reasonable sequence of sentence-level intentions (such as describe, speculate, endorse, introduce, etc.) that are realized through the appropriate **syntactic patterns within sentence and certain common patterns**

in adjacent sentences. For example, a sentence having a syntactic production "VP → VB VP" (a bare verb, often occurring with modals) followed by a sentence with a syntactic production "NP-SBJ → NNP NNP" (named entity as a subject) often occurs, in a corpus of academic writing, where the first sentence proposes a hypothesis or speculation and the next one has a person giving an explanation or opinion about it; the authors note that this pattern "roughly corresponds to a SPECULATE followed by ENDORSE sequence of intentions." J. Li & Hovy (2014) proposed a different syntax-aware model, where a distributed, embeddings-based, representation of a sentence is built recursively from the bottom up—a representation of a phrasal component is a weighted concatenation of the representations of its constituent lexical and phrasal components. The proposed coherence model is a three-layer neural network based on a sliding window of L sentences, which is trained to discriminate coherent windows (coming from the original text) and incoherent ones (sentences out of order). J. Li & Jurafsky (2017) scale up Li and Hovy's window-based coherence modeling approach by avoiding the recursive computation; their discriminative model outperforms strong baselines on the task of predicting the correct ordering of pairs of sentences.

J. Li & Jurafsky (2017) investigate an **end-to-end neural system** in which properties of the meaning transitions between sentences in a (well formed) text can be learned from the data: "Each sentence s_n is associated with a hidden vector representation $z_n \in R^K$ which stores the global information that the current sentence needs to talk about, but instead of obtaining z_n from an upstream model like LDA, z_n is learned from the training data. z_n is a stochastic latent variable conditioned on all previous sentences and z_{n-1}", thus forming a Markov chain across sentences. The authors show qualitative examples of the model being able to provide higher scores to better causal, temporal, and referential sequencing of sentences. Logeswaran et al. (2018) propose an end-to-end neural system for sentence ordering using a Recurrent Neural Network; Gong et al. (2016) use a Pointer network (Vinyals et al., 2015) for this task. T. Wang & Wan (2019) propose a hierarchical neural system with attention, where word-to-sentence and sentence-to-paragraph sequencing are modeled explicitly.

Lai & Tetreault (2018) evaluate a variety of discourse coherence models on data from online forums, emails, and reviews of businesses. Reliable annotation of coherence on these materials is hard (k_q for expert agreement was <0.4; k_q for Mechanical Turk workers was <0.2). Prediction of coherence is studied as both a three-way classification task and as a score prediction task (1 – low coherence, 2 – medium, 3 – high coherence). The authors' propose a method called ParSeq that models coherence as a **three-layer structure of word-sequence-to-sentence, sentence-sequence-to-paragraph, and paragraph-sequence-to-document**. ParSeq generally outperforms entity-grid-based approaches, especially on the score prediction task. Still, the task remains quite challenging, with best Spearman correlations r_s between 0.33 and 0.52 for the different datasets.

Rahimi et al. (2017)'s automated scoring system includes an Organization dimension; the scoring rubric emphasized adherence to the main idea, sense of beginning-middle-end, paragraphic/idea chunking (the extent to which the essay addresses different ideas in turn in multiple paragraphs), and sentence flow (logical and seamless flow from sentence to sentence and from idea to idea). The authors used strong baselines from the coherence modeling literature—entity grid (Burstein et al., 2010) and lexical chaining (Somasundaran et al., 2014). Instead of tracking entities or words, however, the authors **track topics**: Essays are automatically labeled with topics using a window-based algorithm (window size = 10) and the expert-created list of topic words. Features based off the topic grid (such as number of different topics mentioned, average length of a topic chain, distribution of different types of topic transitions) were combined with features that capture organization and essay development without relying on source material (such as number and lengths of paragraphs, LSA similarity across adjacent paragraphs and between sentences in the beginning and the end of the essay, discourse markers) using a random forest classifier; the model scored $\kappa_q = 0.56$ and $\kappa_q = 0.47$ on the two datasets, respectively, against $\kappa_q = 0.52$ and $\kappa_q = 0.42$ for a baseline that combined entity grid and lexical chaining features from prior work.

5.3   SELECTION OF CONTENT: VOCABULARY AND TOPICALITY

These features address the properties of the words selected by the author for use in the essay. VOCABULARY features tend to address general properties of vocabulary selection, such as usage of rarer and longer words or better collocational structures. In contrast, TOPICALITY features tend to address the extent to which the author chose words that are relevant for the specific prompt question. This distinction is easier to make theoretically than in practice, however, as we shall shortly see—mostly because good vocabulary selections for a specific topic tend to be both topically relevant *and* have the desirable general properties.

5.3.1   VOCABULARY

Attali & Burstein (2006) describe a "vocabulary level" feature; each word in the essay is assigned a value based on a **standardized word frequency index** (Breland et al., 1994) and a statistic over this distribution is computed as a scoring feature. According to Haberman (2004), e-rater V2 used the fifth-lowest standardized frequency index value observed in the essay as the feature; he proposes median standardized word frequency as a related alternative with somewhat better psychometric properties. Another feature is the **average word length** in characters across all words in the essay. Both these features are "proxes" (in Page's parlance) for capturing notions such as *precise* and *effective* vocabulary, reasoning that rarer (hence longer[3]) words would support better exactitude and nuance of expression. Indeed, psycholinguistic research has found a strong

---

[3]Zipf (1936) argued that the pressure for efficient communication leads to using shorter words for more frequently used meanings. Zipf has supported his argument by empirical data on word frequency distributions; the relationship is also strong when word frequency and word length measures are aggregated across all the words in the essay. Haberman (2004) reports correlations between -0.759 and -0.606 for median standardized word frequency vs. average word length per essay, in the context of test-taker writing in English.

relationship between word length and the conceptual complexity of the object named by the word, in a variety of languages (Lewis & Frank, 2016). Features based on word length and word frequency tend to garner moderate weights in scoring models—Attali (2011) reports a combined relative weight of .15 to .18 across different writing tasks, for models that also include conventions and discourse features.

Bestgen (2016) investigated a variety of association statistics to measure **collocational usage** in essays written by students of English as a second language (ESL); they found that binning the distribution and using multiple measures of collocation/lexical association improves correlations with scores. For example, in a prior study, Granger & Bestgen (2014) showed that essays written by intermediate and highly proficient ESL students differ in their use of the type of collocations—the less proficient writers used more of the strongly associated high frequency words (as revealed by high values of the t-score measure of association), such as "good example" or "hard work". In contrast, the more proficient writers used more of the strongly associated low-frequency words (as revealed by high values of the point-wise mutual information measure), such as "bated breath" or "preconceived notions". Somasundaran et al. (2015) also showed that a collocation feature was effective for scoring the content of picture-based oral narratives. Interestingly, a feature for assessing collocations based on Futagi et al. (2008), though ostensibly having to do with the right vocabulary choice to complete the pattern, does in fact load with conventions, rather than with vocabulary, in factor analysis (Attali, 2011). This is not surprising given that coming up with good multi-word collocational patterns also involves creating well-formed phrases and is thus a matter of both grammatical and lexical choices. Indeed, mis-collocations that involve incorrect determiners or prepositions are often considered grammatical errors (Gamon et al., 2008). Kochmar & Briscoe (2014) focus on annotation and detection of **semantic mis-collocations** in learner corpora. They classified adjective—nouns pairs extracted from ESL learner data into correct or incorrect collocations using two approaches: (a) depending on whether annotators can think of some appropriate context of use for it; and (b) depending on whether the specific expression was correct in the context that it was used in the learner data. They found greater average inter-annotator agreement on the first version—$\kappa = 0.65$ vs. $\kappa = 0.49$. Using a decision tree classifier over features based on distributional semantic representations of the target words, the phrase, and their semantic neighbors, the authors report classification accuracy of above 0.8 for the out-of-context judgments and 0.65 for the in-context ones. The authors further observed that the system's precision in detecting mis-collocations was quite good, both for out-of-context and for in-context settings (both around 0.7), suggesting that the system is not very likely to erroneously fault the writer for a reasonable usage.

Attali (2011) proposed to derive word quality values based on their **differential usage in high-scoring vs. low-scoring essays**—this computation can be more or less generic, depending on whether every prompt question is considered separately for estimation of per-word quality or whether the estimation is done at the task level—that is, the training data for building the estimates come from a variety of prompt questions used for the same task. Table 5.1 shows the

Table 5.1: Examples of words with high positive or negative values for the differential word usage measure: 20 words with the highest value out of all words with at least 1,000 occurrences in the training data (top), and 20 words with the lowest value out of all words with at least 1,000 occurrences in the training data (bottom)

Type	Examples
highest–value words	necessarily, participant, perhaps, shy, simply, melatonin, similar, determine, significant, sample, furthermore, address, assumption, account, assume, blue, size, impact, while, comparison
lowest–value words	our, good, think, thing, you, get, I, my, so, arguer, always, we, pill, old, every, feel, like, conclude, lot, news

highest- and the lowest-value words according to the differential word use measure for a task-level model for the GRE argument critique task. It is quite apparent that the "better" words tend to be longer and rarer, thus suggesting a relationship between this measure and the other vocabulary measures described above. Indeed, when average differential word use score per essay was added to a scoring model that already included vocabulary, conventions, and discourse features, the combined relative weight of the median word frequency and average word length features dropped from .15 to .05. Note, however, that even the relatively high occurrence cutoff—at least 1,000 occurrences in training data—yielded some words that seem to be quite specific to the argument critique task, such as *sample* and *participant*, suggesting that multiple prompts seem to be targeting a critique based on argument-from-sample (see next chapter for a detailed discussion of types of arguments). Some words also seem to be topic-specific, such as *shy* or *melatonin*, suggesting that the measure might be taking advantage of some *topical* commonalities across prompts. In fact, when additional topicality features are added to the model, the task-level differential word use feature tends to load on the topicality, rather than the vocabulary, factor. We will thus meet the differential word use idea in the next subsection, as well.

5.3.2   TOPICALITY

Topicality, or prompt-relevance, features try to capture whether, or to what extent, the content of the essay is responsive to the topic as set in the prompt question.

Persing & Ng (2014) propose scoring ESL learners' writing for prompt relevance on a seven-point scale (scale of 1 to 4 with half-point increments) using a feature-rich linear regression approach. While they demonstrate that learning one linear regression model per prompt is a useful supervised approach, it means that substantial training data is needed for each prompt in order to build the models. For the task of determining topical relevance, this places a substantial burden on manually annotating texts for each individual prompt. As a result, supervised prompt-specific approaches are impractical and less flexible in an operational setting; if, for example, a new previously unseen prompt is required for an upcoming assessment, the model cannot be applied until a sizeable amount of manually annotated responses are collected and annotated for that prompt. Another important consideration regarding supervised topicality models is the difficulty of creating reliable rubrics for scoring topical relevance; indeed, Persing & Ng (2014) cite a Pearson correlation of only 0.243 between two annotations of topical relevance for a common set of 707 essays.

Beigman Klebanov, Flor, & Gyawali (2016) address the task of assessing the extent to which an essay is on-topic, using word- and essay-level topicality models. Having defined what makes a word topical (based on probabilities of occurrence in and out of a given topic, as well as distribution of other words across topics), they cast the topicality problem as either that of vocabulary (and so has to do with the different word types used in the essay) or of vocabulary and essay development through repetition (using token-based models). They observed that type-based models were generally more effective for predicting essay scores. Furthermore, the authors showed that topicality defined as the proportion of topical words increases with essay score *for essays with similar length*, but is negatively correlated with length, so longer essays generally tend to be less topical, according to the proposed topicality measures. Length-scaled proportion of topical word types in the essay was shown to be the best performing topicality index, in terms of contribution to already strong essay scoring models. A limitation of such an approach is the need to have access to essays responding to all possible prompts in order to build a topical word list for every prompt, but, differently from Persing and Ng's approach, the construction of the topical lists does not require manual intervention.

While the approach in Beigman Klebanov, Flor, & Gyawali (2016) requires data from essays responding to a number of different prompts in order to estimate word topicality for any given prompt, Attali (2011) and Attali & Burstein (2006) present approaches where topicality of a word for the given prompt is estimated based on vocabulary patterns in higher-scoring vs. lower-scoring essays responding to that prompt, thus making it possible to estimate topicality of words for the current prompt without recourse to data from other prompts—albeit it does require training essays from the current prompt to be scored. To be more precise, these features are typically not cast as capturing topicality of words but rather a more general notion of the value of the given word for differentiating between strong and weak essays (and are in this sense more akin to vocabulary features, as discussed in Section 3.1). However, since relevance to the prompt is typically an important part of the scoring rubric, it stands to reason that high scoring essays tend to be more relevant to the prompt than the low-scoring ones, and their usage of vocabulary would reflect that. Attali & Burstein (2006) use content vector analysis to create vectors of weighted frequencies of words at every score point in the training data (so, if the scoring scale is 1 to 6, then six vectors are generated, one for each scoring point). The essay's vector is then compared to each score point vector using a cosine metric, and the nearest score point is the value of one topicality feature; the second feature is the value of the cosine measure for the most similar score point vector. Attali (2011) proposes variants of these features that take into account the full set of six scores instead of just the top one, as well as a variant of the differential word use feature discussed in the vocabulary section above, but this time inducing word-value scores using data restricted to the specific prompt, thus calculating which words tend to be used by stronger vs. weaker writers when responding to the specific question. Evaluating the impact of these features on the performance of the scoring engine, Attali (2011) observes that they have a much larger impact in source-based writing tasks, namely, tasks where the test-taker needs to take the text of the source document into account when crafting an essay. Thus, the addition of the topicality features in source-based tasks leads to a substantial increase in performance–between .05 and .15 increase in Pearson's correlation between human and machine scores, while the figure is about .02–.03 for the tasks where the author is not provided any specific source text. This is not surprising, as the good topical vocabulary for the source-based task is likely to have a narrower extent of variation than in a more open-ended task.

Higgins et al. (2006) addressed the problem of detecting off-topic essays without recourse to on-topic training data using tfidf-weighted content vectors and cosine similarity as building blocks. Unreasonably low semantic similarity to its putative prompt (relative to other essays' similarity to their respective prompts), unreasonably high semantic similarity to another prompt, as well as use of certain strategies employed by uncooperative writers (such as using direct-address terms like *hello* or *thank you*) were features used in models for predicting off-topic status of an essay. The authors reported relatively low false-positive rates (so, bona-fide on-topic essays were generally classified as such, though for some learner data the false positive rate was still about 9%), but not all off-topic essays could be thus captured (the false-negative rate remained at about 30% for some testing contexts). New approaches to representing sentences for the purpose of topicality assessment using representations based on word embeddings have been studied by Rei & Cummins (2016); in particular, their results suggest that directly optimizing word weight parameters for the task of classifying pairs of sentences as belonging to same text or different texts could yield more effective word topicality weights than tfidf-based weighting.

M. Chen & Li (2018) present a neural essay scoring system that uses an extended representation for every essay—a vector that is constructed from the essay is augmented with a vector built using element-wise multiplication of the essay's vector with a vector representing the prompt. A complex architecture is presented, with multiple BiLSTM components and with attention. While the system with all components performs best, the removal of the prompt-to-essay similarity component results in only a slight reduction in average performance (0.007 points in κ_q, from 0.773 to 0.766), so it is not entirely clear that explicit modeling of topicality was consistently effective.

Louis & Higgins (2010) address the problem of detecting off-topic essays when the prompt text is too short to support effective construction of a semantic vector. They expand prompts using morphological variations, synonyms, words that are distributionally similar to those that appear in the prompt, and words that form free associations with prompt words. The authors show that the prompt expansion techniques are effective for reducing false positive rates;

they also show that spelling correction of the essay is important for reducing false positives in ESL learner data. Cummins et al. (2016) propose a different prompt expansion method based on a technique from information retrieval—the prompt serves as a query to a database of Wikipedia articles, and the top retrieved documents are analyzed for selecting expansion terms. Some potential caveats for the latter approach is that coverage of various topics in Wikipedia might be uneven, and also that prompts must be reasonably similar to real topics of public interest likely to be covered in an encyclopedia, as is often the case with state-your-opinion-on-an-issue task, but is not necessarily so for source-based tasks where prompts are often fictitious passages built to illustrate a logical flaw in reasoning, for example.

Jin et al. (2018) address the problem of the system's not having scored on-topic examples at training time, although it is assumed that there are some not-yet-scored essays responding to the target prompt available. Their idea is to train a step-one system using relatively prompt-independent features, such as number of grammar or spelling errors, essay length, depth of parse trees, mean and variance of sentence and word lengths, etc., on pre-existing data from non-target prompts. Then, use this trained system to automatically score essays responding to the target prompt, select those that received very high or very low scores, and use those to train the step-two system using more content-dependent features, based on semantic, POS, and syntactic embeddings. The authors show that this approach performs well across a number of different essay writing tasks, and outperforms strong baselines.[4] A caveat about interpreting the second step as capturing topicality is similar to that discussed earlier for the differential word use feature—topicality is entangled with a more general notion of the "value" of words for differentiating between stronger and weaker writers—some of them could be quite generic. Nguyen & Litman (2016b) explicitly differentiate between what they call argument words (words that are commonly used in argumentative writing, good or bad) such as personal pronouns or comparative adverbs, and what they call domain words that pertain to the specific topic of discussion; it is likely that many of the highly differentiating words would fall under the general argumentative vocabulary within a more-or-less academic register.

Beigman Klebanov, Gyawali, & Song (2017) address the situation where not only are there no *scored* essays responding to the given prompt, but there aren't any such essays at all, namely, the system would need to score a response to a prompt without any prior response data. The idea in that case is to rely on the relatively restricted task–that of scoring argument critique essays. In particular, given that many prompts follow the policy argumentation scheme (X should do Y in order to achieve Z based on evidence W, where X, Y, Z, and W stand for prompt-specific elements), it is very likely that a reasonable on-task (namely, critical) and on-topic response would say that X should *not* do Y and cite various standard problems with W like small or unrepresentative sample, etc. The authors therefore designed hybrid n-gram features, where content words from the prompt are represented as POS tags while function words

---

[4]A more detailed description of this system is given in Chapter 4 Section 4.5.3, in the context of neural architectures for automated essay scoring.

(including modals) remain in their lexical form, to allow capturing features such as "NNP-in-prompt should not VB-in-prompt". The authors show that this technique, together with other features, yields good generalization to unseen prompts for the task of finding critique-bearing sentences related to the prompt.

To summarize the discussion of topicality, the decision regarding which approach to take depends on the available resources. If one has access to scored essays responding to the target prompt and resources to annotate those with prompt-adherence scores, one could obtain the most direct information on topicality with good validity (assuming the annotation is reliable). If the scoring context does not allow for annotation time, but one has access to training essays written in response to the target and other prompts, it is possible to infer topicality by examining vocabulary usage patterns in the current vs. other prompts, or, with some caveats, in higher- and lower-scoring essays responding to the given prompt. Lastly, if one has no in-prompt essays at all, one might need to recourse to comparing the essay to (some representation of) the (expanded) prompt text; to incorporating only the most generalizable information into the feature set, such as marking an essay word as belonging to the prompt; or to inferring topical vocabulary by eliminating from the essay other types of vocabulary that can be assumed to serve a different purpose (for example, argumentation vs. domain words).

5.4   CONVENTIONS

The features reviewed in this section are built to capture the aspect of the scoring rubric that is often phrased along the lines of "demonstrates superior facility with the conventions of standard written English (i.e., grammar, usage, and mechanics)" (for a test that is geared toward both native and non-native speakers of English)[5] or "displays consistent facility in the use of language... though it may have minor lexical or grammatical errors" (for a test that is geared toward non-native speakers of English).[6] We focus on the tasks of detection of errors and on the use of the grammar error/correctness information in the essay scoring context; Y. Wang et al. (2020) provide a survey of approaches to the related task of grammar error correction.

While the precise classification of errors into grammar, usage and mechanics ones is often elusive, the categories are useful in elucidating the kinds of problems that could occur with regards to conventions. GRAMMAR ERRORS generally pertain to a violation of a particular rule of grammar, such as a violation of the number agreement rule between the subject and the predicate of a clause which makes *they makes* an error. USAGE ERRORS are those where the hard-and-fast rule is less clear-cut or its applicability is more difficult to ascertain and might depend on context.[7] Gamon et al. (2013) give the use of indefinite article (a/an) in English as an example. It is

---

[5]https://www.ets.org/gre/revised_general/prepare/analytical_writing/issue/scoring_guide
[6]https://www.ets.org/s/toefl/pdf/toefl_writing_rubrics.pdf
[7]In the big picture of things, rules of grammar are not commandments set in stone that always apply, irrespective of context—they might differ across dialects of the same language, they might be more or less operative in various genres of writing, and they can be flouted for literary effect, e.g., "Yoda speak". The distinction between grammar and usage is therefore not categorical, but a convenience to facilitate the presentation.

required to precede countable nouns, but countability is not a binary property—some nouns are more strongly countable than others, and might be more so in some contexts than others. So, both *I don't drink beer* and *I'd like a beer* are ok, in the right context. Another type of error often classified under usage is confusion between similar-looking or similar-sounding words, like *than* and *then*—one needs to evaluate the specific context of use to judge correctness. MECHANICS ERRORS typically cover spelling, capitalization, punctuation, as well as other orthographic issues like fused words or word-internal hyphenation. The term GRAMMATICAL ERRORS is sometimes used to cover all grammar, usage, and mechanics errors (Leacock et al., 2014, p. 20); we will largely do likewise in this section.

5.4.1   EARLY APPROACHES

A traditional approach to detecting grammatical errors is to craft a set of rules that would identify various specific grammatical problems (Schneider & McCoy, 1998); techniques based on **precision grammars** generally attempt a syntactic analysis of a sentence (that is, attempt to PARSE it), detect a failure in this process, and often categorize failures as instances of specific types of errors; examples of precision grammars include Butt et al. (2002) and Copestake & Flickinger (2000); see Wagner et al. (2007) for further discussion. However, hand-crafting a resource with good coverage is a daunting task. One way to make progress is to use a more flexible parser, such as a **statistical parser** (Klein & Manning, 2003) that would not fail or report an error on ungrammatical input but would always return *some* parse, and build rules operating on outputs of such tools in order to detect specific types of errors such as subject—verb agreement errors (Cai et al., 2009; Y. Wang & Zhao, 2015); one caveat here is that popular statistical parsers are typically not trained on corpora that are rife with grammatical errors, hence their handling of such data might need to be examined in detail and perhaps adjusted (Berzak et al., 2016; Cahill, 2015; Cahill et al., 2014; Geertzen et al., 2013; Huang et al., 2018).

Another approach attempted early on is to rely on **local statistics that do not require a full syntactic analysis**; for example, Chodorow & Leacock (2000) proposed identifying candidate errors by considering low-mutual-information sequences of POS n-grams or hybrid lexical and POS n-grams around a target word, relative to a general reference corpus as well as relative to a sub-corpus focusing on the specific word in question. Yannakoudakis et al. (2011) evaluated language-model-based error rate estimate (an error is declared for every trigram not in the reference data) as a feature for scoring examination essays from the First Certificate in English (FCE) test offered as one of the Cambridge Assessment's English as a Second or Other Language (ESOL) examinations[8] and found that it leads to improved performance ($r = 0.741$ vs. $r = 0.714$) over a strong baseline that contains word and POS n-gram features, essay length, features representing phrase structures detected by a parser, and a measure of syntactic sophistication—longest distance in tokens between a head and a dependent.

---

[8]https://www.cambridgeenglish.org/exams-and-tests/first/

5.4.2   FEATURE-DRIVEN SUPERVISED LEARNING

With the advent of large corpora annotated for grammatical errors (Dahlmeier et al., 2013; Dale & Kilgarriff, 2011; Tetreault & Chodorow, 2008; Yannakoudakis et al., 2011), approaches based on the **feature-engineering paradigm** in supervised machine learning were applied to the task. For an in-depth discussion of the error annotation procedure and a list of annotated corpora for various languages, see Chapter 8 and Appendix A in Leacock et al. (2014). These annotated data, along with prior, smaller-scale studies, allowed for identification of **the most common error types** in various corpora. In particular, it has become clear that beyond spelling errors that are common across the board, native speakers make rather different errors from ESL students (for whom English is not their first language)—half of the ten most frequent errors made by native speakers are negligible in non-native writing. Leacock et al. (2014) note that this does not mean that non-native writers are not making these errors—it is more likely that they simply avoid the kinds of complex sentences where errors such as no comma after an introductory element, in a compound sentence, or in a restrictive clause tend to occur. According to Leacock et al. (2014), the most common error patterns in the Cambridge Learner Corpus (Nicholls, 2003), in contrast, have to do with errors in the choice of content words ("We need to deliver the merchandise on a daily *base*"), prepositions ("Our society is developing *in* high speed"), and determiners ("We must try our best to avoid *the* shortage of fresh water"), these three accounting for about 45% of non-spelling errors, followed by comma errors, inflectional and derivational morphology, wrong verb tense, wrong pronoun, agreement errors, run-on sentences, confused words (like *personal* and *personnel*), conjunction errors, split or joint words, apostrophe errors (not including *it's*), and hyphenation errors. Other error types accounted for less than 1% of the errors each and collectively covered 3% of the errors. Much of the subsequent work has focused on the most frequent error types in ESL writing—wrong articles, prepositions, and collocations, as well as on detection of spelling errors.

Leacock et al. (2014) offer a book-length treatment of various approaches to detection of grammatical errors in the feature-engineering paradigm; we will provide a brief overview here, based on Leacock et al. (2014). In terms of techniques used for detecting the different types of errors, Leacock et al. (2014) comment that detection of article and preposition errors may serve as a kind of paradigm example, since approaches for handling other kinds of errors, such as verb form errors or subject–verb agreement errors, tend to borrow methodology from those more frequent and more extensively studied[9] error types.

Detection of Article and Preposition Errors

Let us start with the **kinds of features** considered for detection of preposition and article errors. These include many of the elements tried in the earlier approaches, now as features to be combined using machine learning: (a) local contextual information, such as n-grams; (b) information about the part of speech of the current token as well as of other tokens that allows, with some

---

[9]Including a shared task dedicated just to article and preposition errors (Dale et al., 2012).

additional processing, to recover some phrasal information as well, such as identification of the syntactic head; (c) information about the syntactic structure of sentence based on the output of a parser or a PHRASE CHUNKER (sometimes also called a shallow parser; a parse where only major phrase boundaries, such as verb and noun phrases, are detected); (d) semantic information that could help determine correct preposition/article usage, such as the tendency of entities denoting organizations to go with the definite article; and (e) the writer's original selection of article/preposition and possibly metadata regarding the writer's native language (L1), due to the observation that writers with different native language backgrounds tend to make different errors in English.[10]

The second element of the data-driven article and preposition error detection systems is **which data is used for training**. Early approaches utilized well-formed training data due to lack of availability of error-annotated data. Within that paradigm, however, methods were proposed to generate artificial errors by replacing some articles (or prepositions) in a well-formed text such as Wikipedia with another article/preposition at various rates, for example, in correspondence with the preponderance of the error in the learner writing, in general or in L1-specific data. Training on such artificially adjusted data proved more effective than using solely the original well-formed text (Dale et al., 2012; Rozovskaya & Roth, 2010a,b). Furthermore, above and beyond texts that are explicitly annotated for errors and well-written texts with artificially introduced errors, it is possible to infer somewhat noisy annotations by scraping online resources offering practice to English language learners, as well as from a pattern of revisions in a large collaboratively built resource such as Wikipedia; Cahill, Madnani, et al. (2013) show that using these to augment training data can help. Additional work on injecting errors into the training data will be reviewed in the context of neural models in Section 5.4.3 below.

The third element in the feature-engineering paradigm is the **machine learning algorithm** used to generate predictions. The error detection task is most commonly cast as a classification task—for a given token, predict whether or not it contains an error, or, when done implicitly as a part of an error correction system, as a multi-class classifier that outputs the best article/preposition for a particular position (a writer's error corresponds to cases where the outputted article/preposition is different from the one originally used); the multi-class classification setup assumes that there are a small number of possible corrections, which is the state of affairs with prepositions and articles since these are closed-class words in English, with relatively few members. A variety of classifier architectures were explored, including: (a) models that compute predictions based on a weighted combination of features represented as a vector, such as Naive Bayes and Averaged Perceptron (Rozovskaya & Roth, 2011), Maximum Entropy (Tetreault & Chodorow, 2008), Support Vector Machines (Oyama & Matsumoto, 2010); (b) probabilistic language models based on n-grams or words, POS tags, or other elements (J. Lee & Seneff, 2006; Turner & Charniak, 2007), and (c) search-engine-based methods where the score for a

---

[10]In fact, Berzak et al. (2014) report substantial success in predicting the typology (structure of language families) of the native languages of students based on syntactic, part-of-speech, and morphological features of their essays in English—that is, speakers of Russian and Polish have more similar grammatical patterns in English than speakers of Russian and French.

given n-gram corresponds to an estimate of total returned results from a commercial search engine (Tetreault & Chodorow, 2009; Yi et al., 2008). Gamon (2010) and Madnani, Heilman, & Cahill (2016) exemplify approaches where both classifier predictions and language model scores were used.

Additional approaches to article and preposition error correction include casting the task as a sequence labeling task, which allows flexible modeling of the dependence of the target element on others in its local vicinity; for example, Gamon (2011) uses a Maximum Entropy Markov Model, and Israel et al. (2013) use a Conditional Random Fields model. Wu & Ng (2013) present an Integer Linear Programming approach to jointly correct all errors in a sentence in a way that optimizes the overall grammaticality of the sentence, thus capturing dependencies between errors ("a cats" could be corrected as "a cat" or "cats" or "the cats", depending on a wider sentence context). Another popular approach in the error correction context is to use statistical machine translation (SMT) methods where models are trained to "translate" the erroneous version into the correct one (Junczys-Dowmunt & Grundkiewicz, 2014; Mizumoto et al., 2012; Yuan & Felice, 2013). Rozovskaya & Roth (2016) combined SMT and classifiers into an effective pipeline; Rozovskaya & Roth (2019) explored a similar approach for Russian.

Spelling Errors

In the literature on spelling errors, a distinction is often made between errors that result in a valid word (real-word errors) and those that result in a non-word. To detect non-word spelling errors, a dictionary lookup is a commonly used procedure; for example, Flor et al. (2019) use a dictionary consisting of 140K single words, 100K multi-word terms, and 130K names, including lexica from WordNet, U.S. Census Data, Wikipedia and other web resources; Reynaert (2004) detail a lexicon generation procedure using frequency-based cutoffs on a large corpus.

To detect real-word spelling errors, approaches based on contextual fit were developed using both classification-based and probabilistic methods (Golding & Roth, 1999; Mays et al., 1991). Hirst & Budanitsky (2005) presented a technique based on semantic similarity for detection of real-word errors, reasoning that an incorrect word would be semantically further from its context than the correct alternative ("It is my sincere *hole/hope* that.."), so any content word that does not have a sufficiently strong relationship with its context but has a close spelling variant that does have such a connection is declared an error. Islam & Inkpen (2009) propose a trigram frequency-based method that takes into account the string similarity between the candidate error and the proposed correction. These algorithms were evaluated on artificially injected errors (Hirst & Budanitsky, 2005; Islam & Inkpen, 2009; Wilcox-O'Hearn et al., 2008). A. J. Carlson et al. (2001) and Golding & Roth (1999) propose an evaluation using confusion sets (pairs of often confused words, like *their* and *there*) in conjunction with well-formed texts that are assumed to have the correct usage; the system is evaluated on picking the right member of the confusion set for a given instance. In an error detection context, the system can predict, for the given candidate, whether it is the correct one to use in the context, or not. The confusion set technique served as the basis and the inspiration of much of the subsequent work on grammatical errors reviewed above, observing that different prepositions (articles), being closed-class words, can be thought of as confusion sets for each other (see Rozovskaya & Roth (2010a) for an overview of this trend).

Due to the clear relationship between proficiency and proportion of misspelled words (see, for example, Flor et al. (2015) on statistics from standardized test datasets), (transformed) counts of misspelled words—both non-word and real word misspellings, also termed word-usage errors—are commonly used in an automated scoring context (Burstein, Tetreault, & Madnani, 2013; Foltz et al., 2013).

Other Grammatical Errors

Cahill, Chodorow, et al. (2013) present a system for detecting missing hyphen errors in English, using a logistic regression classifier over token, stem, and POS-tag unigrams and bigrams, along with dictionary-based, Wikipedia occurrence-based, and sentence configuration-based features. Israel et al. (2012) present a Conditional Random Fields (CRF) (Lafferty et al., 2001) model to detect missing commas, using features such as POS, bi-grams, and distances to the nearest conjunctions; J. Lee et al. (2014) extend this approach to detection of comma splices and utilize parse-tree features in addition. Yeung & Lee (2015) address detection of sentence fragments using a logistic regression model over POS and parse-based features. Tajiri et al. (2012) present a CRF-based method for detection and correction of tense and aspect errors; apart from the standard local-context features, the authors also include features from other verbs in the same sentence. J. Lee & Seneff (2008) present work on detection and correction of verb form errors, capitalizing on the insight that such errors affect parse trees in systematic ways that can be mined for error detection. Rozovskaya et al. (2017) address subject—verb agreement errors using methodology similar to that used by this research group for article and preposition errors (e.g., Rozovskaya et al. (2012)); Flachs et al. (2019) apply a rule-based generator of subject—verb agreement errors and use it to augment the training data for a neural error detection system, showing substantial improvements as a result of data augmentation.

Vincze et al. (2014) present a rule-based system for detection of verb conjugation errors in Hungarian. Rozovskaya & Roth (2019) describe an SMT+classifier system dealing with subject—verb agreement errors and verb aspect errors in Russian. A series of shared tasks addressed correction of errors in Arabic (Mohit et al., 2014; Rozovskaya et al., 2015). Detection of grammatical errors in Chinese was the focus of yearly shared tasks held between 2014 and 2018; see G. Rao et al. (2018) for an overview.

Another related effort is focusing on errors made by mature writers writing in a specific genre—that of *scientific writing*. A dataset of language edits by a professional scientific editing agency was used in a shared task (Daudaravicius et al., 2016) set as classification of sen vs. *correct* (no edits). Although the dataset does not have error-type annotations, the authors observe that many of the edits address genre-specific conventions in use of punctuation, hyphenation, capitalization, abbreviations, rather than "more classical second-language type of errors" such as articles, prepositions, agreement, or misspellings. A variety of traditional supervised learning methods and deep learning methods have been proposed for this task, with most systems exhibiting a strong precision vs. recall imbalance, with the system with the best F_1 score (which uses a combination of a convolutional and a recurrent neural networks (Schmaltz et al., 2016)) achieving $P = 0.54$, $R = 0.74$, and $F_1 = 0.63$.

5.4.3   NEURAL APPROACHES TO DETECTION OF GRAMMATICAL ERRORS

Let us now move to **neural error detection models** that generally do not focus on any particular error type but attempt to detect all errors. Rei & Yannakoudakis (2016) cast the error detection problem as a sequence labeling task. The dataset (from Yannakoudakis et al. (2011)) contains short texts written by ESL learners for an assessment of mastery at the upper-intermediate English proficiency level. The test set contains 2,720 sentences, and training and development data together contain 30,953 sentences. The responses were manually annotated for error spans for 77 types of errors. These were converted to a token level error detection task by labeling each token inside the annotated error span as being incorrect. To capture missing word errors, the error label is assigned to the token immediately after the incorrect gap.

Rei & Yannakoudakis (2016) investigated a number of neural architectures: convolutional, bidirectional recurrent, bidirectional LSTM,[11] and multi-layer variants of each, using a Conditional Random Fields based model as a baseline (Lafferty et al., 2001). They found that a BiLSTM (Bidirectional LSTM) model outperformed all others, beating the CRF model by a large margin ($F_{0.5} = 0.411$ vs. 0.259). The use of $F_{0.5}$ (instead of the more common F_1) is inspired by the feedback application in that it weights precision more than recall (Ng et al., 2014), to reflect the importance of avoiding false positives when declaring errors. The authors also evaluate the effectiveness of the grammar error model for automated essay scoring by adding a new feature—the average probability of each token in the essay being grammatically correct, according to the error detection model—to an already strong baseline from Andersen et al. (2013) that uses similar features to Yannakoudakis et al. (2011) but a different machine learning model—a linear ranking perceptron (Bös & Opper, 1998). The perceptron model achieves $r = 0.751$; with the addition of the new feature performance improves to 0.760.

Continuing the work on the error detection system, Rei (2017) obtains an improvement over the Rei & Yannakoudakis (2016) result by using dropout and by adding a second optimization task of predicting the next token, in addition to predicting the error/non-error label, bringing performance up to $F_{0.5} = 0.485$. Rei et al. (2017) show that a similar extent of improvement ($F_{0.5} = 0.487$) can be achieved by keeping the Rei & Yannakoudakis (2016) model intact but manipulating the training data to inject artificially created errors produced using a statistical machine translation system that has learned to "translate" correct sentences into in-

---

[11]See Chapter 4 for more details about the common neural network architectures.

correct ones; Kasewa et al. (n.d.) further improve on this result by using an off-the-shelf neural machine translation model and an additional data source for error induction ($F_{0.5} = 0.556$). Rei & Yannakoudakis (2017) show that auxiliary prediction tasks such as prediction of POS tags, of grammatical relations, and of the specific error type for the given token can bring performance to $F_{0.5} = 0.508$. The model by Rei & Søgaard (2019) further improves performance (0.521) by having the BiLSTM model learn jointly to predict sentence-level and token-level labels. Variations on the BiLSTM+CRF model were popular in submissions to the shared task on Chinese grammatical error detection (G. Rao et al., 2018). A model that uses the best layer of BERT (Bidirectional Encoder Representations from Transformers (Devlin et al., 2019)) as input for a linear model that makes binary predictions was shown to attain 0.465 (N. F. Liu et al., 2019); Bell et al. (2019) attain $F_{0.5} = 0.573$ by incorporating BERT embeddings into the Rei (2017) architecture; Tsai et al. (2020) show that a 2-layer BiLSTM-CRF model using pre-trained BERT and Flair (Akbik et al., 2018) contextual embeddings as an input representation achieves $F_{0.5} = 0.604$ on this dataset.

5.4.4   GRAMMATICALITY ON A SCALE

Instead of detecting specific erroneous tokens, Heilman et al. (2014) used a variety of features for predicting the overall GRAMMATICALITY of a sentence on a scale of 1-4 (1: incomprehensible; 2: somewhat comprehensible, but can have multiple plausible interpretations; 3: comprehensible, errors if present do not make the sentence unclear; 4: perfect, the sentence is native-sounding). Using features from a precision grammar, a statistical parser, a 5-gram language model, and a spellchecker in a ridge regression model, the authors show that gold grammaticality judgments correlate with those of the system at $r = 0.644$ on the test set. Lau et al. (2015) showed that a similar level of performance ($r = 0.636$) on this dataset can be achieved using predictions from a set of increasingly sophisticated unsupervised models as features, including Bayesian HMM based on Goldwater & Griffiths (2007) and an RNN-based language model from Mikolov et al. (2012), as well as an out-of-the-box spellchecker. Lau et al. (2017) furthermore argue that acceptability judgments (the extent to which a sentence sounds natural) that approximately capture the notion of grammaticality can be predicted with similar models across different languages, and that it is possible that human grammatical knowledge itself is in fact gradient rather than categorical; see therein for a further discussion.

To see how well the prediction models for acceptability judgments deal with specific grammatical errors, Warstadt et al. (2019) interrogated an LSTM model designed to approximate one of the best models in Lau et al. (2015) for its ability to classify sentences into acceptable/unacceptable using a specially constructed dataset containing examples of acceptable and unacceptable sentences culled from the linguistics literature, covering a variety of grammatical phenomena. In particular, they found that the model can quite accurately detect cases of the violation of the subject-verb-object order (e.g., *read the book Bo*) (MCC[12] $= 0.80$), followed by subject—verb agreement errors (e.g., *My friends has to go*) and problems with wh-question formation (e.g., "What did John fry the potato?") (MCC $= 0.60$), but does not handle causative-inchoative alternation well (e.g., *The bubble popped* is ok but not *The bubble blew*) and is not sensitive to problems in the reflexive-antecedent agreement (e.g., *I amused themselves*). The task of predicting binary acceptability judgments using the dataset from Warstadt et al. (2019) is included in the recently introduced GLUE benchmark (A. Wang et al., 2018) that covers a variety of language understanding tasks; recent transformer-based models have demonstrated increasingly strong performance on this task (L. Dong et al., 2019).

---

[12]MCC (Matthews, 1975) is an evaluation metric for binary classifiers. It is a special case of Pearson's r for correlation of two Boolean distributions. On average, any two unrelated distributions will have an MCC of 0, regardless of class imbalance, whereas accuracy would have a majority-class bias.

CHAPTER 6

Genre- and Task-Specific Features

In this chapter, we will discuss features designed specifically to address genre- and task-specific constructs. We consider genres that are most commonly used in education contexts, including argumentative, narrative, and reflective writing, as well as expository source-based writing such as source summarization. The extent of variation in the tasks we review here, as well as in approaches developed for capturing task-specific elements, suggests clearly that assessment of writing is not a one-size-fits-all kind of endeavor.

6.1 WHAT'S IN AN ESSAY?

When one encounters the unqualified term *essay*, one typically envisions a piece of writing that puts forward and supports a claim of some sort; to quote Wikipedia—"An essay is, generally, a piece of writing that gives the author's own argument". While this might be a prototypical essay in the mind of a contemporary reader, a wider, more comprehensive definition has also been proposed: Aldous Huxley famously said that "The essay is a literary device for saying almost everything about almost anything", while also noting that "By tradition, almost by definition, the essay is a short piece".[1]

In the context of education, an essay is a convenient form for practicing one's writing skills. Component skills such as spelling, vocabulary usage, conventions of punctuation and grammar, as well as strategies such as planning and revising are all "necessary for the production of coherently organized essays containing well developed and pertinent ideas, supporting examples, and appropriate detail" (Graham & Perin, 2007b; Needels & Knapp, 1994) during the "learning to write" stage of the educational process. The essay form is also commonly used in assessment of writing skill in the U.S., from upper elementary school, middle, and high school (NAEP[2]) all the way to college and graduate school (ACT,[3] GRE[4]) and professional certification (PRAXIS,[5] FCTE[6]).

---

[1] Aldous Huxley, Preface to *Collected Essays*, published in 1923.
[2] https://nces.ed.gov/nationsreportcard/writing/
[3] https://www.act.org/content/act/en/products-and-services/the-act/test-preparation/writing-sample-essays.html?page=0&chapter=0
[4] https://www.ets.org/gre/revised_general/prepare/analytical_writing/
[5] https://www.ets.org/praxis/about/core/content/
[6] https://www.fldoe.org/accountability/assessments/postsecondary-assessment/ftce/

While versatility and flexibility in terms of purpose, or genre, of writing are necessary for real-world educational, professional, and recreational activities, teachers tend to use certain genres above and beyond others. In lower grades, students are mainly asked to write stories, personal experiences, and other kinds of *narrative writing*. In middle and high school, the emphasis moves to *expository writing*, such as reporting, summarizing and analyzing information, as well as *persuasive writing*—expressing an opinion with the support of reasons and evidence (Graham & Perin, 2007b). According to Persky et al. (2003), 60% of writing assignments in 4th grade, 65% in 8th grade, and 75% in 12th grade are expository in nature; expository writing is also the most frequently assigned writing task at the college level (Bridgeman & Carlson, 1984; Burstein et al., 2016; Mezler, 2014).

In a close correspondence to these instructional tendencies,[7] the U.S. National Assessment of Educational Progress (NAEP) writing assessment of 4th, 8th, and 12th graders in 1998–2007 included writing in persuasive, informative, and narrative modes, explained as follows (National Assessment Governing Board, 2007):

- Persuasive: writing to convince, writing to construct an argument, writing to refute a position;

- Informative: description, explanation, analysis; and

- Narrative: first- and third-person fictional stories, personal essays.

In the 2011 version of the NAEP Writing assessment framework, the definitions of the genres are more closely aligned with the intended overall communicative purpose (National Assessment Governing Board, 2011):

- To Persuade, in order to change the reader's point of view or affect the reader's action;

- To Explain, in order to expand the reader's understanding; and

- To Convey Experience, real or imagined, in order to communicate individual and imagined experience to others.

The later version reflects a recognition that strategies chiefly associated with a particular purpose can be used, by skilled writers, to support other purposes. For example, it is possible to use a first-person mini-narrative in a persuasive essay to support an argument based on personal experience.

In the 2011 NAEP Writing Assessment framework and onwards, writing tasks also specify or clearly imply a particular audience for the writing, such as peers, teachers, or parents (for grade 4), or community leaders and government officials (grades 8, 12); students in 8th and

---

[7]The polemic about the causality in the relationship between instructional and assessment practices is beyond the scope of this book.

12th graders are also allowed a choice of form that best fits the purpose, including letter, essay, or editorial (National Assessment Governing Board, 2011, 2017).

The Persuade and Explain purposes generally dominate the assessment essay types in the context of higher education, persuasive writing often taking the form or an opinion-on-an-issue task (GRE Analyze-an-Issue, TOEFL Independent, Praxis Argumentative, ACT essay task) and explanatory writing often involving presentation of materials from various sources (TOEFL Integrated; Praxis Informative/Explanatory). In a professional certification context, similar purposes would be realized in the specific content domain—for example, in the Written Communication component of the CPA examination, a test-taker might be asked to "recommend a given risk management strategy to executive management or to explain currency exchange rates to a client considering an endeavor into foreign markets",[8] addressing the persuasive/argumentative and explanatory/expository writing genres, respectively.

A legitimate question the reader might have at this point is whether the genre distinctions based on the writer's purpose or intention actually translate into distinct textual patterns in a systematic, measurable way. W. Song et al. (2017) conducted a detailed, sentence-by-sentence analysis of narrative essays written by Chinese middle-school students for a regional test for what the authors called their *discourse mode*—the main purpose of the sentence. Five modes were considered: narration (introduce an event or temporally related series of events); exposition (provide general, uncontested background information); description (show what things are like according to the five senses); argument (persuade the reader of a point of view); and emotion (present the writer's emotions, usually in a subjective, personal and lyrical way). The authors showed that sentences can be annotated for these categories with moderate reliability ($\kappa = 0.55$ in the first round and better in subsequent rounds). About half the sentences belonged to the narration mode, description and emotion were substantially represented, and even argument and exposition were attested, albeit in a small proportion of sentences (1–2%). In computational experiments using hierarchical neural models, sentences belonging to the two most frequent modes were recognized with F_1 scores of around 0.8; emotion and exposition—around 0.7, and the few argument sentences were the hardest to recognize ($F_1 = 0.48$).

Beigman Klebanov et al. (2019) analyzed data from a group of university students each writing in multiple genres (including argumentative, narrative, informational, portraiture, scenic) using DocuScope (Kaufer et al., 2004)—a rhetorical analysis tool geared specifically toward capturing genre distinctions.[9] They found that argumentative and narrative essays exhibited substantial differences; in particular, argumentative writing used reasoned, assertive, public and academic language more than any other genre and it was the least descriptive of them all. Moreover, the authors found that these same characteristics also apply to argumentative writing in other contexts, such as New York Times OpEds and essays written for GRE and TOEFL tests. Curiously, the authors found that the informational genre—which centers on the *explain* rather

---

[8]https://www.gleim.com/cpa-review/blog/bec-written-communications/
[9]Available from http://vep.cs.wisc.edu/ubiq/

than *persuade* goal—was quite close to argumentative writing in its rhetorical profile. Commenting on this finding, the authors observed that the two genres share certain rhetorical elements: "argumentation often engages in providing information from a position of expertise, and, on the other hand, informing the reader is not always free of argumentative framing".

Genre-specific features that will be discussed in this chapter generally go after the distinctive elements of the genre—language of reasons, assertions (claims), and (publicly) demonstrable evidence in **argumentative writing** (Section 6.2), and features related to detailing, characterization, and narration of event sequences in **narrative writing** (Section 6.3). For explanatory/expository writing, we consider specifically the case where the author needs to present information from given source materials—**source-based writing** (Section 6.4). This setting emphasizes the need to relate pre-specified information rather than construct one's own information basis (where perhaps one needs to argue that those pieces of information are relevant, important, and reliable, thereby bringing in some argumentative elements). We also consider **reflective writing** (Section 6.5), often practiced in the context of higher education to deepen the student's learning from experience.

Let us start with persuasive/argumentative writing, a genre that has received by far the most attention in the education-and-NLP community.

6.2 PERSUASIVE/ARGUMENTATIVE WRITING

In this section, we first clarify the distinction between persuasive writing and argumentative writing—to preview, the distinction can be made but it is probably not very useful for the purposes of reviewing the current field of automated scoring of writing. We then turn to reviewing the kinds of features proposed for scoring such essays—features capturing use of evaluative language, figurative language, as well as features for capturing structure and content of arguments.

6.2.1 PERSUASION VS. ARGUMENTATION

A distinction is sometimes made between argumentative and persuasive writing along the following lines.[10]

- The **goal** of ARGUMENTATION is to get the reader to acknowledge that your side is valid and deserves consideration as another point of view. The general **technique** of argumentative writing is to offer the reader relevant reasons, credible facts, and sufficient evidence to support that the writer has a valid and worthy perspective.

- The **goal** of PERSUASION is to get the reader to agree with your point of view. Typical **techniques** include blending facts and emotion in an attempt to convince.

Let us first consider the goals. A related distinction is made between a *discussion*, where the interlocutors "search honestly and without bias for the best solution to a controversial prob-

---

[10]from https://www.middlesex.mass.edu/ace/downloads/tipsheets/persvsargu.pdf.

lem" and a *debate*, where "partisans of opposed settled convictions defend their respective viewpoints" (C. Perelman & Olbrechts-Tyteca, 1969). Presumably, an argumentative essay is being set up for a discussion, while a persuasive one is being set up for a debate. In *New Rhetoric: A Treatise on Argumentation*, Perelman and Olbrechts-Tyteca continue the analysis of discussion vs. debate by pointing out that although this distinction is theoretically useful, it is "only through a rather schematic view of reality that the determination of the weight of arguments can be compared with the weighting of ingots", that is, it is rather hard to take biases out of any actual discussion. Moreover, in a debate, "a defender of a particular point of view is very often convinced that he is sustaining what is objectively the best thesis and that its triumph will be that of the best cause". In a similar vein, while an argumentative essay is "an invitation to decide" (Kaufer & Butler, 2000), leaving the reader the ultimate choice whether to accept the writer's recommendation, it is still the case that the writer seeks to bring the reader to a particular decision and "the best argument writing transforms an external recommendation into one that the reader can mistake for his own free deliberations" (Kaufer & Butler, 2000). Viewed form this angle, the best argumentative writing is a subtler form of persuasion, through creating an illusion of persuasion-through-discussion instead of persuasion-through-debate.

Let us consider now the distinction between argumentative and persuasive techniques, one engaging in solid reasoning while the other doing whatever it takes to convince. Since Aristotle's *Rhetoric*, it has been recognized that gaining adherence of an audience to a particular idea or a course of action might require different types of *appeals*—emotional appeals (those based on *pathos*) and appeals based on the credibility of the speaker (those based on *ethos*); *logos*-based appeals that prioritize logical reasoning from premises to conclusions; as well as appeals related to the timeliness, the here and now (*kairos*). The distinction between argumentative and persuasive techniques cited earlier in this section seems to limit the former to logos-based arguments whereas the latter is allowed to cover the different aspects of persuasion more comprehensively. Indeed, analyzing premises used to support claims on *Change My View*, a reddit.com forum, Hidey et al. (2017) found that 44% of the premises contained logos-based appeals, 29% contained pathos-based ones, and 3% contain ethos-based appeals; thus, the different types of appeals were all attested in the persuasion-oriented data.

As with the distinction between a discussion and a debate, the differentiation might be theoretically useful but not so easily drawn in practice. A personal attack on the opponent as a means to support the argument that their opinion is wrong (*ad hominem* argument) could be logically fallacious or not; personal considerations could be relevant for judging a person's willingness to tell the truth (Fearnside & Holther, 1959; Walton, 1992). Emotion-based considerations can be brought into a reasoned argument by, for example, using emotively loaded language to explain positive or negative consequences of some policy or action (Feng & Hirst, 2011; Walton & Macagno, 2015). Figurative language is notoriously effective in *covertly* affecting reasoning: Thibodeau & Boroditsky (2011) demonstrated that changing a single word ("Crime is a virus/beast ravaging the city of Addison") in an otherwise identical description that additionally includes charts and numbers has an effect on what policies are proposed to deal with the problem. Depending on the metaphor, experiment participants proposed predominantly social-reform-based policies (fix the economy, improve education, provide healthcare) or punitive ones (building more jails, stricter enforcement), without realizing the metaphor's influence on their thinking (people pointed to charts and numbers as justifications). Where does reason stop and empathy or fear begin?

Beyond the blurriness of the distinctions in both goals and methods, the distinction between argumentation and persuasion is also not a very consequential one from the point of view of automated scoring of essays—so far, with very few exceptions to be discussed below, the *reasonableness* of the argument provided has not been the focus of the argumentation features. Furthermore, even if the task is of the persuasive writing kind, providing logical, well-reasoned arguments in support of your position isn't against the rules. For example, in the TOEFL Independent writing task, the test-taker is asked to agree or disagree with a statement, and then told that "you'll be expected to use specific reasons and examples to support your answer".[11] Finally, while expression of an author's opinion might be more explicit and prominent in some persuasive/argumentative contexts than in others, a writing task in this genre is unlikely to ask the author to take his or her opinion out of the essay entirely; that would take the task outside of the scope of this genre. For example, the TOEFL Integrated task, where the author is asked to summarize other people's positions without taking one himself or herself is not an argumentative/persuasive writing task, *per se*, but a form of writing best aligned with the *explain* purpose. Therefore, we will henceforth use persuasive and argumentative interchangeably, unless a nuanced distinction is necessary.

6.2.2   FEATURES BASED ON USE OF EVALUATIVE LANGUAGE

Farra et al. (2015) address the use of evaluative language in a persuasive essay, stating that "sentiment expressions reveal a writer's judgments, evaluations and feelings, and are likely to be employed to express a preference for a particular position, or to point out the shortcomings of an alternative position".[12] In particular, the authors propose features to assess the extent to which the writer uses evaluative language about topically-relevant concepts. The authors used the MPQA (Multi-perspective Question Answering) lexicon (T. Wilson et al., 2005) as well as a sentiment lexicon specially developed for automated essay scoring (Beigman Klebanov et al., 2012, 2013) to detect expressions of sentiment, and a topic signature-based approach to detect topically-relevant concepts (C.-Y. Lin & Hovy, 2000). The authors build sentiment-target pairs, namely, instances where a sentiment expression and a word co-exist in the same sentence. For example, the sentence "At school, I always learned the most from teachers who encouraged me" would be tagged as positive (due to the positive opinion words *learned*, *most*, and *encouraged*)

---

[11]https://www.ets.org/toefl/test-takers/ibt/about/content/writing/independent-transcript
[12]Note the way in which evaluative language is expected to straddle both the debate-like explicit position-taking in the essay as well as the discussion-like aspect of pointing out problems.

and the words *school*, *teachers*, *learned*, and *encouraged* would be considered targets of the positive sentiment (under the resolve-sentence method; see paper for more detail). The authors also used an *arguing* lexicon with explicit expression of argumentative intent such as "for these reasons, I claim with confidence" (Burstein et al., 1998) as another version of opinionated language, and build arguing-target pairs as well.

The opinion-target system is then built using linear regression over features that include counts of sentiment-target and arguing-target pairs, ratios of topical targets to all targets, as well as features based on consistency and/or flipping of sentiment. The opinion-target system was able to predict essay scores above and beyond the impact of essay length, showing partial correlation (controlling for length) of 0.23 with essay scores on TOEFL Independent data. In the feature analysis, the authors point out that the bulk of the effect is carried by sentiment-target pairs, rather than the arguing-target ones, and suggest as a possible explanation that more skilled writers might be using more subtle expressions of argumentative intent than those encoded in the arguing lexicon.

Using the VADER system for sentiment analysis (Hutto & Gilbert, 2014), Janda et al. (2019) assigned a <positive,negative,neutral> distribution to each sentence in an essay (each dimension has a real-valued score between 0 and 1, all three scores sum up to 1) and aggregate those into an overall essay sentiment profile. The positive, negative, and neutral scores survived feature selection and were shown to contribute above and beyond syntax-based and topic-development-based features on average across all the data in the ASAP evaluation dataset;[13] positive and negative polarity features were particularly strong predictors of scores for the two persuasive subsets in the ASAP dataset (see datasets 1 and 2 in Figure 17 in Janda et al. (2019)), further supporting the importance of assessing the use of evaluative language in this genre of writing. As a caveat, Janda et al. (2019) do not present an evaluation that would clearly show that these features provide information above and beyond a length baseline.

6.2.3   FEATURES BASED ON USE OF FIGURATIVE LANGUAGE

Figurative language, especially metaphors, can be effective persuasion devices, often through strategically highlighting some aspects of the issue and hiding others using a suggestive metaphor—a process termed *framing* and much studied in a political science context (Entman, 2003; Lakoff, 1991). Metaphors also often contribute an evaluative component—for example, a *solid* foundation is usually a good thing, while a *shaky* one is not, whether you are talking about actual construction practices or career development. Being able to harness an apt metaphor for one's argument is a useful skill,[14] and it is exercised (more or less effectively) by some essay writers in the educational assessment context. For example, using the *building/foundation* metaphor, writers argue in support of "Originality does not mean thinking something that was never thought before; it means putting old ideas together in new ways" and in opposition to "It

---

[13]https://www.kaggle.com/c/asap-aes/
[14]See Section 7.1.3 in Veale et al. (2016) for a further discussion of metaphor comprehension and use as a skill.

is better to have broad knowledge of many academic subjects than to specialize in one specific subject", respectively, as follows (words belonging to the source domain of building/foundation are italicized).

> History is a progressive passing on of ideas, a process of *building on the foundations laid* by the previous generations. New ideas cannot *stand* if they are without *support* from the past.

> I found the focus necessary and very important at a certain late stage of the personal working career or academic career. The reason behind this you *build up* some "*spikes* of knowledge" on a *broad* knowledge *platform*. These *sharp spikes* of knowledge will allow you to promote yourself and to *pull* with you the society *forward*.

Beigman Klebanov & Flor (2013a) developed an annotation protocol for detection of **metaphors** in argumentative essays, by focusing on metaphors that are noticeable to sophisticated readers not trained in metaphor theory and those that support the writer's arguments; this is in contrast to a more standard Metaphor Identification Procedure (Pragglejaz, 2007) that emphasizes formal properties of metaphors more than their alignment with the writer's specific purpose. Beigman Klebanov, Leong, & Flor (2018) provide a large-scale evaluation of the relationship between metaphor use and holistic essay score, using a computational model to detect metaphors and evaluating on tens of thousands of essays written by various populations of test-takers in response to six different tasks. They found that scaled frequency of metaphorically used content words correlated significantly with essay scores after controlling for essay length, and was stronger for the persuasive essay tasks where the writers were given a short general prompt (like the ones cited above) without any additional source material. The authors hypothesized that without the necessity to draw on provided sources, writers had more freedom in their argumentative and lexical choices, hence the extent of metaphoricity provided a stronger differentiation between writers.

Flor & Beigman Klebanov (2018) investigated the use of **idioms** in persuasive essays written for the TOEFL test—namely, essays written by non-native speakers typically applying to college in the U.S. Using a large list of English language idioms, a search procedure, and a subsequent human verification of the results, the authors found that 1,017 essays out of 10,670 scanned during the search (9.5%) actually used one or more of the idioms on the list. It is an open question exactly what they used the idioms for, namely, whether the usage is tied specifically to argumentation.

W. Song et al. (2016) studied the use of **parallelism** in argumentative and narrative essays written by Chinese senior high school students during mock examinations. The authors define parallelism as "two or more coherent text spans (phrases or sentences), which have similar syntactic structures and related semantics, and express relevant content or emotion together". An example of parallelism is a famous line from *Julius Caesar* "I came, I saw, I conquered" (translated). The authors found that in argumentative essays students use parallelism to emphasize different aspects of support they are offering for the thesis; the parallel sentences are therefore often located in either consecutive positions or in parallel positions in different paragraphs. The authors found that detection of parallelism can be automated, achieving precision, recall, and F_1 scores around 0.80 for detection of parallel sentence pairs, using features capturing positions of the two sentences in the essays, word-similarity-based scores, sequence-based, and syntax-based alignment between the two sentences. Using the automated system to analyze a new set of argumentative and narrative essays, the authors show that for both argumentative and narrative data, essays with parallelism tend to have significantly higher scores than those without, with the trend much more pronounced in argumentative essays: The correlation between essay score and number of parallel chunks in an essay is $r = 0.29$ for argumentative writing, vs. $r = 0.16$ for narratives. Dai et al. (2018) reported parallelism detection performance on data that includes mainly essays to be above 0.9 in precision, recall, and F_1 score using a neural classifier.

6.2.4   FEATURES BASED ON ARGUMENT STRUCTURE

Argument Components and Argument Relations

Substantial recent research has been conducted at the intersection of argument mining and essay scoring. In particular, that arguments—especially those based on *logos*—often have recurrent and recognizable components has been known at least since Aristotle's syllogisms. A syllogism is an instance of reasoning where from a combination of a general statement (e.g., "All men are mortal") and a specific statement (e.g., "Socrates is a man"), a conclusion is deduced ("Socrates is mortal"). More generally, and broadly consistently with argumentation theory (Toulmin, 2003)[15] and with prior computationally oriented work on argument analysis such as Mochales-Palau & Moens (2009) and Peldszus & Stede (2013), Stab & Gurevych (2017a) define a minimal set of ARGUMENT COMPONENTS, namely, a CLAIM (a controversial statement) and a PREMISE (justification or refutation of the claim); justification (support) or refutation (attack) are, in turn, the possible ARGUMENT RELATIONS between premises and claims. Elaborating further on the argumentation structures beyond the minimal claim—premise pair, one claim can have multiple premises (a convergent argument), one premise can support multiple claims (divergent argument), a chain structure where a sequence of premises support a claim is also possible, as well as a linked structure where two premises jointly support a claim, each one separately being insufficient.[16]

Argument Structures in Essays

Applying these general configurations to persuasive essays, Stab & Gurevych (2017a) identify a set of the most relevant argument components: a MAJOR CLAIM, corresponding to the main

---

[15]Toulmin (2003) uses the terms *claim* and *data* for claims and premises, respectively: "We already have, therefore, one distinction to start with: between the claim or conclusion whose merits we are seeking to establish (C) and the facts we appeal to as a foundation for the claim—what I shall refer to as our data (D)" (p. 90).

[16]An Aristotelian syllogism would be an instance of a linked argument, where the general and the specific statements are premises that together support the claim that Socrates is mortal.

thesis of the essay that is typically stated in the introductory and concluding sections of an essay, followed by a sequence of *claims* that either support or attack the major claim, and each claim is supported or attacked by one or more *premises*. The authors allow for convergent argument structures (multiple premises independently supporting one claim) and chain argument structures (a premise can support another premise which, in turn, supports a claim). The excerpt below exemplifies some of the structures: $Premise_1$ supports $Claim_1$, and $Premise_2$ and $Premise_3$ each independently support $Claim_2$. Both $Claim_1$ and $Claim_2$ support the major claim (made elsewhere in the essay) that cloning technology is beneficial to humanity. Note also that discourse markers, intentionally left outside of the claims and premises structure, help the reader follow the argument, namely, understand which statements are related to which other statements, and which constitute claims vs. premises.[17]

> Second, scientists use animals as models in order to learn about human diseases$_{Premise_1}$ and therefore cloning animals enables novel developments in science$_{Claim_1}$. Furthermore, infertile couples can bear children that are genetically related$_{Premise_2}$. Even same sex couples can have children$_{Premise_3}$. Consequently, cloning can help couples have children$_{Claim_2}$.

In the Stab & Gurevych (2017a) annotation campaign, 402 persuasive essays were annotated for argument structures, of which 80 were annotated by three people to obtain reliability estimates. Major claims and premises yielded better inter-annotator agreement (>0.8 in chance-corrected coefficients), while claims were more difficult to agree upon, both at the level of classifying sentences for presence/absence of claims and for identifying textual spans for claims (0.5–0.6 coefficients). The overall reliability of the classification into major claims, claims, premises, and non-argumentative at the span level was 0.767, using a version of Krippendorf's alpha coefficient, a commonly used metric for measuring inter-rater reliability. The agreement on whether a sentence contained a claim that supported the major claim, a claim that attacked the major claim, or contained no claim at all was similar to claim vs. non-claim classification results, suggesting that differentiating claims into those supporting and attacking the major claim generally does not generate additional disagreement beyond detecting the presence of a (any) claim.

Next, the authors evaluated the argument structures, namely, which components are related by support relations or attack relations to which other components. Taking all allowable pairs of argument components within a paragraph, the authors generated a list of 4,922 possibly related pairs, and obtained an agreement of $\kappa = 0.7$ on classifying those into support relationship or not; the agreement was at the same level for the classification into attack relationship or not.

The distribution of argument components in essays was such that an essay containing on average 366 words organized into 5 paragraphs had 15 argument components, such that 10 were

---

[17]The inclusion of "even" in $Premise_3$ is in the original (Stab & Gurevych, 2017a).

premises, 2 were major claims, and 4 were claims.[18] The four claims on average per essay were split into three claims that support a major claim and one that attacks it; the ten premises were split into nine supporting premises and one attacking premise. The observed scarcity of attack relations corresponds to the general observation in the argumentation literature that student-produced written argumentation tends to be insensitive to alternative perspectives (Ferretti & Graham, 2019), although use of counterarguments, alternative standpoints and rebuttals can be encouraged through targeted instruction (Y. Song & Ferretti, 2013).

Automated Detection of Argument Structure

Turning to the computational experiments, Stab & Gurevych (2017a) perform **argument component identification**, using Conditional Random Fields to induce an IOB tagging of tokens in a sentence, so that ARG-B tokens begin an argument component, ARG-I tokens are inside one, and ARG-O tokens are outside of argument components. The system uses essay and paragraph position features, punctuation, part of speech and parse-based information, including lexicalized parse features, and transition probability between classes, and achieves $F_1 > 0.8$ for every category (ARG-B, ARG-I, ARG-O), and a macro-F_1 score of 0.867. Ajjour et al. (2017) improved the score to 0.885 using a Bi-LSTM model that uses a wider document-level context in addition to features similar to those in Stab & Gurevych (2017a). Mensonides et al. (2019) reported a macro-F_1 score of 0.887 using a multi-tasking neural network that not only detects and classifies argument components but also does POS-tagging and phrase chunking.

For **argument component classification** in Stab & Gurevych (2017a), the single most effective set of features are positional features (called "structural" in the original[19]), that include component length, number of tokens preceding and following the component in the sentence, proportion of sentence covered by component, as well as location of the component—first or last in paragraph, in introduction or conclusion, relative position in paragraph; these features are especially effective for identifying major claims. Detection of claims and of major claims can be further improved by adding a large variety of features studied by the authors, including lexical (unigrams and common dependency tuples), syntactic (parse-based, tense of main verb, presence of modals), discourse features (PDTB-discourse relations) extracted from the component and its surrounding text, as well as features capturing lexical indicators of a forward progression from supporting statement to its target (such as "Consequently"), a backward progression from a target to its support (such as "In addition"), indicators of thesis (e.g., "Overall") and of a rebuttal (e.g., "Admittedly"), as well as first person indicators. Overall, a SVMs system using all features achieves a macro F_1 score of 0.794 on test data, with F_1 scores of 0.891 and 0.879 for major claims and premises, respectively, and a lower score of 0.611 for detecting claims. Results from Nguyen & Litman (2015) suggest that identifying argumentation-related and topic-related

---

[18]The total of claims and premises is 16 rather than 15, probably due to rounding.
[19]We reserve the term "argument structure" to the whole system of interlinked claims and premises.

vocabulary from a separate development set of essays can help argument component classification.

A separate **component linking** model is trained that classifies pairs of components as linked or not; similar types of features (adjusted to work with pairs of components instead of single ones) are extracted from both the components, along with some new features, such as shared nouns, or association of the component's words with being part of a supporting/attacking component ("source") or a component being supported/attacked ("target"). For example, "therefore" is likelier to participate in a target component, while "because" is likelier to appear in a source component. An SVM-based system performs at $F_1 = 0.917$ for non-linked pairs but only at $F_1 = 0.508$ for the linked ones. The relatively large number of components that are left unlinked by the system motivated a joint-modeling approach using Integer Linear Programing to concurrently optimize classification and linking using outputs of the two base classifiers. The joint model yields substantial improvements in detection of claims and in detection of linked pairs, from $F_1 = 0.611$ to 0.682 and from $F_1 = 0.508$ to $F_1 = 0.585$, respectively. Niculae et al. (2017) reported a performance of up to $F_1 = 0.601$ on the detection of argument component links, using factor graphs in a structured SVM model that captures higher-order structures such as chain arguments and convergent arguments. Potash et al. (2017) further improve these results to $F_1 = 0.732$ and $F_1 = 0.608$, for the claim detection and link detection tasks, respectively, using a joint linking and classification model based on a pointer network architecture with attention. Kuribayashi et al. (2019) further pushed the performance on the detection of linked pairs to $F_1 = 0.678$ by using joint span, linking, and classification learning using an LSTM model that explicitly provides separate encodings to (a) the argument component itself and (b) the discourse marker that precedes it in the sentence. The authors' analysis suggests that their system improves upon the prior models on linking the components of *deep* arguments (such as chain arguments); this could be due to the model's ability to track sequences of discourse markers. Persing & Ng (2016a) propose another Integer Linear Programing-based approach to jointly detect, classify and link argument components, without making use of the annotated argument components; error analysis shows that problems in mis-detection of argument components, false positives in particular, propagate to the component classification and link detection tasks and substantially hurt performance.

After linking, Stab & Gurevych (2017a) accomplish the next step of classifying linked pairs into **support relations** and **attack relations** using an SVM classifier with similar features as before along with sentiment-based features; Stab & Gurevych (2017a) report excellent performance on support relations ($F_1 = 0.947$) but much weaker performance on attack relations ($F_1 = 0.413$). Nguyen & Litman (2016a) proposed expanding the context and using discourse relations extracted using sentences surrounding the target pair. The joint learning model developed by Kuribayashi et al. (2019) improves the performance on support and attack classification to $F_1 = 0.967$ and $F_1 = 0.611$, respectively.

Argument Structure and Essay Quality

To investigate the relationship between argument structure characteristics and essay scores, Ghosh et al. (2016) annotated 107 essays from the TOEFL11 corpus (Blanchard et al., 2013) using a slightly earlier version of the Stab and Gurevych annotation scheme (Stab & Gurevych, 2014). The essays in the corpus are released with coarse-grained holistic scores: low, medium, and high. Ghosh et al. (2016) used approximately stratified sampling from the three score levels. Argument components and argument relations were annotated at clause level. Using the annotations, the authors created feature sets based on argument components (number of claims, number of premises, proportion of sentences containing argument components), argument relations (number and percentage of supported claims, number and percentage of claims with no premises, number of attack relations, number of attacks against the major claim), as well as argument topology (number of claims supported by a chain of premises, number of claims with multiple same-level premises, number of claims supported by a deeper structure including other claims and premises). Different features were combined using logistic regression.

Baseline performance using essay length in sentences was $\kappa_q = 0.535$. The authors show that each family of features yields an improvement when added to the baseline (κ_q between 0.735 and 0.770), and adding all of them to the baseline yields the best performance of $\kappa_q = 0.803$. Based on feature weights in logistic regression, the authors observed that the number and proportion of claims with no premises were strong negative features, while the proportion of sentences containing argument components and the non-chain topology features had strong positive weights; the authors also observe the scarcity of attack relations and the resultant ineffectiveness of features based on attacks. These results show that argument structures, if correctly identified, can contribute substantially to score predictions.

Ghosh et al. (2016) also investigate automated argument analysis using many of the features from an earlier version of the Stab and Gurevych's system discussed above. They train an argument analysis system using the Stab and Gurevych essays and test on TOEFL essays; they observe somewhat weaker performance than that reported by Stab and Gurevych, which could be due to the stratified nature of the TOEFL dataset where very poorly written essays (low score) constitute a full one third of the dataset. Automatically generated features yield a system with a lower agreement with essay scores than those based on human annotations, but the system combining all features still achieved performance of $\kappa_q = 0.737$, compared to 0.784 using human-annotated features; the authors did not report results for automatically generated features added to the baseline essay length feature.

Beigman Klebanov, Stab, et al. (2016) investigated the effectiveness of argument-structure based features for holistic scoring using a much larger set of TOEFL essays. Features included the numbers of any argument components; the numbers of major claims, claims, premises, supporting and attacking premises, arguments against, arguments for, and the average number of premises per claim; the authors did not consider features based on argument topology. The features were combined using a linear regression model trained to predict essay scores. They found that argument-structure-based features had moderate correlations with coarse-grained holistic scores on their own ($\kappa_q = 0.344$), and yielded an improvement when added on top of the length baseline: $\kappa_q = 0.517$ for length-only and $\kappa_q = 0.540$ when augmented with argumentation features.

Nguyen & Litman (2018) showed that performance can be improved by using a stronger baseline (word, sentence, and character counts, average word and sentence length; number and proportion of spelling errors, stop words, prompt words, academic vocabulary; features based on punctuation) that scores $\kappa_q = 0.604$, and by adding on top of it features based on argument structures. The features include counts and proportions of various argument components, sentences, and paragraphs containing argument components; average number of premises per claim; paragraphs containing pairs of components of different types; number of supported vs. dangling claims, supporting premises; and features that capture argument topology—number of chain arguments and tree arguments, number of paragraphs that contain such structures. While the system with all argument structure features scored $\kappa_q = 0.607$, the authors show that ablating the argument topology features resulted in a better performance of $\kappa_q = 0.618$. Nadeem et al. (2019) use argument structure based features from Nguyen & Litman (2018) as well as length features and features based on various types of discourse connectives generated by the addDiscourse toolkit (Pitler & Nenkova, 2009); their system achieves $\kappa_q = 0.642$ on the TOEFL dataset.

Additional research with the ultimate goal of assessment and feedback on argumentation was conducted to identify specific types of **structural deficiencies** in arguments. Stab & Gurevych (2017b) showed that it is possible to detect insufficiently supported arguments with high accuracy; Stab & Gurevych (2016) addressed the task of identifying essays that contained no opposing arguments, that is, no evidence of engagement with an opposing point of view (myside bias). Wachsmuth et al. (2017) show that given perfectly identified argumentation structures (argument components, component linking, and argument relations, modeled as labeled trees rooted in major claims) and positional information in an essay, the existence of myside bias can be predicted nearly perfectly. For example, the configuration where a premise/claim precedes the major claim and attacks it occurs substantially more frequently in essays without myside bias.

Cross-Domain Generalization of Argument Structure Detection

Researchers have also considered approaches that move away from fully supervised learning; cross-domain generalization of argument structure detection is also an area of active research. Ferrara et al. (2017) experimented with classifying sentences into those containing some argument component or not by using an unsupervised metric that combined information about position in the essay and the extent to which the sentence is focused on a single topic, using LDA for unsupervised topic modeling. Petasis & Karkaletsis (2016) investigated the use of techniques based on extractive summarization for argument structure analysis, reasoning that "a claim is expected to share similar concepts with other text fragments that either support or attack the claim". They show that a version of TextRank (Mihalcea & Tarau, 2004) where the text is represented as graph of sentences with tfidf-based similarity weights on the edges can detect the sentence containing the major claim in the essay with an accuracy of 0.29 (vs. 0.13 accuracy for a random pick) in the Stab and Gurevych test data.

Deguchi & Yamaguchi (2019) investigate a method that uses both unsupervised and supervised elements in identification of argument components: They adapt the sentence similarity function of the TextRank algorithm to use the probability of a link between two sentences as predicted by a neural-net based classifier trained to predict the existence of a link between argument components; the system had an accuracy of 0.54 for finding the major claim of an essay, using cross-validation on the 402 essays from Stab & Gurevych (2017a). We note that the neural network was trained on in-domain (essay) data, so the question of whether analysis of essays can be helped by utilizing argument-component-annotated data from another domain was left open. Lippi & Torroni (2015) developed their models on data from another domain, using a rich feature set of partial tree kernels for detecting claims; subsequent cross-validation on essay data showed competitive performance, though the authors did not address cross-domain generalization of the trained models.

This question has been addressed by Daxenberger et al. (2017)—feature-based and neural systems were trained and evaluated in-domain and cross-domain for various argumentation-component-annotated datasets. For the essay data in particular, training on out-of-domain (non-essay) materials resulted in a precipitous decline in performance for claim detection—from claim-F_1 scores in the low 0.6 in-domain to the mid 0.4 range for cross-domain generalization; Ajjour et al. (2017) reported similar results for in-domain vs. cross-domain argument component identification for essays. Al-Khatib et al. (2016) show promising performance in terms of generalization of a system trained on different data to essay data: The authors collected a large set of passages marked for argumentativeness and non-argumentativeness at the sentence level by distant supervision, namely, using metadata from the idebate.org portal. A classifier trained on the idebate data using lexical and syntactic features scored just 3 F_1 points below the same classifier trained on in-domain essay data.

Improvement in performance and robustness of the various pieces of the argument structure detection pipeline is an active area of current research. While many effective and promising techniques have been proposed, the extent to which these variations in techniques impact the downstream essay scoring application has not been investigated yet.

6.2.5   FEATURES BASED ON ARGUMENT CONTENT

Stance Detection

Perhaps the most basic element of the argumentative content in a defend-your-position-on-an-issue type of essay is exactly *what* the author's position is with respect to the issue. This task has been referred to as STANCE classification, namely, determining whether the author's overall position is *for* or *against* the statement in the prompt. Faulkner (2014) conducted a stance annotation on 1,320 argumentative essays from the International Corpus of Learner English (ICLE, Granger (2003)) and showed good agreement ($\kappa = 0.68$) between an expert and a majority vote of crowdsourced annotation for a three-way classification into *for*, *against*, and *neither*; there were relatively few essays in the latter class (5%), while the rest were split approximately equally between *for* and *against*. The author comments that the *neither* category generated substantial disagreement—only 22 out of 122 cases of *neither* marked by the expert were marked as such by the crowd, and 22 out of 69 in the other direction. These cases often corresponded to situations where the writer agreed with part of the proposition and disagreed with another part, so, it isn't so much that the writer hasn't taken a stance but that it might be a nuanced one (in case it made sense to annotators) or a confusing one.

The author then proceeded to devise two types of features to capture stance in essays. The first set of features captures stance-attitude profiles. Using lexicons of stance expressions (e.g., *assert, believe, could, demonstrate* for *for*-stance; *allege, cannot, deny, lack, without* for *against*-stance) and the MPQA subjectivity and sentiment lexicon (e.g., *abuse, absurd, fictitious, fiasco* are all strongly subjective and negative; *fidelity, first-rate, opportunity, peaceable* are all strongly subjective and positive) (T. Wilson et al., 2005), the authors create stance-attitude pairs by extracting cases of an attitude expression in the immediate or embedded clause relative to the clause containing a stance expression. The second set of features captures the prompt-relevance (or topicality) aspect of stance-taking, scoring words in propositions in the scope of stance expressions by their semantic relatedness to the prompt, using a measure based on hyperlink structure of Wikipedia developed by Milne & Witten (2008). The author reported a classification accuracy of 82% using an SVM classifier on a subset of data that did not contain the *neither* class.

Working with a different subset of ICLE data, Persing & Ng (2016b) attempted a more fine-grained classification of stance—both by expanding the scale to include *somewhat agree* and *somewhat disagree* categories and by breaking prompts down into sets of claims and annotating the stance of an essay written in response to the prompt with respect to each claim separately. Out of the total 1,593 pairs of <prompt-part, essay>, 56% were classified as *strongly agree*, 26% as *strongly disagree*, and below 10% for each of the other classes. The authors build on Faulkner's feature set by extracting somewhat different dependency-based subtrees and additionally requiring them to be prompt-relevant, as well as by adding features that specifically consider negation and hedging patterns to target the more nuanced classes. The authors found that while their system outperformed their replication of Faulkner's on the two strong-stance classes, neither system had more than a single-digit F_1 score on any of the classes apart from *strongly agree* and *strongly disagree*, suggesting that nuanced stance is a fairly rare occurrence in the essay data examined and therefore hard to learn; in addition, when it does occur, it is not expressed in a very straightforward way but rather in a way that would require substantial world knowledge to figure out. To the best of our knowledge, the relationship between essay score and aspects of stance expression has not yet been addressed.

Assessment of Thesis Strength

Assessment of the essay's thesis statement is the next step into the analysis of an essay's argument content. According to Ke et al. (2019), "a THESIS statement summarizes the main point the author is trying to argue for in her essay in the form of a claim (i.e., a statement that is controversial and therefore can be argued) and states why the essay is important and worth reading. Hence, in addition to being clear, concise, specific, and relevant to the prompt the essay is written for, a strong thesis statement should briefly provide evidences for the author's claim, justifications for the importance of the claim, and possibly a roadmap for the essay".

Ke et al. (2019) developed a holistic rubric for judging **thesis strength** (on a scale of 1–6), as well as rubrics for specific dimensions such as argue-ability, clarity, specificity, eloquence, conciseness, relevance to prompt, confidence, and justification. The authors report an inter-rater agreement of $\alpha = 0.635$ for the thesis-strength rubric; the version of distance metric in the α coefficient is not specified. The specific dimensions have a range of reliability scores, all above 0.5. We note that many of the dimensions show extremely skewed distributions, with fewer than 10% of the instances in the non-majority category; thus, nearly all observed thesis statements were arguable, clear, concise, and confident, and very few really managed the task of directing the development of the essay.

Ke et al. (2019) showed that automating thesis identification and thesis strength assessment are challenging tasks. A surprising finding is that a first-major-claim baseline using a strong system for argument component identification and argument relation classification (Eger et al., 2017) performs quite poorly, below F_1 of 0.2. It could be that the notions of thesis and major claim diverge somewhat; in particular, 37% of the essays contain thesis statements that span two sentences or more, and some of the dimension annotations suggest that the authors included material that could perhaps be classified as claims rather than major claims, namely, concise justifications of the major claim. In prior work, thesis clarity was specifically considered (Persing & Ng, 2013), with human-human agreement being an issue (36% exact agreement on a 7-point scale, 62% adjacent agreement, plus a skewed distribution where 83% of the cases are in the top three scores). Falakmasir et al. (2014) investigated the task of detecting reasonably good thesis statements in argumentative writing—namely, only thesis statements classified as "simple but acceptable" or "sophisticated" were treated as positive examples in the detection experiments, while candidate thesis statements classified as "vague or incomplete" were re-classified as non-thesis-statements. The authors showed promising performance of a feature set that contains positional (last sentence; first paragraph), syntactic, summary-like (usage of most frequent words in the essay), and prompt overlap features, achieving 0.83 F score for detecting thesis statements using decision trees in a corpus of first draft essays written by high school students. Essay-level classification into essays that contained an acceptable thesis statement or not was F = 0.74. Jabbari et al. (2016) improve the essay-level classification using an SVM model with SMOTE oversampling to achieve $F = 0.77$ (average F score across *thesis* and *no-thesis* categories), and $F_1 = 0.83$ for the *thesis* category.[20]

Annotation of Argument Quality in Position-on-an-Issue Essays

Persing & Ng (2015) considered the task of holistic assessment of **argument strength**, on a scale of 1–4 with 0.5-point increments: 1 means "does not make an argument or unclear what the argument is", 2 means "essay makes a weak argument for its thesis or sometimes argues against it", 3 means "essay makes a decent argument for its thesis and could convince some readers", 4 means "essay makes a strong argument for its thesis and would convince most readers". The authors used ICLE data in their study. The task is quite difficult for raters to agree upon: 84% of the essays were given the score of 2.5 or 3, suggesting that two raters randomly giving scores would be expected to agree within 0.5 point at least 71% of the time, which is roughly what the authors observed (67% agreement within 0.5 score point). Gao et al. (2019) used a six-point scale for assessing argument quality (among other dimensions) in essays written by college students in a STEM major. Trained raters agreed better on some dimensions than on others, with an average correlation of $r = 0.75$; yet, scores given by trained raters correlated only moderately with scores given by the tutors who originally graded the assignments. For the argument quality dimension specifically, the correlation between raters' and tutors' grades was $r = 0.34$.

Horbach et al. (2017) experimented with assessing argument quality as one of the many dimensions of essay quality, for a dataset of essays written by highly proficient writers. The authors assessed inter-rater reliability for six annotators on a three-point scale using the %ModAgree metric, which is the proportion of essays where a rater agrees with the mode score. While the authors report a high measurement of 0.85 for quality of argumentation, the measure is not chance-corrected, and the distribution of scores is highly skewed toward the highest score of 3.

Carlile et al. (2018) worked at the level of single arguments using a subset of the Stab and Gurevych essay data. Each premise is annotated with strength, which is used to decide on the persuasiveness of the claim supported by it, which, in turn, is used to decide on the persuasiveness of the major claim it supports. At the level of a claim, which would correspond to the level of a single argument (since the claim and its premises are evaluated as a bundle for persuasiveness of the claim), the authors present agreement of $\alpha = 0.7$ on a six-point scale; the version of distance metric in the α coefficient is not specified. The annotations show that writing a persuasive argument (scored as 6 or 5 on the scale, "very strong, clear argument" and "a strong, pretty clear argument", respectively) is quite difficult, as fewer than 10% of the annotated arguments got one of the top two scores, and only 21% received a score in the top half (that is, including score 4 that covers "decent, fairly clear" arguments). The authors also annotated certain characteristics of claims and premises and assessed their relationship with persuasiveness, to improve the understanding of what it is about the argument that goes with being persuasive. Beyond gen-

---

[20]Falakmasir et al. (2014) use F rather than F_1 in the paper, though it appears possible from the context of the discussion that F_1 (for thesis category) is intended. This conclusion is supported by the $F_1 = 0.73$ reported in Jabbari et al. (2016) for "our previous fine-tuned SVM model" which seems to correspond to Falakmasir et al. (2014) with slight modifications.

eral traits like being eloquently put, having good evidence, and being specific, the authors noted that having premises that relied on real examples and statistics correlated with persuasiveness, although the correlations are relatively weak (<0.25). Generally, it appeared that it was possible to use premises of different kinds (real example, invented instance, analogy, testimony, statistics, definition, common knowledge) and make claims of different types (something is good or bad, true of false, worth or not worth doing) resulting in more or less persuasive arguments. To summarize, argument strength is not easy to annotate reliably and it generally remains an open question *under what conditions* certain types of premises and claims work and others do not.

Argument Quality in Critique Essays

For a typical opinion-on-an-issue task, what kind of arguments work seems like a rather open-ended question—surely there is any number of arguments that one could bring to bear on a fairly general topic such as whether reliance on technology hampers people's ability to think for themselves, or whether a broad or a specialized college education is better. Y. Song et al. (2017) circumvent this potential open-endedness problem by considering a type of argumentative writing where the task is that of criticizing an argument put forward in an extended prompt; the task is taken from a high-stakes standardized test given to relatively advanced (post-college-graduation) test-takers. To clarify the nature of the critique task, consider the following prompt from Y. Song et al. (2017):

> The following appeared in a memorandum from the new president of the Patriot car manufacturing company.

> "In the past, the body styles of Patriot cars have been old-fashioned, and our cars have not sold as well as have our competitors' cars. But now, since many regions in this country report rapid increases in the numbers of newly licensed drivers, we should be able to increase our share of the market by selling cars to this growing population. Thus, we should discontinue our oldest models and concentrate instead on manufacturing sporty cars. We can also improve the success of our marketing campaigns by switching our advertising to the Youth Advertising agency, which has successfully promoted the country's leading soft drink".

In the ARGUMENT CRITIQUE task, writers are asked to analyze the reasoning in the provided argument, consider any assumptions, and discuss how well any evidence that is mentioned supports the conclusion.

Using Walton's theory of argumentation schemes (Walton, 1996), Y. Song et al. (2017) analyzed arguments given in different prompts of the argument critique task. They found that across 20 prompts selected for analysis, 6 different argumentation schemes were used, with up to 4 schemes per prompt. Causal arguments were used in 15 out of 20 prompts, followed by policy arguments (a scheme derived by Song et al. based on multiple Walton's schemes), arguments from sample, example, comparison, and position to know. The quoted prompt is a fairly typical case—it has an over-arching policy argument (proposal of a specific plan to solve a specific practical problem) as well as an implicit causal argument (that the proposed plan would in fact achieve the goal).

The key observation based on these analyses and on Walton's argumentation scheme theory is that it is possible to define a set of all **critiques that can reasonably be made** when attacking an argument belonging to a particular scheme. Staying on the subject of cars, let's say the proposal is for a car manufacturer to paint a line of cars pink in order to increase appeal to young women, based on a poll where young women said they love pink cars. This argument includes a policy scheme, a causal scheme, and a sample scheme. We address each in turn.

Given a policy argument, namely, an argument for or against a decision to implement a particular solution to a practical problem, there are six types of critiques one might raise. First, is there really a problem? (Perhaps our sales with the young women demographic are already strong.) Second, how desirable/important is it to solve the problem? (Is it important to appeal to this demographic in particular? Perhaps young women are generally an increasingly small proportion of buyers of new cars.) Third, is it practically possible to carry out the proposed solution? (Is anyone producing the desired quantities of pink car paint?) Fourth, is the implementation plan well defined? (Exactly which line of cars? Are we going to paint the whole car or just some parts?) Fifth, are there undesirable side effects that would occur if the policy is implemented? (Are all other demographics going to turn away from the car?) Sixth, are there better alternative plans that would achieve the goal? (Perhaps we can sell a nicely designed—pink!—add-on like a wheel cover, instead of introducing pink paint in the production line? That would be cheaper.)

Policy arguments are often accompanied by causal arguments, namely, the claim that the proposed solution will lead to the problem being solved. Causal arguments can be attacked on the grounds of: First, is there really a causal mechanism or merely a coincidence between the cause and the effect? (Do young women actually buy a pink version of a product, all else being equal?) Second, is the causal mechanism strong enough to actually produce the desired effects? (Is the preference toward pink objects so strong that it would be a deciding factor in car acquisition?) Third, does the causal mechanism apply in the current case? (Perhaps young women buy pink hats and gloves, but not cars.) Fourth, are there intervening factors that could undermine the causal mechanism? (Using rare and expensive pink paint would raise the cost of the car, so they might like it better but not buy due to a higher price).

Finally, the third argumentation scheme in our example, namely, the poll cited in support of the proposal, goes with its own set of six critical questions, including representativeness and size of the sample, among others (see Y. Song et al. (2017) for more detail).

In summary, given a particular argument, it is possible to derive a relatively limited set of reasonable argument critiques. Note that this is not to say that any critique would be as strong or persuasive as any other; for example, whether there is sufficient paint to be obtained to carry out the car painting plan might not be a strong objection—presumably, it would not be difficult to commission a particular company to deliver a large order of pink paint, given sufficient time.

Yet, this critique would be a reasonable one in the context of the prompt, even if not the most damning for the proposed plan.

In the annotation campaign described in Y. Song et al. (2017), two pairs of annotators worked on argument critique essays written in response to three different prompts each, for a total of four prompts covered between the two pairs. Only essays that received a high holistic score were chosen for the task, on the grounds that these essays are likelier to contain a large number of valid critiques and are less likely to suffer from ambiguity or lack of clarity in expressing arguments than essays with lower scores. The annotators were trained in the argumentation schemes present in every prompt and in the critical questions that are appropriate for each scheme. During annotation, they marked a stretch of text where a specific critical question was raised and labeled it with scheme and question. The inter-annotator agreement for the binary classification of sentences into those that contain some critique (any scheme, any question) and those that were left unmarked (termed "generic") was $\kappa = 0.65$ on average, ranging between 0.54 and 0.72 for different pairs of annotators and different prompts. Agreement for specific categories for specific prompts for a specific pair of annotators ranged between $\kappa = 0.54$ and $\kappa = 0.94$, apart from a single case of $\kappa = 0.37$. The authors thus demonstrated the feasibility of a moderately reliable detailed analysis of the content of the arguments, in the context of an argument critique task and for well-written essays.

The authors applied the same protocols to randomly sampled essays, resulting in κ of 0.57 and 0.60 for two prompts for the classification of sentences into generic and non-generic (Y. Song et al., 2014) and later to a set of randomly sampled essays responding to 10 different prompts, with an inter-annotator agreement of $\kappa = 0.67$ (Beigman Klebanov, Gyawali, & Song, 2017). Using the annotations, Y. Song et al. (2014) reported that a scoring feature derived from the annotations—the proportion of sentences that were non-generic—produced an improvement in the performance of a state-of-art essay scoring system, suggesting that the information about the extent to which an essay raises reasonable critiques is potentially a useful scoring feature.

Experiments on automating the detection of argument critiques (non-generic sentences) have been carried out by Y. Song et al. (2014) and Beigman Klebanov, Gyawali, & Song (2017). In the first, the authors used 260 training and 40 test essays to evaluate predictions of generic vs. non-generic sentences within each prompt, using word n-grams (n = 1–3) in current, previous, and next sentences, relative position of the sentence in the essay, POS features, and prompt-relevance/topicality features based on Jaccard similarity between sentence and prompt. While the feature set performed reasonably well when the training and testing essays belonged to the same prompt, the authors noted that training on one prompt and testing on the other resulted in a dramatic drop in performance. This is problematic for a practical use of the feature, since the release schedule of the scoring engine and the release schedule of new prompts are not always aligned, so it is possible that the scoring engine would need to score operational essays responding to a completely unseen new prompt.

To address the problem of cross-prompt generalization specifically, Beigman Klebanov, Gyawali, & Song (2017) conducted 10-fold cross-validation leave-one-prompt-out experiments on annotated data from 10 prompts, with the goal of reducing the difference in performance between the average across 10 prompts and the worst-case performance. The Y. Song et al. (2014) system that served as a baseline showed average classification accuracy of 0.678 for generic vs. non-generic sentences, with 0.642 for the worst-case fold. To support cross-prompt generalization, the authors (a) introduced structural features based on discourse parse output, including discourse labels of current, previous, and next sentences, and (b) generalized n-gram features to hybrid lexico—syntactic features where content words from the prompt were represented as their POS while the rest remained at lexis level; generalized n-grams could then capture patterns like "will not VB" that would capture parts of a causal mechanism critique toward different actions recommended in the different policy prompts. The resulting system performed at 0.706 on average, with the worst-case performance just two points below, at 0.686.

6.2.6 DISCUSSION: BETWEEN CONTENT AND STRUCTURE

Beigman Klebanov, Stab, et al. (2016) investigated the question of the relationship between sentences containing argument components as predicted by the Stab and Gurevych model and sentences annotated as containing non-generic materials—germane argument critiques—in Y. Song et al. (2014). They found that the presence of a premise in a sentence provided the best clue to the sentence being non-generic; that is, it is in the justifications of attack claims on the prompt argument that the critical questions predicted by the argumentation scheme theory were raised. However, the correspondence was not perfect; in particular, the argument component system over-generated, with a 3:1 ratio of false positives (something that looks like a premise but is not marked as non-generic) to false negatives (something that does not look like an argument component but is marked as non-generic). That is, students quite often wrote things that looked like justifications of a claim but weren't actually reasonable justifications, and also, more rarely, things that did not look like premises yet were part of a germane critique— seemingly fact-seeking questions are an example cited for the latter case ("What was it 3 or 4 years ago?" is used to cast doubt on the causal mechanism described in the prompt to account for the current situation).

Musi et al. (2016) addressed the task of classifying all <claim, major claim> and <premise, claim> pairs annotated in a subset of the Stab and Gurevych essays for the argumentation scheme instantiated by the pair. The authors reported a large number of pairs where the annotators could find no appropriate argumentation scheme. They found that <claim, major claim> pairs are often such that the claim is a rephrasing of the major claim, so the support relation between them "is justified if redundancy is considered as a stylistic strategy for achieving consensus on a certain stance", but there is no argument scheme connecting the pair. The authors also noted cases where a <premise, claim> pair only works as a scheme-based argument if additional material for the essay is included; cases where the argument-scheme-like relation was reversed; and cases where no argumentation scheme could be found that supported the <premise, claim> link. These observations are in general agreement with those in Beigman Klebanov, Stab, et al. (2016)—that the structural analysis over-generates with respect to argumentation-scheme-relevant content and that premises are the most likely loci where scheme-relevant argumentation is to be found.

Ong et al. (2014) reported a finding that is consistent with the structure vs. content observations above. Their corpus of human-scored essays written for a freshman psychology course averaged 3.03 (median 3) on the scale of 0–5; the scoring rubric included not only grammar, usage, flow, and organization, but also "logic behind their argumentation". An automated rule-based scoring system identified argument structures: claims, supporting and opposing premises backed by citations, as well as more task-specific categories called "hypothesis" (the task was "write an argumentative essay supporting two separate hypotheses that they created based on data they were given") and "current study". The authors observed that the automated system that identified the categories based on discourse connectives, citation format, and specific key vocabulary (such as *conflict, oppose, evidence, suggests, predict, study, research,* and a few more) and credited the writer for mentioning the necessary components tended to over-score the low-scoring essays, with the mean of 3.4 and a median of 3.5, which could suggest that something that is recognizably formed like an argument component quite often was not actually credited as such by a human rater—possibly because its content did not quite make sense or was not really an argument.

Additional research considered the question of whether information about the content of the argument component is necessary for recovery of aspects of argument structure. Opitz & Frank (2019) studied to what extent a system that knows nothing about what is actually said inside the argument component[21] can identify attack relations and support relations between components. The authors extracted features from the argument component and its context separately for content-based and content-ignorant models, respectively. Features include unigrams, features based on constituency parse, positional features, PDTB-based discourse features (Z. Lin et al., 2014; Prasad et al., 2008), word embeddings-based features, as well as sentiment features aligned with syntactic trees as described in Socher et al. (2013). The authors found that content-ignorant models generally performed better than the content-based ones, and were generally not far behind—only 2 macro-F_1 score points—the replicated Stab & Gurevych (2017a) results. In a similar vein, Mensonides et al. (2019) show that macro-F_1 score of 0.798 on the argument component identification task can be achieved by a version of the system that does not look at the words inside the argument components at all—only at their context (compare to 0.867 for the Stab and Gurevych system).

It is not surprising that writers who come up with a reasonable argument also tend to articulate and sign-post it in a way that makes it easy for the reader—and a machine—to recognize

---

[21]Recall that the discourse markers are generally left outside of the argument component in Stab and Gurevych's annotation, hence these would be features of context.

and link its various components. After all, persuasive writing, just like any kind of writing, should be *clear* if it is to achieve its purpose. However, this connection between content and structure can provide grounds for some gaming strategies—some of the discourse-connective-tissue, so to speak, or what Opitz & Frank (2019) termed the context of an argument component, can be used even if the test-taker is struggling to come up with an actual argument, in the hopes that a system would be fooled by a vaguely argumentative-looking structure. Madnani et al. (2012) refer as *shell* to those pieces in persuasive writing that are used to "organize the persuader's tactics and claims rather than to express them". Thus, in "It must be the case that this diet works since it was recommended by someone who lost 20 pounds on it", Madnani et al. (2012) identify *it must be the case that* and *since* as shell elements, while the sentence as a whole is an instance of a (well-organized) argument from a position to know. We will return to the question of full vs. empty shells in the discussion of gaming in Chapter 12.

6.3   NARRATIVE WRITING/CONVEY EXPERIENCE

Computational analysis of written narratives is of interest not only in the educational context, but also in clinical diagnostics (Bourassa et al., 2017; Fraser et al., 2014; Lynn et al., 2018; Roemmele et al., 2017), financial communication (Mahmoud El-Haj et al., 2019), literary analysis (Bamman et al., 2014; Elson et al., 2010), among others.

Experiments with computational modeling of some of the elements of narrative has been done recently in the context of the Story Cloze, Narrative Cloze, and Narrative Event Ordering tasks (Chambers & Jurafsky, 2008; Z. Li et al., 2019; Mostafazadeh et al., 2016, 2017), where a system needs to predict the ending of a short narrative, a missing event, and a sequence of events in a narrative, respectively. Representation of narrative units/events is an active research topic (Goyal et al., 2010; Ludwig et al., 2018; Weber et al., 2018), as well as work on automated generation of stories (B. Li et al., 2013; Martin et al., 2018; McIntyre & Lapata, 2009); see the proceedings of the 2019 Workshop on Narrative Understanding for a snapshot of the most recent work (Bamman et al., 2019), as well as Mani (2012) for an in-depth review of narratological concepts and approaches to their computational modeling.

6.3.1   SCORING NARRATIVE ESSAYS

Somasundaran et al. (2018) specifically considered the task of scoring narrative essays. They worked with a corpus of 942 narrative essays written by students in grades 7, 10, and 12 in response to 18 different prompts related to personal experiences (e.g., write a story about your proudest moment), hypothetical situation (e.g., pretend that you've become a teacher for a day–what happened?), or a fictional story (e.g., write a story about finding a message in a bottle). They used a rubric for scoring NARRATIVES developed in the Smarter Balanced Assessment Consortium,[22] where narratives are assessed for organization, development, and conventions.

---

[22]http://portal.smarterbalanced.org/library/en/performance-task-writing-rubric-narrative.pdf

The organization trait assesses the structure of the narrative—plot, characters, setting, events, sequencing, and transitioning between events, while the narrative development rubric addresses the use of elaboration techniques such as detailing, dialogue, description, user of sensory, concrete, and figurative language, appropriate style, etc. The conventions rubric covers grammar, usage, and mechanics. In the manual scoring study, the authors report inter-rater reliability of $\kappa_q = 0.71$ for organization and $\kappa_q = 0.73$ for development, both judged on a scale of 1–4, with 0 score given to essays that are "insufficient, written in a language other than English, off topic, or off-purpose". The reliability of the conventions rubric (scale of 1–3) is lower, with $\kappa_q = 0.46$. The authors noted that organization and development scores were highly correlated ($r = 0.88$).

For automated scoring experiments, the authors used linear regression to combine a variety of features modeled to capture aspects of the narrative organization and narrative development traits. They design a set of features to capture properties of **event cohesion and coherence**, where an *event* is defined as a verb and a pair of events is a pair of verbs that share argument fillers in the text (e.g., <broke, door> and <hit,door> are an event pair). Event cohesion features include (1) total count of event pairs in the essay; (2) proportion of in-essay event pairs that are found in a separately constructed event database (using Gigaword corpus (Parker et al., 2011) automatically annotated for typed dependency information (Napoles et al., 2012)); and (3) proportion of in-essay event pairs that have substantial association (using point-wise mutual information (Church & Hanks, 1990)). To capture the coherence of event sequencing, the authors compute event chains, defined as sequences of events that share the same actor or object, in subject or direct object role (Chambers & Jurafsky, 2008). Features derived from event chains include the lengths of the longest and the second-longest chains, association scores of the longest, highest-scoring, lowest-scoring chains (sum of PMI values for all event pairs in the chain), as well as versions of these features that are normalized by the log of essay length (wordcount).

Another set of features addresses clarity of **transitioning** between events, using a transition-cue lexicon compiled from the Penn Discourse Treebank (PDTB) manual (Prasad et al., 2008) and from web sources; the lexicon includes, for example, words and phrases that provide locational or temporal connection. The transitioning features include raw and essay-length-normalized counts of transition cues.

Going after elements of narrative development, the authors also constructed feature sets that capture **subjective and evaluative language** often used to describe characters or their private mental states in detail (e.g., foolish, smart; sadness, happiness), using subjectivity lexicons from the literature (Beigman Klebanov et al., 2012; T. Wilson et al., 2005). A separate **detailing** feature set includes presence and count features for parts of speech that tend to be used for providing detailed descriptions of characters or actions (proper nouns, adjectives, and adverbs). Development features calculated off the essay's word-type **graph** from Somasundaran et al. (2016) were also included (see Chapter 5 for a more detailed exposition). Essay graphs were constructed where each content word type was a node and links were drawn between nodes of two words if they appeared in adjacent sentences in an essay. Graph-based features include proportion of nodes with degree one/two/three, highest/second-highest/median degree, top three and median PageRank values in the graph, as well as essay-length-normalized versions of the features.

Additional features included counts and normalized counts of first and third person singular **pronouns** which indicate the story's point of view, **lexical density** (proportion of content words in an essay), as well as features capturing vocabulary that is less typical of narrative such as use of **modals** (e.g., could, shall) and **stative verbs** (e.g., know, prefer, copular uses of "to be"; stative verbs contrast with dynamic ones that typically carry events in a narrative).

As a baseline, Somasundaran et al. (2018) use e-rater (Attali & Burstein, 2006), that includes features capturing grammar, usage, and mechanics conventions, as well as aspects of organization and development through identification of discourse elements (Burstein et al., 2003). The baseline performs at $\kappa_q = 0.47$ and 0.51 for organization and development traits, respectively. The authors combine their features using linear regression, studying different feature types separately, as well as various subsets of feature types, including the baseline. For organization, the best feature set includes detailing, pronouns, modals, lexical density, graph, subjectivity, and transitioning), and achieves $\kappa_q = 0.60$. For narrative development, the best feature set includes detailing, modals, lexical density, graph, statives, and transitioning, and performs at $\kappa_q = 0.63$.

The authors noted that the baseline (e-rater) is not part of the best performing system, as well as the curious absence of the event feature set from the best performing models for both organization and development—this being the feature set that most directly aligns with elements of the organization scoring rubric such as having a natural/logical sequence of events. The authors interpreted this result as suggesting that even though the events feature set on its own has some predictive power (κ_q of 0.39 and 0.43 for organization and development, respectively), "other features, correlated with events, must be stronger indicators of narrative competence". The single best-performing feature type was graph features that scored $\kappa_q = 0.49$ and $\kappa_q = 0.54$ for organization and development, respectively, seconding the authors' earlier finding of the effectiveness of these features for scoring both narrative and argumentative essays (Somasundaran et al., 2016). The authors also noted that essays that are well-written, long and elaborated but non-narrative, or "off-purpose", constitute a challenge for the automated scoring system; a case in point is an essay that ostensibly was written in response to the prompt "describe a travel experience" but in fact mainly contained a discussion of educational advantages of travel in general. The authors conjectured that a possible solution could be running a binary narrative classifier that would flag non-narrative essays and prevent them from being submitted to the scoring system.

Flor & Somasundaran (2019) explored the relationship between lexical concreteness and narrative scores (organization plus development scores from Somasundaran et al. (2018)), showing a positive correlation ($r = 0.22$ using all content words) that is mostly carried by nouns ($r = 0.25$) and adjectives ($r = 0.30$). The authors' results also suggest that the associations might be stronger for certain types of narratives (fictional more than personal, for example, with correlations of $r = 0.41$ vs. $r = 0.14$, respectively). The authors have not benchmarked the results against length-informed baselines.

6.3.2   SCORING TRANSCRIPTS OF ORAL NARRATIVES

A related application of narrative analysis in the educational context is assessment of oral narratives by young children with the goal of diagnosing language disorders as well as for monitoring progress in the development of narrative skills; see Deane et al. (2019) for a recent review of the literature on narrative skill development in children. Children with language disorders often produce narratives that are less complex and not as well organized as those told by typically developing children of the same age; see Petersen (2011) for a review of narrative interventions administered to children with language impairments. Petersen et al. (2008) review assessments of recorded oral narratives produced by children between 3 and 12 years old (for different assessments); all methods reviewed therein rely on manual scoring.

Assessments typically involve measurements of macrostructure and/or microstructure of the narratives. Macrostructure, sometimes also referred to as story grammar, has to do with setting (reference to time and place) and episodes (initial motivating event, goal-directed actions, and outcomes related to the initiating event); microstructures include specific types of expressions, such as coordinating and subordinating conjunctions (e.g., for, but, yet), elaborated noun-phrases, metacognitive verbs (think/believe) (Gillam et al., 2017).

Jones et al. (2019) explored automated scoring of macrostructure elements in 414 transcribed children's narratives also scored by humans using the rubric from Gillam et al. (2017). In particular, human scores ranging from 0 (not present) to 3 (mastered) for each of the following macrostructure elements were used for evaluation: Character, Setting, Initiating Event, Plan, Action, Consequence. The authors reported very high κ_q agreement between predictions automatically generated by BERT (Bidirectional Encoder Representations from Transformers (Devlin et al., 2019)) and human scores, with 0.79 being the lowest score for Consequence. For each macrostructure element, BERT was trained to predict a continuous score (in a regression mode) using the whole narrative as a single instance; the continuous scores were then rounded to the nearest integer for computing κ_q. As a caveat, the authors note that human scores assigned by trained undergraduates diverged quite substantially from expert human scores assigned to a 50-item subset of the data; BERT correlations with expert scores were likewise substantially lower than those observed for the undergraduate scorers. A larger expert scored corpus is needed to validate the excellent performance of the automated system.

Rouhizadeh et al. (2013) explore automated methods for distinguishing narrative retellings produced by typically developing children from those produced by autistic children, using a measure of usage of unexpected words in the narrative; they showed that children with autism produced significantly higher rates of unusual words, both when the words were identified by human raters and automatically. Regneri & King (2016) also address narratives produced by neurotypical and autistic individuals, showing that a measure combining normalized average length of a coreference chain and average proportion of sentences with at least one anaphoric link both correlates with human-assigned scores of narrative cohesion and significantly differs between the populations of interest. Somasundaran et al. (2015) addressed the task of scoring the content of picture-based oral narratives, and showed that features that capture narrative elements such as detailing (increased usage of proper names, adjectives, and adverbs) and use of subjectivity helped improve over a baseline scoring model that focused on the oral delivery aspect of the task.

6.4   EXPOSITORY WRITING BASED ON SOURCES

In education, writing from sources is commonly used in assessing and fostering comprehension of the source material. Graham & Hebert (2011) conducted a meta-analysis of research on writing techniques shown to enhance students' reading. Their findings are unequivocal: "The evidence from this meta-analysis shows that having students in grades 2–12 write about material read enhances their comprehension of it. ... Confidence can be placed in our findings, as we replicated them repeatedly and the quality of studies was relatively high". Indeed, many of the studies of source-based writing by children and adolescents to be reviewed in this section were conducted in the context of assessment of reading comprehension.

Before we turn to automated assessment of source-based writing, let us take a quick look at the major relevant developments in the computational linguistics research. A series of large-scale evaluations of automated summarization systems have been held as part of the U.S. government-funded Document Understanding Conferences[23] (2001–2007) and the Summarization track of the Text Analysis Conferences (TAC) [24] (2008–2011, 2014). For the 2008 TAC competition (Dang & Owczarzak, 2008), for example, a total of eight evaluators (a) prepared four reference summaries for each source (one or a set of multiple source documents to be covered in a single summary); (b) scored two top summaries per participating team per source for content using the manual Pyramid method (Nenkova & Passonneau, 2004) based on the four reference summaries, as well as scored these summaries for readability ("fluency and structure of the summary, independently of content, based on such aspects as grammaticality, non-redundancy, referential clarity, focus, structure, and coherence") and responsiveness (a holistic score that considers content and linguistic quality). In addition to manual evaluations, all submitted summaries were scored using automated summary assessment methods–ROUGE (C.-Y. Lin, 2004; C.-Y. Lin & Hovy, 2003) and BE-HM (E. Hovy et al., 2005). More recent research on automated summarization focuses mostly on news data, on development of both extractive summaries (those that copy selected material from the sources) and abstractive ones (where the important points are detected and paraphrased), as well as on the application of neural networks to improve the summary generation process; see Kryscinski et al. (2019) for a recent review and a critique, as

---

[23]https://duc.nist.gov
[24]http://www.nist.gov/tac

well as a book-length review in Nenkova & McKeown (2011) and a review specifically focused on evaluation metrics in Lloret et al. (2018).

The Pyramid method for manual evaluation of summary content has been applied to analysis of human summaries as well; we will discuss it in detail in Section 6.4.5. ROUGE and BE-HM are methods for automatically comparing the target summary to a set of reference summaries using small building blocks—n-grams in the case of ROUGE and head-modifier syntactic tuples in the case of BE-HM; these inspired some of the methods for assessing human summaries, and will be mentioned as needed.

Generally, SOURCE-BASED writing tasks require the writers to (a) select which information in the source text is most important (CONTENT SELECTION); (b) organize ideas from the text into a coherent whole; (c) reflect on the content of the text through review, re-examination, and critique; (d) get personally involved with the text to make active decisions regarding what is to be written and how it is to be treated; and (e) transform or manipulate the language of the text to put ideas into their own words (Graham & Hebert, 2011). Selection of important information from the source and its reasonable organization in the essay are central constructs for most, if not all, source-based writing contexts we will review in this section. Transformation of the original language (non-plagiarism) might or might not be of importance, depending on the specific task—when the source text is available during writing, one would expect direct copying to be discouraged; when the task involves recall from a source that is not immediately available, recalling verbatim text from the source might be positively evaluated. Reflection and personal involvement, through examination of the material and articulation of a personal reaction or a critique, might or might not be part of the construct of a source-based writing task. We have discussed a task where the writer's argument critique of the source is the central construct (see Section 6.2.5); reflective writing will be reviewed in Section 6.5. In this section, we address cases where articulating the writer's own opinion on the subject matter is not the main construct to be assessed; indeed, in some cases it is explicitly discouraged, writers being asked to focus on **retelling** or **summarizing** the source material.

6.4.1 SCORING HUMAN SUMMARIES–AN OVERVIEW

Methods for scoring human-produced summaries focus on two aspects of the summary: (a) closeness to a reference that represents the content that a good summary should address; and (b) good organization and development of the summary itself, including coherence, signposting important transitions using discourse cues, good use of sophisticated vocabulary, appropriate length. Since methods proposed to capture (b) are similar to those proposed for the more generic scoring of essays as reviewed in Chapter 5, we will focus the discussion on methods proposed to address (a), although coherence features will also be mentioned, as needed.

To address (a), one needs to address two challenges: First, **how to represent the desired content,** and second, **how to compare** a given summary to the content model. As far as comparison goes, there are two general strategies—**verbatim overlap,** often using n-gram-based methods, and **semantic similarity**, often using latent semantic space models such as Latent Semantic Analysis or word embeddings-based representations; in many approaches both methods are used.

It is in the design of the representation of the desired content that the most substantial variation across methods occurs. The source document itself is the simplest representation; however, it is often insufficient since a good summary does not merely represent *some* information from the source but only *important* information. The central research question is therefore how to **systematically capture important information** from the source. The proposed approaches include use of source text (reviewed in Section 6.4.2), of one or more expert or peer/crowdsourced summaries (Section 6.4.3), of an explicit expert-provided model of the desired content (Section 6.4.4), as well as ways to transform both source text and reference summaries into representations that are effective for automated scoring of an incoming summary (Section 6.4.5). This section is thus organized based on the proposed solutions for systematic capture of important content, as a part of a scoring system for source-based writing. We will **boldface** the element that corresponds to the content capture in the description of each system that is reviewed below, to help the reader track the structure of this section.

6.4.2   APPROACHES THAT USE SOURCE DOCUMENT AS THE SOLE REFERENCE

The simplest type of source-based task is that of retelling a previously read story; it is used, in an oral version, in the context of a reading assessment of young children (Bernstein et al., 2017, 2018). Children read a short story out loud, and then are asked to retell it, without access to the original text. Such retellings are then scored on the scale of 0–6, where 0 corresponds to a silent, irrelevant, or unintelligible response, 1 is a minimal response; 2 is a limited response that has some concept sequences but misses major concepts and main narrative arc of the story; 3 is a partial response that covers part of the main narrative; 4 is an adequate response mentioning enough major and minor concepts to suggest the main narrative logic; 5 is a good response where the major and minor concepts convey main narrative and causal logic; and 6 is a complete response with close narrative fidelity. The scoring rubric thus emphasizes selection of the right information (major/minor/relevant) and its reasonable sequencing (narrative arc, narrative logic). J. Cheng (2018) reports inter-rater correlation of $r = 0.786$ for this rubric and presents a system for automated scoring of retellings using a dataset of 1,262 rated retellings from 94 students in grades 2–4 (3 retellings per student, 4.5 ratings per retelling), distributed as follows: 0 (2%), 1 (10%), 2 (14%), 3 (23%), 4 (21%), 5 (16%), 6 (14%). A measure of **word types in common** between the source story and the human transcription of a retelling normalized by the number of word types in the source story was strongly correlated with human score ($r = 0.87$); the author comments that this good performance is most likely due to the good-faith nature of the retellings from young children, that is, extensive but completely incorrect use of the words and phrases from the source story—telling a different story with the same words—was unlikely.

It is interesting to note that no importance weighting of the words nor a sequencing model were required to achieve the high correlation; it must be the case that children who recalled more also recalled the more important elements in a reasonable order.

Crossley et al. (2019) addressed scoring of summaries using a main-ideas-based scoring rubric. Summaries were written by Amazon Mechanical Turk workers (792 summaries, each person was asked to summarize three different texts) and by low-literacy adults (adults who read at less than 9th grade level; 231 summaries, each person was asked to summarize two different texts). Source texts were simplified news stories on unrelated topics, between 128 and 452 words long, at Flesch–Kincaid grade level between 4th and 8th grades; 33 source texts were used in total, with between 20 and 129 participant summaries per text. All summaries were assigned an expert classification into low-scoring (mention some or no main ideas from the text) and high-scoring (mention most or all main ideas from the text). The authors show that type-token ratio for all words and for content words specifically, average word frequency of the words in the summary in spoken English, as well as **word2vec-based similarity between the summary and source** were all significant predictors for classifying essays into low and high. High-scoring summaries were more similar to the source, had a higher type-token ratio for all words but a lower one for content words (that is, repeated the same words less frequently overall but more frequently for content words), and used vocabulary that is less frequent in spoken English. The model achieved 81.6% classification accuracy on the test partition.

H. Li et al. (2018) consider semantic-similarity-based scoring of summaries using source text as a baseline against which other content representation methods are evaluated. The authors work with 1,440 summaries (180 for each of 8 expository texts of 200–400 words, at Flesch–Kincaid grade levels of 8–12 grades) written by 240 Amazon Mechanical Turk workers, each writing a 50–100 word summary for each of the source texts (some data was excluded due to non-compliance with the task). The summaries were scored using a 4-dimensional rubric, where a writer could gain between 0 and 2 points on each dimension; thus the final scores ranged from 0 to 8. The dimensions were: (a) whether there is a clear topic sentence that states the main ideas; (b) whether the summary includes major points in a logical order, and does not contain minor points or author's reflections; (c) whether the summary is free of grammar, usage, mechanics, and spelling errors; and (d) whether the summary uses clear and accuracy signal words (discourse connectives) to connect information. Summaries that contained a copy of 10 or more consecutive words from the source were disqualified. Four English native senior Ph.D. students graded the summaries, achieving an interclass correlation coefficient of 0.80. A 300-dimension Latent Semantic Analysis space was built using 37,520 texts (10.9M words) from the TASA corpus (Touchstone Applied Science Associates, Inc., renamed Questar Assessment Inc.). Texts in the TASA corpus have nine genres and span K–12 grade levels. The baseline method assigned a score using **LSA similarity between the source text and the essay**; this method scores Pearsons's $r = 0.40$ on average across the 8 topics.

Louis & Nenkova (2009) present a method of scoring machine-generated summaries without a gold standard, by computing the **Jensen Shannon divergence between word frequency distributions in the source text and in the summary**. The authors show that this method can rank systems very effectively—using a system's average score over a large number of summaries, the correlation between the proposed method and human score of content selection is Spearman's $r_s = 0.74$. Louis & Nenkova (2009) remark that their method is not as effective in a micro-context, where an accurate score of a particular summary is the goal. Considering the scores for a given summary, the authors note that the Spearman correlation between their scores and human scores was not significant for 27% of the cases, suggesting that for a non-negligible proportion of inputs the method did not assign correct scores to the different summaries. This limitation makes this method less useful in the context of automated scoring of human summaries where each person writes one or a very small number of summaries and the score given to an individual summary is consequential.

6.4.3   APPROACHES THAT USE SOURCE DOCUMENT AND EXPERT/PEER SUMMARIES AS REFERENCES

H. Li et al. (2018) investigate similarity-based scoring against other human produced summaries as an alternative to scoring based on similarity to source text. Their method, termed CrowdsourcingLSA, is to concatenate all summaries on the given topic apart from the summary-to-be-scored into a single long document and assign the score that is based on the **LSA similarity with the concatenated peer summaries**. This method scores $r = 0.44$, which is not significantly better than source-text-based scoring but somewhat more consistent: The CrowdsourcingLSA models ranged between $r = 0.40$ and $r = 0.49$ across the different prompts, while the source-text-based model ranged between $r = 0.29$ and $r = 0.48$. The authors also included a system using **LSA comparison to a single expert summary** in their evaluation; that version scored $r = 0.45$, not significantly different form source-text and CrowdsourcingLSA versions. A version of CrowdsourcingLSA that used only good peer summaries (with human scores of 6–8 points) scored $r = 0.48$, which was not significantly different from CrowdsourcingLSA that did not require pre-scoring of peer summaries.

Madnani et al. (2013) report on a study with children in grades 6–9 where the participants were asked to write a summary of a passage in the context of assessment of their reading comprehension. In the authors' example, students read a three-paragraph expository passage and were asked to write a summary such that "The first sentence of your summary should be about the whole passage. Then write three more sentences. Each sentence should be about one of the paragraphs". The first sentence should identify the "global" concept of the passage, and the rest of the sentences should address three main points, called "local concepts". Written summaries were scored holistically on a scale of 0 to 4, where 0 was given to off-topic responses and to "I don't know" responses, as well as responses that demonstrate no understanding of the passage; 1 – to summaries that demonstrate minimal local understanding (include 1 local concept only) or contain only verbatim text; 2 – to summaries with moderate local understanding (2–3 local concepts but no global), with or without verbatim text, contain at most 1 inaccuracy, or global understanding only with no local concepts; 3 – to summaries with good global understanding and at least 2 local concepts, with or without some verbatim text, with at most 1 inaccuracy; 4 – to summaries that demonstrate excellent global understanding and understanding of 3 local concepts, does not include verbatim text of 3+ words copied from the passage, and contains no inaccuracies. Note that, in contrast with the retelling from memory task we reviewed above, in this summary writing task students had access to the passage while writing the summary, and substantial verbatim repetition of phrases from the original passage was penalized by the scoring rubric.

Madnani et al. (2013) develop a set of positive and negative features for scoring written summaries. Negative features focused on the extent of **verbatim overlap between the passage and the essay**: BLEU (Papineni et al., 2002)—a metric commonly used to score machine translations—that captures n-gram (n = 1 . . . 4) overlap between the passage and the summary; ratio of the sum of lengths of all three-word (or longer) sequences that are copied from the passage to the (a) length of the summary (CopySumm), (b) length of the passage (CopyPassage); length of the longest word sequence in the summary copied from the passage. Positive features focused on recall of the right content and its coherent arrangement: ROUGE (C.-Y. Lin & Hovy, 2003)—a metric used for scoring automatically generated summaries—that captures **lexical and phrasal overlap between the given summary and a model summary (randomly selected from score four summaries responding to the same prompt)**; number of sentences in the summary; coherence—token counts of common discourse connectors; and a feature that assesses the extent to which the first sentence of the summary has global coverage, by counting the number of passage sentences that the first sentence of the summary borrows two-word or longer sequences from. A logistic regression classifier using these features achieves .52 and .65 exact match performance versus human scores for two passages (a separate model is trained for each passage), beating a most common score baseline by .2 and .14 points, respectively. The analysis of the models shows that features perform consistently across the two passages, with BLEU, ROUGE, and CopySumm in the top three features using an information gain metric; BLEU and CopySumm had a negative weight while ROUGE had a positive weight, as expected based on the scoring rubric.

Sladoljev-Agejev & Šnajder (2017) worked in the context of using summaries to assess reading comprehension in English, with data from 114 first-year business undergraduate students with mostly upper intermediate and advanced competency in English as L2. In this study, two articles from *The Economist* of about 900 words each were presented to the participants; they were asked to read an article and write a summary of about 300 words that should clearly present the main ideas to a third person who did not read the article. The summaries were scored by human raters on dimensions related to both content (accuracy, completeness, relevance) and organization and writing quality (coherence, cohesion, organization); each dimension was rated on a four-point scale. Inter-rater reliability measured by weighted kappa ranged from 0.64 for accuracy to 0.83 for cohesion. The authors do not address the issue of inter-correlation between various dimensions. For their automated scoring experiments, Sladoljev-Agejev & Šnajder (2017) used features from Madnani et al. (2013) as well as additional features from Coh-Metrix (Graesser et al., 2004), including features measuring mean and std of paragraph and sentence lengths, average word length in syllables and letters, referential cohesion (content overlap between adjacent sentences), and use of various types of connectives (adversarial, logical, additive, etc.). The authors found that Ridge regression models using a selected set of features outperformed the average human score baseline on all dimensions, showing accuracies between 44.5 for organization to 55.9 for cohesion. Interestingly, features capturing **verbatim repetition of material from the prompt** (BLEU and Madnani et al. (2013) copying features) had a positive weight in the model predicting accuracy of the summary but a negative weight on all other dimensions, while **ROUGE (calculated with respect to expert-created reference summaries)** was selected for only three out of the six dimensions (relevance, cohesion, and organization) and always had a negative weight. Vocabulary sophistication features describing average word length in syllables and letters entered only accuracy and relevance models, with positive weights. Thus, for accuracy, essays that had more sophisticated vocabulary and borrowed more verbatim material from the source tended to have a higher score, whereas for completeness, it is essays with more sophisticated vocabulary that borrowed less verbatim material from the source that tended to score higher. Šnajder et al. (2019) investigated rhetorical structure-based features for scoring coherence and cohesion of summaries; since these dimensions do not deal with the source-based nature of the task, we will not review those here (but see Chapter 5 for a discussion of models of coherence).

Jorge-Botana et al. (2015) explore a summary task delivered in the context of distance higher education. The participants were 242 third-year undergraduate psychology students. The source text was a 3,660-words excerpt from a psychology textbook. The task required students to read the text and summarize it, with no time limit and no limit on the length of the summary. Three judges evaluated the summaries on the scale of 0–10, taking into account "the quality of the content (i.e., main ideas), use of adequate writing style, length, use of correct technical words, coherence, and personal elaboration of the summary produced (i.e., lack of very close paraphrases of the textual sentences that were just read)". Thus, as in Madnani et al. (2013), excessive borrowing from the source text was to be evaluated negatively, although the students were not specifically instructed to avoid plagiarism. Inter-rater correlations ranged between $r = 0.38$ and $r = 0.49$ for different pairs; the authors note that sensitivity to plagiarism was a major source of disagreements. The authors removed from the sample 34 summaries with disagreements above a threshold (see paper for more detail). Scores from the three judges were averaged to obtain the gold standard scores. For the automated scoring model, the authors used (1) a measure of plagiarism–a harmonic-mean of (1a) **proportion of summary trigrams shared with the source** out of all trigrams in the summary and (1b) proportion of source trigrams shared with the summary out of all trigrams in the source; (2) a measure of good content selection—**LSA similarity to an expert summary**; and (3) a measure of local coherence–average paragraph-to-paragraph LSA similarity for pairs of adjacent paragraphs. A multiple regression model on the training partition of the data (164 summaries) showed significant contributions from each of the measures—negative for the plagiarism measure and positive from the other two.[25] The model achieved $r = 0.72$ with average human scores on the test partition (44 summaries). The content-selection component alone achieved $r = 0.67$ on test data.

Xia et al. (2019) investigated automated scoring of summaries written by English language learners at various degrees of proficiency; 411 such summaries from 137 learners were used for testing their proposed methods; 300 simulated summaries (proficient writers were asked to write good and bad summaries, as language learners would) were used for training and development. Summaries were scored on the scale of 0 to 5, where score 5 was assigned when "The summary demonstrates excellent understanding of the original passage: Content covers all the main points of the passage. All content included is accurate, with no irrelevant details or repetitions. Target reader is fully informed"; score 1 was assigned when "The summary demonstrates very little understanding of the passage: Most of the content is of limited relevance, with repetitions or verbatim borrowing from the original text. In some paraphrased parts of the text, inaccuracy of content or omissions of main points are evident. Target reader is minimally informed". The pairwise correlation between human annotators ranged between 0.690 and 0.794. The authors use the original text as reference and create four types of features: (1) **verbatim overlap with the source text** using BLEU and ROUGE; (2) features based on semantic similarity between words and sentences in the summary vs. the original text, using embeddings trained on Wikipedia, including **word2vec** (Mikolov, Sutskever, et al., 2013), as well as (3) semantic spaces trained on Simple English Wikipedia using LSA, LDA, doc2vec (Le & Mikolov, 2014), tfidf for document-level **summary-to-source semantic similarity**; and (4) features based on length, type-token ratio, and manually assigned reading difficulty level of the passage using the Common European Framework of Reference for Languages (CEFR). A Kernel Ridge Regression (KRR) model using these features attained $r = 0.636$ with the human scores, against a ROUGE baseline that scored $r = 0.499$. The authors investigated **machine-generated summaries as an alternative reference** instead of the source text, but the resulting models showed inferior performance. The authors show that performance can be raised to $r = 0.665$ using, in addition to the KRR model, an attention LSTM and a CNN using a full sentence-by-sentence similarity matrix between source text and essay, although the CNN and LSTM models on their own did not improve over the ROUGE baseline.

So far, we have discussed methods where borrowing from source texts and matching model summaries were used as separate features for scoring summaries. Kakkonen and colleagues (Kakkonen et al., 2006, 2008, 2005; Kakkonen & Sutinen, 2004) used both source ma-

---

[25]While Jorge-Botana et al. (2015) discuss a way to turn plagiarism features into originality features, it is the plagiarism features that were used in the final model; confirmed by personal communication with the authors.

terials and pre-scored essays to derive a source-use score for an essay: **pre-scored essays were compared using LSA to relevant passages from a textbook** on which the course-final essays were supposed to be based, to derive similarity thresholds that corresponded to essay scores. The authors reported Spearman correlations with human holistic scores in the range of $r_s = 0.57$–0.90, for essays written for different courses in the Finnish higher education context, using relatively small samples of <150 essays per course. The authors also evaluated pLSA (Hofmann, 2001) and LDA (Blei et al., 2003) as alternatives to LSA but found their performance to be generally inferior.

6.4.4 APPROACHES THAT USE ADDITIONAL EXPERT-PROVIDED MATERIALS AS REFERENCES

In this section, we review approaches that utilize expert provided materials that are not summaries, such as lists of key concepts, topics, and examples.

Srihari et al. (2008) investigate automated scoring of a summary writing task using *handwritten* essays from 8th grade students.[26] The students were required to read a source text titled "American First Ladies" and respond in writing to the prompt "How was Martha Washington's role as First Lady different from that of Eleanor Roosevelt?" Three hundred responses to this prompt were manually scored using a six-point holistic rubric, where score 1 was given to essays that were brief, repetitive, and showed understanding of only some sections of the text; 2 – readable but not logical essays, showing limited understanding; 3 – partial understanding; 4 – logical and accurate but only literal understanding of the article; 5 – an organized essay showing understanding of the roles of first ladies, but without a thorough elaboration; and 6 – understanding similarities and differences between roles and of characteristics of the first ladies; complete, accurate, and insightful; focused, fluent, and engaging. The holistic rubric thus emphasized evidence of increasingly more nuanced understanding of the source material and coherent and well-elaborated presentation. The authors review in detail the relevant work on optical handwriting recognition (OHR), and present a pipeline that achieves a 57% word recognition rate against human transcriptions. The authors then explore two scoring methods—(a) using LSA in a way similar to T. Landauer et al. (2003) (reviewed in Chapter 4), by comparing the semantic vector generated for the essay with pre-scored essays at various score points; and (b) using a small set of features in a supervised machine learning paradigm using a small neutral network with a four-node hidden layer. For system (b) for scoring handwritten essays, the following features were used: number of words from the automated segmentation; number of lines; average number of characters in line; total number of characters in document; counts of "and" and of a small number of **manually provided key concepts** ("Washington's role", and "differed from" or "was different from") generated using word-spotting in the automatic transcription. The features thus capture mainly elaboration, connectivity, and whether the essay mentioned

---

[26]The authors also report results on a more complex multi-source writing task given to grade 5 students, but since the scoring rubric and the specific features used to score these are not elaborated, we omitted the presentation from this review.

the key concepts of roles and comparison. The LSA-based system showed 25% exact match and 58% within-one-point match relatively to human scores, while the feature-based system showed better performance, with 33% exact match and 71% within-one-point match. The authors hypothesized that the feature-based system was more robust to OHR errors since it did not require accurate identification of all words but only of a small subset of words in the essay.

Rahimi, Litman, and colleagues (Rahimi et al., 2017, 2015, 2014) studied methods of automatically scoring student essays using a detailed expert annotation of source text. Short essays were written by students in grades 5–6 (mean length 161 words, sd 92, $N = 1,569$) and 6–8 (mean length 208 words, sd 105, $N = 809$) based on a single source document—an article from "Times for Kids" about a UN effort to eradicate poverty in a rural village in Kenya. The teacher read the text aloud while students followed along with their own copy, including a guided discussion during the read aloud. Students then wrote an essay where they were asked to make a claim and support it using details from the text. All essays were scored on five dimensions, including Evidence, on a scale of 1–4, using the rubric from Correnti et al. (2013). The Evidence dimension is related to demonstrating integral use of selected details from the text to support the claim. Inter-annotator agreement ranged from $\kappa_q = 0.67$ and $\kappa_q = 0.73$ for the two datasets, respectively.

To build Evidence models, **exhaustive list of topics, important topic words, and examples** mentioned in the source texts were identified manually by experts. Thus, four main topics identified in the source text were: (1) Hospitals (evidenced by 19 keywords including health, treatment, doctor); (2) Malaria (12 keywords, including bed, net, infect, mosquito); (3) Farming (12 keywords, including fertilizer, irrigation, crop); and (4) School (17 keywords, including student, lunch, book, attend). An exhaustive list of examples for all topics—the four main ones and four secondary ones—was also compiled. For example, for topic 2 (Malaria), examples include (malaria, common, disease, preventable), (mosquitoes, carry, malaria infect, people, biting), (kids, die, malaria, adult, sick, 20,000, day), (bed, nets, mosquitoes, away, people, save, millions, lives), (bed, nets, cost, 5, $, dollar), and (cheap, medicine, treat, malaria).

The scoring rubric for Evidence emphasized (a) the number of pieces of evidence (0-1 pieces for score 1, at least 2 for score 2, and at least 3 for scores 3 and 4); (b) relevance of the selected evidence; (c) specificity of the evidence; and (d) elaboration of evidence. The authors created features in close alignment with the rubric. For number of pieces of evidence, a window-based algorithm with window size = 6 was used—**a window contains evidence related to a main topic if there are at least two words from the list of words for that topic**. The number of different topics found is the value of the feature. Relevance is modeled as a binary feature that is set to 1 if there are fewer than three sentences with any topic words. To capture specificity, the number of examples mentioned for each of the topics was counted. Elaboration was approximated by word count. The features were combined using random forest classifier. The authors show that a model with all features outperforms the unigram baseline $\kappa_q = 0.64$ to 0.62 (5–6 grade dataset) and $\kappa_q = 0.62$ to 0.56 (6–8 grade dataset), the latter improvement being significant. The specificity feature set performed particularly well, with $\kappa_q = 0.61$ and 0.60, for the two datasets, respectively. The word count feature scored $\kappa_q = 0.39$ and $\kappa_q = 0.31$, respectively. The authors also show that their system is more consistently applicable across grades—training on one dataset and testing on the other yielded $\kappa_q = 0.61$ and 0.62 for the two directions, while the unigram baseline scored $\kappa_q = 0.58$ for a case where the system is trained on 5–6 grade data and tested on 6–8 and only $\kappa_q = 0.46$ in the opposite direction. In another evaluation of the Evidence scoring model on the 5–6 grades' data, H. Zhang & Litman (2017) show that **using skip-gram embeddings trained on in-domain data to augment the exact match with topic and example lists** during feature extraction can improve performance,[27] especially on data from younger children (4–6 grades); in particular, the model is able to match "poverty" with a mis-spelled "proverty", which is important for construct validity, since spelling is not part of the evaluation rubric for the Evidence dimension. H. Zhang & Litman (2018) show that performance can be brought up to $\kappa_q = 0.68$–0.70 by using a co-attention neural network to model the relationship between the source text and the essay. The co-attention mechanism relies on a similarity matrix of each sentence in the source and each sentence in the essay; the system thus assigns "attention", or importance, scores for different sentences in an essay. This model does not require human-supplied topic lists and is thus more resource-lean; however, it remains to be explored whether essays are credited by the system for using vocabulary similar to that specified in human topic and examples lists.

6.4.5 APPROACHES THAT USE TRANSFORMED TEXT AND/OR EXPERT/PEER SUMMARIES AS REFERENCE

In this section, we review a number of methods where the source text and/or expert or peer summaries were transformed in some way before they were used as reference. The transformations include explicit importance weighting of elements of the source text (Section "Explicit Importance Weighting of Elements of Source Text"), adjustment of the semantic space in which similarities are measured to better align with the scoring rubric (Section "The Inbuilt Rubric Method"), and extraction of importance-ranked content nuggets from a set of peer summaries (Section "The Pyramid Method").

Explicit Importance Weighting of Elements of Source Text
Beigman Klebanov et al. (2014) consider an integrative summarization task used in an assessment of English proficiency for non-native speakers applying to higher education institutions in the USA. They use both source material and a large number of available peer summaries of varying quality and propose **weighing source n-grams by the proportion of high-scoring summaries from a development set that use that n-gram**; a development set of 750 essays was used, out of which about one third were high-scoring. An essay is then assigned a source-use score that is the sum of weights of all n-grams in the overlap between the essay and the score,

---

[27] See Mikolov, Chen, et al. (2013) for skip-gram embeddings.

normalized by essay length. These source-use scores (with n = 1,2,3,4) did not improve over a naive source—essay unigram overlap model that weights all words in the overlap uniformly, in terms of correlation with human holistic scores of essay quality. This result is somewhat surprising given that the scoring rubric heavily emphasized the need to include the most important information from the source in the summary: for score 5, the writer "successfully selects the important information", for score 4—"is generally good in selecting the important information", for score 3—"contains some important information", for score 2—"contains some relevant information", for score 1—"provides little or no meaningful or relevant coherent content" from the source. The authors hypothesized that the highest-weighting source words tended to correspond to general topical and function words, rather than the most important specific information in the source, and so did not differentiate well between high-quality essays and on-topic essays that failed to select the critical information nuggets from the source. In an attempt to reduce the weight of such words, the authors modified the **weight to be the difference between the use of the n-gram in high-scoring vs. low-scoring essays,** that is, taking into account not only similarity in source usage with good examples but also a dis-similarity with poorly written summaries. This measure showed a stronger performance, with $r = 0.54$ with human holistic scores for unigrams, $r = 0.42$ for bigrams, and $r = 0.32$ for trigrams, all significantly outperforming the naive unigram overlap baseline (which scored $r = 0.24$).

The source-based writing task addressed by Beigman Klebanov et al. (2014) is a somewhat more complex one that includes usage of multiple sources—writers were asked to "read a passage, then to listen to a lecture discussing the same topic from a different point of view, and to summarize the points made in the lecture, explaining how they cast doubt on points made in the reading". This type of task is sometimes called **contrastive** summarization (Paul et al., 2010). Source-use features addressing the selection of important information from the lecture were described above; the authors also considered features for capturing contrast between the sources. Since the lecture and the reading addressed the same topic, they are expected to share words and phrases. The authors hypothesized that important material in the lecture would tend to be something that is unique to the lecture rather than shared with the reading. Therefore, each n-gram in the overlap between lecture and summary was **weighted by the difference in the n-gram's occurrence count in the lecture vs. the reading to emphasize material that is unique to the lecture**. The contrastive feature correlated with human holistic scores of the essay at $r = 0.31$ for trigrams, significantly above the $r = 0.24$ baseline.

Lemaire et al. (2005) investigated automated assignment of importance scores to each sentence in the source document. A total of 278 students in grades 8–11 were given an expository (18 sentences averaging 29 words per sentence) or a narrative (24 sentences averaging 16 words per sentence) text and asked to "underline three to five sentences that seemed to be the most important". The authors hypothesized that more important sentences would have higher LSA semantic similarity to the text taken as a whole. Indeed, that was the case for the expository text, where the authors observed a correlation of $r = 0.64$ between the human importance scores and those provided by the **LSA comparison of each sentence to the vector representing the whole text**; the correlation for the narrative text was not significant. The authors also evaluated the hypothesis that more important sentences would be highly LSA—similar to a larger number of other sentences in the text; this measure yielded a similar correlation of $r = 0.66$ for the expository text and a non-significant correlation for the Narrative text. The difference in performance on expository vs. narrative texts could be due to genre differences; it is also possible that the method performs better on longer sentences.

The Inbuilt Rubric Method

Olmos et al. (2016) propose making use of experts not to write full model summaries but in order to provide **wordlists to seed the dimensions to adjust the LSA space so that instead of opaque, difficult to interpret dimensions, the top k dimensions of a scoring model would be aligned with specific k concepts that the summary should mention**. A three-step procedure is proposed: (1) experts provide descriptors (3–6 words) for each key concept; and (2) LSA vectors for all descriptors of the same concept are averaged to produce a concept vector. An iterative procedure between (1) and (2) is described where the concept vector is evaluated by inspecting its 100 nearest neighbors in the LSA space to ensure that they capture the intended concept; descriptors are removed and added until the inspection provides satisfactory results. The k concept vectors are then substituted instead of the original k vectors in the LSA space; call the resulting matrix M. (3) The matrix M is transformed, using the Gram–Schmidt method, into an orthogonal matrix such that each of the k new basis vectors is close to one of the k concept vectors before the transformation, respectively. This new concept matrix is used to project vectors in the original LSA space into a space with interpretable first k dimensions. To generate a score for a summary, the summary is projected into this transformed space, and **the score assigned to the summary is the sum of values on the first k dimensions, following the reasoning that the value along a dimension reflects the extent to which the summary addresses that dimension**. The authors refer to this scoring process as an Inbuilt Rubric method.

To evaluate the Inbuilt Rubric method, two judges were asked to score each summary by providing a sub-score between 0 and 2 to each of the four key dimensions ($k = 4$); the total score was then the sum of dimension scores. The inter-rater reliability for the total score was $r = 0.89$. The two human scores were averaged to create the human total score for the subsequent experiments. Olmos et al. (2016) show that the Inbuilt Rubric method outperforms ($r = 0.82$ vs. $r = 0.66$) the more standard method where LSA vectors (in the original space) are compared to gold summaries, on a corpus of 78 student essays. To validate the claim that the top four dimensions each represent a particular concept, respectively, the authors ran four multiple regression experiments. In the first experiment, the human sub-score for the first concept—a number between 0 and 2—was the dependent variable, while the independent variables were the scores produced for each of the first four dimensions by the Inbuilt Rubric method. The authors sought to see whether the beta standardized regression coefficient for the first dimension—

the one that by construction should represent the first concept—is bigger than for the other dimensions. The authors found that although all dimensions were significant predictors of the score on the first dimension, it was the first dimension that had the biggest coefficient (0.782 for first vs. < 0.360 for all other dimensions). For multiple regression modeling human sub-scores on the second concept, the second dimension score was the strongest predictor (beta = 0.727 vs. < 0.290 for all other dimensions). The differences were not as large for the other two concepts (concept 3: 0.436 for third dimension vs. < 0.270 for the rest; concept 4: 0.376 for the fourth dimension vs. < 0.160 for the rest), but in all cases the expected dimension had the largest weight in the respective sub-score prediction model. These results suggest that the Inbuilt Rubric method yielded scoring dimensions that were sensitive to specific target concepts. Jorge-Botana et al. (2019) further adjust the method to take into account meaning elements that are shared by the target k concepts, not only what is distinctive to each, as well as to avoid the situation where the first expert-generated concept received a better representation than the subsequent ones.

The Pyramid Method

Passonneau et al. (2018) applied the "wise crowd" (Surowiecki, 2005) approach to generating **an importance-ranked representation of the source content**. As a "wise crowd", the authors collected summaries from five masters students whose grades were high, attending a highly competitive private university, who performed the same summarization task as the study population. These writers were expected to be more skilled in both summarization and content presentation than the study population—academically unprepared students attending a community college. **The summaries contributed by the "wise crowd" are manually analyzed using the Pyramid method to derive content units** (Nenkova & Passonneau, 2004). A content unit has three components: (1) **a set of phrases from "wise crowd" summaries that express the same meaning**; (2) a descriptive label that captures the shared meaning, provided by the annotator; and (3) **the weight of the content unit, calculated as the number of "wise crowd" summaries that expressed that idea**, in this case an integer between 1 and 5. In the authors' example, a content unit could be labeled "Matter has volume and mass" and have phrases *matter contains both volume and mass, it takes up space defined as volume and contains a certain amount of material defined as mass, matter is anything that has mass and takes up space (volume)*, and *it contains volume and mass*. The weight of this unit is 4, since the phrases come from four "wise crowd" summaries. The authors note that content unit weights tend to have a Zipfian distribution, with a small number of units with large weights and a large number of units with small weights. The inter-rater reliability of the content model (the set of content units based on the "wise crowd" summaries) was 0.87, using an adjusted alpha coefficient.

The set of all content units found in the "wise crowd" summaries is then used to score target summaries. **A target summary is manually analyzed into its own content units, and those that match model content units are given the respective score; scores for all matches are summed up to produce the raw total score of the target summary.** The authors experimented with a larger "wise crowd" but found that between 4 and 5 "wise crowd" summaries were sufficient to produce stable scores. The authors cite inter-rater reliabilities between 0.78 and 0.86 (adjusted alpha coefficient) from prior studies where machine-produced summaries were scored using this method. Note that in the original Pyramid Method as presented in Nenkova & Passonneau (2004), summaries were scored using the ratio of the weighted sum of content units in the current summary to an optimal summary with the same number of content units that would including all the higher-weighted units before including any of the lower-weighted ones.

To evaluate the wise-crowd approach to content representation, Passonneau et al. (2018) compared the ranked idea units produced by their procedure to those produced by experts: "Fourteen main ideas in the source text were identified by a panel of three researchers who first worked independently, then came to a consensus on the final list. Main ideas in students' summaries were counted, and reported as a proportion of the total". Inter-rater reliability was $r = 0.92$. All 14 concepts from the main ideas rubric were found in the "wise-crowd" model with weight ≥ 3. The total scores given to target summaries using the expert main ideas rubric and using the "wise crowd" content model were correlated at $r = 0.88$ on a set of 20 student summaries.

Passonneau et al. (2018) next address **automation of the procedure for assessing a target summary using the "wise crowd" content model**. The PyrScore method (Passonneau et al., 2013) breaks the target summary into a large set of n-grams (in the authors' example, $n = 1..14$), and compares those n-grams to descriptors and phrases in the content units of the "wide crowd" model, using vector-space-based comparison techniques. Each sentence in the target summary is assigned multiple segmentations into n-grams, each with its weight for matching content units. Passonneau et al. (2018) use an approximation algorithm *wmin* (Sakai et al., 2003) to solve a packing problem—distribution of a set of objects (content units) into containers (sentences); see Passonneau et al. (2018) for details of parametrization of PyrScore. The total PyrScore assigned to the 20 student summaries that were also manually scored using the "wide crowd" content model yielded a correlation of $r = 0.95$. The total PyrScore assigned to 120 student summaries also scored by a human using the expert main idea rubric was $r = 0.83$. These results suggest that once a "wise crowd"-based content model is in place, it is possible to automatically score target summaries, achieving a high agreement score with expert assessment of the content of these summaries.

In a further step toward automation, Passonneau et al. (2018) evaluate the PEAK method (Q. Yang et al., 2016) that **automates both the construction of the content model from the "wise crowd" summaries and the scoring of target summaries** using the automatically constructed content model. The algorithm uses ClauseIE (Del Corro & Gemulla, 2013) to extract all <s,p,o> (<subject, predicate, object>) triples from all the "wise crowd" summaries. The resulting set is then analyzed to identify anchor triples—those with at least two salient components (*s* and *p*; *s* and *o*; or *p* and *o*) where salience is defined as being semantically similar to respective components in at least three other triples. Once anchors are identified, all triples from the other model summaries are considered as potential contributors to the content units described by the anchor; up to one most similar triple from each of the other summaries is added to the anchor's content unit. In the next step, content units with similar anchors are merged; the weight of the final content unit is the maximal weight of its member anchors. To score a target summary, the summary is also split into <s,p,o> triples and similarity scores are assigned between those triples and content units from the content model. To find the maximal score for a target summary while ensuring that the assignment between target triples and content units is one-to-one, the authors use the Munkres–Kuhn algorithm (Kuhn, 1955). The authors show that the PEAK method yields scores that correlate at $r = 0.70$ with human scores assigned using the expert main idea rubric, on the same set of 120 summaries on which the PyrScore method achieved the 0.83 correlation. The results for the PEAK method suggest that a fully automated utilization of a small number of "wise crowd" summaries may be feasible. PyrEval is another algorithm from the PyrScore/PEAK family for automated construction of content model (pyramid) from reference summaries and for its use in summary scoring.

Passonneau et al. (2007) applied the manual Pyramid method to a set of oral retellings of a story collected from 10 very young children (ages 5–7). Retellings were collected during three consecutive days, to examine any patterns in the recall of story details. Their findings highlight an important aspect of a method that relies on *secondary* sources to obtain information about the importance of material in the *primary* source—the authors found that as the days went by, children tended to incorporate more and more *inferred* information into their retellings, that is, information that was not explicitly present in the original story. Moreover, multiple children inferred similar pieces of information. According to the Pyramid method, these inferences are part of the content of the source; this could be a desirable property of the model (a consistent inference is as good as stated, so the content model includes elements of the background knowledge underlying the source text) or not, if part of the task is to not impute material that was not explicitly there.

6.5   REFLECTIVE WRITING

In their seminal book on the subject of reflection, Boud et al. (1985b) summarize succinctly—in the book's title—what it is that REFLECTION is centrally about: "Reflection: Turning Experience into Learning". Reflection is one of two ways of turning personal experience into learning, the other being trial and error. According to Dewey (1933), it is the reflective activity that enables problem-solving to take place. To reconstruct, analyze, and ultimately learn from an experience, learners "need to describe their experience, to work through the attitudes and emotions which might color their understanding, and to order and make sense of the new ideas and information which they have retained". Boud et al. (1985a) similarly define reflection as "a generic term for those intellectual and affective activities in which individuals engage to explore their experiences in order to lead to a new understanding and appreciation" (p. 19); see K. Mann et al. (2009) for reviews of the literature on reflection in the context of education.

In reflective writing one would therefore expect to see a description of a specific personal experience—the "**what happened**" part of reflection, as well as some evidence of the reader's thinking about the experience, in terms of understanding **why** it happened and perhaps also how to best use the newly acquired insight—**what next**. Keeping these broad categories in mind will help us appreciate the similarities between the studies to be reviewed in this section, as they all address a variety of learning contexts (language, performance, science, and engineering) using various theoretical models of reflection and, therefore, also different rubrics/categories. In terms of technical approaches to modeling reflection, we will see that lexical categories—namely, words grouped together based on their meanings—are the most commonly used type of feature, and that the diversity of the contexts together with the similarities in some of the most effective features testify to the existence of certain quantifiable meaning-based patterns one generally expects to see in reflective writing. These often correspond to first-person perspective, past tense (for what happened) and future tense (for what next), as well as language of feelings, insight, and causality. For each study we review below, we will <u>underline</u> the domain of application, and use **boldface** to emphasize the features that were found to be effective for assessing reflections.

Kovanović et al. (2018) present a computational study of reflection in students' writing. Reflection was conceptualized as a process of perceiving and analyzing behavior in terms of goals, effects, and designs for an improved action; the specific categories were based on prior literature in the context of medical training to encourage students to become mindful practitioners (Hulsman et al., 2009). Kovanović et al. (2018) examined students' self-reflection in their short annotations of video recordings of their own musical performances. The data comes from 4 undergraduate courses in <u>performing arts</u> in a Canadian university, from the total of 77 students. Students used an annotation tool to create time-stamped annotations associated with specific parts of the video, as well as a general annotation that contained comments or a summary of the video. All annotations were coded at the sentence (or sometimes sentence fragment) level using three categories that describe elements of reflection: Observation (the student observes something about their own behavior but does not indicate why the behavior occurred: "I still continue to have problems making eye contact"); Motive (what they observed and why it occurred; "being up there made me insecure... which led to my eyes dropping frequently"); Goal (what they will do next time or what they need to work on; "what I really want to avoid is ending up just mirroring everything"); as well as an Other category for sentences that did not match any of the reflection categories. These categories very clearly align with the "what-why-what next" framework: What happened? (Observation) Why did it happen the way it did? (Motive) What is to be done next? (Goal). In total, 3.3K sentences containing 4.4K units of analysis were annotated by two coders, with inter-annotator agreement of $\kappa = 0.75$. In the data, Goal was the most frequent category (55%), followed by Observation (34%), Motive (5%), and Other (4%).

Kovanović et al. (2018) then proceeded to build an automated model to classify sentence segments into the reflection categories, using a random forest classifier with the following four types of features. First, n-grams—100 most frequent uni-, bi-, and trigrams, build after removal of stopwords. Top n-grams included *need, think, music, practice, left hand, eye contact, need work, front mirror, practice front mirror, third goal would.* Second, the authors used Linguistic Inquiry and Word Count (LIWC) (Tausczik & Pennebaker, 2010) features that include wordlists capturing various physiological and psychological processes (perceptual, cognitive, affective, social), topics (work, leisure, family), as well as linguistic categories such as parts of speech, for a total of 93 categories. The third resource used in the study is Coh-Metrix (Graesser et al., 2011, 2004), which provides 109 indices of text cohesion (i.e., referential, causal, temporal, spatial, and structural cohesion), several measures of text complexity and readability, and measures of usage of various linguistic categories. Fourth, a binary feature "first_in_sentence" was used to indicate whether the segment was the first in the sentence; the authors hypothesized that Observations would tend to appear in sentence-initial position. The system achieved 0.75 classification accuracy and $\kappa = 0.51$ on a held out set.

The authors then inspected the top 20 most discriminating features, and observed that the list was largely dominated by LIWC and Coh-Metrix categories, with only two bigrams making the list. Vocabulary of **perceptual processes** (liwc.see) was the strongest discriminator between reflection categories and Other; this could be due to the nature of the reflection task—visual observation of performance through video. Focus on the **past** (past tense of verbs and words such as 'ago') and language of **insight** were most characteristic of Motive and Observation, occurring less frequently in Goal and Other; language of **causality** was more prominent in Motive than in other categories. Moving to Coh-Metrix features, use of causality (ratio of causal particles to causal verbs), use of agent-less passive voice, and higher syntactic complexity characterized Motive segments.

While Kovanović et al. (2018) did not directly address assessment of the quality of reflection with the goal of scoring or feedback, their results suggest that theoretically postulated phases of the refection process—the what happened, why, and what next—can be moderately reliably identified in students' reflective notes, which opens up the possibility of assessment and feedback, for example, whether the full cycle of reflection behaviors has been attested in a students' response.

G. Cheng (2017) analyzed students' written reflection on their learning experiences. Participants of this study were students from various academic disciplines enrolled in a 13-week, credit-bearing language enhancement course entitled "Advanced English for University Studies" given at the English Language Centre (ELC) of the Hong Kong Polytechnic University. In the course, students were required, among other assignments, to reflect on their **English language learning experiences** and achievements and document the reflection in a written entry of at least 170 words.

Using the A-S-E-R theoretical framework adapted from prior work in the context of teacher education, G. Cheng (2017) defined four elements of reflection and scored each essay on the scale of 1 (developing) to 4 (competent) on each of the dimensions. The dimensions are Analysis (A), Strategy (S), External influences (E), and Report of events (R). The theoretical framework is thus different from that used in the Kovanović et al. (2018) study, but the categories can still be loosely aligned with what happened (Report), why (Analysis), what next (Strategy), with the External Influences category probably falling under "why".

The data included 748 reflective entries by 398 students, with an average length of 239 words (or 13 sentences) per entry. Each entry was manually and independently annotated by two researchers; the authors do not provide inter-annotator agreement estimates. The basic unit of annotation was either a single sentence or an aggregate of consecutive sentences belonging to one category. If a unit has the properties of more than one category, it will be labelled with multiple categories.

G. Cheng (2017) performed automated scoring experiments on each dimension in isolation. For each dimension, each text passage was classified into one of five categories (0, 1, 2, 3, 4), where 0 means that the text segment does not contain any language relevant to the dimension, and 1–4 correspond to the "developing" to "expert" scores for the given dimension. A system based on **LSA** was developed for automating the scoring—a sentence is classified into a category for which it shows the highest cosine similarity with training sentences belonging to the category. If multiple sentences in a given category were found in an essay, a rounded average rating was assigned to the essay overall. For example, if an essay had a score 2 sentence and a score 3 sentence for dimension S, the essay would be assigned score 3 for dimension S. The system performed at $\kappa = 0.60$ to $\kappa = 0.73$ for the various dimensions, for essay-level classification.

Luo & Litman (2016) addressed a somewhat different reflection context, that of **immediate monitoring of learning of STEM content**. Students listened to a lecture delivered as part of their university coursework and were asked to "describe what was confusing or needed more detail" at the end of the lecture. In order to provide automated immediate feedback on these reflections, such as "Could you provide more detail?" for vague reflection like "everything was confusing!", the authors developed a system to analyze quality of reflection. Responses were scored on the scale of 0–3 for quality of reflection: 0 was given to irrelevant or empty responses; 1 was given to vague reflections, where the student re-stated a broad concept or a title from a lecture slide, or perhaps reflected on an organizational rather than content aspect of a course; 2 was given to insufficiently deep/detailed statements about content; 3 was given to deep/specific reflection statements about the course content, such as "Part III on worksheet in class, comparing metals. I was confused about why each metal was selected". The rubric thus gives higher scores to active or constructive reflections that are expected to facilitate learning; indeed, prior research has shown that the quality of reflection score correlates significantly with learning gains from a course (Menekse et al., 2011). This reflection task seems to emphasize the what and the why aspects of reflection—a specific observation of an instance of confusion and a possible reason for that occurrence. Based on a sample of 100 responses, the inter-annotator agreement for the scores was $\kappa = 0.73$.

To automate the scoring of reflections, the authors build an SVM classifier using a number of feature types. The following binary features were implemented: (a) whether or not the response was empty; (b) whether or not the response was about the course at all (using matching stems of keywords such as *lecture, slide, activity, discussion*); and (c) whether the reflection refers to the organization of class or any course assignments (instead of the content, as instructed), using keywords like *organization, assignment, homework*. Specificity score was generated by the Speciteller tool (J. Li & Nenkova, 2015). Another feature to capture detailing is the length of the response. Title features were used to capture the rubric "is reflection simply an exact repetition of a title in slides?": titles from the lecture slides were extracted, then compared to the response to see whether a statement repeats part of a title or its entirety; number of title words in a statement; and ratio of title words. Finally, unigram features were also extracted.

The data came from two cohorts of students taking an undergraduate course on introductory materials science and engineering: 27 students with 108 reflections for 4 lectures (cohort 1) and 53 students with 1149 reflections for 23 lectures (cohort 2). The system performed at $\kappa_q = 0.859$ in 10-fold cross validation on the cohort 2 data; $\kappa_q = 0.834$ on leave-one-lecture-out cross-validation with 23 lectures; and $\kappa_q = 0.835$ on leave-one-topic-out cross-validation, where topic is a group of related lectures. In cross-cohort evaluation the system performed at $\kappa_q = 0.515$, suggesting that moving to a new group of learners might not be an easy transition, even if course materials and instructor are kept the same. In particular, the score distribution varied across cohorts, with 17.5% of responses at score level 0 in cohort 1 and 38.9% of responses at score level 0 in cohort 2. Response characteristics at the same score point also differed somewhat between the two cohorts: in cohort 1, the top-scoring responses averaged only 7.1 words in length, while in cohort 2 it was 13.1 words. Interestingly, a system without the length and unigram features, namely, a system that did not specifically check the content of the response beyond title check and a check for a small number of keywords for the binary features, performed at $\kappa_q = 0.730$–0.759 for the 10-fold, lecture, and topic evaluations, and $\kappa_q = 0.439$ in the cross-cohort evaluation. That is, making sure that students complied with the rubric requirements to not submit empty responses, not talk about course logistics, not copy titles, and mention something specific along with "lecture" or "slide" already goes a long way toward accurate scoring of responses. The results highlight the effectiveness of designing features closely aligned to the scoring rubric, as well as the promise of a **sentence-level specificity model** to capture an important aspect of reflection, namely, making *specific* (and detailed) observations.

Birney (2012) examined the relationship between depth of reflection scores based on theories of reflective practice and usage of various linguistic features, using 18 relatively **long blog and journal entries** written as part of **professional education**. The samples, averaging 908 words in length, were written as part of course assignments by students pursuing a higher Diploma in Business Systems Analysis and students pursuing a BSc in Nursing. The assignments emphasized analysis of a personal experience in the context of the material being studied: The Nursing students were asked to "Identify an issue/scenario from your practice that demonstrates your development of competence... and demonstrates evidence of your critical reflection", and the Business System Analysis students were asked to choose a concept from the studied material and "reflect on how this theory may be applied to practice" and give examples of "where you have seen evidence of this concept applied to a real-world situation (this could be related to work, everyday situations etc.)". The scoring rubric considered indicators of increasingly higher levels of reflection: While all writers in the sample provided a clear description of context—(lowest level), increasingly fewer succeeded in identification of issues, analysis, creative synthesis (level 2), considering implications of issues, examining multiple perspectives, and linking to broader social structures (level 3), and even fewer show evidence of learning, insight, self-awareness, change in beliefs, and discuss revision to future practice (level 4). Thus, while everybody covered the "what happened" aspect of reflection, the "why" part and especially the "what next" parts were not as readily supplied by the writers. To derive a reflection score, a weighted sum of all instances of specific indicators was calculated, with lower-lever indicators having a lower weight. A set of linguistic indicators based on Ryan (2011) was used. The author shows that linguistic features such as use of **first person voice**, **thinking and sensing verbs** (e.g., *believe, feel, consider, decide, guess, imagine*), explicit **causal language** (e.g., *therefore, consequently, hence, because*), **appraisal** adjectives and adverbs (e.g., *thorough, elaborate, consistent, remarkable, mediocre, vague; successfully, suddenly, unexpectedly, deliberately, doubtfully*), use of **future tense** (e.g., *am going to, intend, will ensure, mean to, will try*), and adverbs describing **different outcome possibilities** (e.g., *under these conditions, in view of, taking into account, differently, depending on, conditionally*) were all strongly correlated with depth-of-reflection scores (Pearson's $r > 0.5$). The author also notes that the length of the entry did not significantly correlate with the depth-of-reflection score.

Ullmann (2019) explored computational modeling of a detailed construct of reflective writing, including reflection, description of an experience, feelings, personal belief, awareness of difficulties, perspective, lessons learned, and future intention. This more detailed rubric is still generally aligned with the "what, why, and what next" framework with description (what), feelings, beliefs, and awareness of difficulties (why), and perspective, lessons learned, and future intentions (what next). The dataset contained 77 essays written by students from across academic disciplines, in response to both reflective and non-reflective prompts. Each sentence (5,030 in total) was annotated by multiple crowdsourced workers; the authors selected for further experiments only those instances on which there was a majority agreement, thus concentrating on the relatively clear-cut instances. Various classifiers (Random Forest, SVM, Naive Bayes) over word unigram features were used to classify sentences into expressing a relevant dimension or not (a binary classifier for each dimension). The system performed above majority baseline for most dimensions. Inspecting the most important features, the authors found, consistently with Birney (2012), that variations on the **first person singular pronoun**—*I, me, my*—were the strongest predictors of the *reflection* class as well as for a number of the more specific dimensions. This result emphasizes that reflective writing tends to be *personal*, relating the writer's own experience from the writer's own perspective. An explicit connection between first person perspective and reflection is made, for example, in Lindsay et al. (2010). Words of **feeling** (*feel, felt*) were also predictive for multiple dimensions. Dimension-specific predictors included **past tense verbs** for Experience (*had, was, were*) and **contrast connectives** for Awareness of Difficulties (*but, however, not*).

Beigman Klebanov, Burstein, et al. (2017) address automated scoring of essays submitted in response to a Utility Value (UV) writing intervention. A person finds UV in study materials if he or she believes it is useful and relevant beyond the immediate situation, for other tasks or aspects of a person's life. For example, a biology student might say that "I will really need this for medical school," or "This material will be important when I take over the family farm". A **Utility Value** intervention where a student is asked to write **how specific course topics are relevant to their own lives** or useful for themselves or others has been shown to boost course performance in various disciplines (biology, psychology, math) in college and high school students (Gaspard et al., 2015; Harackiewicz et al., 2016; Hulleman et al., 2010; Hulleman & Harackiewicz, 2009).

Beigman Klebanov, Burstein, et al. (2017) worked with data from the Harackiewicz et al. (2016) study, where writing samples were collected from first-year students enrolled in introductory biology courses at the University of Wisconsin, Madison, 2012–2014. The UV task assigned to the students was as follows: "Select a concept or issue that was covered in lecture and formulate a question. Write an essay addressing this question and discuss the relevance of the concept or issue to your own life. Be sure to include some concrete information that was covered in this unit, explaining why this specific information is relevant to your life or useful for you. Be sure to explain how the information applies to you personally and give examples". The utility value and control writing assignments were coded by research assistants for the level of utility value articulated in each essay, on a scale of 0–4, based on how *specific* and *personal* the utility value connection was to the individual. A "0" indicates no utility; a "1" indicates general utility applied to humans generically; a "2" indicates utility that is general enough to apply to anyone, but is applied to the individual; a "3" indicates utility that is specific to the individual; and a "4" indicates a strong, specific connection to the individual that includes a deeper appreciation or future application of the material. In terms of "what, why, and what next" categories, this task emphasizes the what (specific course material that the student has learned) and the what next (how this would help the student in a future personal situation). According to Harackiewicz et al. (2016), inter-rater reliability with this coding rubric was $\kappa = 0.88$. The 3,935 essays averaging 508 words in length written across 6 biology topics were partitioned into train (70%), development (20%), and test (10%) data for the computational experiments. In the training data, the scores were distributed as follows: 4% score 0; 15% score 1; 9% score 2; 38% score 3; 34% score 4.

Beigman Klebanov, Burstein, et al. (2017) used random forest regression from the scikit-learn toolkit (Pedregosa et al., 2011) to generate scoring models using the following families of features, each separately and all together. The first family of features is targeting extent of **references to self and other humans through grammatical means**, namely, pronouns; features in this family include log frequency per 1,000 words counts of first person singular, first person plural, second person, possessive determiners (e.g., *their*), and indefinite pronouns (e.g., *anyone*). The frequency of **first person singular pronouns** (e.g., *I, mine*) was highly predictive of the UV score ($r = 0.714$), all the features in the family together produced $r = 0.759$, on development data. The second family of features is built around the observation that relatively to the technical content covered in a biology unit, expression of utility would be **non-technical**, using more everyday, non-academic vocabulary, which includes shorter, more frequent, and more concrete words, as well as have higher lexical diversity due to the need to cover both the technical and the non-technical vocabulary. Measures in this family yielded all together a correlation of $r = 0.302$ with the UV score. The next family of features—called **ArgNar**—is based on the observation that essays addressing UV tend to incorporate, in addition to the typical expository/informational presentation of the course material, a personal mini-narrative–background with details about events in the author's life that motivates the particular UV statement, as well as some argumentative elements, as the writer needs to put forward a claim regarding the relationship between their own or other people's lives and biology knowledge, along with necessary qualifications. Usage of past tense verbs and of common action, mental, and desire verbs (e.g., *get, go, know, put, think, want*) that could signal sequences of actions and personal stance toward those were used to capture the extent of narration; argument development and hedging/boosting wordlists were used to capture the argumentation elements. The ArgNar family of features yielded $r = 0.289$ with the UV score. Finally, the last family of features targets **content** that is likely to produce personal connections with topics studied in the introductory biology class, based on development data, namely issues related to health, food, risk, social and personal relationships, as well as expressions of **affect/appraisal** and **insight**; these were modeled using the relevant LIWC (Tausczik & Pennebaker, 2010) categories. The content family produced $r = 0.306$ with the scores. Combining the four families together yielded $r = 0.787$ on the development set and $r = 0.779$ on test data. We note that the pronoun family alone achieved r of 0.759 and 0.766, respectively. Beigman Klebanov, Burstein, et al. (2016) show that adding n-grams (n = 1,2,3) features pushes the test set performance to $r = 0.798$. Beigman Klebanov, Priniski, et al. (2018) explored generalization of the UV scoring models and of the features to successively different contexts: using data as above, they evaluated essays produced in a different institution in an introductory biology course ($r = 0.70$) and in an introductory psychology course ($r = 0.57$, with $r = 0.60$ for a model without the LIWC features). The authors also used the features but retrained classifiers for data from yet another institution with physics, chemistry, and biology courses where a variant of utility value task was used—the task emphasized communal, rather than personal, utility, therefore almost all essays received UV scores below 3 using the original rubric. Classifiers for no-utility (0) vs. some-utility (1 and up) were trained and performed better than majority class but not by much (all accuracies ≤ 0.70, about 5 points above majority baseline). These results show that while the original features do capture some properties of utility-value writing across various contexts, it is important to evaluate applicability of features and systems for every new context, as "shifts to a new institution (and, thus, a new student population), a new subject matter course, or a new variant of the original task may result in systematic changes in the textual features that render the original system inapplicable to the new context".

6.6 OTHER TASKS/GENRES

Kuzi et al. (2019) addressed automated assessment of a complex writing task administered to veterinary students—**a written analysis of case studies**. Case study analysis is a mixed genre that includes source-based aspects, such as "The student should identify at least two major differential diagnoses for the animal and defend his/her choices with evidence from the case and information from the literature" (Diagnosis) and "The students should identify the clinical observations in the case to support his/her problem list and diagnosis" (Evidence); form-based requirements such as "The authors should provide references that helped them understand the case" (References); as well as personal elements, such as "The student should identify and explain at least 2 personal learning issues from the exercise" (Personal). Responses to such a complex assignment averaged 2.4K words—much longer documents than a typical persuasive essay. Each assignment was graded by three peers (also students in the class), on a scale of 0–4 for each of the dimensions, as well as a holistic score. The Personal rubric showed the best inter-annotator agreement (2.8 of the peers agreed on the score, on average), followed by References (2.6), with Diagnosis (2.3) and Evidence (2.1) showing lower agreement. Two hundred ninety-four responses to a single case study were used in the study. The authors explore ranking such assignments using lexical (unigram) and topic model-based features using LDA. The topic feature for topic j for segment i in the response is the KL divergence of the word probability distributions in j and i. A 5-topic model is induced for a given set of responses to be ranked, then SVMrank (Joachims, 2002) is used to learn the optimal combination and weighting of the topical and lexical features using the training set (160 responses) and evaluated on the test set (134 responses). An evaluation using Kendall's τ shows this task to be quite difficult—no model scored more than 0.45 on any of the dimensions. Yenaeng et al. (2014) studied scoring of medical case studies using SVMs over term frequency based representations.

Another writing task that has been addressed by researchers is **scientific writing**, in the context of edits by professional proofreaders that are predominantly focused on the disciplinary conventions in scientific writing. Daudaravicius et al. (2016) report on a shared task on classifying sentences into those that "need improvement" or not. The data was a collection of text extracts from 9,919 published journal articles (mainly from Physics and Mathematics) with data before and after language editing, as performed by professional language editors. In the authors' example, the sentence "For example, separate biasing of the two gates can be used to implement capacitor-less DRAM cell in which information is stored in the form of charge in the body region, at the back channel surface near to the source" was edited for hyphenation, articles, and phrase order to read "For example, separate biasing of the two gates can be used to implement a capacitorless DRAM cell in which information is stored at the back-channel surface near to the source in the form of charge in the body region". The task proved to be quite difficult, with the best performance, by a deep learning based system, being $\kappa = 0.36$ on the test data. Analyzing the results, the authors show that while edits based on misuse of articles, punctuation, and hyphenation were detected by most systems, more subtle problems such as domain-appropriate lexical choices were more difficult to detect. The authors call for error-type annotation to gain a better understanding of the unique characteristics of this task. Another task addressing analysis of the quality of scientific writing is that of predicting whether a scientific article will be accepted or rejected at a conference or predicting scores assigned by reviewers (Kang et al., 2018; Leng et al., 2019; Shen et al., 2019; P. Yang et al., 2018); differently from scientific editing, which mostly focuses on improving the clarity and precision of writing, acceptance decisions (presumably) involve a more comprehensive evaluation, including originality and substance.

6.7   SUMMARY

In this chapter, we have surveyed the work on computational modeling of genre- and task-specific aspects of writing. Thus, while all writing, whether it is a persuasive essay on a general topic, a narration, a critique, a summary, or a reflection, should be clear, well-organized, and well-developed (see Chapter 5 for a survey of the work on those), in this chapter we focused on constructs that might be important in some types of writing tasks but not in others.

Specifically, we have surveyed the field of computational approaches to modeling details of argumentation in essays, including argument structure (claims, premises) and the content of an argument. In the last few years, argumentation mining has become a hot topic in the computational linguistics/NLP community at large, with some of the earlier influential work considering argumentation in the context of persuasive essays and making available essay data for argument structure detection benchmarks, hence a relatively large number of studies addressing argument structure detection in student essays. We have also reviewed work attending to other aspects of argumentation, such as usage of evaluative and figurative language, presence of stance and thesis, as well as aspects of the quality of the arguments, the latter mostly in the context of argument critique essays.

Another relatively extensively researched type of task is source-based expository writing, such as a summary. The interest in this line of work in the computational linguistics/NLP universe was mostly spurred by the interest in automated generation and evaluation of summaries. Some of this work was also applicable to assessment of human summaries, with summary evaluation measures like ROUGE and BLEU being commonly used as features for scoring summaries and the application of the Pyramid method to scoring human summaries. It is interesting to observe that automated methods for performing the critical task of identifying the most important information in a source text often use additional human-generated resources such as good, bad, or expert human summaries or lists of topical or keywords, in addition to the source text itself. The task of automatically identifying important pieces using just the source text itself is quite difficult; background knowledge against which humans perceive some elements of the text to be more central than others is still to be modeled. Progress on this task would contribute to advancement in other education-related tasks, such as automated generation of advanced reading comprehension questions based on text passages.

We have also reviewed more nascent fields of assessing narrative writing and reflective writing, the first focusing on relaying an experience and the second on learning from it. The field of reflective writing specifically is quite fragmented at the moment, with a large variety of rubrics and tasks, from short reflections of performance to long journal entries. There is a preponderance of certain lexical and grammatical categories, such as personal pronouns, future and past tense, and language of insight and causality, in good reflective writing, yet consistent document-level structures beyond lexis–parallel to the hierarchical organization of an argument (thesis, claims, premises) or to a story-grammar structure of narratives—are yet to be clearly articulated and computationally addressed.

Overall, we hope to have demonstrated in this chapter that assessment of writing is not a one-size-fits-all endeavor—there is variation in the tasks with a concomitant variation in the construct that are being assessed through the writing task and the properties of essays that respond to those tasks. Thus, when building an automated essay scoring system one needs to attend both to modeling the more general aspects such as clarity, relevance, elaboration, and coherence, and to modeling the more task-specific aspects of the rubric that assess the extent to which the writer can hone the general essay form to the specific goal of his or her writing, be it persuasion, critique, explanation, communication of experience, demonstration of learning from experience, or a complex task with multiple communicative goals.

CHAPTER 7

Automated Scoring Systems: From Prototype to Production

7.1 INTRODUCTION

In the previous chapters, we described the considerations that must be taken into account for maximizing the accuracy of an automated scoring system. However, the set of desiderata—and challenges—for deploying large-scale automated scoring applications in production environments is naturally quite different. Like any complex operational application that is expected to interact with a large user-base and deliver results relatively quickly (Atchison, 2016), automated scoring applications must also be designed to satisfy certain important criteria. Specifically, reliability, scalability, and flexibility are the salient desirable characteristics of such applications, and it is often easy to optimize one of these at the expense of others. Lotteridge & Hoefer (2020) describe additional considerations such as audit trails, data storage and security, as well as the software lifecycle of an automated scoring application (versioning, monitoring, score reproducibility). Habermehl et al. (2020) describe further architectural desiderata for implementing a more synergistic human and machine scoring pipeline where active learning is used to select responses to be scored by humans; this data is then used to continuously retrain the automated scoring system. Thus, operational automated scoring pipelines have many moving parts, have multiple stakeholders, and typically involve numerous teams within an organization. Therefore, it is critical that they be developed within a framework that can support the challenges of competing demands.

In this chapter, we first briefly describe the salient technical characteristics that are needed in a modern automated scoring application. Next, we present an example architecture for automated scoring applications, designed to be scalable, robust, as well as flexible. This architecture builds on an open-source framework and extends it to address some limitations. We also compare this architecture to a more traditional architecture in terms of speed and, finally, we illustrate the details of the architecture by using it to build the basic automated scoring system from Chapter 2. Some of the material below is derived from a previous paper published by one of the authors (Madnani, Cahill, et al., 2018).

7.2   CRITERIA

In this section, we briefly describe the characteristics that are important to look for in an architecture being considered for operational automated scoring applications.

1. **Reliability**. The reliability (stability) of a production-based automated scoring application is crucial. If a system is unstable (e.g., crashes or fails to deliver scores or feedback with low latency) this effectively renders it useless to most test-takers or clients.

2. **Scalability**. At the same time, the ever-increasing number of student responses that are passed to large-scale scoring applications puts pressure on them to scale quickly to increased volumes of data (particularly when the increase is spiked as in during a test administration). Like with other real-time services, clients expect (and often have contractual guarantees) to receive scores (or automated feedback) from a scoring application in a given amount of time and will not tolerate a slowdown in performance due to high load.

3. **Flexibility**. Business demands also require that new functionality or customizations be frequently added to keep up with new populations and forms of writing. This involves multiple software developers who all need to be able to contribute to the codebase concurrently. A modular design facilitates efficient development by multiple developers (Burstein & Marcu, 2000). Another facet of flexibility arises during the development phase of the application: it can be that, within an organization, multiple programming languages are used (particularly where a research group is responsible for continued enhancement of the features in such an application) and a flexible architecture should allow this in some limited fashion.

7.3   EXAMPLE ARCHITECTURE

There are not many publications in the literature on automated essay scoring that discuss architectures suitable for automated essay scoring applications. There are several software development frameworks designed to batch-process large amounts of data that could be considered, e.g., Apache Hadoop. However, these frameworks are not designed to support real-time processing, which has a fundamentally different set of requirements.

In this section, we present an example architecture that was proposed in a previous publication by one of the authors (Madnani, Cahill, et al., 2018). This example architecture leverages the open-source, distributed, message-based computation system called **Apache Storm**.[1]

7.3.1   PRELUDE: APACHE STORM

Before describing how Apache Storm is better able to meet our requirements, we briefly introduce some of the Apache Storm terminology that is necessary to follow this chapter. APACHE STORM is a *stream-processing framework* (Stonebraker et al., 2005), i.e., it performs computations over data as it enters the system, e.g., computing features and scores for written or spoken

---

[1]http://storm.apache.org

student responses in real time. Compared to a batch-processing paradigm where computational operations apply to an entire dataset, stream processors define operations that are applied to each individual data item as it passes through the system. A difference between Apache Storm and Apache Spark, another stream-processing framework, is that Spark performs data-parallel computations while Storm performs task-parallel computations. A Storm application is composed of three major components.

- **Spouts** produce the data streams to be processed by the application.

- **Bolts** consume data streams, apply operations to them, and produce the results of the operation as additional data streams.

- A **Topology** is a network of spouts and bolts, usually organized as a directed acyclic graph with edges denoting data dependencies between the bolts. A final bolt is added at the end of the graph to produce the final result of the application.

Next, we discuss the significant advantages that Storm provides for building applications that not only process data streams at scale but also provide results in real time—the specific use case of operational automated scoring applications.

- **Scalable**. Storm can scale to millions of data streams per second by simply increasing the parallel processing settings in the topology and adding more compute nodes to the cluster. It also automatically handles running bolts in parallel to maximize throughput.
- **Robust**. Storm also provides strong guarantees that every data stream *will* be processed and never be dropped. In case of any faults during a computation, e.g., hardware failures, Storm automatically reassigns tasks to other nodes to ensure that an application can run forever (or until explicitly stopped).
- **Programming language agnostic**. Storm topologies, bolts, and spouts can be defined in *any* programming language. This is particularly important in NLP where high quality open-source libraries are available in many programming languages, e.g., StanfordNLP/Java (Klein & Manning, 2003), NLTK/Python (Bird et al., 2009), and WordNet::Similarity/Perl (Pedersen et al., 2004).
- **Customizable**. Since bolts can be shared across topologies, it is very easy to have a central repository containing all bolts. Each new instantiation of a Storm topology (e.g., an automated scoring application) can be easily created by selecting relevant bolts and defining the information flow through them. This also allows for convenient "plug and play" experiments with different NLP core components such as parsers or taggers.

7.3.2   ARCHITECTURE DETAILS

In their simplest form, automated scoring applications can be seen as machine learning applications where an automated scoring model is (a) trained on a large set of human-scored responses,

(b) evaluated for accuracy, fairness, as well as validity on held-out data, and (c) deployed in a production setting requiring high throughput and low latency. Although this is a fairly simplified view of such applications—for example, it ignores monitoring components that automatically detect anomalous conditions such as drifts in machine scores and application failures—it should suffice for the goal of this chapter.

Although Storm affords several advantages to stream-based NLP applications in general, it has some gaps in the case of building automated scoring applications. Specifically:

1. Although Storm has support for multiple programming languages, it does not actually provide any reliable Perl and Python bolt and spout implementations out of the box even though these languages are commonly used in NLP libraries and components.

2. Storm does not provide a way to identify and group data streams, i.e., there is no way to say "I want the output from all the bolts in the topology for the same student response together".

3. If a response causes an exception in one of the bolts (e.g., the parser times out because a response is too long), Storm will retry the same response forever instead of bypassing its processing in any downstream bolts.

Our example architecture extends Storm in order to address all of the above issues. The core of this enhanced architecture is a custom implementation of a Storm bolt that we term a FeatureService. FEATURESERVICE is an abstract class with implementations in Java, Perl, and Python. Each object inherited from this class represents a *service* that performs a simple, discrete task on the data streams that pass through it. The Perl and Python implementations of FeatureService use the IO::Storm[2] and the streamparse[3] open-source libraries respectively and bring them up to par with the corresponding Storm-native Java implementation.

FeatureService encapsulates an extremely easy-to-use interface for developers: after sub-classing FeatureService in their preferred programming language, they only need to implement two methods: setup() to load any resources required and calculate() to perform the processing. Finally, FeatureService implements data stream grouping: developers specify which other feature services are its prerequisites (i.e., which inputs it needs) and the calculate() method *automatically* receives the values of all of its prerequisites as a hash or a dictionary at runtime.

For the interested reader, Figure 7.1 shows stubs for three services written using Python, Perl, and Java and for a topology defining a toy application using these services. The application takes a student response, tokenizes it into sentences, assigns part-of-speech tags to each sentence, and then computes the proportion of words in the student response that are misspelled.

---

[2]http://github.com/dan-blanchard/io-storm
[3]http://github.com/Parsely/streamparse

```
class SentencesService(FeatureService):

  prereqs = ['essay']

  def setup(self):
    # load PunktTokenizer model from NLTK

  def calculate(self, repr_dict):
    # rep_dict['response'] contains the response
    # use PunktTokenizer to split into sentences
    # return list of sentences

                                             1
```

```
public class StanfordTaggerService extends FeatureService {

  Set<String> prereqs = new HashSet(Arrays.asList("words"));

  public void setup() {
    // load Stanford Tagger model from disk
  }

  @Override
  protected Object calculate(JSONObject reprDict) {
    // reprDict.get("sentences") contains list of sentences
    // iterate and tag each sentence
    // return list of POS-tagged sentences
  }
}
                                             2
```

```
package MisspelledWordsService;

extends 'FeatureService';

has '+prereqs' => (
  default  => sub { ['sentences'] }

);
sub setup {
  # initialize the spell checker
}

sub calculate {
  # $repr_dict->{'sentences'} contains
  # list of sentences from the response
  # iterate over the each word in each
  # sentence and check if it's a spelling error
  # return the proportion of words that are misspelled
}
                                             3
```

```
(ns example_topology.bolts

  (def SPOUT "response")

  (def BOLTS-LIST
    {

      "sentences" ;; name of output key
      ["python" "SentencesService" ;; how service is run
      ["response"]] ;; pre-requisites needed by service

      "tagged_sentences"
      ["java" #(StanfordTaggerService.)
      ["sentences"]]

      "misspelled_words"
      ["perl" "MisspelledWordsService"
      ["sentences"]

    })
)                                            4
```

Figure 7.1: Illustrating Storm services and topologies. Boxes 1, 2, and 3 show stubs for three different services (`FeatureService` bolts) written in Python, Java, and Perl, respectively. Box 4 shows the stub of a topology (written in Clojure) that defines a toy scoring application composed of these bolts.

7.3.3   EVALUATION

In order to illustrate the positive impact of the example service-based architecture, we compare the throughput (measured in responses scored per hour) of two different versions of two commonly used automated scoring applications—one that scores responses for writing quality using features for discourse structure, vocabulary use, and English conventions (Attali & Burstein, 2006) and a second application that scores responses for understanding of content (Heilman & Madnani, 2015; Madnani, Cahill, & Riordan, 2016). Unlike writing quality, content-scoring

Table 7.1: Throughputs for two different scoring applications (measured in student responses scored per hour), for a traditional version and for the version that uses the proposed Storm-based service architecture

		Version	
		Traditional	*Service-based*
Score Type	*Quality*	6058	12091
	Content	57285	70491

generally ignores misspellings and grammatical errors. We will examine content-scoring in more detail in Chapter 10.

The first version of each of the two applications does not use the service-based architecture; it is structured as a traditional application and lacks any significant task parallelization. The second version uses the service-based architecture with each component implemented as a bolt inheriting from the `FeatureService` class and participating in a pre-defined topology. This version is able to take full advantage of Storm's automatic parallelization. Table 7.1 shows their throughput values.[4] For both scoring applications, using the service-based architecture leads to a significant increase in the throughput.

Student responses processed by the writing quality scoring application are, on average, 3–4 times longer than the responses processed by the content scoring application which leads to lower throughput values for the former in general. In addition, the writing quality scoring application uses many more features than the content scoring application leading to more opportunities for parallelization and, hence, a larger increase in throughput over the traditional version.

For the purpose of this chapter, we focus on the throughput metric since it is generally the metric used by IT departments when running performance tests on automated scoring systems. Furthermore, no metrics can effectively measure the intangible benefits provided by this example architecture such as improved collaborative development, ease of integrating multiple programming languages, and sharing code across different automated scoring systems in the form of modular services.

7.3.4   ILLUSTRATING THE ARCHITECTURE

As an example how the service-based architecture can be used, we take the basic system that we discussed in Chapter 2 and illustrate an implementation using this architecture.

Recall that the basic system from Chapter 2 uses five features:

---

[4]The throughput was measured by scoring 250,000 responses for writing quality and 135,000 responses for content. Each application was run on the same single server. The responses were written to questions from a mixture of low- and high-stakes assessments.

- The log of the number of word tokens (LOGWORDS) and word types (LOGTYPES) in the response indicating elaboration.

- The mean word length in the response (MEAN_WORDLEN) indicating vocabulary sophistication.

- The proportion of words in the response that are number—i.e., are tagged with the cardinal tag (CD)—indicating precision.

- The proportion of words in the response that are misspelled (PROP_MISSPELLED) indicating knowledge of English conventions.

Figure 7.2 shows a visualization of the Storm topology for our basic automated scoring system that uses the above five features. Each oval in the figure represents a Storm bolt. There are 10 bolts in total. All student responses to be scored enter the topology at the **Spout** and are passed on to the **ResponseReader** bolt which uses statistical language identification models and a set of simple rules to automatically detect responses that may be written in bad faith, e.g., responses in other languages or non-scorable responses of the form "idk", "i don't know", etc. All such bad-faith responses are directed to a human scorer. Any responses not filtered out here are then passed to the subsequent bolts that compute intermediate representations (sentences, words, part-of-speech tags) and to bolts that compute the features used in the basic system (described in Chapter 2).[5] Once these features are computed, they are passed to the final bolt that uses a pre-trained machine learning model to compute a score for the response. The service-based architecture automatically handles parallelization, e.g., while a response is being tagged in the **Part-of-Speech Tagger** bolt, other bolts are processing other responses. It also allows for multiple instances of a bolt, so throughput can be further improved by having multiple instances of slower bolts (e.g., taggers or syntactic parsers).

The service-based architecture has already been used to build several operational educational NLP systems: (a) the e-rater® automated essay scoring system (Burstein, Tetreault, & Madnani, 2013) that is used to score student essays written to the GRE® and the TOEFL® tests; (b) the c-rater™ system (Madnani, Cahill, et al., 2018; Madnani, Cahill, & Riordan, 2016) that automatically scores content knowledge in student responses to questions on the PRAXIS® teacher-licensure tests; (c) the Language Muse® web app (Burstein et al., 2017; Madnani, Burstein, et al., 2016) that helps teachers build language activities for language learners in their classrooms; and (d) the Writing Mentor™ Google Docs add-on (Madnani, Burstein, et al., 2018) that provides feedback to struggling post-secondary writers and helps them improve their writing in a self-paced, self-regulated fashion.

---

[5]Note that the Part-of-Speech Tagger bolt takes the output of the Sentence Tokenizer bolt as input, and not the output of the Word Tokenizer bolt. Similarly, the Misspelled Word Counter bolt takes the output of the ResponseReader bolt as input rather than the output of either of the tokenizer bolts. We assume that, in this example, these two software components perform their own internal word (and sentence) tokenization. This can be easily changed if consistent tokenization across bolts is important.

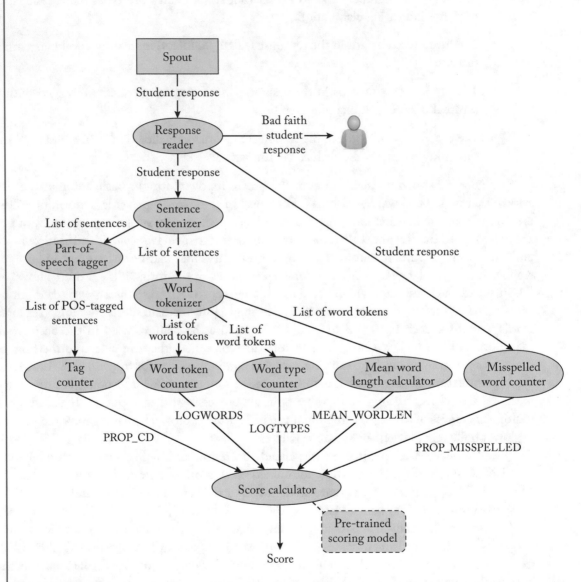

Figure 7.2: Illustrating the service-based topology for the basic automated scoring system from Chapter 2. Each oval represents a bolt and each edge between bolts represents a data stream connection. The final bolt uses a pre-trained, pre-loaded model to compute the score for a response, based on the five feature streams.

7.4   CONCLUSIONS

The goal of this chapter was to provide insights into the rarely discussed topic of transitioning an automated scoring system from a small-scale research prototype into a production system that can process millions of student responses reliably and with low latency.

We described an example architecture that can be used to successfully execute such a transition. This architecture employs a robust, service-based framework that extends Apache Storm—which provides several advantages out of the box in terms of scalability, robustness, and fault-tolerance. The extensions made to the Storm framework as part of this architecture address some specific limitations pertaining to its use in automated scoring applications. We also presented an evaluation showing that using this architecture leads to significant improvements in processing throughput, ease of development, and scalability. Finally, we showed an example implementation for the basic automated scoring system described previously in Chapter 2 as an illustration of how the architecture can be used.

CHAPTER 8

Evaluating for Real-World Use

8.1 INTRODUCTION

In Chapter 2, we used quantitative metrics such as Pearson's correlation and quadratically weighted Kappa to evaluate the predictive performance of the automated essay scoring systems we built as part of our hands-on exercises. In the same chapter, we alluded to the fact that it is also important to consider additional factors such as construct-relevance and fairness when evaluating such systems. In this chapter, we discuss in detail some of these additional factors. While incorporating these factors into the evaluation process will certainly require additional effort from the NLP practitioner, we consider it necessary to produce scores that can be trusted by the test stakeholders.

Test scores, whether assigned by human raters or computers, can have a significant effect on people's lives—especially when deployed as part of high-stakes tests such as the GRE® and the TOEFL®—and, therefore, must be scrutinized beyond simple accuracy. Automated essay scoring systems may offer some advantages over human raters, e.g., higher score consistency (Williamson et al., 2012). Yet, like any other machine learning algorithm, models used for essay score prediction may inadvertently encode discrimination into their decisions due to biases or other imperfections in the training data, spurious correlations, and other factors (Romei & Ruggieri, n.d.; von Davier, n.d.). Given that the educational measurement community has been conducting significant research into such issues for a long time, our primary goals in this chapter are the following.

1. Draw awareness of the NLP community toward the significant research that the educational measurement community has been conducting on using factors other than accuracy for evaluating essay scores. We attempt to do this by summarizing the salient aspects of this research and by providing references to the relevant psychometric literature.

2. Describe a solution that would allow an NLP practitioner interested in building automated essay scoring systems to incorporate the findings of educational measurement research into their evaluations.

8.2 VALIDITY

An overarching concept in psychometric literature is that of VALIDITY which is defined as the "degree to which evidence and theory support the interpretations of scores assigned to a test (whether by humans or by automated systems) for proposed uses of tests" (AERA, 2014). A test itself is neither valid or invalid—it's only the proposed interpretation of the test scores for a particular use case that needs to be validated. For example, the scores assigned for a science test might be used to endorse a certification or to inform admission decisions. Each of these uses implies a different interpretation of the scores—whether the test-taker has mastered a particular curriculum or whether the test-taker is likely to be successful in a more advanced course, respectively. The chosen interpretation must then be evaluated in terms of its validity by collecting supporting statistical and psychometric evidence.

As an example, let us consider the proposed use of the aforementioned science test to predict success in an advanced course. The relevant evidence for interpreting the test scores for this proposed use would need to support the following propositions:

1. that the content domain of the science test is consistent with the prerequisite skills needed for the advanced course,

2. that the scores assigned to the test-takers are not unduly impacted by "irrelevant" skills such as writing ability (more on this below),

3. that "success" in the advanced course can also be measured in a valid manner, and

4. that test-takers with higher scores on this science test are likely to be more successful in the advanced course than their counterparts with lower scores.

To understand the framework of validity more broadly, we will draw more on the idea of the "construct"—which we introduced back in Chapters 2 and 3. We defined the CONSTRUCT as a set of related knowledge, skills, and other abilities that a particular test is designed to measure. Examples include logical reasoning, language proficiency, reading comprehension, etc.

Two common ways in which the validity of a particular use case might be challenged are *construct under-representation* and *construct-irrelevance*.

Construct under-representation refers to the situation when a test might fail to capture the salient aspects of the purported construct to some degree. This could occur because, say, the test inadequately samples the domain content or only allows certain ways in which test-takers can respond to the test questions even though there are other ways of responding warranted by the construct. For example, if a test of English language proficiency contained *only* questions that require writing a response and none that require speaking a response, the use of such a test's scores to inform graduate school admissions could plausibly be challenged on the basis of construct under-representation.

Construct irrelevance refers to the situation when the scores for a test might be systematically affected by processes or factors that are deemed extraneous to the intended purpose of that test, i.e., its construct. Returning to our hypothetical English language proficiency test, if it turned out that test-takers who were more familiar with the subject matter of the reading passages used in the writing questions *systematically* received higher scores than those that were not as familiar, this would be considered a source of construct-irrelevant variance in said scores and the use of such scores to inform graduate school admissions would likely be considered invalid.

8.3   FAIRNESS

The Standards for Educational and Psychological Testing (AERA, 2014) cites fairness as a "fundamental validity issue" that requires careful consideration throughout *all* stages of the testing process including test development, test administration, test scoring, and score interpretation (Angoff, 2012; Bridgeman et al., 2003; Duong & von Davier, n.d.; Y.-H. Lee & von Davier, n.d.; J. Liu & Dorans, 2016; Oliveri & von Davier, 2016; Zieky, 2016). Such FAIRNESS considerations dictate that the test reflects the same construct(s) for the entire test-taking population, that scores from a fair test have the same meaning for the test taking population, and that a fair test does not offer undue advantages (or disadvantages) to some individuals because of their characteristics such as those associated with race, ethnicity, gender, age, socioeconomic status, or linguistic or cultural background.

For example, the notion of *accessibility* requires that all test-takers should be given an unimpeded opportunity to demonstrate their standing on the construct being measured by a test. For, say, test administration, this might mean that standard print and electronic formats might impede examinees with visual impairments and some older adults. Such an impediment would be deemed unfair if visual acuity is construct-irrelevant.

At the same time, one must be aware of the complex interplay between adaptations made to a test to increase its accessibility and the validity of the scores for the intended uses of the test. For example, it may be the case that by making changes to the standardization practices to make the testing set up more accessible, one might change the actual construct being measured which can then compromise the validity of the intended use of the scores.

For the benefit of NLP practitioners who constitute the core readership of this book, we now restrict the broader definition of fairness to one that is more quantitatively oriented and applies specifically to test scoring. Under this definition, we describe a FAIR TEST as one with no *consistent* differences in the scores due to construct-irrelevant factors, irrespective of whether said scores are produced by human raters or by automated scoring models. More specifically, while the unequal distribution of socio-economic status and educational resources means some differences in performance across subgroups are to be expected, it must be ensured that systematic and/or large differences in the scores assigned to the various subgroups result *only* from differences in skills and not from construct-irrelevant factors—e.g., age, gender, race, etc.

In the next section, we specifically examine possible sources of bias when it comes to both human and automated scoring of constructed responses, including essays.

8.4   FAIRNESS FOR ESSAY SCORING

Recent studies in machine learning and NLP have highlighted that algorithms can often introduce their own biases either due to an existing bias in the training data or due to a minority group being inadequately represented in the training data (Feldman et al., 2015; D. Hovy & Spruit, 2016). With the advent of deep learning methods in NLP, biases may also be encoded into word representations learned in an unsupervised fashion from large amounts of data (Agarwal et al., 2019; Bordia & Bowman, 2019; Caliskan et al., 2017; Sweeney & Najafian, 2019) requiring explicit de-biasing techniques that may or may not be effective (Gonen & Goldberg, 2019; Kaneko & Bollegala, 2019; Sun et al., 2019). Finally, it is also possible to inadvertently encode socio-economic status into a model by using nothing more than morpho-syntactic features derived from informal writing such as social media posts (Basile et al., 2019).

Educational NLP applications are also affected by biases and require a careful consideration of broader issues pertaining to equity and fairness (Mayfield et al., 2019). More specifically for essay scoring, it is well understood that even human scoring of constructed responses is a subjective process. The same response can sometimes receive different scores from different human raters. Among the factors that can impact the assigned scores are rater fatigue (Ling et al., 2014), differences between novice and experienced raters (Davis, 2015), and the effect of raters' linguistics background on their evaluation of the language skill being measured (Carey et al., 2011). To guard against such rater inconsistencies, responses for high-stakes tests are often scored by multiple raters (Penfield, 2016; Z. Wang & von Davier, 2014).

The proponents of automated scoring of constructed responses claim that it can overcome many such issues inherent to human scoring: computers do not get tired, do not have personal biases, and can be configured to always assign the *same* score to a given response. However, automated essay scoring is certainly not immune to biases and, in fact, several studies have documented differing performance of automated scoring models for test-takers with different native languages or with disabilities (An et al., 2016; Bridgeman et al., 2012; Burstein & Chodorow, 1999; Loukina, Beigman Klebanov, et al., 2017; Ramineni & Williamson, 2018; Z. Wang & von Davier, 2014; Z. Wang et al., 2016). Furthermore, the performance of automated scoring systems is obviously only as good as the human ratings that they learn from; human rater bias has the potential to impact the performance of such systems significantly (Amorim et al., 2018).

Biases can also arise because of techniques used to develop new features for automated essay scoring models. The automated score may be based on features which are construct-irrelevant despite being highly correlated with the human scores in the training data. As an example, consider that more proficient writers tend to write longer responses. Therefore, one almost always observes a consistent positive correlation between essay length and human proficiency score (L. Perelman, 2014; Shermis, 2014). This is acceptable since verbal fluency—a correlate of response length—is considered an important part of the construct of writing proficiency. Yet, longer essays should not *automatically* receive higher scores. Therefore, without proper model validation to consider the *relative* impact of such features, decisions might be made that are biased against subgroups of test-takers.

Another source of bias might arise if the performance of the automated scoring model varies substantially across writing prompts. In such a scenario, for tests such as TOEFL® where different writing prompts may be assigned to different test-takers, the scores assigned by the automated system might be affected by construct-irrelevant variance—namely the identity of the prompt they were assigned which has nothing to do with their writing skills. Therefore, such cross-prompt variation would need to be measured and analyzed on a large variety of prompts before deploying such a model for automated essay scoring.

8.5   RSMTOOL

Due to the aforementioned sources of potential bias, psychometric guidelines require that if automated scoring models are to be used for making high-stakes decisions for college admissions or employment, the NLP researchers developing those models should perform model validation to ensure that construct-irrelevant factors are not causing such models to produce significant differences in scores across different subgroups of test-takers or across different writing prompts designed for the same task.

Several standard analyses have been used in the psychometric literature to evaluate the fairness of automated essay scoring systems across test-taker subgroups. One example is *standardized mean difference* (or SMD) which is computed as follows: first calculate the difference between the mean automated score and the mean human score and then divide this difference by the standard deviation based on either one or both sets of scores, depending on whether scores are available for the same set of essays and how well the sample of essays approximates the overall test-taker population. SMD is a well-known measure of "effect size" which represents a quantitative measure of a phenomenon; in this case, it represents how strongly the automated scores differ from the human scores for, say, a particular test-taker subgroup of interest (Yan & Bridgeman, 2020). If the differences are larger than some pre-determined threshold, they might be the result of a biased scoring model. Other more recent analyses include analyzing the performance of individual features using differential feature functioning (M. Zhang et al., 2017) or computing the variance in mean model residual across groups (Yao et al., 2019).

However, it is not practical to assume that NLP practitioners will either be familiar with existing psychometric analyses or be able to keep up with new ones. A convenient solution to this dilemma is an open-source tool called RSMTool (Madnani, Loukina, von Davier, et al., 2017)—which we already used for our hands-on exercises in Chapter 2! RSMTool incorporates *both* the standard machine learning pipeline necessary for building an automated essay scoring model and a set of psychometric and statistical analyses aimed at detecting possible biases in the trained model's performance. More specifically, RSMTool offers the following benefits to an NLP practitioner working on automated essay scoring.

1. The code for RSMTool is entirely open-source under the Apache 2.0 license.[1] This is important so that the psychometric and educational measurement community cannot only audit the source code of the already available analyses to ensure their compliance with fairness standards but also easily contribute new analyses which are then immediately made available to NLP practitioners.

2. RSMTool builds on top of the popular scikit-learn machine learning library (Pedregosa et al., 2011) which means that most of the well-known and well-understood machine learning algorithms are available to the practitioner for modeling automated essay scoring.

3. RSMTool comes pre-packaged with several psychometric analyses that have been developed to detect biases in scores produced by the automated essay scoring model. For example, it can generate subgroup analyses based on standardized mean differences (SMD) and differential feature functioning (DFF). RSMTool also includes analyses based on essay length, a potentially construct-irrelevant factor. For example, it computes the contribution of essay length itself to the score as well as the contribution of any (non-length) feature to the score beyond what is already encoded in essay length. Finally, RSMTool also includes analyses based on estimates of the TRUE SCORES. According to classical test theory, the true score is defined as the average score that would be assigned to an essay by a hypothetical, infinite population of human raters. The true score is always a latent variable but its variance can be approximately estimated from a finite number (N) of human scores, with the quality of the approximation improving as N increases. Evaluating automated scoring systems against approximated true scores can produce performance estimates that are robust to errors in human scores and remain stable even when human–human agreement varies (Loukina et al., 2020).

4. The output of RSMTool is a comprehensive HTML report that is entirely self-contained (including any figures) and can be easily shared and viewed in any modern browser.

5. RSMTool has been designed to make it easy for the user to add new evaluations and analyses. The evaluation and report-generation components of RSMTool (including the fairness analyses) can be run on predictions from *any* machine learning system, not just the ones that are provided by RSMTool itself. Each section of the report is implemented as a separate Jupyter notebook (Kluyver et al., 2016). The practitioner can choose which sections should be included into the final HTML report and in which order. Furthermore, practitioners who want to use different evaluation metrics or custom fairness analyses can provide them in the form of new Jupyter notebooks; these analyses are dynamically executed and incorporated into the final report along with the existing analyses or even in their place, if so desired, without modifying a single line of code. RSMTool also provides a well-documented API which allows practitioners to integrate various components of RSMTool into their own applications, if so needed.

---

[1]https://github.com/EducationalTestingService/rsmtool

An example RSMTool report can be seen at `https://bit.ly/fair-tool`—see (Madnani, Loukina, von Davier, et al., 2017) for more details on the data for which this report was generated. We also refer the interested reader to the extensive online documentation available for RSMTool.[2]

8.6   POSTSCRIPT: CONNECTIONS TO FATML

We conclude this chapter by drawing connections between the research on validity and fairness of automated scoring systems that is being conducted by the psychometric community and the recent research efforts on ensuring fairness, accountability, and transparency for machine learned models from—what is now referred to as—the FATML community (Kamiran & Calders, 2009; Kamishima et al., 2012; Luong et al., 2011; Zemel et al., 2013).

Friedler et al. (2016) proposed a formal framework for conceptualizing the idea of fairness. Within that framework, the authors define the idea of "structural bias": the unequal treatment of subgroups when there is no clear mapping between the features that are easily observable for those subgroups (e.g., culturally and historically defined characteristics that are irrelevant to scoring) and the "true" features on which algorithmic decisions should actually be based (the construct). Our conceptualization of fairness for automated scoring models in this chapter–avoiding systematic biases in test scores across subgroups due to construct-irrelevant factors–fits perfectly in this framework.

Friedler et al. (2016) also showed—along with Berk et al. (2018)—that there are many different ways to formally define algorithmic fairness and that it may be impossible to achieve fairness according to each and every one of these definitions at the same time. Loukina et al. (2019) recently showed that similar observations can also be made regarding automated scoring of spoken responses.

More notably, Hutchinson & Mitchell (2019) draw explicit connections between the fairness criteria proposed by the educational measurement community—resulting from decades of research into test fairness—and the ML fairness criteria that have more recently been proposed by the machine learning and data mining community.

Another possible avenue of work in automated scoring that can be inspired by the work of the FATML community is that of bias mitigation. So far, we have primarily discussed techniques for *detecting* potential biases in automated scoring models. We showed that there are multiple sources of possible bias which makes it unlikely that there would be a single "silver bullet" that can make automated scores completely bias-free. The approach currently favored in the educational measurement community is to try and reduce susceptibility to construct-irrelevant factors by design. This includes an expert review of each feature before it is added to the model to ensure that it is theoretically and practically consistent with the skill set being measured by the test. These features are then combined in an easily interpretable model (usually linear regression) which is trained on a representative sample of test-taker population.

---

[2]`https://rsmtool.readthedocs.io`

However, simpler scoring models may not always be the right solution. For one, even simpler models may still exhibit bias. In addition, recent studies on scoring test-takers' knowledge of content rather than writing proficiency have shown that using more sophisticated—and hence, less transparent—models yields non-trivial gains in the accuracy of the predicted scores. An alternative to using simpler models might be to use more sophisticated subgroup analyses which can improve model fairness without necessarily sacrificing model performance (Gardner et al., 2019). Overall, building fair automated scoring at large requires complex, nuanced solutions.

The machine learning community has identified several broad approaches to deal with discrimination that could, in theory, be used for automated scoring models, especially those using more complex nonlinear algorithms: the training data can be modified (Feldman et al., 2015; Hajian & Domingo-Ferrer, 2013; Kamiran & Calders, 2012; Mancuhan & Clifton, 2014), the algorithm itself can be changed so that it optimizes for fairness as well as the selection criteria (Calders & Verwer, 2010; Kamishima et al., 2012; Zemel et al., 2013), and the output decisions can be changed after-the-fact (Kamiran et al., 2012). A survey of such approaches is provided by Romei & Ruggieri (2013).

PART IV

Further Afield: Feedback, Content, Speech, and Gaming

CHAPTER 9

Automated Feedback

9.1 WHAT IS FEEDBACK?

So far in this book we have discussed automated scoring of essays—along a single holistic dimension or along multiple dimensions that capture different aspects of essay quality. A score can be a type of FEEDBACK, defined by MacMillan dictionary as "comments about how well or how badly someone is doing something, which are intended to help them do it better".[1] A score is a specific kind of "comment"—a numerical one—on the writer's performance, and it is often meant to help the writer improve, especially when scores are given on interpretable dimensions. According to the dictionary, feedback is often qualified with *constructive, effective, useful, encouraging, positive, negative, immediate, instant,* and *initial.* These adjectives point to the common evaluative feedback (positive/negative), to the timing of its arrival (immediate), to its continuous nature (initial), and to its usefulness to the person given the feedback.

Automated systems providing feedback on writing clearly address the timeliness and continuity concerns—one can typically submit many drafts and receive instantaneous feedback. In cases where it can be clearly determined that the user has made an error—such as in spelling or grammar, or by failing to provide a conclusion to an essay—the feedback can also be evaluative (negative); positive feedback could be implicit (in that no errors have been pointed out) or explicit, either in the form of a comment (like "Well done!") or perhaps a visual representation of the system's success in finding certain expected elements in an essay (such as highlighting thesis or conclusion statements, as done in Criterion (Burstein et al., 2004), for example).

In some cases, it is not easy to automatically determine whether the user has done a good or a bad job with a particular aspect of writing, because the system does not have sufficient information about what the user has intended to do. For example, the claim detection feedback in Writing Mentor (Burstein et al., 2018) can show the strong claims (e.g., "John must visit his sister") and the more cautious, hedged claims (e.g., "This might be a good idea") used in an argumentative essay, but it cannot assess them[2] because doing so requires knowing whether the observed claim modulation accords with the user's intention. It is the user who is meant to reflect on the essay and the feedback on claims and edit the essay accordingly, to make sure the wording reflects the writers' confidence in the claim. This type of feedback might not be covered under the MacMillan's definition of feedback cited above, because there is no explicit quality signal from the feedback itself, but it would be covered under a more generous definition of

---

[1] https://www.macmillandictionary.com/us/dictionary/american/feedback
[2] Beyond the encouragement to write more if the system failed to find any claims.

"information about a person's performance of a task which is used as a basis for improvement" (from Oxford Languages dictionary used in Google).

9.2   FEEDBACK SYSTEMS

A lot of work has been done under the broad umbrella of more or less evaluative, immediate, and continuous writing feedback. In fact, for nearly every aspect of essay quality captured in the scoring features we discussed in Chapters 5 and 6, there are attempts to give users feedback (beyond the score) to help them improve that aspect of writing. In this section, we survey a number of writing feedback systems described in the literature, pointing out the genre or feature of writing that the system focuses on. Our main goal is to exemplify the range of the work rather than to exhaustively review the literature; thus, only one or two systems are mentioned for each genre of feature. We intentionally omit spell checkers and grammar checkers due to their ubiquity in daily practice.

For example, Wambsganss et al. (2020) describe AL (short for *Argumentation Learning*), a feedback system intended to support **argumentative writing**. The system detects argument components and argument relations between them following the approaches described in Chapter 5, and then shows students the detected components and relations by highlighting claims and premises in the text, as well as by showing the argument structure as a graph (premises are connected to claims they support, etc.); the tool shows problems such as unsupported claims, as well as scores for persuasiveness, coherence, and readability of the arguments. In a small-scale study, the authors showed that students who used the tool provided more and more convincing arguments than students using a more traditional alternative.

ArgReWrite[3] (F. Zhang et al., 2016) is another feedback system for supporting argumentative writing. Students make revisions to their first draft, the system automatically labels revisions with their estimated purpose, such as Evidence and Reasoning, as well as the traditional "surface" revisions such as grammar and spelling. The system's labels are presented to the user; if the identified purpose does not match the user's intentions, "it indicates that the effect of the writer's change might have not met the writer's expectation, which suggests that the writer should revise their revisions". The system also allows the teacher to correct the automatically generated labels, and the student can either receive completely automated feedback immediately, or teacher-corrected feedback after some delay.

Nguyen et al. (2016) present a kind of a **critique** task, where the writer is asked to review a peer's essay. In particular, reviewers often focus exclusively on identifying a problem but not on proposing solutions, thus making the critical review less constructive and therefore less useful for the writer of the original essay. The system described in Nguyen et al. (2016) helps writers of peer reviews by flagging draft reviews without solutions; the authors show evidence that revised versions of the flagged reviews tended to contain solution proposals.

---

[3]http://argrewrite.cs.pitt.edu/

The eRevise system developed by E. L. Wang et al. (2020) is an example of feedback on **use of source material** in an essay. Students write in response to a fixed prompt that is pre-annotated with hierarchically structured information nuggets (main topics and detailed keywords covering aspects of subtopics) that could be effectively mentioned in the essay as pieces of evidence to support the writer's arguments. Based on the automated analysis, students received automatically generated feedback such as "provide additional evidence", "provide more detail for the already presented evidence", "explain why the specific pieces of evidence were picked", and "connect the evidence to the overall argument". The authors noted that while in many cases the student responded to feedback with an effective revision along the lines suggested by the feedback, there were also instances where the revision did not seem to align with the feedback, as well as cases where an attempt was made but was insufficient to improve the quality of the essay, such as adding details that are not pertinent, repeating evidence that was already stated in the essay, adding evidence that was not in the source, or recycling the same explanation for multiple pieces of evidence.

Wade-Stein & Kintsch (2004) describe Summary Street, an early feedback system that helps middle school students write better summaries; in particular, LSA is used to provide feedback on the **summary's coverage of the source text**. The source text is split into sections (often using the author's subheadings); section coverage is determined by calculating the cosine of the summary to each section, and using empirically derived thresholds to judge the coverage as sufficient or not. The students are shown a bar chart where each bar represents a topic/section to be covered and its height represents the extent of coverage in the current draft of the summary; the visualization also includes the target extent of coverage, which the student strives to surpass in their revisions. Summary Street also provides feedback on redundancy (two sentences that are exceedingly semantically similar are flagged) and relevance (sentences that are insufficiently related to any of the target topics are flagged); these are meant to induce the student to reflect on succinctness and relevance of their summaries, even if the specifically flagged sentences turn out, on students' reflection, to be non-redundant or relevant. The authors show that summaries produced with the tool tend to have better coverage, especially of later sections of the source material that students not using the tool often neglected.

G. Cheng (2017) used their system for analyzing reflective writing (described in Chapter 6) to provide evaluative feedback on the **quality of reflection**. Essay sentences are automatically classified into reflection categories (roughly aligned with what happened, why, and what next), and each essay gets scores on the scale of 1 (developing) to 4 (competent) on each of the reflection categories through sentence-level aggregation. The output of the system was used to provide feedback to students in the form of labeling of their entry with the relevant categories, explanation of categories, as well as general suggestions for improvement with examples. In the post-implementation survey, 67% of respondents agreed or strongly agreed that the system's feedback could help improve their reflective skills in L2 learning. In a focus group study, the authors found that while students found the feedback helpful, some commented that getting the scores could be demotivating for those who got a low score after investing a substantial effort. Gibson et al. (2017) describe another feedback system designed to assist with reflective writing; the system detects evidence for a somewhat different set of reflection categories (challenge, change, and context), the extent to which the reflection along these categories is personal (Link2Me), and reflection type (emotive, epistemic, critique). The system uses specially developed pattern-matching rules for detection. Category membership and personalization of sentences are visualized through markup in the text. The authors report positive user experience from a group of pharmacy students tasked with writing weekly reflective statements about various incidents as part of a curriculum built to prepare students to make more informed decisions and clinical judgments.

Glosser, as described in Calvo & Ellis (2010) and Villalón et al. (2008), provides feedback on **topicality** by automatically extracting key topics from the essay and the sentences that address them. The system uses LSA to analyze the term-passage matrix for a given document; after applying singular value decomposition, eigenvectors with the largest eigenvalues correspond to main topics, and passages aligned with the chosen dimension are shown as those addressing the topic. The topics are shown accompanied by reflection questions, such as "Are the ideas used in the essay relevant to the question?" or "Would the essay be better if it took into account other ideas or references?". Writing Mentor (Burstein et al., 2018) provides feedback on the **main topic** that can be applied to a draft-in-development rather than a complete draft of an essay—the system presents the largest set of related keywords it found in the draft, inviting a reflection on whether the highlighted keywords represent the topic the writer most wanted to discuss. Writing Mentor also allows the user to edit the main topic and define additional topics for automatic keyword tracking. Both tools also provide feedback related to **topic development**—Glosser shows an automatically constructed concept map, while Writing Mentor shows the distribution of main topic and any additional topics defined by the user across the different sections of the text, advises the user to consider both focus and development ("It can be confusing for readers to encounter a paragraph that discusses multiple ideas") and points out a connection between sections in the text and topical distribution through guidelines such as "Does your title signal the main content of your paper?" and "Do section headers signal the content of that section?".

Both Glosser and Writing Mentor also provide feedback related to the **coherence** of the essay. Glosser identifies consecutive paragraphs that are far apart in the latent semantic space and flags the transition as a potential break in coherence, along with questions for reflections such as "Do you understand how each paragraph and sentence follows from the previous one?" or "Could the ideas in the essay be organized in a clearer way?". Writing Mentor points out transition terms, exceedingly long sentences, and pronouns, for the user to check that the transitions are signaled as intended and pronouns are not missing referents; feedback relating topic development to sectioning is also shown under the coherence tab, with a suggestion to use topical keywords to give more informative section titles.

Criterion (Burstein et al., 2004, 2003) provides feedback on the dimension of **organization** by automatically identifying and showing to the user sentences in the essay that correspond to the following discourse categories: background, thesis, main ideas, supporting ideas, and conclusion.

Han et al. (2019) provide feedback on **grammatical constructions** using a database of leveled grammatical patterns based on the Common European Framework of Reference for Languages (CEFR) proficiency levels, each accompanied with a set of "can-do" statements, such as "A1: Can use 'and' to join a limited range of comparative adjectives", etc.[4] The authors mention feedback on **vocabulary** using a leveled sense inventory (for example, "cattle" is classified as B1; "albeit" as C2; "as" is classified as A1, A2, B1 for its "job", "use", and "while" senses,[5] respectively). Relevant patterns in the students' essays are matched and patterns from the next proficiency level are suggested to help the user produce a more advanced piece of writing. Wanner et al. (2013) describe designs for systems that would propose alternatives to a detected **miscollocation**, while Tarp et al. (2017) describe a prototype of an auto-complete-style writing assistant, based on collocational information. Y. Liu et al. (2019) conduct preliminary evaluations for a system that proposes idioms in order to improve the **stylistic appeal** of an essay; Tan et al. (2018) describe a system that recommends a fitting quotation.

9.3 EVALUATION OF FEEDBACK SYSTEMS

The reader might have noticed that we have omitted from the discussion so far what is perhaps the most important attribute of feedback—its usefulness. A question that naturally arises in this context is how to measure usefulness, which, in turn, leads to the question—usefulness for what purpose? In particular, is it useful for **improving the current draft** of the essay or for **improvement in skill** so that the first draft of the *next* essay is better than it would have been without using the feedback system on the previous essay?

In this first type of context, the primary evaluation criterion for the system is some evidence of improvement of the written product over the writer's first draft while using the feedback system. Indeed, measurements of improvement across drafts and evidence of students making corrections following feedback are often used for evaluation (Attali, 2004; Chapelle et al., 2015; Foltz et al., 2014; Lipnevich & Smith, 2008).

Evaluation of a feedback tool through a demonstration of skill-improvement–the efficacy of the tool—is a complicated endeavor. To demonstrate that the observed improvement in skill is specifically due to the use of the writing tool, and not due to something else happening in a student's life and education at the same time requires a research design that can take other potential sources of variation in outcomes into account, such as the one used in randomized controlled studies often used to assess interventions, including in education (Connolly et al.,

---

[4]https://www.englishprofile.org/component/grammar/
[5]https://www.englishprofile.org/wordlists/evp

2018); some such studies have been performed with respect to writing feedback tools (Rock, 2007; J. Wilson & Roscoe, 2020).

Many writing feedback tools seem to position themselves somewhere between the skill-improvement and the product-improvement purposes, perhaps assuming that quantity will eventually turn into quality, namely, extensive work on improving the written product might lead to internalization and generalization of the skill to new contexts. This might or might not be true. Feedback that helps the user fix an error quickly by pointing it out and by suggesting a correction might be good in a product-oriented context, but not in a skill-oriented context; letting the user pinpoint and fix the error himself or herself might be a better skill-development strategy (Hyland & Hyland, 2006). According to the meta-analysis of writing interventions for adolescents by Graham & Perin (2007a), explicit grammar instruction tended to be ineffective; this finding is cited by the developers for Writing Pal to support their decision to forgo giving explicit feedback on grammar (D. McNamara et al., 2013), in contrast to most other systems that do provide such feedback.

A writer's general attitude toward feedback could play a role in achievement and in effectiveness of feedback. Calvo & Ellis (2010) found that students who viewed writing feedback as an invitation to reflect tended to have higher writing achievement than students who perceived feedback as a recipe to help complete the task. While many automated writing evaluation systems incorporate invitation-to-reflect kind of feedback, it takes two to make it work, in that the user needs to have a mindset receptive to that kind of feedback.

CHAPTER 10

Automated Scoring of Content

10.1 INTRODUCTION

In this chapter, we will examine another application of automated scoring—scoring assessments that use open-ended tasks not to measure the quality of what's being written, but instead to gather evidence of what the test-takers know, have learned, or can do in a specific subject area. We refer to these types of assessments as content-based and to the systems that score them as automated CONTENT SCORING systems. Figure 10.1 shows an example content-based question and its corresponding scoring rubric.

Although multiple-choices (or "selected response") questions can provide one possible way to assess the understanding of content, such questions may not always provide the most complete picture of test-takers' knowledge. This is due to the fact that selected response questions test, in part, test-takers' ability to recognize and select an answer from a list of options. It is difficult to be certain whether the correct answer would have been provided by the test-taker if it had *not* been included as one of the multiple-choice options.

On the other hand, allowing test-takers to write a free-text response is able to better provide a more complete assessment of their understanding. Figure 10.2 shows example responses written by actual students from each score point as graded by human raters. This clearly illustrates the differences between open-ended content-based responses and selected responses.

However, having humans grade open-ended, free-text responses requires a lot more time and is more expensive. Using multiple-choice questions is, therefore, usually a practical decision. Automated scoring systems that can accurately and fairly grade content-based responses can enable more accurate assessment of how well test-takers have understood or learned specific concepts.

An important consideration that makes automated scoring of content different from automated scoring of writing quality is that, more often than not, it is not important if the test-taker makes some spelling mistakes or grammatical errors as long as the desired content (e.g., scientific principles, trends in a graph, details from a reading passage, or missing information from an experiment) is included in the response. The scoring rubric for the example question in Figure 10.1 clearly illustrates this ("Minor errors will not necessarily lower the score"). This point is further reinforced by the actual example responses for score point 3 in Figure 10.2—spelling errors such as *measureing*, *contaneir*, etc., have not lowered the scores assigned by the human raters.

Prompt—Acid Rain

A group of students wrote the following procedure for their investigation.

Procedure:
1. Determine the mass of four different samples.
2. Pour vinegar in each of four separate, but identical, containers.
3. Place a sample of one material into one container and label. Repeat with remaining samples, placing a single sample into a single container.
4. After 24 hours, remove the samples from the containers and rinse each sample with distilled water.
5. Allow the samples to sit and dry for 30 minutes.
6. Determine the mass of each sample.

The students' data are recorded in the table below.

Sample	Starting Mass (g)	Ending Mass (g)	Difference in Mass (g)
Marble	9.8	9.4	−0.4
Limestone	10.4	9.1	−1.3
Wood	11.2	11.2	0.0
Plastic	7.2	7.1	−0.1

After reading the group's procedure, describe what additional information you would need in order to replicate the experiment. Make sure to include at least three pieces of information.

(a)

Score 3

The response is an excellent answer to the question and describes three additional pieces of information that would be needed to accurately replicate the experiment. It is correct, complete, and appropriate and contains elaboration, extension, and/or evidence of higher-order thinking and relevant prior knowledge. There is no evidence of misconceptions. Minor errors will not necessarily lower the score.

Score 2

The response is a proficient answer to the question and describes two additional pieces of information that would be needed to accurately replicate the experiment. It is generally correct, complete, and appropriate, although minor inaccuracies may appear. There may be limited evidence of elaboration, extension, higher-order thinking, and relevant prior knowledge, or there may be significant evidence of these traits but other flaws (e.g., inaccuracies, omissions, inappropriateness) may be more than minor.

Score 1

The response is a marginal answer to the question and describes one additional piece of information that would be needed to accurately replicate the experiment. While it may contain some elements of a proficient response, it is inaccurate, incomplete, and/or inappropriate. There is little evidence, if any, of elaboration, extension, higher-order thinking, or relevant prior knowledge. There may be evidence of significant misconceptions.

Score 0

The response, though possibly on topic, is an unsatisfactory answer to the question and describes little or no accurate or relevant information from the acid rain investigation. It may fail to address the question, or it may address the question in a very limited way. There may be no evidence of elaboration, extension, higher-order thinking, or relevant prior knowledge. There may be evidence of serious misconceptions.

(b)

Figure 10.1: A content-based question (a) taken from the Automated Short Answer Scoring Prize contest (`https://www.kaggle.com/c/asap-sas`) organized by the Hewlett Foundation and its corresponding scoring rubric (b).

Score 3

You would need many more pieces of information to replicate the experiment. You would need the type of samples to begin with in the procedure. You would also need to know the amount of vinegar used in each container. You would also need to know exactly how to mass the samples and what types of container to use (plastic for example, might alter the results).

Some additional information you will need are the material. You also need to know the size of the containeir to measure how the acid rain effected it. You need to know how much vineager is used for each sample. Another thing that would help is to know how big the sample stones are by measureing the best possible way.

Score 2

There are two pieces of additional information neccisary to replicate the experiment. Fipst of all the procedure does not officialy specify what the four samples are. Also,the procedure does not specify how much vinigar to pour for each container. A good procedure would have specified this

After reading the groups procedure I would need to know what type of vinegar they were using because it could of been any type, what was the measure of containers because the containers could have been 3 different sizes and they wouldn't have valid results, and they also should have told me what they were holding constant because I wouldn't know what variables to use or control.

Score 1

They should add how much vinegar to add to each sample. For this lab to be more accurate they should have also added more trials as well as adding a constant variable such as a rock in just water.

In order to replicate this experiment, I would need to know what the different mauterials were. I would also need to know how many different materials there were and what the starting mass of each material was.

Score 0

Well what i understand about this procedure is that you take four samples, put them in different containers that look the same, put vinegar on every sample + finally rinse them out with normal water + let them sit for 30 minutes till they dry. Then your finally going to see the difference between those samples.

I will need to know what's the purpose for this experiment, know the difference in mass for each sample, and I need to know an esimate of what they thought the starting and ending mass was.

Figure 10.2: Sample responses from each score point written by students to the question in Figure 10.1. These scores were assigned by human raters.

A final note on terminology: Content scoring is sometimes also referred to in the literature as "short-answer" scoring. Although it is true that many content-based questions tend to be very specific and elicit responses that are relatively short, this is not always the case. Previously published studies have considered responses that span a range of lengths—from a few words (Basu et al., 2013) to a few dozen words (Horbach et al., 2013; Madnani et al., 2013) to a few hundred words (Madnani, Cahill, & Riordan, 2016). Given that the primary facet of interest is the content of the response and not its length, we refer to the task as "content scoring" in this chapter.

10.2   APPROACHES

Content scoring approaches fall into two general categories.

1. **Reference-based Approach**. Responses are scored on the basis of their similarity to *reference* answers provided by the authors of the question or selected from existing high-scoring responses (Alfonseca & Pérez, 2004; Horbach et al., 2013; Meurers et al., 2011; Nielsen et al., 2008; Pado & Kiefer, 2015; Sukkarieh et al., 2011). Specifically, this approach requires enumerating in advance either a large set of correct answers or a core set of underlying "concepts" that the responses are then matched against. The degree to which a response and the references match is generally expressed via a small number of continuous-valued features. A single automated scoring model can usually be learned for multiple questions since the features tend not to be question-specific.

2. **Response-based Approach**. More recent approaches sidestep the requirement of manually enumerating the set of correct responses or concepts—an onerous task even for moderately open-ended questions—and instead rely on the use of a large number of detailed features extracted from the student responses themselves (e.g., word n-grams, etc.) and human scores assigned to the responses to learn an automated scoring model (Dzikovska et al., 2013; Madnani, Loukina, & Cahill, 2017; Mohler et al., 2011; Ramachandran et al., 2015; Zesch, Heilman, & Cahill, 2015; Zhu et al., 2016). Response-based approaches generally require learning a separate scoring model for each question since the features used are heavily lexicalized and extracted from the responses themselves.

The choice of whether the reference-based approach is better than the response-based approach depends on the open-ended nature of the question and on whether there is a sufficient number of human-scored responses available. Sakaguchi et al. (2015) explored the combination of the two types of approaches and observed that if sufficient human-scored data is available, response-based approaches often work better than reference-based approaches.

In general, response-based approaches represent the state of the art in computational linguistics and related fields. Systems using this approach have demonstrated excellent performance on responses from different content areas—including science, reading comprehension, and mathematics—in public competitions (Shermis, 2015), shared tasks (Dzikovska et al.,

2013), for systems deployed for formative assessments in classrooms (O. L. Liu et al., 2014; Mao et al., 2018; Zhu et al., 2016), as well as for summative assessments (Madnani, Cahill, et al., 2018; Madnani, Cahill, & Riordan, 2016).

For these reasons, we focus on response-based approaches for the rest of this chapter. We refer the reader to Burrows et al. (2015) for a more comprehensive survey of literature on content-scoring.

10.3   RESPONSE-BASED SCORING

In this section, we describe a typical response-based automated content scoring model. For such a model, a reasonable amount of data with one or more human scores for each response needs to be available for training. The size and other characteristics of the training data (e.g., the number of responses available for each score level on the scale) can have an impact on the performance of the trained system (Heilman & Madnani, 2015).

10.3.1   FEATURES

Once the training data is available, linguistic features are then extracted to represent each response. Such features may include:

1. Character n-grams including whitespace and punctuation.
2. Word n-grams—usually unigrams and bigrams.
3. Syntactic features such as triples extracted over dependency parses.
4. Some representation of response length, e.g., discretized bins computed as follows: whether the log of the number of characters in the response, rounded down to the nearest integer, equal x—for all possible x in the training set.

Usually the features are binary indicating either the presence or absence of the aspect under consideration. Such features are generally motivated by their ability to approximate what makes a good response to a content-based question: they generally contain (a) the right concepts (approximately captured by the word n-grams), (b) the right syntactic relationships between those concepts (approximately captured by the syntactic features), and (c) the right amount of detail (coarsely captured by the response length features).

The character n-grams serve a special purpose: they capture spelling and morphological variations such that responses are not excessively penalized for misspellings or for using the incorrect morphological variants. For example, if the correct response to a question must contain the phrase "temperature increased", a test-taker response containing the phrase "temprature increase" (with a misspelling and an incorrect verb form) can still get credit for that concept.

This is by no means an exhaustive list of features that can be extracted from responses. We only focus on these features as they are easy to extract and yet have been shown to provide good performance across a range of content genres.

10.3.2   MODEL

Once the features are extracted, a machine learning model can then be trained to predict scores for new responses to the same question. The training objective for the machine learning model is to maximize agreement with the human scores for the training data, as measured by metrics such as the κ_q or, preferably, mean squared error (MSE). Madnani, Loukina, & Cahill (2017) compared a range of different machine learning models (classifiers and regressors) on a large dataset containing multiple content-based questions and provided specific model-training recommendations—the most important one being to properly tuning the hyper-parameters of any scoring model.

As with models used for automated scoring of writing quality (discussed in Chapter 4), the choice of the model should be a compromise between performance (scoring accuracy) and post-hoc interpretability (Lipton, 2016). One option may be to choose more interpretable models and sacrifice some performance. Another option may be to apply recent techniques that allow interpreting the workings of more sophisticated "black box" models (Koh & Liang, 2017; Ribeiro et al., 2016). However, the latter may require careful tuning or adaptation of the interpretability technique to the model and feature space under consideration (Doshi-Velez & Kim, 2017).

10.4   EMERGING TREND: DEEP NEURAL NETWORKS

As with many other NLP applications, recent work on automated content scoring has also explored the use of deep neural network architectures with moderate success. The deep learning approach has been applied to *both* reference-based scoring as well as response-based scoring.

Sakaguchi et al. (2015) use word embeddings for candidate and reference answers to compute additional similarity features which are then combined with response-based features using support vector regression. Kumar et al. (2017) use an LSTM-based architecture with an explicit layer that computes a similarity metric over the candidate and test-taker state vectors from the previous layers. Riordan et al. (2017) adapt an existing network architecture that was previously applied to automated scoring of writing quality (Taghipour & Ng, 2016). They use word embeddings for the responses as the *only* input (reference answers are not used) with a convolutional layer extracting "features" as inputs for the subsequent LSTM layer. They also compare many different hyper-parameter settings for the neural network. Marvaniya et al. (2018) and Saha et al. (2018) enhance the set of existing reference answers with additional pre-graded candidate answers and then use similarity-based features computed over sentence embeddings—obtained from a state-of-the-art LSTM-based architecture—as well as over the answer tokens to predict the score using a multinomial logistic regression model. Deep learning approaches have also been recently applied to score content in more specialized domains such as clinical notes (Yim et al., 2019), mathematical equations and expressions (Cahill et al., 2020), and science explanations (Riordan et al., 2020). Other recent work has investigated how the performance of deep neural networks is affected by using character-level representations (to augment word representations) (Riordan et al., 2019) or by explicitly incorporating the scoring rubric into the network architecture (T. Wang et al., 2019).

The tradeoff between explainability and predictive performance that we discussed in Chapter 4 still applies to deep neural network approaches used for response-based content scoring. However, it is somewhat mitigated by the fact that even the non-neural approaches used for content scoring tend to use more complex, non-linear models due to the highly sparse, lexicalized feature set that is commonly employed.

10.5   SUMMARY

In this chapter, we described a different type of automated-scoring task: that of scoring responses to content-based questions where the goal is not to assess the quality of the written responses but rather to assess, for example, whether the test-takers have correctly understood a given concept as it was taught in the classroom or whether they possess the requisite specific knowledge in a particular area. We outlined the differences between automated content scoring and automated essay scoring. We also described the two popular approaches to automated content scoring in the literature and briefly discussed the nascent use of deep learning approaches to content scoring.

With the increasing use of intelligent tutoring systems and other technology-based formative assessment tools in classrooms and the prevalence of more specialized assessments in educational institutions and in the workplace, automated content scoring is an extremely important area of NLP research.

CHAPTER 11

Automated Scoring of Speech

11.1   INTRODUCTION

We have so far considered automated scoring of *written* responses. A neighboring field of automated scoring of *spoken* responses shares certain characteristics with our primary field of interest; we therefore provide a brief overview. We refer a reader interested in learning more to the recently published edited volume on automated assessment of speech (Zechner & Evanini, 2020); the discussion in this chapter is informed by that work.

Spoken responses in assessment tasks range from *scripted* speech (that is, reading out loud or repetition of the prompt) to *spontaneous* speech, namely, responses to open-ended questions such as "Describe your recent vacation". Intermediate locations on the scripted-vs.-spontaneous spectrum are also possible, for example, a task with moderately predictable speech where the test-taker produces a sentence using certain key words, or a picture narration task where the target vocabulary is somewhat restricted to the detail of the picture (Loukina, Zechner, et al., 2017).

Early work on speech scoring concentrated on scripted speech and, therefore, on the accuracy of the content (the extent to which what the test-taker said matches the prompt) and on its DELIVERY (fluency and pronunciation; e.g., overall pronunciation accuracy, number of disfluencies, stress patterns, intonation). Both of these aspects of speech production are assessed in moderately open-ended tasks as well; measurement of accuracy becomes somewhat more involved, since there is no one correct answer and many close variants are acceptable. Moderately open-ended tasks could also support measurement of what is called *language use*—typically covering vocabulary choice and grammar.

For spontaneous speech, and especially tasks that elicit extended spoken responses, delivery and language use elements in the scoring rubric are often joined by discourse and topic development considerations. One can clearly perceive parallels to the essay scoring world, with grammar, pronunciation, and prosody conventions (of spoken, rather than written, English), vocabulary, and discourse-level aspects of a spoken composition being assessed.

The scripted-vs.-spontaneous dimension is relevant for the design of the speech scoring system for at least two reasons. The first is similar to the distinction between scoring for content and scoring for proficiency that we discussed in the context of written responses (see Chapter 10). The more open-ended the question, the harder it is to operationalize the notion of a *correct* response in terms of content accuracy; on the other hand, open-ended tasks allow test-takers to demonstrate proficiency in terms of use of nuanced vocabulary, topic development, coherence, etc. The second reason is more specific to the speech scoring pipeline—the first step in automated scoring of speech is automated recognition of the words uttered by the test-taker, and the larger the possible vocabulary, the harder the task.

In this chapter, we start with reviewing the typical components of an automated speech recognition system (ASR)—a foundational building block of speech scoring systems. We then proceed to review the main elements of a system for scoring spontaneous speech, using research on SpeechRater®—a state of the art system for scoring spontaneous speech. We review features capturing aspects of delivery, vocabulary, and discourse, and draw parallels to the text-based work we discussed in the rest of the book.

11.2   AUTOMATED SPEECH RECOGNITION FOR SPEECH SCORING

Automated speech recognition (ASR) is a process that converts the speech signal in a digital audio recording into text. The speech signal—voiced sounds, unvoiced sounds, and silences—is measured at regular short intervals across various frequencies. These measurements serve as the input into an ACOUSTIC MODEL, whose job it is to translate them into phonemes or sequences of phonemes. Acoustic models are typically implemented using a hybrid Deep Neural Network and Hidden Markov Model approach (DNN–HMM).

The next component of an ASR system is a *pronunciation dictionary* that maps the orthographic form of a word to its sequence of phonemes. The words listed in the pronunciation dictionary are the words that the ASR system can recognize.

The components mentioned so far can generate a candidate sequence of words based on the acoustic signal; a *language model* helps pick the likelier sequences. Language models are usually implemented as n-gram models, with a trigram model being the most popular.

The process of speech recognition is a search for the most probable sequence of words uttered in the given recording, given the acoustic measurements, the acoustic model, the pronunciation dictionary, and the language model; we note that some of the current end-to-end systems do not explicitly contain all of these components.

The standard measure used to evaluate an ASR system is WORD ERROR RATE (WER)—the discrepancy between the ASR-hypothesized sequence of words and that provided by a human transcriber. The ASR hypothesis and the transcription are first aligned using dynamic programming, minimizing the *edit distance* between the hypothesis and the transcription—the number of edits (insertions, deletions, or substitutions) needed to change one string into the other. Using the optimal alignment, three types of ASR errors are recorded: (a) insertion (ASR produced a word where no word was transcribed), (b) deletion (ASR produced no word where a word was transcribed), and (c) substitution (ASR and transcription have different words). The WER is the sum of the counts of the three types of errors divided by the number of words in the transcription; the lower the value, the better the system's performance.

Recent advances in ASR (largely enabled by the advent of deep neural networks) have resulted in near-human levels of recognition in some contexts. For example, Xiong et al. (2017) report WER of 5.8% for their ASR system on the popular Switchboard corpus (Godfrey et al., 1992) of unscripted conversations between two native speakers of English; the WER of one human transcriber against the other was 5.9% in their study, with 5.1% reported in a different study using a more elaborate human transcription methodology (Saon et al., 2017). Both human and ASR performance is substantially worse for data from non-native speakers. Zechner (2009) reported average human WERs of 15–20% for data from an English proficiency exam;[1] human error rate was higher for responses of lower audio quality, responses from lower-proficiency speakers, and for shorter responses. According to Qian et al. (2020), the current state-of-the-art ASR WER for non-native spontaneous speech from the TOEFL iBT speaking assessment is about 20–25%.

Discussing factors that impact the performance of an automated speech recognition system, Qian et al. (2020) mention characteristics of the recording (such as audio quality and audio channel variability), as well as characteristics of the task (more scripted, more predictable speech is easier to recognize than the more open-ended, less predictable speech).

11.3 FEATURES FOR ASSESSING SPONTANEOUS SPEECH

11.3.1 DELIVERY: PRONUNCIATION, FLUENCY

The DELIVERY dimension of the scoring rubric for the TOEFL iBT speaking tasks is as follows.[2]

Score 4 Generally well-paced flow (fluid expression). Speech is clear. It may include minor lapses, or minor difficulties with pronunciation or intonation patterns, which do not affect overall intelligibility.

Score 3 Speech is generally clear, with some fluidity of expression, though minor difficulties with pronunciation, intonation, or pacing are noticeable and may require listener effort at times (though overall intelligibility is not significantly affected).

Score 2 Speech is basically intelligible, though listener effort is needed because of unclear articulation, awkward intonation, or choppy rhythm/pace; meaning may be obscured in places.

Score 1 Consistent pronunciation, stress, and intonation difficulties cause considerable listener effort; delivery is choppy, fragmented, or telegraphic; frequent pauses and hesitations.

According to Lennon (2000), FLUENCY can be measured "by speech rate, and by such dysfluency markers as filled and unfilled pauses, false starts, hesitations, lengthened syllables,

---

[1]Zechner (2009) showed that human consensus can be improved using a more elaborate protocol that includes transcribers considering draft transcriptions from other transcribers.

[2]https://www.ets.org/s/toefl/pdf/toefl_speaking_rubrics.pdf

retraces, and repetitions" (p. 25). SpeechRater features capture the fluency construct by looking at breakdowns, speed, and repairs (Hsieh et al., 2020), as detailed below.

Breakdowns are measured through filled pause rate (number of filled pauses, such as *uh*, *em*, per second), number and duration of silences (a silence is defined as a gap of more than 0.145 seconds between two words), rate of silences (number of silences to total number of words or to total duration of response), as well as distribution of silences with respect to clauses (syntactically defined long phrases and sentences).

Speed is measured by speaking rate (number of words per second in the duration of the response, removing leading and trailing silences), articulation rate (number of words per second in the duration of speech, namely, after removing durations of silences and filled pauses), and mean length of a run (contiguous sequence of words without long or filled pauses).

Repairs are captured using repetitions and the notion of an INTERRUPTION POINT—the point in the utterance where an abandoned or repaired speech ends and a new clause or phrase begins.

To measure **pronunciation**, one would typically compare the patterns observed in a given response to native speaker patterns. SpeechRater uses a score produced by an acoustic model trained mostly on native speech in order to compute a number of scoring features for pronunciation;[3] a separate feature looking specifically at the divergence in vowel durations from native patterns is also used. Prosody is additionally measured by considering patterns of stress (e.g., frequency of stressed syllables, mean distance between stressed syllables, in syllables and in seconds), tone, and rhythm (e.g., proportion of speech that consists of vowels, as well as measures of variation in durations of syllables and other types of segments[4]). See Hsieh et al. (2020) and research cited therein for more details regarding the delivery features and for a review of relevant research on L2 prosody.

Looking back at the world of writing, it is possible, in principle, to measure **writing fluency** using keystroke logs. For example, Sinharay et al. (2019) experiment with features such as mean duration of pauses between words, number of bursts (analogous to *runs* in the speech fluency terminology), time on task, typing speed, rate of correction of typos, pauses at sentence junctures vs. between-word and in-word pauses, minor or major edits, retyping, and many other features capturing the writing *process* rather than its *product* (the final submitted essay). Sinharay et al. (2019) show that process features combined using linear regression can successfully predict holistic essay scores, with correlations of $r = 0.761$ and $r = 0.678$, for two datasets of persuasive writing from 6th–9th graders collected as a part of writing assessment using software with keystroke log capture. Thus, students who write their essay faster, in longer and more frequent bursts, and spend more time on task tend to produce better essays. While predictive, these features are not used in essay scoring models because the fluency of the writing process is not part

---

[3]Note that the acoustic model used for speech recognition is trained on predominantly non-native data that reflects the test-taker population of the TOEFL iBT test.

[4]More variation in durations of syllables and other segments, namely, less rhythmic speech, typically indicates lower speaking proficiency.

of the scoring rubric for essays. Still, the construct of writing fluency is a measurable one and can be used in appropriate contexts.

11.3.2 LANGUAGE USE: VOCABULARY, GRAMMAR

The TOEFL iBT scoring rubric for the language use dimension is as follows.

Score 4 The response demonstrates effective use of grammar and vocabulary. It exhibits a fairly high degree of automaticity with good control of basic and complex structures (as appropriate). Some minor (or systematic) errors are noticeable but do not obscure meaning.

Score 3 The response demonstrates fairly automatic and effective use of grammar and vocabulary, and fairly coherent expression of relevant ideas. Response may exhibit some imprecise or inaccurate use of vocabulary or grammatical structures or be somewhat limited in the range of structures used. This may affect overall fluency, but it does not seriously interfere with the communication of the message.

Score 2 The response demonstrates limited range and control of grammar and vocabulary. These limitations often prevent full expression of ideas. For the most part, only basic sentence structures are used successfully and spoken with fluidity. Structures and vocabulary may express mainly simple (short) and/or general propositions, with simple or unclear connections made among them (serial listing, conjunction, juxtaposition).

Score 1 Range and control of grammar and vocabulary severely limit or prevent expression of ideas and connections among ideas. Some low-level responses may rely heavily on practiced or formulaic expressions.

The scoring rubric emphasizes the range and sophistication of grammatical construction and vocabulary. Consequently, SpeechRater's **grammar features** (M. Chen & Zechner, 2011; Yoon et al., 2020) include occurrence and frequency of various types of clauses (dependent infinitival, finite dependent) and phrases (noun, verb, prepositional phrases, complex nominals, coordinate phrases), as well rates per word of noun phrases and verb phrases. Additional features result from comparing part of speech sequences in the response to those observed in other responses to the same test at different score levels (Bhat & Yoon, 2015). These features are based on the observation that various POS sequences tend to occur more or less frequently in responses at different levels of proficiency. For example, the lowest scoring responses tend to not contain tags like WP (e.g., *whom*) and WDT (e.g., *whichever*), which, in declarative sentences, tend to signal relative clauses. Complex verb formations such as passive (VBD_VBN, e.g., *was seen*), gerund (VBG, e.g., *picking*), infinitive (TO_VB, e.g., *to come*) tend to occur more often in higher scoring responses, whereas the lower scoring responses tend to use simple tenses (e.g., VBZ—present tense verbs, e.g., *picks*). Some constructions could signal incorrect grammatical forms and their use declines with increasing proficiency; for example, RBR_JJR—a comparative adverb followed by a comparative adjective—is related to a common double-marking error in expressions such as *more easier*. Additional parts of speech tags specifically pertain to spoken discourse, such as UH (filler words such as *uh* or *um*) or GW (word fragments); their frequency declines with more fluent speech.

Variation in syntactic complexity with increasing L2 English proficiency was observed in **writing** as well. For example, Lu (2010) reported that features such as mean length of clause, proportion of dependent and coordinated clauses out of all clauses, number of complex nominals per clause and other features reflecting syntactic sophistication showed significant differences by proficiency level. Bhat & Yoon (2015) implemented Lu et al.'s features for the spoken language context, and found that most of them did not correlate significantly with speaking proficiency scores, the best correlation being $r = 0.14$ for the DCC feature (mean number of dependent clauses per clause). The authors hypothesized that one reason for the poor performance of the writing-based features in the speech context is that these features, operating at the deeper, clausal level of syntactic structures, are more prone to compounding of errors from the multi-stage processing required for their calculation. For example, errors in automated speech recognition and in sentence and clause boundary detection in spoken utterances could hamper the effectiveness of these features. The POS-based features require a somewhat more shallow automated analysis and are hence generally more robust to recognition errors than features that require a full syntactic parse of the sentence.

While the observations above suggest caution in borrowing writing-based features for scoring speech due to the additional layer of error inherent in the preliminary automated speech recognition step as well as to the added difficulty of identifying syntactically relevant units in the stream of speech without the help of punctuation, the work of Biber and colleagues (Biber & Gray, 2013; Biber et al., 2016) suggests that the reverse borrowing should also be conducted cautiously. In particular, there are systematic differences in grammatical (and lexical) patterns used in speech and in writing. For example, TOEFL test-takers are more likely to use colloquial features (e.g., pronouns, modal verbs) in speech than in writing, and they are more likely to use grammatical devices such as passive voice verbs and nominalizations in written responses. These differences do not pertain only to TOEFL test-takers; Biber & Gray (2013) comment that "In almost every regard, the patterns of linguistic variation found in TOEFL iBT responses parallel these more general patterns of variation found across spoken and written registers in English" (p. 64). Thus, while grammatical features might be good differentiators of proficiency in both speech and writing, the specific differentiating features for the two modalities might be different.

Features for capturing sophistication of **vocabulary** in SpeechRater are quite similar to those considered in the essay scoring context—type-token ratio and various features calculated off general word frequencies of the vocabulary in the response. As in writing, the length of the response and the number of different words used in the response are strong predictors of speaking proficiency; the feature counting the number of word types correlates at $r = 0.49$ with the TOEFL iBT speaking proficiency score (Yoon et al., 2020).

11.3.3 TOPIC DEVELOPMENT: CONTENT, DISCOURSE

The TOEFL iBT scoring rubric for the topic development dimension is as follows.

Score 4 Response is sustained and sufficient to the task. It is generally well developed and coherent; relationships between ideas are clear (or clear progression of ideas).

Score 3 Response is mostly coherent and sustained and conveys relevant ideas/information. Overall development is somewhat limited, usually lacks elaboration or specificity. Relationships between ideas may at times not be immediately clear.

Score 2 The response is connected to the task, though the number of ideas presented or the development of ideas is limited. Mostly basic ideas are expressed with limited elaboration (details and support). At times relevant substance may be vaguely expressed or repetitious. Connections of ideas may be unclear.

Score 1 Limited relevant content is expressed. The response generally lacks substance beyond expression of very basic ideas. Speaker may be unable to sustain speech to complete the task and may rely heavily on repetition of the prompt.

This aspect of the scoring rubric emphasizes topic development and coherence; in both of these areas, the approaches are similar to those employed for written responses, with some modifications.

For **topicality**, version 5.0 of SpeechRater included a feature based on content vector analysis that is very similar to that described in Attali & Burstein (2006).[5] Content vectors are constructed using pre-scored responses for each score point, and the incoming response is compared to each of the score point vectors, with the score point of the closest matching vector being used as a feature (max_cos). For the open-ended, defend-your-position-on-an-issue TOEFL Independent speaking task,[6] L. Chen, Zechner, et al. (2018) report a correlation of $r = 0.37$ with the human scores when the model vectors are built using human transcribed responses; when using automated speech recognition, the correlation is $r = 0.30$. Much like in the essay scoring literature, additional approaches to building the vectors were investigated, including using LSA (Xie et al., 2012), WordNet synsets (M. Chen & Zechner, 2012), and doc2vec (Tao et al., 2016).

For the TOEFL Integrated speaking task, where the test-taker is asked to use information provided in reading and listening stimuli to answer a question about certain specific details mentioned in the stimuli, L. Chen, Zechner, et al. (2018) report higher correlations for the max_cos feature ($r = 0.50$ when using human transcribed responses to build the model vectors) and better robustness to ASR errors ($r = 0.49$). For the same task, Evanini et al. (2013) found that a feature that looks at words used by the test-taker that overlap with the listening stimulus but not

---

[5]We discussed content vector analysis in the context of writing in Chapter 5.
[6]https://www.ets.org/s/toefl/pdf/speaking_practice_sets.pdf

with the reading one provide a strong quality signal; a parallel finding has been reported for the TOEFL Integrated writing items (Beigman Klebanov et al., 2014). The contrastive prompt use feature has the advantage that no pre-scored test-taker responses are required for its calculation, so it can be used with new, unseen prompts.

The work on assessment of the **coherence** of a spoken response is based on the relevant work in the essay scoring context. Wang and colleagues (X. Wang & Evanini, 2020; X. Wang et al., 2013; X. Wang, Evanini, et al., 2017) adapted the guidelines for annotation of discourse coherence on a 3-point scale from Burstein et al. (2010); annotators were asked to mark specific awkward points in an essay if they gave it a coherence rating of 2. The authors reported that the construct of coherence can be captured reasonably reliably for spoken responses ($k_q = 0.68$), and correlates at $r = 0.656$ with the holistic proficiency score; the number of awkward points correlated at $r = -0.626$ with the holistic score.

To automatically approximate coherence, "surface" features capturing frequencies of various grammatical cohesion-creating devices were created, such as counts of pronouns, conjunctions, discourse connectives; ratio of pronoun tokens to noun types; number of types of discourse connectives; features that capture the similarity of the chains of connectives in the given response to those derived from reference responses. Counts of types and tokens of discourse connectives had the highest correlations with human coherence scores ($r > 0.3$), both using transcribed data and automatically recognized data. Adding a coherence score predicted by the model with the "surface" features to a competitive SpeechRater baseline for predicting holistic scores resulted in an improvement in correlations from $r = 0.736$ to $r = 0.752$ (X. Wang & Evanini, 2020). X. Wang et al. (2013) experimented with entity-grid based features for modeling coherence (see Section 5.2.3 in Chapter 5); the authors show, consistently with the findings for the essay scoring context, that augmenting the entity-grid-based features with features measuring grammar, usage, mechanics improves the models.

X. Wang, Bruno, et al. (2017) report a study on enriching the discourse representation of a spoken response with annotation of its rhetorical structure. Adapting the Rhetorical Structure Theory based Discourse Treebank manual (L. Carlson & Marcu, 2001) originally developed for written newspaper text to account for phenomena specific to oral English language learner production, X. Wang, Bruno, et al. (2017) added relations such as disfluency (a disfluent span such as a false start or a self-correction is a satellite of a fluent span), awkward, unfinished utterance, discourse particle (such as *you know* or *all right*, treated as satellites of adjacent spans). X. Wang, Gyawali, et al. (2019) and X. Wang & Evanini (2020) report evaluations of features derived from the output of a rhetorical structure parser for prediction of coherence and holistic proficiency of spoken responses of non-native speakers. Type and token counts of rhetorical relations (excluding disfluencies and awkward relations) found in the response correlated at $r > 0.5$ with coherence scores and at $r = 0.3$–0.4 with proficiency scores.

11.4   SCORING MODELS

Linear regression and its variants are commonly used assessment contexts, due to their easy interpretability that makes them the models of choice even if other, more complex models can deliver a slightly better performance. In fact, a large scale evaluation of 7 different models, including random forest and support vector machines, showed no performance benefits over linear regression, on non-native spontaneous speech assessment data (Loukina et al., 2018). For some neural models for scoring of speech see L. Chen, Tao, et al. (2018); Craighead et al. (n.d.); Qian et al. (2018).

Another similarity to the essay scoring context is the need for a filtering model to reduce the chance of invalid scores due to a problematic characteristic of certain responses. Such non-scorable responses include technical problems with the recordings, as well as responses from non-cooperative test-takers, such as responses that are not in the target language, off-topic responses, canned (memorized) responses, extensive repetition, plagiarism; in the next chapter, we provide a brief review of research on detecting such responses, some of it coming from speech scoring contexts.

CHAPTER 12

Fooling the System: Gaming Strategies

12.1 INTRODUCTION

In Chapters 1 and 8, we introduced the notion of **construct validity** which said that the scores assigned by an automated scoring system *must* be aligned with the writing construct—the actual set of writing skills that the test is supposed to measure. However, if a test-taker employs external, *construct–irrelevant* means (unrelated to their writing skills) to obtain a higher score from the automated scoring system (or even human raters), perhaps by explicitly trying to exploit a weakness in the system, then those scores can no longer said to be valid. Furthermore, such scores also compromise test fairness since scores assigned to other test-takers who only put forth a good-faith effort are unfairly lower.

Even Page (1966) prognosticated that an automated scoring system might induce students to try and "game" it.

> *Won't this grading system be easy to con? Can't the shrewd student just put in the proxies which will get a good grade?*

It is true that test-takers can and do employ GAMING strategies to discover and exploit weaknesses of automated scoring systems. In fact, the use of these strategies is one of the more serious threats to score validity when it comes to high-stakes standardized tests given that the incentives to obtain a higher score are also significantly higher. Such strategies can involve repeating the same paragraphs over and over, deliberately varying sentence structure, replacing words with more sophisticated variants, re-using words from the prompt, using general academic words, plagiarizing from other responses or from material found on the Internet, inserting unnecessary *shell language*—linguistic scaffolding for organizing claims and arguments—and automated generation of essays (Bejar et al., 2014, 2013; Higgins & Heilman, 2014; Powers et al., 2001; Sobel et al., 2014). This is one of the primary reasons why it is not recommended that high-stakes standardized tests be scored *solely* by an automated scoring system but also by a human rater.

Gaming strategies are generally handled by building in filters or flags or advisories for aberrant responses or by changing the questions on the test frequently. However, developers of automated scoring systems can never anticipate all possible strategies and may have to react quickly as new ones are discovered in use, by developing new methods to identify them.

In this chapter, we discuss a few examples that illustrate the use of such strategies along with the corresponding solutions that can help detect their use.

12.2 SHELL LANGUAGE

The first case study we discuss is related to the use of SHELL LANGUAGE that we first introduced in Chapter 6. Recall that shell language can be defined as sequences of words used in persuasive writing or speaking to provide an organizational framework for an argument (Madnani et al., 2012). Therefore, the "shell" is the scaffolding that helps organize the parts that actually express the specific claims or evidence, or the "meat" of the argument. As an example, consider the following sentence from a hypothetical essay on whether schools should start later in the day: "I do not agree with the presented argument that we should begin the school day later because the evidence does not support the fact that a delayed school start helps with students' concentration". In this sentence, the underlined parts represent the shell while the non-underlined parts represent the meat.

How should shell language be treated when it comes to scoring essays? It is evident that shell language is a *necessary* component of writing a good persuasive essay. It would be near impossible for a proficient writer to construct convincing arguments without the help of the organizational support that shell expressions provide. Therefore, from a validity perspective, it is important to ensure that essays containing shell language are not inadvertently rewarded or punished for that reason alone.

The astute reader will notice that shell language is quite generalized in nature and does not necessarily include specific details related to the prompt to which the essay is being written. It is this property of shell language that makes it susceptible to potential use in a gaming strategy. One specific strategy that has been detected among some GRE® test-takers is the use of shell language to lengthen a response in a construct-irrelevant fashion. More specifically, the presence of *unnecessary* shell language can inflate scores since automated scoring systems tend to learn that longer essays are, for the most part, higher-scoring essays. Additional inflation in automated scores can also occur if the scoring system is looking for words related to argumentation as evidence of the writer's argumentation skill. Note that dealing with this strategy is a bit tricky: the goal is to distinguish responses that have been *artificially* lengthened—by inserting unnecessary shell language or "empty shells"—from responses that are appropriately longer due to a more detailed elaboration of an argument, for example.

Bejar et al. (2013) conduct a large-scale study on the prevalence of shell language in GRE® essays to determine whether *human* raters are fooled by "empty shells" into awarding higher scores. They first evaluate the shell language detection tool proposed by Madnani et al. (2012) on a corpus of 200,000 GRE® essays written to a total of 219 different prompts in the period between 2006 and 2010. They find that the shell language identified by the tool agreed reasonably with the characterization of shell in those essays by two expert human raters. This agreement is measured by computing overlaps between the shell spans reported by the software and those reported by each of the human raters. The authors find that the overlap of each rater with the tool is about 50%. Furthermore, the overlap of the shell scores produced by the tool with two different raters is also found to be positively related with an R^2 of .53.

In the second part of the study, the tool is used to sample essays with differing amounts of shell language. These sampled essays are then re-scored by two (different) expert human raters who are not told anything specific about the nature of the study but are simply asked to score the essays. The primary question for this experiment is whether human raters under *operational conditions* might be overly influenced by any unnecessary shell language in the essays and, therefore, assign high scores than said essays deserve. If this were the case, then having the essays re-scored by a different set of human raters under more relaxed, *non-operational* conditions will lead to discrepancies in scores. The authors report that although minor discrepancies were found, they were *not* a function of the amount of shell language in the essay. Therefore, the conclusion was that human raters tasked with assigning scores to GRE® essays in an operational setting are adequately trained to handle unnecessary shell language.

12.3   ARTIFICIALLY GENERATED ESSAYS

Automated scoring systems do not actually "read" the essays in the same way that human raters do but rather rely on features that are computed either by directly measuring an essay characteristic or by computing an approximation for it. The process of covering the desired construct with computationally feasible features can often leave cracks, allowing essays written using construct-irrelevant strategies to sneak through.

The presence of such cracks can be illustrated by automatically generating entire essays with characteristics that are specifically designed to target known weaknesses of automated scoring systems. For example, the Babel essay generation system (Sobel et al., 2014) is a tool that is specifically designed to generate such essays. Babel takes as input a list of keywords which is then used to randomly generate an essay that is syntactically well-formed and uses sophisticated English vocabulary but is completely incoherent semantically. For example, let us reconsider our hypothetical prompt on whether schools should start later in the day. If we provide the keywords "school", "day", and "late" to the Babel generator app,[1] it generates an essay with the following two first paragraphs.

> *School to ligations will always be a part of mankind. Humankind will always accuse twenty-four hour period; whether on conjecture or for the study of semiotics. The vastly intrepid late lies in the area of literature in addition to the search for semiotics. Why is solar day so precipitous to parsimony? The solution to this query is that late is piscine.*
>
> *As I have learned in my reality class, twenty-four hour period is the most fundamental atelier of human society. Despite the fact that the neutrino of proclamations emits orbitals, the same brain may catalyze two different gamma rays on the dictum. The same neuron may*

[1] http://babel-generator.herokuapp.com/

produce two different plasmas with the agronomist that is indubitably or considerately enormous to process gravity. A pendulum is not the only thing a brain for axioms spins; it also reacts at mean solar day. If the people involved solicit hagiolatry and advance, inconsistency by community with late can be more tensely amplified. Because organisms are abandoned to school, affronts which admonish the interlopers in question quarrel also of school.

As is evident from this excerpt, the generated essay means absolutely nothing but contains complete sentences containing long, rare words strung together in a syntactically well-formed fashion. The goal of the tool is to generate essays targeted at systems that produce a score based on surface characteristics such as grammar (counts of various types of grammatical constructions or grammatical errors) or vocabulary (e.g., average word length or word frequency) but not on features pertaining to the underlying meaning of a response. Given that such measures are indeed correlated with high-scoring essays, one could imagine many automated scoring systems being fooled into giving Babel-generated essays a high score.

Interestingly enough, the targeting strategy employed by the Babel essay generator might itself provide sufficient clues to detect the essays it generates. Such essays display characteristics that lie at the extreme opposite ends of the scale. The coherence contained in these essays is remarkably low while their syntactic well-formedness and vocabulary sophistication are both strikingly high.[2] Quantitatively, this divergence is very likely to be exhibited in the distributions of features representing these characteristics.

Cahill et al. (2018) confirmed this intuition for the e-rater® scoring engine; they found that the distributions of the grammaticality feature—a continuous value indicating how grammatical, on average, the essay is based on a trigram language model and n-gram counts—and the median word frequency feature for Babel-generated essays were *statistically significantly different* ($p < .001$) from their counterparts for actual essays written in good-faith. Due to this statistical property, they were able to develop a random-forest classifier that detected Babel-generated essays with 100% accuracy. This classifier was then adapted into an ADVISORY, a program that runs on any new incoming essay *before* the actual scoring system to flag aberrant responses, such as Babel-generated essays, and route them directly to a human rater—someone not very likely to be fooled—rather than letting the automated system assign a potentially invalid score.

Readers might observe, correctly, that generating an essay using a tool like Babel seems completely impractical in a real test setting. However, it is possible for a determined test-taker to pre-generate an essay using the tool, memorize (parts of) it, and reproduce it from memory at test time.

---

[2]See Chapter 5 for a detailed discussion on models of coherence and vocabulary sophistication.

12.4   OFF-TOPIC RESPONSES

Another strategy that test-takers might employ upon encountering an unfamiliar or difficult topic in a test is to instead write about a different topic altogether, one that they are either more familiar with or have memorized a response to. Such responses are termed *off-topic*. Of course, it is entirely possible that test-takers may unintentionally write an off-topic response based on, say, a good-faith misinterpretation of the assigned topic. In any case, it is best that such cases be judged by a human rater who is in a better position to determine whether the off-topicness of the response was inadvertent or deliberate. Therefore, it is important to develop automated approaches for detecting off-topic responses. Over the years, many such approaches have been developed and most, if not all, of them rely on computing some measure of similarity between the text of the question and the response text, usually by projecting both texts in a semantic vector space and computing their cosine similarity (J. Cheng & Shen, 2011; Higgins et al., 2006; Louis & Higgins, 2010). While we focus here on off-topicness, it is worth pointing out that we discussed more general models for quantifying essay topicality in Chapte 5. Next, we present a more interesting approach to detecting off-topic responses inspired by image recognition techniques.

X. Wang, Yoon, et al. (2019) present a unique approach to computing the similarity between a given response and the prompt text. They create what they term "similarity grids", two-dimensional grids with the (content) words from the prompt text laid out from left to right and the words from the response (automatically transcribed to text using automated speech recognition) laid out from top to bottom. Each cell (i, j) in the grid contains a value of the similarity between the ith content word from the response and the jth content word from the prompt text. The authors then make the insightful link that these two-dimensional grids can, in fact, be thought of as *grayscale images* with "lighter" cells indicating higher similarity and "darker" ones indicating lower similarity. See Figure 12.1 for an example illustrating these "images". Of course, there is no reason that such grids have to be graysale images; they can also be "RGB images" with three channels per image, each "channel" providing additional information to the network. For example, the other two channels in an RGB image could contain the IDF values for the response and prompt words, respectively, converting an unweighted similarity measure to a weighted measure with more important words contributing more.

Once we arrive in the realm of images, the next step follows somewhat naturally: use supervised deep learning techniques from computer vision to solve a binary classification problem—classify the darker grids as class 1 (off-topic) and the lighter ones as class 0 (on-topic). The authors use the powerful Inception networks from the computer vision literature (Szegedy, Ioffe, et al., 2016; Szegedy, Vanhoucke, et al., 2016)—very deep neural networks consisting of dozens of layers of CNNs. These networks are chosen because of their strong performance on the task of image recognition. The authors train the Inception networks on approximately 184,000 spoken responses from 283 different test questions designed for a high-stakes English speaking assessment. Of course, the number of authentic off-topic responses in the corpus is significantly

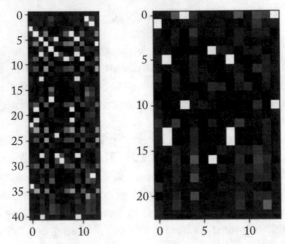

Figure 12.1: Grayscale images representing the two-dimensional similarity grids for an on-topic response on the left and an off-topic one on the right. It is clear that the off-topic response contains more darker cells than the on-topic response. Figure reproduced from X. Wang, Yoon, et al. (2019).

low leading to a highly imbalanced classification problem. To get around this issue for any given topic, the authors simply sample responses from different, unrelated topics as the off-topic responses, maintaining an equal proportion for on-topic and off-topic responses.

The authors show that the best performing network in their proposed approach attains 93% F1 on the off-topic detection task on their artificially constructed dataset, handily beating a baseline approach using a random-forest classifier with various word-embedding based similarity measures as features. Although this work focuses on spoken responses, it can easily be ported to the writing setting since the response used to create the similarity grid is plain text, not audio.

12.5   PLAGIARISM

In the previous section, we described how X. Wang, Yoon, et al. (2019) use image recognition techniques to detect off-topic responses where the primary characteristic is that there is *too little* shared content between the essay and the prompt. However, one could also flip the problem around and use the *same* technology to detect cases where there is *too much* shared content between the essay and some other external material. This, of course, is the definition of PLAGIARISM—copying material from other sources and passing it off as original content—and is one of the most common strategies that students and test-takers can employ.

There has been a lot work on detecting plagiarism (Bär et al., 2012; Kakkonen & Mozgovoy, 2010; Potthast et al., 2014) and, like its complementary problem of off-topic detection, most of it relies on computing similarity measures between different essays or between the essays and sources such as Wikipedia articles or other well-known reference material from the Internet. For example, *Turnitin*—one of the most popular tools used for detecting plagiarism—has indexed more than 70 billion online resources against which teachers can check students' writing submissions (Walchuk, 2016).

However, in a standardized test setting, test-takers are usually not allowed access to the Internet and have a limited amount of time to write. Plagiarism manifests in a different fashion in such settings. For higher-stakes tests such as IELTS®, GRE®, and TOEFL®, there is generally a large number of example essays available either as part of test preparation courses or shared by other test-takers in online communities and discussion forums. Test-takers interested in employing this strategy can memorize such essay (or parts of them) that they can then reproduce as CANNED RESPONSES (responses containing memorized segments from external sources such as test prep websites) when taking the test. The techniques used to detect canned responses are mostly the same (X. Wang, Evanini, et al., 2019) with the modification that a response needs to be compared to multiple potential sources of plagiarism whereas off-topic responses only have to be compared to the prompt text. Additionally, in order to effectively apply such similarity-based plagiarism techniques, test developers have to monitor the test preparation materials being shared online and periodically update the index of materials that is used by the plagiarism checker.

12.6   OTHER RELATED WORK

So far, we have discussed specific gaming strategies and techniques that have been developed to detect their use. In this section, we will focus on more general studies that analyze different types of gaming behavior and placing them in broader frameworks.

Powers et al. (2001) conduct a study to determine how easy it is to fool an automated scoring system by asking several writing experts to compose essays explicitly targeting the system. The group of experts recruited for the study is quite diverse; it includes members of the writing community known to be skeptics of automated scoring, members of the test-development team from the Educational Testing Service, computational linguists, among many others. Participants are given two GRE® prompts along with a detailed description of the e-rater® automated scoring, the scoring rubric for each prompt, and samples of previously scored essays for each prompt. They are then asked to write two essays for each prompt—one that they think would be assigned a *higher* score than it deserved and another they think would be assigned a *lower* score than deserved. They are also asked to provide their reasoning behind their predictions of higher or lower scores. The essays written by the experts are then scored by e-rater as well as by two trained human raters on a scale of 1 to 6. The human raters were aware of the provenance of the essays but not of the specific strategies that the writer might have employed. At the end, the difference between the e-rater score and the average score of the two raters is computed for each submitted essay.

In total, 27 participants submitted a total of 63 essays. The 2 human raters agreed exactly or within 1 score point of one another 92% of the time for the scores they awarded. e-rater agreed exactly or within one score point with each of the two raters 65% of the time. The study participants predicted that they would receive a higher e-rater score than the average human score for 30 essays and were correct 87% of the time (26 out of the 30 did get a higher e-rater score). The predictions of lower e-rater score were only accurate 42% of the time (10 actual out of 24 predicted). The top strategies that writers employed to fool e-rater into giving a higher score are: (a) write several paragraphs and then repeat them multiple times (5 point difference in the worst case![3]); (b) use varied sentence structure, words related to the prompt, and discourse cue words but provide no actual critical analysis of the argument in the prompt (3.5 point difference); and (c) write an essay that "rambles on", uses faulty logic or uses a "haphazard" progression of ideas but sprinkle in some relevant content words and a few complex sentences (3 point difference). Conversely, it proved much more difficult to get e-rater to award lower scores than human raters. Only two essays managed to obtained differences of greater than 1 point in that direction. One made extensive use of metaphors and literary allusion while avoiding the use of specific words that e-rater pays attention to.

This valuable adversarial study shows that it is indeed possible for responses employing construct-irrelevant strategies to trick the system into awarding unnecessarily high scores. Since this study was published, e-rater has gained a plethora of advisories that can detect a variety of bad-faith behavior and route the responses directly to a human (Breyer et al., 2014; Ramineni et al., 2015; M. Zhang et al., 2013, 2016).

In a similar vein, Higgins & Heilman (2014) attempt to quantify how susceptible an automated scoring system may be to different gaming strategies. Their specific use case is the automated scoring of short content-focused responses (like those we discussed in Chapter 10). As part of their experimental setup, they use the top three different open-source automated scoring systems entries from the Automated Short Answer Scoring Prize (ASAP2) contest that we also described in Chapter 10. Their experiments consist of artificially modifying the responses in the original ASAP2 dataset to reflect the use of three different gaming strategies: (1) using longer responses; (2) re-using words from the prompt text; and (3) over-using general academic words. The modified responses are then scored by the three chosen systems and their scores examined for any systematic impact of the three gaming strategies. The simulations carried out show that the chosen, relatively simple gaming strategies show varying degrees of effectiveness across the three systems, and across the ten content scoring tasks in the dataset. For specific combinations of systems and tasks, gaming strategies range from having almost no effect to producing a mean increase of more than a full score point. The authors also show that it is not always easy to predict which gaming strategy will influence a system based solely on the system architecture. Given these observations, the authors conclude with a recommendation

---

[3] For the 26 essays that were correctly predicted to get a higher score from e-rater than from human raters, three had a difference of 3 or more points, five of 2 to 3 points, 12 of 1 to 1.5 points, and six of .5 points.

to explicitly measure the impact of gaming strategies *before* any scoring system is operationally deployed such that appropriate filter or advisories can be developed and deployed along with the system to ensure valid scores.

In another study, Yoon et al. (2018) describe a general operational processing pipeline for detecting non-scorable responses, i.e., atypical responses for which an automated scoring system is not likely to predict valid scores. Some non-scorable responses are simply the result of unintentional system errors, e.g., background noise for spoken responses or a malfunction in the text capture systems for written responses. However, some non-scorable responses are user-initiated, e.g., off-topic responses, canned responses, responses in a foreign language, or responses that only contain keyboard banging. The authors apply the pipeline to both automated speech scoring as well as automated essay scoring and focus on different parts of the pipeline at which such non-scorable responses can be detected: (1) at the input stage when the essay enters the automated scoring pipeline, (2) during the feature generation stage, and (3) during the score generation stage. For example, off-topic responses would generally be detected at the input stage while automatically generated essays from Babel would be detected during the feature generation stage.

12.7   SUMMARY

In this chapter, we described the basic idea behind construct-irrelevant response strategies or gaming strategies—the idea of using means other than the writer's own skill to obtain a higher score than is deserved. We looked at a few specific gaming strategies that are employed by test-takers, especially in high-stakes contexts, and also discussed potential methods to detect them. Finally, we discussed a few studies that helped us think about gaming strategies in a more general way. As long as automated scoring systems are used to score consequential tests, test-takers will be incentivized to compromise such systems in ingenious ways, in turn requiring system developers to think up their own ingenious methods for detecting the test-takers strategies, and so on.

PART V

Summary and Discussion

CHAPTER 13

Looking Back, Looking Ahead

In this final chapter of the book, let us take stock of the ground we have covered and look ahead to what is next for automated essay evaluation. Going back to the beginning and to the 1966 Ellis Page's eloquent argument in support of the endeavor of automated essay scoring, let us first consider how far the field has come, against the backdrop of the expectations and the hurdles laid out in that paper. The discussion in this chapter draws heavily on the theme paper on automated essay scoring presented by the authors at the 2020 meeting of the Association for Computational Linguistics (Beigman Klebanov & Madnani, 2020).

13.1 REPORT CARD: WHERE ARE WE NOW?

13.1.1 ACCOMPLISHMENTS

Page's minimal desiderata have certainly been achieved—AWE systems today can score in agreement with the average human rater, at least in some contexts. For example, Pearson's Intelligent Essay Assessor™ (IEA) scores essays written for the Pearson Test of English (PTE) as well as for other contexts: "IEA was developed more than a decade ago and has been used to evaluate millions of essays, from scoring student writing at elementary, secondary and university level, to assessing military leadership skills".[1] Besides sole automated scoring as for PTE, there are additional contexts where the automated score is used in addition to a human score, such as for essays written for the Graduate Record Examination (GRE®)[2] or for the Test of English as a Foreign Language (TOEFL®).[3]

During the course of this book, we took a deep dive into what makes an automated scoring system tick. We went hands-on to build and evaluate an actual (albeit simplistic) automated scoring system on real data in Chapter 2. We discussed the nuances of what it takes to create an automated scoring system in the real world in Chapter 3. Next, we discussed in detail the two core components of automated scoring systems: the machine learning models that power them (Chapter 4) and the features that the models use—both generic writing features, e.g., those measuring discourse, organization, coherence (Chapter 5), and genre- and task-specific ones such as those used for scoring persuasive writing versus narrative writing (Chapter 6). Next, we briefly discussed areas related to automated essay scoring such as scoring for content (Chapter 10) and scoring open-ended spoken responses (Chapter 11).

---

[1]https://pearsonpte.com/the-test/about-our-scores/how-is-the-test-scored/
[2]https://www.ets.org/gre/revised_general/scores/how/
[3]https://www.ets.org/toefl/ibt/scores/understand/

Does this mean that the problem of automated writing evaluation is solved? Well, not exactly.

13.1.2   NEEDS IMPROVEMENT

As we discussed in Chapter 1, Page (1966) anticipated some difficulties for AWE systems—many of them are still work in progress.

Originality

Page worried that an original writer would be underscored by the computer—perhaps because the features taken into account are but approximations of the real properties of good writing and so could fail to capture some of the instances thereof—especially those that are not *typically* displayed by good essays. In Chapter 1, we observed that there exists some recent work on capturing aspects of essays that are often considered creative, such as use of figurative language; we also noted that the testing context might not be conducive to displaying creativity, since more creative, out-of-the-ordinary writing goes with a higher risk of mis-interpretation—by humans, not only by machines.

Having reviewed in detail the variety of features for essay scoring, in general (Chapter 5) and for specific genres (Chapter 6), we may add that the best defense against mis-scoring original essays is to make sure that the scoring system is as comprehensive as possible in its assessment of the complex and multi-faceted construct of writing quality. Research on automated scoring systems has come a long way since Page's set of relatively simplistic features—not only have such elusive constructs as topicality or coherence been explored and quantified, but much more genre-specific constructs such as form and quality of arguments, development of a narrative, coverage of a summary, or type of reflection activity evidenced in writing have been modeled computationally. Assuming that any *good* essay—original or less so—complies with the stated requirements of a scoring rubric, modeling these requirements as closely and comprehensively as possible would help do justice to good essays and correctly give lower scores to essays that do not adhere to those requirements.

Gaming

Students and test-takers do employ gaming strategies to discover and exploit weaknesses of AWE systems. We have reviewed some such strategies in Chapter 12, including use of unnecessary formulaic language (shell), off-topic responses, plagiarism, as well as usage of automatically pre-generated essays. Such strategies are generally handled by building in filters, or advisories, for aberrant responses. However, it is challenging for developers of automated scoring systems to keep up to date with the evolving strategies employed by motivated test-takers. This is most often the case in high-stakes standardized tests where test-takers have a larger incentive to gain a higher-than-deserved score to aid admission to an institution of higher education or to obtain professional certification. This is one of the reasons standardized tests are often not scored *solely* by an AWE system but also by a human rater. We will return to the standardized testing context in Section §13.2.2.

Content

Work has been done over the last decade on automated evaluation of written responses for their content and not their general writing quality; in Chapter 10, we have reviewed reference-based and response-based approaches, as well as the emergent trend of using deep neural networks for this task. Scoring for content focuses primarily on what students know, have learned, or can do in a *specific* subject area such as Computer Science, Biology, or Music, with the fluency of the response being secondary. For example, some spelling or grammar errors are acceptable as long as the desired specific information (e.g., scientific principles, trends in a graph, or details from a reading passage) is included in the response. Note that most current content scoring systems ascertain the "correctness" of a response based on its similarity to other responses that humans have deemed to be correct or, at least, high-scoring; they do not employ explicit fact-checking or reasoning for this purpose.

Considerations of the quality of the content are also often incorporated into automated essay scoring systems, to a certain extent. For example, we discussed ways to measure the extent to which an essay is on-topic (Chapter 5, Section 5.3.2), or that is uses good arguments (Chapter 6, Section 6.2.5), or that a source-based essay touches upon the major points made in the source text (Chapter 6, Section 6.4). Generally speaking, depending on the specific task and genre, there might be more or less focus on the *correctness* of the content, and a valid scoring system for the task needs to cover the content-related aspects of the scoring rubric, if present, along with the more generic ones related to flow, conventions, grammatical, and lexical sophistication.

Feedback

In Chapter 11, we briefly discussed some common desiderata for feedback, such as evaluation, timeliness, continuity, and usefulness. We also observed that many of the aspects of writing quality that are captured in scoring features are also the ones on which automated feedback can be provided in order to encourage the user to improve that aspect of writing. Examples include feedback on argument construction, on source text coverage, quality of reflection, topic development, coherence, vocabulary, and others.

Can we then put a green check-mark against Page's agenda for automated feedback, which "may magnify and disseminate the best human capacities to criticize, evaluate, and correct"? Alas, not yet; research on effectiveness of automated feedback on writing is inconclusive (Bai & Hu, 2017; J. Choi, 2010; Englert et al., 2007; Grimes & Warschauer, 2010; Ranalli et al., 2017; Roscoe & McNamara, 2013; Shermis et al., 2008; J. Wilson, 2017; J. Wilson & Czik, 2016). One potential reason for the different outcomes is difference in user populations—feedback that works for L1 writers might not work for L2 writers; differences in ages, skill levels, presence, or absence of learning disabilities could all play a role. Adjustment of the evaluation methodology to the specific *purpose* of the writing assistance tool is another issue for consideration; we will return to this issue in Section §13.3.

13.2   GOING OFF THE PAGE

So far, Page's outline of the promises and challenges of AWE have provided a good framework for surveying the field. There are also a number of developments that were not mapped on Page's chart; let us now consider those.

13.2.1   ASSESSING WRITING IN MULTIPLE LANGUAGES

In order to advance the work on understanding and assessing writing quality, there is clearly a need for a multi-lingual perspective, since methods developed for one language or dialect may not work for another. This consideration does not appear in Page (1966), yet it is an active line of subsequent work. While this book has focused on English, various aspects of writing evaluation, e.g., annotation, detection of various types of errors, and building AWE systems, have been researched for a variety of languages: W. Song et al. (2016), G. Rao et al. (2017), Shiue et al. (2017) worked with data in Chinese, Lorenzen et al. (2019) in Danish, Berggren et al. (2019) in Norwegian, Amorim & Veloso (2017) in Portuguese, Stymne et al. (2017) in Swedish, Berkling (2018) and Weiss & Meurers (2019) in German, Mezher & Omar (2016) in Arabic, Kakkonen et al. (2005) in Finnish, Loraksa & Peachavanish (2007) in Thai, Lemaire & Dessus (2001) in French, and Ishioka & Kameda (2006) in Japanese. The list is by no means exhaustive; see Flor & Cahill (2020) for a recent review.

13.2.2   STANDARDIZED TESTING

The use of automated evaluation technology envisioned by Page was as a service to reduce a teacher's burden; to eventually "lift from the shoulders of the English teacher, that brave and harried soul, his perpetual pressure of unassigned papers, or his unassuaged guilt". While such use has certainly been made (Burstein et al., 2004; Grimes & Warschauer, 2010), the most visible use case for AWE technology has arguably evolved to be in the context of standardized testing, be it for a test of English such as TOEFL® or PTE, a broader, more advanced psychometric examination such as the GRE® or GMAT, or for professional licensure such as AICPA or PRAXIS®.

This development of often high-stakes usage has led to somewhat different challenges from those that Page had anticipated. These challenges generally fall under the purview of the field of educational measurement (Bennett & Bejar, 1998; Clauser et al., 2002; Williamson et al., 2012): How to ensure that the automatic scores assigned to test-takers are (1) *valid*, i.e., they actually measure the skill that the test developer designed the test to measure, (2) *defensible*, i.e., there is a reasonably clear explanation of why test-takers received the particular scores they did, and (3) *fair* to all the test-takers.

We addressed construct validity in detail in Chapters 1 and 8 where we discussed how construct irrelevance and construct under-representation can both be considered serious threats to the validity of an automated system's scores. We addressed defensibility by discussing the notion of interpretability of automated scoring models in Chapter 4—more powerful and sophisticated machine learning models can certainly have better predictive performance but they might be lacking in explainability which is why linear regression and its variants are still the more defensible choice. We summarize fairness in the next section.

An additional challenge of high-stakes usage is how to architect scoring systems for large-scale, low-latency use which requires them to be reliable, scalable, flexible, and selective in terms of software and application frameworks. We discussed these architectural considerations in detail in Chapter 7.

13.2.3   INCREASED ATTENTION TO FAIRNESS

It would probably not be an overstatement to say that fairness in AI is quickly becoming its own sub-field, with a new annual ACM conference on Fairness, Accountability, and Transparency having been inaugurated in 2018[4] and relevant research appearing at many impactful publication venues, such as Science (Caliskan et al., 2017), NIPS (Kim et al., 2018; Pleiss et al., 2017), ICML (Kearns et al., 2018), ACL (D. Hovy & Spruit, 2016; Sap et al., 2019; Sun et al., 2019), KDD (Speicher et al., 2018), AAAI (J. Zhang & Bareinboim, 2018), and others (Dwork et al., 2012; Hajian & Domingo-Ferrer, 2013). There is also recent work that examines fairness and ethical considerations when using AI in education (Gardner et al., 2019; Mayfield et al., 2019).

The educational measurement community has long been studying fairness in automated scoring (AERA, 2014; Ramineni & Williamson, 2013; Williamson et al., 2012) and in that field, fairness considerations dictate that the test reflects the same construct(s) for the entire test taking population, that scores from the test have the same meaning for all the test taking population, and that a fair test does not offer undue advantages (or disadvantages) to some individuals because of their characteristics—such as those associated with race, ethnicity, gender, age, socioeconomic status, or linguistic or cultural background—or the test characteristics itself, e.g., the different prompts shown to different test-takers at test time. We described this measurement-driven notion of fairness as the absence of differential subgroup performance in more detail in Chapter 8.

The recent progress made by the NLP community toward enhancing the usual accuracy-based evaluations with some of these psychometric analyses—from computing indicators of potential biases in automatic scores across various demographic sub-groups to computing new metrics that incorporate measurement theory to produce more reliable indicators of system performance—is quite promising (Loukina et al., 2019; Madnani, Loukina, von Davier, et al., 2017).

---

[4]https://facctconference.org/

13.2.4   PERVASIVENESS OF TECHNOLOGY

Page's *gedankenexperiment* on the potential of automated essay evaluation in a classroom context no doubt appeared audacious in 1966 but nothing back then could have prepared his readers to the pervasiveness of technology we are experiencing today. Today you can very literally carry your AWE system in your pocket; you can even carry several. You can use them (almost) at any time and at any place—not only in classrooms, but at home, at work, and even while texting with a friend.

This is perhaps the biggest issue that Page's vision did not address: the possibility of universal availability and the concomitant co-optation of a tool beyond its original intended purpose. Much like the calculator—invented by Blaise Pascal to help his father with the tedious arithmetic of tax collection—ended up "freeing" people from the burden of figuring out their intended tip at a restaurant through mental arithmetic, a future writing aid meant to help a student improve his argument writing assignment for a class could end up being used by a lawyer for composing her closing argument. Since such usages are on the horizon, we should consider the implications now.

13.3   DISCUSSION

Once an invention is out in the open, it is difficult to predict what specific uses people would put it to. How do we go about evaluating the tool if we don't know what the user's goal is? While it isn't possible to anticipate all specific uses, it is possible, we believe, to consider the *types* of uses that suggest different evaluation strategies. From the current vantage point, we see three types of uses.

13.3.1   SUPPORT CONSEQUENTIAL DECISION MAKING

The first use is where a consequential decision about the writer or a related entity (such as a class or a school) is being made based on the written product. This use is exemplified by the application of automated scoring in a standardized testing context to decide on admissions to an institution of higher education or the granting of a professional licenses; other cases such as course placement decisions, coursework grading, or even extension of a job offer (where the submission of a writing sample is a part of the job application process) would belong to this type of use. In all such cases, the automated system needs to provide valid and fair scores (or other types of feedback), since the livelihood or professional trajectory of people might depend on the outcome. We have dealt with the particulars of this case in detail in Section §13.2.2.

We observe that sometimes consequential decisions might be made based on an evaluation of a writing sample for a construct that is different from quality of writing, per se. For example, we mentioned cases where writing is taken to be a reflection of the user's knowledge (as in content scoring) or experience (as in reflective writing), and writing evaluation methods can be built to assess those constructs, not necessarily the construct of writing quality.

It has long been known that writing style is a quantifiable and sufficiently personal characteristic to enable attribution of a written text to its author; see, for example, the classic study on the attribution of the disputed Federalist papers to Hamilton vs. Madison based on a contrastive analysis of function word usage (Mosteller & Wallace, 1963), or the early neural network classifier that learned to attribute plays to either Shakespeare or Marlowe based on features derived from function word distributions (Merriam & Matthews, 1994). Evaluation from the point of view of authorship attribution goes beyond literary scholarship, however; it can support highly consequential decisions in contexts such as criminal law, civil law, forensics; see Stamatatos (2009) for a review of methods and applications. Evaluation of writing (or transcripts of speech) can also target detection of clinically relevant conditions such as depression or mental disorders (Gutierrez et al., 2017; Resnik et al., 2013; Roark et al., 2011). In these applications, as well, the notions of validity, fairness, and defensibility of the automated evaluation come into play.

13.3.2   CREATE A BETTER WRITTEN PRODUCT

The second type of use is one where the focus is on the final product, namely, the actual piece of writing produced following the writer's use of AWE technology. In this context, it does not much matter exactly what part of the final product is due to the human and which part is due to the machine—perhaps the machine only corrected misspellings, or suggested improvements for the human to vet, or maybe the human only contributed the very first ideation, and the machine has done the rest. Perhaps all the human writer contributed was the thesis ("I think school should start at 8 rather than 7") and then clicked "submit" to get back an essay making a cogent and convincing case in support of the thesis. Mining large textual databases for arguments and evaluating them are feasible today as recently demonstrated by IBM's Debater technology[5] (Gretz et al., 2019; Levy et al., 2017; Rinott et al., 2015); introduce some figuration to make it more appealing (Veale, 2018; Veale et al., 2017) and storify it (Radford et al., 2019; Riegl & Veale, 2018), et voilà!

This type of use is essentially a machine's augmentation of human ability, and is hinted at, for example, in a customer testimonial for Grammarly: "Grammarly allows me to get those communications out and feel confident that I'm putting my best foot forward. Grammarly is like a little superpower, especially when I need to be at 110%". The human presumably remains at the same level of ability, but the product of the machine—human collaboration is superior to what the human alone could have produced. Indeed, for this use case, measures capturing improvement across drafts are often used for evaluation.

Within the product-centered evaluation paradigm, there could be various specific objectives other than the improvement of the holistic quality of the piece of writing; it could be an increase in the speed of production, or the maximization of click-through rate in an advertisement text, for example.

[5]https://www.research.ibm.com/artificial-intelligence/project-debater/

13.3.3   HELP THE USER LEARN TO WRITE BETTER

The third type of use for AWE software is to help the writer improve his or her writing skill. Scores or other types of feedback are designed, in this context, to provide tutoring or guidance, not for fixing specific problems in the current piece of writing but to help the user learn more general skills that would make the first draft of their *next* essay better than the first draft of their current essay.

Evaluation of a tool though a demonstration of skill-improvement—the efficacy of the tool—is a complicated endeavor; we briefly outlined how such evaluations could proceed in Chapter 11. A tool that allows for monitoring of improvement in skill (even if the improvement is due to other factors such as school instruction or participation in some activity or community) could also be useful in the broader context of skill-oriented use, as the learner and the teacher would be able to tell that improvement is happening, even if we do not know exactly why. Improvement in important aspects of learning such as motivation and self-efficacy could also provide value to the learner (Grimes & Warschauer, 2010; J. Wilson & Roscoe, 2020).

13.3.4   RELATIONSHIPS BETWEEN TYPES OF USE

One could argue that an ideal automated writing assistant would support all the different goals at once—help one produce better writing, help one learn, and do both in a psychometrically responsible fashion—benefits are not restricted to certain types of users more than others—so that decision-making based on the outcome of the usage of the tool can also be supported.

Indeed, the uses are not necessarily mutually exclusive. For example, the human augmentation and consequential decision use cases could apply at the same time. It is possible that, at some future point in time, spelling will be deemed to lie outside of the construct targeted by the consequential assessment of writing and spell-correction software will be made available to test-takers. However, this would require a careful examination of the impact of correction on the distributions and interpretations of the scores. In particular, I. Choi & Cho (2018) found that manually vetted correction of spelling errors yielded a significant increase in scores assigned to the essays by trained raters, and that, even after controlling for the error quantity and quality predictors, the magnitude of the average gain in the score was smaller for responses with higher original scores. Add to the mix the finding that automated spelling correction is more accurate on essays that are of better quality to begin with (Flor, 2012), and it's likely that the automated assessment of an automatically spell-corrected version of an essay might show an unexpected relationship with original scores that would need to be closely examined for bias or for an increase in construct-irrelevant variance.

Human augmentation and consequential decision could also be somewhat at odds, in certain contexts. For example, the machine's input could dilute the evidence for an evaluation from the authorship attribution point of view. Had the infamous Unabomber used Writing Mentor's transition terms feedback to diversify his discourse connectives, perhaps the case against Theodore Kaczynski would not have been so strong, seeing as some of his signature items included expressions like *at any rate*, *moreover*, and *on the other hand* (Coulthard et al., 2016, p. 163); actually, he might not even have been found had an automated assistant decided to nix some instances of "cool-headed logician" from his manifesto.[6,7]

It is also possible that the effect of using a tool optimized for one use case could be the opposite of what another use case requires. If "use it or lose it" has any truth to it, a potential consequence of extensive, consistent, and pervasive human augmentation for producing superior written products is an adverse impact on the skill of the human in the human—machine team. If the near universal adoption of calculators is any guide, once a skill (long division) can be reliably outsourced to a machine, humans stop valuing it in daily practice and, therefore, might set out to lose it in the long run.[8] Spelling is a likely candidate writing skill where reliable access to high quality correction software could make humans stop worrying about it rather than invest effort in improving it.

13.4 CONCLUSION

In his visionary paper from 1966, Ellis Page provided a proof-of-concept demonstration of the possibility of automated grading of essays, as well as outlined some potential challenges to its adoption. Subsequent research and practice have delivered on Page's minimum desiderata for an AWE system; current research is working to address the outstanding challenges dealing with a variety of languages, content domains, and writing tasks.

The field of AWE has thus progressed according to the trajectory charted by Page to a large extent, though not completely. In particular, while Page imagined the main use case of AWE to be in the service of a harried teacher and his feedback-thirsty students, in reality, the most visible use case has arguably evolved to be automated scoring of essays for standardized testing, which, in turn, has led to new challenges, such as ensuring the validity and fairness of scores, as well as the scalability of the scoring system.

The other development that Page could not anticipate is the sheer pervasiveness of technology in people's daily lives; AWE software can be made available not only in classrooms to be used under the watchful eye of the English teacher, but (almost) anywhere and at any time, including on mobile devices. While it is difficult to predict specific uses people would find for such software, we outlined a number of *types* of use, depending on the goal: (a) consequential decision making about the user; (b) delivery of the best possible written product in partnership

---

[6]"A term in Ted Kazinscki's (unibomber) manifesto that was recognized by his brother, causing him to call the FBI". (The Urban Dictionary)

[7]See Coulthard et al. (2016) pages 162–163 for a short account of the Unabomber case; Foster (2000) for a more detailed report. The 2017 Discovery Channel miniseries "Manhunt: Unabomber" narrates this triumph of forensic linguistics.

[8]1989 Curriculum and Evaluation Standards for School Mathematics from the National Council of Teachers of Mathematics recommend in the Summary of Changes to Content and Emphasis in K-4 Mathematics (p. 21) decreasing the attention devoted to long division specifically and to "complex paper-and-pencil computations" in general; the recommendation for grades 5–8 is likewise to decrease emphasis on "tedious paper-and-pencil computations" (p. 71). https://archive.org/details/curriculumevalua00nati. The document has sparked substantial controversy, including with regards to long division (Klein & Milgram, 2000).

with the user; and (c) assisting the user in improving her writing skills. We believe that we, as researchers, can help users find *value* in our technology by considering the goals, engaging partners from other relevant disciplines, and designing the tools as well as their e*valu*ations to focus on specific types of use.

Definitions-in-Context

Index

References

AERA. (2014). *Standards for Educational and Psychological Testing*. American Educational Research Association.

Agarwal, O., Durupınar, F., Badler, N. I., & Nenkova, A. (2019). Word Embeddings (Also) Encode Human Personality Stereotypes. In *Proceedings of the Eighth Joint Conference on Lexical and Computational Semantics (*SEM 2019)* (pp. 205–211). doi: http://dx.doi.org/10.18653/v1/s19-1023

Aggarwal, C. C. (2018). *Neural Networks and Deep Learning*. Springer International Publishing. doi: http://dx.doi.org/10.1007/978-3-319-94463-0

Ajjour, Y., Chen, W.-F., Kiesel, J., Wachsmuth, H., & Stein, B. (2017). Unit Segmentation of Argumentative Texts. In *Proceedings of the Workshop on Argument Mining* (pp. 118–128). doi: http://dx.doi.org/10.18653/v1/w17-5115

Akbik, A., Blythe, D., & Vollgraf, R. (2018). Contextual String Embeddings for Sequence Labeling. In *Proceedings of the International Conference on Computational Linguistics (COLING)* (pp. 1638–1649).

Alfonseca, E., & Pérez, D. (2004). Automatic Assessment of Open Ended Questions with a BLEU-Inspired Algorithm and Shallow NLP. In *Advances in Natural Language Processing* (pp. 25–35). Springer. doi: http://dx.doi.org/10.1007/978-3-540-30228-5_3

Alikaniotis, D., Yannakoudakis, H., & Rei, M. (2016). Automatic Text Scoring Using Neural Networks. In *Proceedings of the Annual Meeting of the Association for Computational Linguistics (ACL)* (pp. 715–725). doi: http://dx.doi.org/10.18653/v1/p16-1068

Al-Khatib, K., Wachsmuth, H., Hagen, M., Köhler, J., & Stein, B. (2016). Cross-Domain Mining of Argumentative Text through Distant Supervision. In *Proceedings of the Conference of the North American Chapter of the Association for Computational Linguistics: Human Language Technologies (NAACL-HLT)* (pp. 1395–1404). doi: http://dx.doi.org/10.18653/v1/n16-1165

Allen, L., Crossley, S., Snow, E., & McNamara, D. (2014). L2 Writing Practice: Game Enjoyment as a Key to Engagement. *Language Learning & Technology*, *18*(2), 124–150.

Amorim, E., Cançado, M., & Veloso, A. (2018). Automated Essay Scoring in the Presence of Biased Ratings. In *Proceedings of the Conference of the North American Chapter of the Association for Computational Linguistics: Human Language Technologies (NAACL-HLT)* (pp. 229–237). doi: http://dx.doi.org/10.18653/v1/n18-1021

Amorim, E., & Veloso, A. (2017). A Multi-Aspect Analysis of Automatic Essay Scoring for Brazilian Portuguese. In *Proceedings of Conference of the European Chapter of the Association for Computational Linguistics: Student Research Workshop)* (pp. 94–102). doi: http://dx.doi.org/10.18653/v1/e17-4010

An, J., Kieftenbeld, V., & Kanneganti, R. (2016). *Fairness in Automated Scoring: Screening Features for Subgroup Differences.* Presented at the Annual Meeting of the National Council on Measurement in Education, Washington DC.

Andersen, Ø. E., Yannakoudakis, H., Barker, F., & Parish, T. (2013). Developing and Testing a Self-Assessment and Tutoring System. In *Proceedings of the Workshop on Innovative Use of NLP for Building Educational Applications (BEA)* (pp. 32–41).

Angoff, W. H. (2012). Perspectives on Differential Item Functioning Methodology. In P. Holland & H. Wainer (Eds.), *Differential Item Functioning* (pp. 3–23). Taylor & Francis.

Ariel, M. (1988). Referring and Accessibility. *Journal of Linguistics*, *24*(1), 65–87. doi: http://dx.doi.org/10.1017/s0022226700011567

Atchison, L. (2016). *Architecting for Scale: High Availability for Your Growing Applications* (1st ed.). O'reilly Media, Inc.

Attali, Y. (2004). Exploring the Feedback and Revision Features of Criterion. *Journal of Second Language Writing*, *14*, 191–205.

Attali, Y. (2007). Construct Validity of E-Rater®in Scoring TOEFL®Essays. *ETS Research Report Series*, *2007*(1), i–22. doi: http://dx.doi.org/10.1002/j.2333-8504.2007.tb02063.x

Attali, Y. (2011). A Differential Word Use Measure for Content Analysis in Automated Essay Scoring. *ETS Research Report*, *RR-11-36*. doi: http://dx.doi.org/10.1002/j.2333-8504.2011.tb02272.x

Attali, Y. (2013). Validity and Reliability of Automated Essay Scoring. In *Handbook of Automated Essay Evaluation: Current Applications and New Directions* (p. 181-198). Routledge. doi: http://dx.doi.org/10.4324/9780203122761.ch11

Attali, Y. (2016). A Comparison of Newly-Trained and Experienced Raters on a Standardized Writing Assessment. *Language Testing*, *33*(1), 99-115. doi: http://dx.doi.org/10.1177/0265532215582283

Attali, Y., & Burstein, J. (2004). AUTOMATED ESSAY SCORING WITH E-RATER® V.2.0. *ETS Research Report Series*, *2004*(2), i-21. doi: http://dx.doi.org/10.1002/j.2333-8504.2004.tb01972.x

Attali, Y., & Burstein, J. (2006). Automated Essay Scoring with E-Rater V. 2. *The Journal of Technology, Learning and Assessment*, *4*(3), 1–30. doi: https://dx.doi.org/10.1002/j.2333-8504.2004.tb01972.x

Attali, Y., & Powers, D. (2008). A Developmental Writing Scale. *ETS Research Report Series*, *2008*(19), i–59. doi: http://dx.doi.org/10.1002/j.2333-8504.2008.tb02105.x

Baayen, H. (2001). *Word Frequency Distributions*. Dordrecht: Kluwer. doi: http://dx.doi.org/10.1007/978-94-010-0844-0

Bachman, L., Lynch, B., & Mason, M. (1993). Investigating Variability in Tasks and Rater Judgments in a Performance Test of Foreign Language Speaking. In *Paper Presented At the 15th Language Testing Research Colloquium*.

Bai, L., & Hu, G. (2017). In the Face of Fallible AWE Feedback: How Do Students Respond? *Educational Psychology*, *37*(1), 67-81. doi: http://dx.doi.org/10.1080/01443410.2016.1223275

Bamman, D., Chaturvedi, S., Clark, E., Fiterau, M., & Iyyer, M. (Eds.). (2019). *Proceedings of the First Workshop on Narrative Understanding*. doi: http://dx.doi.org/10.18653/v1/w19-24

Bamman, D., Underwood, T., & Smith, N. A. (2014). A Bayesian Mixed Effects Model of Literary Character. In *Proceedings of the Annual Meeting of the Association for Computational Linguistics (ACL)* (pp. 370–379). doi: http://dx.doi.org/10.3115/v1/p14-1035

Bär, D., Zesch, T., & Gurevych, I. (2012). Text Reuse Detection Using a Composition of Text Similarity Measures. In *Proceedings of the International Conference on Computational Linguistics (COLING)* (pp. 167–184).

Baroni, M., Lenci, A., & Onnis, L. (2007). ISA Meets Lara: an Incremental Word Space Model for Cognitively Plausible Simulations of Semantic Learning. In *Proceedings of the Workshop on Cognitive Aspects of Computational Language Acquisition* (pp. 49–56). doi: http://dx.doi.org/10.3115/1629795.1629802

Barzilay, R., & Lapata, M. (2008). Modeling Local Coherence: an Entity-Based Approach. *Computational Linguistics*, *34*(1), 1–34. doi: http://dx.doi.org/10.1162/coli.2008.34.1.1

Basile, A., Gatt, A., & Nissim, M. (2019). You Write Like You Eat: Stylistic Variation as a Predictor of Social Stratification. In *Proceedings of the Annual Meeting of the Association for Computational Linguistics (ACL)* (pp. 2583–2593). doi: http://dx.doi.org/10.18653/v1/p19-1246

Basu, S., Jacobs, C., & Vanderwende, L. (2013). Powergrading: a Clustering Aapproach to Amplify Human Effort for Short Answer Grading. *Transactions of the Association for Computational Linguistics, 1,* 391–402.

Beigman Klebanov, B., Burstein, J., Harackiewicz, J., Priniski, S., & Mulholland, M. (2016). Enhancing STEM Motivation through Personal and Communal Values: NLP for Assessment of Utility Value in Student Writing. In *Proceedings of the Workshop on Innovative Use of NLP for Building Educational Applications (BEA)* (pp. 199–205). doi: http://dx.doi.org/10.18653/v1/w16-0522

Beigman Klebanov, B., Burstein, J., Harackiewicz, J., Priniski, S., & Mulholland, M. (2017). Reflective Writing About the Utility Value of Science as a Tool for Increasing STEM Motivation and Retention–Can AI Help Scale Up? *International Journal of Artificial Intelligence in Education, 27*(4), 791–818. doi: http://dx.doi.org/10.1007/s40593-017-0141-4

Beigman Klebanov, B., Burstein, J., Madnani, N., Faulkner, A., & Tetreault, J. (2012). Building Subjectivity Lexicon(S) from Scratch for Essay Data. In *Proceedings of CICLING* (pp. 591–602). doi: http://dx.doi.org/10.1007/978-3-642-28604-9_48

Beigman Klebanov, B., & Flor, M. (2013a). Argumentation-Relevant Metaphors in Test-Taker Essays. In *Proceedings of the First Workshop on Metaphor in NLP* (pp. 11–20).

Beigman Klebanov, B., & Flor, M. (2013b). Word Association Profiles and Their Use for Automated Scoring of Essays. In *Proceedings of the Annual Meeting of the Association for Computational Linguistics (ACL)* (pp. 1148–1158).

Beigman Klebanov, B., Flor, M., & Gyawali, B. (2016). Topicality-Based Indices for Essay Scoring. In *Proceedings of the Workshop on Innovative Use of NLP for Building Educational Applications (BEA)* (pp. 63–72). doi: http://dx.doi.org/10.18653/v1/w16-0507

Beigman Klebanov, B., Gyawali, B., & Song, Y. (2017). Detecting Good Arguments in a Non-Topic-Specific Way: an Oxymoron? In *Proceedings of the Annual Meeting of the Association for Computational Linguistics (ACL)* (pp. 244–249). doi: http://dx.doi.org/10.18653/v1/p17-2038

Beigman Klebanov, B., Kaufer, D., Yeo, P., Ishizaki, S., & Holtzman, S. (2016). Argumentative Writing in Assessment and Instruction: a Comparative Perspective. In *Genre in Language, Discourse and Cognition* (p. 111-121). Berlin: Mouton De Gruyter. doi: http://dx.doi.org/10.1515/9783110469639-008

Beigman Klebanov, B., Leong, C. W. B., & Flor, M. (2018). A Corpus of Non-Native Written English Annotated for Metaphor. In *Proceedings of the Conference of the North American Chapter of the Association for Computational Linguistics: Human Language Technologies (NAACL-HLT)* (pp. 86–91). doi: `http://dx.doi.org/10.18653/v1/n18-2014`

Beigman Klebanov, B., & Madnani, N. (2020). Automated Evaluation of Writing – 50 Years and Counting. In *Proceedings of the Annual Meeting of the Association for Computational Linguistics (ACL)* (pp. 7796–7810). doi: `http://dx.doi.org/10.18653/v1/2020.acl-main.697`

Beigman Klebanov, B., Madnani, N., & Burstein, J. (2013). Using Pivot-Based Paraphrasing and Sentiment Profiles to Improve a Subjectivity Lexicon for Essay Data. *Transactions of the Association for Computational Linguistics*, *1*, 99–110. doi: `http://dx.doi.org/10.1162/tacl_a_00213`

Beigman Klebanov, B., Madnani, N., Burstein, J., & Somasundaran, S. (2014). Content Importance Models for Scoring Writing from Sources. In *Proceedings of the Annual Meeting of the Association for Computational Linguistics (ACL)* (pp. 247–252). doi: `http://dx.doi.org/10.3115/v1/p14-2041`

Beigman Klebanov, B., Priniski, S., Burstein, J., Gyawali, B., Harackiewicz, J., & Thoman, D. (2018). Utility-Value Score: a Case Study in System Generalization for Writing Analytics. *Journal of Writing Analytics*, *2*, 314–328. doi: `http://dx.doi.org/10.37514/jwa-j.2018.2.1.13`

Beigman Klebanov, B., Ramineni, C., Kaufer, D., Yeoh, P., & Ishizaki, S. (2019). Advancing the Validity Argument for Standardized Writing Tests Using Quantitative Rhetorical Analysis. *Language Testing*, *36*(1), 125-144. doi: `http://dx.doi.org/10.1177/0265532217740752`

Beigman Klebanov, B., Stab, C., Burstein, J., Song, Y., Gyawali, B., & Gurevych, I. (2016). Argumentation: Content, Structure, and Relationship with Essay Quality. In *Proceedings of the Third Workshop on Argument Mining (Argmining2016)* (pp. 70–75). doi: `http://dx.doi.org/10.18653/v1/w16-2808`

Bejar, I. (2017). Threats to Score Meaning in Automated Scoring. *Validation of Score Meaning for the Next Generation of Assessments: the Use of Response Processes*, 75. doi: `http://dx.doi.org/10.4324/9781315708591-7`

Bejar, I., Flor, M., Futagi, Y., & Ramineni, C. (2014). On the Vulnerability of Automated Scoring to Construct-Irrelevant Response Strategies (CIRS): an Illustration. *Assessing Writing*, *22*, 48-59. doi: `http://dx.doi.org/10.1016/j.asw.2014.06.001`

Bejar, I., VanWinkle, W., Madnani, N., Lewis, W., & Steier, M. (2013). Length of Textual Response as a Construct-Irrelevant Response Strategy: the Case of Shell Language. *ETS Research Report Series*, *2013*(1), 1–39. doi: http://dx.doi.org/10.1002/j.2333-8504.2013.tb02314.x

Bell, S., Yannakoudakis, H., & Rei, M. (2019). Context is Key: Grammatical Error Detection with Contextual Word Representations. In *Proceedings of the Workshop on Innovative Use of NLP for Building Educational Applications (BEA)* (pp. 103–115). doi: http://dx.doi.org/10.18653/v1/w19-4410

Bennett, R. E., & Bejar, I. I. (1998). Validity and Automad Scoring: It's Not Only the Scoring. *Educational Measurement: Issues and Practice*, *17*(4), 9–17. doi: http://dx.doi.org/10.1111/j.1745-3992.1998.tb00631.x

Berggren, S. J., Rama, T., & Øvrelid, L. (2019). Regression or Classification? Automated Essay Scoring for Norwegian. In *Proceedings of the Workshop on Innovative Use of NLP for Building Educational Applications (BEA)* (pp. 92–102). doi: http://dx.doi.org/10.18653/v1/w19-4409

Bergstra, J., Breuleux, O., Bastien, F., Lamblin, P., Pascanu, R., Desjardins, G., ... Bengio, Y. (2010). Theano: a CPU and GPU Math Expression Compiler. In *Proceedings of the Python for Scientific Computing Conference (Scipy)* (Vol. 4, pp. 1–7).

Berk, R., Heidari, H., Jabbari, S., Kearns, M., & Roth, A. (2018). Fairness in Criminal Justice Risk Assessments. *Sociological Methods & Research*, 004912411878253. doi: http://dx.doi.org/10.1177/0049124118782533

Berkling, K. (2018). A 2nd Longitudinal Corpus for Children'S Writing with Enhanced Output for Specific Spelling Patterns. In *Proceedings of the Eleventh International Conference on Language Resources and Evaluation (LREC 2018)*.

Bernstein, J., Cheng, J., Balogh, J., & Rosenfeld, E. (2017). Studies of a Self-Administered Oral Reading Assessment. In O. Engwall, J. Lopes, & I. Leite (Eds.), *Proceedings of the International Workshop on Speech and Language Technology in Education (Slate)* (pp. 180–184). doi: http://dx.doi.org/10.21437/slate.2017-30

Bernstein, J., J.Cheng, Balog, J., & Downey, R. (2018). Artificial Intelligence for Scoring Oral Reading Fluency. In H. Jiao & R. Lissitz (Eds.), *Applications of Artificial Intelligence to Assessment*. Charlotte, NC: Information Age Publisher.

Berzak, Y., Kenney, J., Spadine, C., Wang, J. X., Lam, L., Mori, K. S., ... Katz, B. (2016). Universal Dependencies for Learner English. In *Proceedings of the Annual Meeting of the Association for Computational Linguistics (ACL)* (pp. 737–746). doi: http://dx.doi.org/10.18653/v1/p16-1070

Berzak, Y., Reichart, R., & Katz, B. (2014). Reconstructing Native Language Typology from Foreign Language Usage. In *Proceedings of the Eighteenth Conference on Computational Natural Language Learning* (pp. 21–29). doi: http://dx.doi.org/10.3115/v1/w14-1603

Bestgen, Y. (2016). Using Collocational Features to Improve Automated Scoring of EFL Texts. In *Proceedings of the Workshop on Multiword Expressions* (pp. 84–90). doi: http://dx.doi.org/10.18653/v1/w16-1813

Bhat, S., & Yoon, S.-Y. (2015). Automatic Assessment of Syntactic Complexity for Spontaneous Speech Scoring. *Speech Communication*, *67*, 42 - 57. doi: http://dx.doi.org/10.1016/j.specom.2014.09.005

Biber, D., & Gray, B. (2013). Discourse Characteristics of Writing and Speaking Task Types on the TOEFL Ibt®Test: a Lexico-Grammatical Analysis. *ETS Research Report Series*, *2013*(1), i–128.

Biber, D., Gray, B., & Staples, S. (2016). Predicting Patterns of Grammatical Complexity Across Language Exam Task Types and Proficiency Levels. *Applied Linguistics*, *37*(5), 639–668. doi: http://dx.doi.org/10.1093/applin/amu059

Bird, S., Loper, E., & Klein, E. (2009). *Natural Language Processing with Python*. O'reilly Media Inc.

Birney, R. (2012). *Reflective Writing: Quantitative Assessment and Identification of Linguistic Features* (Unpublished doctoral dissertation). Waterford Institute of Technology.

Blanchard, D., Tetreault, J., Higgins, D., Cahill, A., & Chodorow, M. (2013). TOEFL11: a Corpus of Non-Native English. *ETS Research Report Series*, *2013*(2), i–15. doi: http://dx.doi.org/10.1002/j.2333-8504.2013.tb02331.x

Blei, D., Ng, A., & Jordan, M. (2003). Latent Dirichlet Allocation. *Journal of Machine Learning Research*, *3*, 993–1022. doi: http://dx.doi.org/10.1109/asru.2015.7404785

Bordia, S., & Bowman, S. R. (2019). Identifying and Reducing Gender Bias in Word-Level Language Models. In *Proceedings of the Conference of the North American Chapter of the Association for Computational Linguistics: Student Research Workshop* (pp. 7–15). doi: http://dx.doi.org/10.18653/v1/n19-3002

Bös, S., & Opper, M. (1998). Dynamics of Batch Training in a Perceptron. *Journal of Physics a: Mathematical and General*, *31*(21), 4835. doi: http://dx.doi.org/10.1088/0305-4470/31/21/004

Boud, D., Keogh, R., & Walker, D. (1985a). Promoting Reflection in Learning: a Model. In D. Boud, R. Keogh, & D. Walker (Eds.), *Reflection: Turning Experience Into Learning* (p. 18-40). London: Routledge.

Boud, D., Keogh, R., & Walker, D. (Eds.). (1985b). *Reflection: Turning Experience Into Learning*. London: Routledge.

Bourassa, K. J., Manvelian, A., Boals, A., Mehl, M. R., & Sbarra, D. A. (2017). Tell Me a Story: the Creation of Narrative as a Mechanism of Psychological Recovery Following Marital Separation. *Journal of Social and Clinical Psychology*, *36*(5), 359-379. doi: `http://dx.doi.org/10.1521/jscp.2017.36.5.359`

Boyd, A., Hana, J., Nicolas, L., Meurers, D., Wisniewski, K., Abel, A., ... Vettori, C. (2014). The MERLIN Corpus: Learner Language and the CEFR. In *Proceedings of the Language Resources and Evaluation Conference* (pp. 1281–1288).

Breiman, L. (2001). Random Forests. *Machine Learning*, *45*(1), 5–32. doi: `http://dx.doi.org/10.1007/0-387-21529-8_16`

Breland, H. M., Jones, R. J., Jenkins, L., Paynter, M., Pollack, J., & Fong, Y. F. (1994). THE COLLEGE BOARD VOCABULARY STUDY. *ETS Research Report Series*, *1994*(1), i-51. doi: `http://dx.doi.org/10.1002/j.2333-8504.1994.tb01599.x`

Breyer, F. J., Attali, Y., Williamson, D. M., Ridolfi-McCulla, L., Ramineni, C., Duchnowski, M., & Harris, A. (2014). A Study of the Use of the E-Rater®Scoring Engine for the Analytical Writing Measure of the GRE®Revised General Test. *ETS Research Report Series*, *2014*(2), 1–66.

Bridgeman, B., & Carlson, S. (1984). Survey of Academic Writing Tasks. *Written Communication*, *1*, 247–280. doi: `http://dx.doi.org/10.1177/074108838400100200`

Bridgeman, B., Lennon, M. L., & Jackenthal, A. (2003). Effects of Screen Size, Screen Resolution, and Display Rate on Computer-Based Test Performance. *Applied Measurement in Education*, *16*(3), 191-205. doi: `http://dx.doi.org/10.1207/s15324818ame1603_2`

Bridgeman, B., Trapani, C., & Attali, Y. (2012). Comparison of Human and Machine Scoring of Essays: Differences by Gender, Ethnicity, and Country. *Applied Measurement in Education*, *25*(1), 27–40. doi: `http://dx.doi.org/10.1080/08957347.2012.635502`

Brin, S., & Page, L. (1998). The Anatomy of a Large-Scale Hypertextual Web Search Engine. *Computer Networks and ISDN Systems*, *30*(1-7), 107–117. doi: `http://dx.doi.org/10.1016/s0169-7552(98)00110-x`

Burrows, S., Gurevych, I., & Stein, B. (2015). The Eras and Trends of Automatic Short Answer Grading. *International Journal of Artificial Intelligence in Education*, *25*(1), 60–117. doi: `http://dx.doi.org/10.1007/s40593-014-0026-8`

Burstein, J., & Chodorow, M. (1999). Automated Essay Scoring for Nonnative English Speakers. In *Proceedings of the Symposium on Computer Mediated Language Assessment and Evaluation in Natural Language Processing* (pp. 68–75). doi: http://dx.doi.org/10.3115/1598834.1598847

Burstein, J., Chodorow, M., & Leacock, C. (2004). Automated Essay Evaluation: the Criterion Online Writing Service. *AI Magazine, 25*(3), 27-36.

Burstein, J., Elliot, N., Klebanov, B. B., Madnani, N., Napolitano, D., Schwartz, M., … Molloy, H. (2018). Writing Mentor: Writing Progress Using Self-Regulated Writing Support. *Journal of Writing Analytics, 2*, 285–313.

Burstein, J., Elliot, N., & Molloy, H. (2016). Informing Automated Writing Evaluation Using the Lens of Genre: Two Studies. *CALICO, 33*(1), 117–141. doi: http://dx.doi.org/10.1558/cj.v33i1.26374

Burstein, J., Kukich, K., Wolff, S., Lu, J., & Chodorow, M. (1998). Enriching Automated Essay Scoring Using Discourse Marking. In *Proceedings of the Workshop on Discourse Relations and Discourse Marking.*

Burstein, J., Madnani, N., Sabatini, J., McCaffrey, D., Biggers, K., & Dreier, K. (2017). Generating Language Activities in Real-Time for English Learners Using Language Muse. In *Proceedings of the Fourth (2017) ACM Conference on Learning @ Scale* (pp. 213–215).

Burstein, J., & Marcu, D. (2000). Benefits of Modularity in an Automated Essay Scoring System. In *Proceedings of the Workshop on Using Toolsets and Architectures to Build NLP Systems* (pp. 44–50).

Burstein, J., Marcu, D., & Knight, K. (2003). Finding the WRITE Stuff: Automatic Identification of Discourse Structure in Student Essays. *IEEE Intelligent Systems, 18*(1), 32–39. doi: http://dx.doi.org/10.1109/mis.2003.1179191

Burstein, J., & Sabatini, J. (2016). The Language Muse Activity Palette: Technology for Promoting Improved Content Comprehension for English Language Learners. In *Adaptive Educational Technologies for Literacy Instruction* (pp. 275–280). Taylor & Francis, Routledge: NY.

Burstein, J., Tetreault, J., & Andreyev, S. (2010). Using Entity-Based Features to Model Coherence in Student Essays. In *Proceedings of the Conference of the North American Chapter of the Association for Computational Linguistics:Human Language Technologies (NAACL-HLT)* (pp. 681–684).

Burstein, J., Tetreault, J., & Chodorow, M. (2013). Holistic Discourse Coherence Annotation for Noisy Essay Writing. *Dialogue & Discourse, 4*(2), 34–52. doi: http://dx.doi.org/10.5087/dad.2013.202

Burstein, J., Tetreault, J., & Madnani, N. (2013). The E-Rater Automated Essay Scoring System. In M. Shermis & J. Burstein (Eds.), *Handbook of Automated Essay Evaluation: Current Applications and Future Directions*. New York: Routledge. doi: `http://dx.doi.org/10.4324/9780203122761.ch4`

Burstein, J., & Wolska, M. (2003). Toward Evaluation of Writing Style: Overly Repetitious Word Use. In *Proceedings of the Conference of the European Chapter of the Association for Computational Linguistics (EACL)*.

Butt, M., Dyvik, H., King, T. H., Masuichi, H., & Rohrer, C. (2002). The Parallel Grammar Project. In *COLING-02: Grammar Engineering and Evaluation*. doi: `http://dx.doi.org/10.3115/1118783.1118786`

Cahill, A. (2015). Parsing Learner Text: to Shoehorn or Not to Shoehorn. In *Proceedings of the Linguistic Annotation Workshop (LAW)* (pp. 144–147). doi: `http://dx.doi.org/10.3115/v1/w15-1616`

Cahill, A., Chodorow, M., & Flor, M. (2018). Developing an E-Rater Advisory to Detect Babel-Generated Essays. *Journal of Writing Analytics, 2,* 203–224. doi: `http://dx.doi.org/10.37514/jwa-j.2018.2.1.08`

Cahill, A., Chodorow, M., Wolff, S., & Madnani, N. (2013). Detecting Missing Hyphens in Learner Text. In *Proceedings of the Workshop on Innovative Use of NLP for Building Educational Applications (BEA)* (pp. 300–305).

Cahill, A., Fife, J. H., Riordan, B., Vajpayee, A., & Galochkin, D. (2020). Context-Based Automated Scoring of Complex Mathematical Responses. In *Proceedings of the Workshop on Innovative Use of NLP for Building Educational Applications (BEA)* (pp. 186–192). doi: `http://dx.doi.org/10.18653/v1/2020.bea-1.19`

Cahill, A., Gyawali, B., & Bruno, J. (2014). Self-Training for Parsing Learner Text. In *Proceedings of the First Joint Workshop on Statistical Parsing of Morphologically Rich Languages and Syntactic Analysis of Non-Canonical Languages* (pp. 66–73).

Cahill, A., Madnani, N., Tetreault, J., & Napolitano, D. (2013). Robust Systems for Preposition Error Correction Using Wikipedia Revisions. In *Proceedings of the Conference of the North American Chapter of the Association for Computational Linguistics: Human Language Technologies (NAACL-HLT)* (pp. 507–517).

Cai, D., Hu, Y., Miao, X., & Song, Y. (2009). Dependency Grammar Based English Subject-Verb Agreement Evaluation. In *Proceedings of the Pacific Asia Conference on Language, Information and Computation (PACLIC)* (pp. 63–71).

Calders, T., & Verwer, S. (2010). Three Naive Bayes Approaches for Discrimination-Free Classification. *Data Mining Journal; Special Issue with Selected Papers from ECML/PKDD*. doi: http://dx.doi.org/10.1007/s10618-010-0190-x

Caliskan, A., Bryson, J. J., & Narayanan, A. (2017). Semantics Derived Automatically from Language Corpora Contain Human-Like Biases. *Science*, *356*(6334), 183–186. doi: http://dx.doi.org/10.1126/science.aal4230

Calvo, R. A., & Ellis, R. A. (2010). Students' Conceptions of Tutor and Automated Feedback in Professional Writing. *Journal of Engineering Education*, *99*(4), 427–438. doi: http://dx.doi.org/10.1002/j.2168-9830.2010.tb01072.x

Carey, M. D., Mannell, R. H., & Dunn, P. K. (2011). Does a Rater's Familiarity with a Candidate's Pronunciation Affect the Rating in Oral Proficiency Interviews? *Language Testing*, *28*(2), 201–219. doi: http://dx.doi.org/10.1177/0265532210393704

Carlile, W., Gurrapadi, N., Ke, Z., & Ng, V. (2018). Give Me More Feedback: Annotating Argument Persuasiveness and Related Attributes in Student Essays. In *Proceedings of the Annual Meeting of the Association for Computational Linguistics (ACL)* (pp. 621–631). doi: http://dx.doi.org/10.18653/v1/p18-1058

Carlson, A. J., Rosen, J., & Roth, D. (2001). Scaling Up Context-Sensitive Text Correction. In *IAAI* (pp. 45–50).

Carlson, L., & Marcu, D. (2001). Discourse Tagging Reference Manual. *ISI Technical Report ISI-TR-545*, *54*, 56.

Chambers, N., & Jurafsky, D. (2008). Unsupervised Learning of Narrative Event Chains. In *Proceedings of the Annual Meeting of the Association for Computational Linguistics: Human Language Technologies (ACL)* (pp. 789–797). doi: http://dx.doi.org/10.3115/1690219.1690231

Chapelle, C., Cotos, E., & Lee, J. (2015). Validity Arguments for Diagnostic Assessment Using Automated Writing Evaluation. *Language Testing*, *32*(3), 385–405. doi: http://dx.doi.org/10.1177/0265532214565386

Chen, H., & He, B. (2013). Automated Essay Scoring by Maximizing Human-Machine Agreement. In *Proceedings of the Conference on Empirical Methods in Natural Language Processing (EMNLP)* (pp. 1741–1752).

Chen, L., Tao, J., Ghaffarzadegan, S., & Qian, Y. (2018). End-to-End Neural Network Based Automated Speech Scoring. In *Proceedings of the IEEE International Conference on Acoustics, Speech and Signal Processing (ICASSP)* (pp. 6234–6238). doi: http://dx.doi.org/10.1109/icassp.2018.8462562

Chen, L., Zechner, K., Yoon, S.-Y., Evanini, K., Wang, X., Loukina, A., … Gyawali, B. (2018). Automated Scoring of Nonnative Speech Using the Speechratersm V. 5.0 Engine. *ETS Research Report Series*, *2018*(1), 1-31. doi: `http://dx.doi.org/10.1002/ets2.12198`

Chen, M., & Li, X. (2018). Relevance-Based Automated Essay Scoring Via Hierarchical Recurrent Model. In *Proceedings of the International Conference on Asian Language Processing (IALP)* (p. 378-383). doi: `http://dx.doi.org/10.1109/ialp.2018.8629256`

Chen, M., & Zechner, K. (2011). Computing and Evaluating Syntactic Complexity Features for Automated Scoring of Spontaneous Non-Native Speech. In *Proceedings of the Annual Meeting of the Association for Computational Linguistics: Human Language Technologies (ACL-HLT)* (pp. 722–731).

Chen, M., & Zechner, K. (2012). Using an Ontology for Improved Automated Content Scoring of Spontaneous Non-Native Speech. In *Proceedings of the Seventh Workshop on Building Educational Applications Using NLP* (pp. 86–94).

Cheng, G. (2017). Towards an Automatic Classification System for Supporting the Development of Critical Reflective Skills in L2 Learning. *Australasian Journal of Educational Technology*, *33*(4). doi: `http://dx.doi.org/10.14742/ajet.3029`

Cheng, J. (2018). Real-Time Scoring of an Oral Reading Assessment on Mobile Devices. In *Pcoeedings of Interspeech* (pp. 1621–1625). doi: `http://dx.doi.org/10.21437/interspeech.2018-34`

Cheng, J., & Shen, J. (2011). Off-Topic Detection in Automated Speech Assessment Applications. In *Proceedings of the Twelfth Annual Conference of the International Speech Communication Association* (pp. 1597–1600). doi: `http://dx.doi.org/10.21437/interspeech.2011-479`

Chodorow, M., & Leacock, C. (2000). An Unsupervised Method for Detecting Grammatical Errors. In *Proceedings of the Conference of the North American Chapter of the Association for Computational Linguistics: Human Language Technologies (NAACL-HLT)*.

Choi, I., & Cho, Y. (2018). The Impact of Spelling Errors on Trained Raters' Scoring Decisions. *Language Education & Assessment*, *1*(2), 45–58. doi: `http://dx.doi.org/10.29140/lea.v1n2.61`

Choi, J. (2010). *The Impact of Automated Essay Scoring (AES) for Improving English Language Learner's Essay Writing*. University of Virginia Charlottesville, VA.

Church, K., & Hanks, P. (1990). Word Association Norms, Mutual Information and Lexicography. *Computational Linguistics*, *16*(1), 22–29. doi: `http://dx.doi.org/10.3115/981623.981633`

Clauser, B. E., Kane, M. T., & Swanson, D. B. (2002). Validity Issues for Performance-Based Tests Scored with Computer-Automated Scoring Systems. *Applied Measurement in Education*, *15*(4), 413–432. doi: `http://dx.doi.org/10.1207/s15324818ame1504_05`

Connolly, P., Keenan, C., & Urbanska, K. (2018, 9). The Trials of Evidence-Based Practice in Education: a Systematic Review of Randomised Controlled Trials in Education Research 1980-2016. *Educational Research*. doi: `http://dx.doi.org/10.1080/00131881.2018.1493353`

Copestake, A., & Flickinger, D. (2000). An Open Source Grammar Development Environment and Broad-Coverage English Grammar Using HPSG. In *Proceedings of the International Conference on Language Resources and Evaluation (LREC)*.

Correnti, R., Matsumura, L. C., Hamilton, L., & Wang, E. (2013). Assessing Students' Skills At Writing Analytically in Response to Texts. *The Elementary School Journal*, *114*(2), 142–177. doi: `http://dx.doi.org/10.1086/671936`

Cortes, C., & Vapnik, V. (1995). Support-Vector Networks. *Machine Learning*, *20*(3), 273–297. doi: `http://dx.doi.org/10.1007/bf00994018`

Coulthard, M., Johnson, A., & Wright, D. (2016). *An Introduction to Forensic Linguistics: Language in Evidence*. Routledge. doi: `http://dx.doi.org/10.4324/9781315630311`

Cozma, M., Butnaru, A., & Ionescu, R. T. (2018). Automated Essay Scoring with String Kernels and Word Embeddings. In *Proceedings of the Annual Meeting of the Association for Computational Linguistics (ACL)* (pp. 503–509). doi: `http://dx.doi.org/10.18653/v1/p18-2080`

Craighead, H., Caines, A., Buttery, P., & Yannakoudakis, H. (n.d.). Investigating the Effect of Auxiliary Objectives for the Automated Grading of Learner English Speech Transcriptions. In *Proceedings of the Annual Meeting of the Association for Computational Linguistics (ACL)*. doi: `http://dx.doi.org/10.18653/v1/2020.acl-main.206`

Crossley, S. A., Kim, M., Allen, L., & McNamara, D. (2019). Automated Summarization Evaluation (ASE) Using Natural Language Processing Tools. In *Proceedings of the International Conference on Artificial Intelligence in Education* (pp. 84–95). doi: `http://dx.doi.org/10.1007/978-3-030-23204-7_8`

Cummins, R., Yannakoudakis, H., & Briscoe, T. (2016). Unsupervised Modeling of Topical Relevance in L2 Learner Text. In *Proceedings of the Workshop on Innovative Use of NLP for Building Educational Applications (BEA)* (pp. 95–104). doi: `http://dx.doi.org/10.18653/v1/w16-0510`

Dahlmeier, D., Ng, H. T., & Wu, S. M. (2013). Building a Large Annotated Corpus of Learner English: the NUS Corpus of Learner English. In *Proceedings of the Workshop on Innovative Use of NLP for Building Educational Applications (BEA)* (pp. 22–31).

Dai, Y., Song, W., Liu, X., Liu, L., & Zhao, X. (2018). Recognition of Parallelism Sentence Based on Recurrent Neural Network. In *Proceedings of the IEEE International Conference on Software Engineering and Service Science (ICSESS)* (p. 148-151). doi: http://dx.doi.org/10.1109/icsess.2018.8663734

Dale, R., Anisimoff, I., & Narroway, G. (2012). HOO 2012: a Report on the Preposition and Determiner Error Correction Shared Task. In *Proceedings of the Seventh Workshop on Building Educational Applications Using NLP* (pp. 54–62).

Dale, R., & Kilgarriff, A. (2011). Helping Our Own: the HOO 2011 Pilot Shared Task. In *Proceedings of the European Workshop on Natural Language Generation (ENLG)* (pp. 242–249).

Dang, H., & Owczarzak, K. (2008). Overview of the TAC 2008 Update Summarization Task. In *Proceedings of the Text Analysis Conference (TAC)*.

Daudaravicius, V., Banchs, R. E., Volodina, E., & Napoles, C. (2016). A Report on the Automatic Evaluation of Scientific Writing Shared Task. In *Proceedings of the Workshop on Innovative Use of NLP for Building Educational Applications (BEA)* (pp. 53–62). doi: http://dx.doi.org/10.18653/v1/w16-0506

Davis, L. (2015). The Influence of Training and Experience on Rater Performance in Scoring Spoken Language. *Language Testing*, *33*, 117–135. doi: http://dx.doi.org/10.1177/0265532215582282

Daxenberger, J., Eger, S., Habernal, I., Stab, C., & Gurevych, I. (2017). What is the Essence of a Claim? Cross-Domain Claim Identification. *Arxiv Preprint Arxiv:1704.07203*. doi: http://dx.doi.org/10.18653/v1/d17-1218

Deane, P. (2013). On the Relation Between Automated Essay Scoring and Modern Views of the Writing Construct. *Assessing Writing*, *18*(1), 7–24. doi: http://dx.doi.org/10.1016/j.asw.2012.10.002

Deane, P., Somasundaran, S., Lawless, R. R., Persky, H., & Appel, C. (2019). The Key Practice, Building and Sharing Stories and Social Understandings: the Intrinsic Value of Narrative. *ETS Research Report Series*, *2019*(1), 1-78. doi: http://dx.doi.org/10.1002/ets2.12266

Deguchi, M., & Yamaguchi, K. (2019). Argument Component Classification by Relation Identification by Neural Network and Textrank. In *Proceedings of the Workshop on Argument Mining* (pp. 83–91). doi: http://dx.doi.org/10.18653/v1/w19-4510

Del Corro, L., & Gemulla, R. (2013). Clausie: Clause-Based Open Information Extraction. In *Proceedings of the International Conference on World Wide Web* (pp. 355–366). doi: `http://dx.doi.org/10.1145/2488388.2488420`

Deng, J., Dong, W., Socher, R., Li, L.-J., Li, K., & Fei-Fei, L. (2009). Imagenet: a Large-Scale Hierarchical Image Database. In *Proceedings of the Conference on Computer Vision and Pattern Recognition*. doi: `http://dx.doi.org/10.1109/cvpr.2009.5206848`

Devlin, J., Chang, M.-W., Lee, K., & Toutanova, K. (2019). BERT: Pre-Training of Deep Bidirectional Transformers for Language Understanding. In *Proceedings of the Conference of the North American Chapter of the Association for Computational Linguistics: Human Language Technologies (NAACL-HLT)* (pp. 4171–4186).

Dewey, J. (Ed.). (1933). *How We Think*. Boston: DC Heath. doi: `http://dx.doi.org/10.1037/10903-000`

Diederich, P., French, J., & Carlton, S. (1961). Factors in Judgments of Writing Ability. *ETS Research Bulletin, RB-61-15*. doi: `http://dx.doi.org/10.1002/j.2333-8504.1961.tb00286.x`

Dong, F., & Zhang, Y. (2016). Automatic Features for Essay Scoring – an Empirical Study. In *Proceedings of the Conference on Empirical Methods in Natural Language Processing (EMNLP)* (pp. 1072–1077). doi: `http://dx.doi.org/10.18653/v1/d16-1115`

Dong, F., Zhang, Y., & Yang, J. (2017). Attention-Based Recurrent Convolutional Neural Network for Automatic Essay Scoring. In *Proceedings of the Conference on Computational Natural Language Learning (Conll)* (pp. 153–162). doi: `http://dx.doi.org/10.18653/v1/k17-1017`

Dong, L., Yang, N., Wang, W., Wei, F., Liu, X., Wang, Y., ... Hon, H.-W. (2019). Unified Language Model Pre-Training for Natural Language Understanding and Generation. In *Advances in Neural Information Processing Systems* (pp. 13063–13075).

Doshi-Velez, F., & Kim, B. (2017). Towards a Rigorous Science of Interpretable Machine Learning. *Corr, abs/1702.08608*.

Dronen, N., Foltz, P. W., & Habermehl, K. (2015). Effective Sampling for Large-Scale Automated Writing Evaluation Systems. In *Proceedings of the Second (2015) ACM Conference on Learning @ Scale* (p. 3–10).

Duong, M. Q., & von Davier, A. (n.d.). Heterogeneous Populations and Multistage Test Design. In R. E. Millsap, L. A. van der Ark, D. M. Bolt, & C. M. Woods (Eds.), *New Developments in Quantitative Psychology: Presentations from the 77th Annual Psychometric Society Meeting* (pp. 151–170). doi: `http://dx.doi.org/10.1007/978-1-4614-9348-8_10`

Dwork, C., Hardt, M., Pitassi, T., Reingold, O., & Zemel, R. (2012). Fairness through Awareness. In *Proceedings of the Innovations in Theoretical Computer Science Conference* (p. 214–226). doi: http://dx.doi.org/10.1145/2090236.2090255

Dzikovska, M., Nielsen, R., Brew, C., Leacock, C., Giampiccolo, D., Bentivogli, L., ... Dang, H. T. (2013). Task 7: the Joint Student Response Analysis and 8th Recognizing Textual Entailment Challenge. In *Proceedings of Semeval* (pp. 263–274).

Eger, S., Daxenberger, J., & Gurevych, I. (2017). Neural End-to-End Learning for Computational Argumentation Mining. In *Proceedings of the Annual Meeting of the Association for Computational Linguistics (ACL)* (pp. 11–22). doi: http://dx.doi.org/10.18653/v1/p17-1002

Elsner, M., & Charniak, E. (2008). Coreference-Inspired Coherence Modeling. In *Proceedings of the Annual Meeting of the Association for Computational Linguistics: Human Language Technologies (ACL-HLT)* (pp. 41–44). doi: http://dx.doi.org/10.3115/1557690.1557702

Elsner, M., & Charniak, E. (2011). Extending the Entity Grid with Entity-Specific Features. In *Proceedings of the Annual Meeting of the Association for Computational Linguistics: Human Language Technologies (ACL-HLT)* (pp. 125–129).

Elson, D. K., Dames, N., & McKeown, K. R. (2010). Extracting Social Networks from Literary Fiction. In *Proceedings of the Annual Meeting of the Association for Computational Linguistics (ACL)* (pp. 138–147).

Englert, C., Zhao, Y., Dunsmore, K., Collings, N. Y., & Wolbers, K. (2007). Scaffolding the Writing of Students with Disabilities through Procedural Facilitation: Using an Internet-Based Technology to Improve Performance. *Learning Disability Quarterly*, *30*(1), 9-29. doi: http://dx.doi.org/10.2307/30035513

Entman, R. (2003). Cascading Activation: Contesting the White House?S Frame After 9/11. *Political Communication*, *20*, 415–432. doi: http://dx.doi.org/10.1080/10584600390244176

Evangelopoulos, N., Zhang, X., & Prybutok, V. R. (2012). Latent Semantic Analysis: Five Methodological Recommendations. *European Journal of Information Systems*, *21*(1), 70–86. doi: http://dx.doi.org/10.1057/ejis.2010.61

Evanini, K., Xie, S., & Zechner, K. (2013). Prompt-Based Content Scoring for Automated Spoken Language Assessment. In *Proceedings of the Workshop on Innovative Use of NLP for Building Educational Applications (BEA)* (pp. 157–162).

Falakmasir, M. H., Ashley, K. D., Schunn, C. D., & Litman, D. J. (2014). Identifying Thesis and Conclusion Statements in Student Essays to Scaffold Peer Review. In *Proceedings of the*

International Conference on Intelligent Tutoring Systems (pp. 254–259). doi: `http://dx.doi.org/10.1007/978-3-319-07221-0_31`

Farag, Y., Yannakoudakis, H., & Briscoe, T. (2018). Neural Automated Essay Scoring and Coherence Modeling for Adversarially Crafted Input. In *Proceedings of the Conference of the North American Chapter of the Association for Computational Linguistics: Human Language Technologies (NAACL-HLT)* (pp. 263–271). doi: `http://dx.doi.org/10.18653/v1/n18-1024`

Farra, N., Somasundaran, S., & Burstein, J. (2015). Scoring Persuasive Essays Using Opinions and Their Targets. In *Proceedings of the Workshop on Innovative Use of NLP for Building Educational Applications* (pp. 64–74). doi: `http://dx.doi.org/10.3115/v1/w15-0608`

Faulkner, A. (2014). *Automated Classification of Argument Stance in Student Essays: a Linguistically Motivated Approach with an Application for Supporting Argument Summarization*. Doctoral Dissertation, City University of New York.

Fearnside, W., & Holther, W. (1959). *Fallacy: the Counterfeit of Argument*. Englewood Cliffs, NJ: Prentice-Hall. doi: `http://dx.doi.org/10.2307/355996`

Feldman, M., Friedler, S. A., Moeller, J., Scheidegger, C., & Venkatasubramanian, S. (2015). Certifying and Removing Disparate Impact. *Proceedings of the ACM SIGKDD International Conference on Knowledge Discovery and Data Mining (KDD)*, 259-268. doi: `http://dx.doi.org/10.1145/2783258.2783311`

Feng, V., & Hirst, G. (2011). Classifying Arguments by Scheme. In *Proceedings of the Annual Meeting of the Association for Computational Linguistics: Human Language Technologies (ACL-HLT)* (pp. 987–996).

Ferrara, A., Montanelli, S., & Petasis, G. (2017). Unsupervised Detection of Argumentative Units Though Topic Modeling Techniques. In *Proceedings of the Workshop on Argument Mining* (pp. 97–107). doi: `http://dx.doi.org/10.18653/v1/w17-5113`

Ferretti, R., & Graham, S. (2019). Argumentative Writing: Theory, Assessment, and Instruction. *Reading and Writing*, *32*, 1345–1357. doi: `http://dx.doi.org/10.1007/s11145-019-09950-x`

Flachs, S., Lacroix, O., Rei, M., Yannakoudakis, H., & Søgaard, A. (2019). A Simple and Robust Approach to Detecting Subject-Verb Agreement Errors. In *Proceedings of the Conference of the North American Chapter of the Association for Computational Linguistics: Human Language Technologies (NAACL-HLT)* (pp. 2418–2427). doi: `http://dx.doi.org/10.18653/v1/n19-1251`

Flor, M. (2012). Four Types of Context for Automatic Spelling Correction. *Traitement Automatique Des Langues (TAL)*, *53*(3), 61–99.

Flor, M., & Beigman Klebanov, B. (2018). Catching Idiomatic Expressions in EFL Essays. In *Proceedings of the Workshop on Figurative Language Processing* (pp. 34–44). doi: http://dx.doi.org/10.18653/v1/w18-0905

Flor, M., & Cahill, A. (2020). Automated Scoring of Open-Ended Written Responses – Possibilities and Challenges. In *Innovative Computer-Based International Large-Scale Assessments*. Springer Science Publishers.

Flor, M., Fried, M., & Rozovskaya, A. (2019). A Benchmark Corpus of English Misspellings and a Minimally-Supervised Model for Spelling Correction. In *Proceedings of the Workshop on Innovative Use of NLP for Building Educational Applications (BEA)* (pp. 76–86). doi: http://dx.doi.org/10.18653/v1/w19-4407

Flor, M., Futagi, Y., Lopez, M., & Mulholland, M. (2015). Patterns of Misspellings in L2 and L1 English: a View from the ETS Spelling Corpus. *Bergen Language and Linguistics Studies*, 6. doi: http://dx.doi.org/10.15845/bells.v6i0.811

Flor, M., & Somasundaran, S. (2019). Lexical Concreteness in Narrative. In *Proceedings of the Second Workshop on Storytelling* (pp. 75–80). doi: http://dx.doi.org/10.18653/v1/w19-3408

Foltz, P., Rosenstein, M., Dronen, N., & Dooley, S. (2014). Automated Feedback in a Large-Scale Implementation of a Formative Writing System: Implications for Improving Student Writing. In *Paper Presented At the Annual Meeting of the American Educational Research Association, Philadelphia, PA*.

Foltz, P., Streeter, L., Lochbaum, K., & Landauer, T. (2013). Implementation and Application of the Intelligent Essay Assessor. In M. Shermis & J. Burstein (Eds.), *Handbook of Automated Essay Evaluation: Current Applications and New Directions* (pp. 68–88). New York: Routhledge.

Foster, D. (2000). *Author Unknown: on the Trail of Anonymous*. Macmillan.

Fraser, K. C., Meltzer, J. A., Graham, N. L., Leonard, C., Hirst, G., Black, S. E., & Rochon, E. (2014). Automated Classification of Primary Progressive Aphasia Subtypes from Narrative Speech Transcripts. *Cortex*, *55*, 43–60. doi: http://dx.doi.org/10.1016/j.cortex.2012.12.006

Freedman, D. A. (2009). *Statistical Models: Theory and Practice*. Cambridge University Press. doi: http://dx.doi.org/10.1017/cbo9781139165495

Friedler, S. A., Scheidegger, C., & Venkatasubramanian, S. (2016). On the (Im)Possibility of Fairness. *Corr*, *abs/1609.07236*.

Futagi, Y., Deane, P., Chodorow, M., & Tetreault, J. (2008). A Computational Approach to Detecting Collocation Errors in the Writing of Non-Native Speakers of English. *Computer Assisted Language Learning*, *21*(4), 353–367. doi: http://dx.doi.org/10.1080/09588220802343561

Gamon, M. (2010). Using Mostly Native Data to Correct Errors in Learners' Writing. In *Proceedings of the Conference of the North American Chapter of the Association for Computational Linguistics: Human Language Technologies (NAACL-HLT)* (pp. 163–171).

Gamon, M. (2011). High-Order Sequence Modeling for Language Learner Error Detection. In *Proceedings of the Workshop on Innovative Use of NLP for Building Educational Applications (BEA)* (pp. 180–189).

Gamon, M., Chodorow, M., Leacock, C., & Tetreault, J. (2013). Grammatical Error Detection in Automatic Essay Scoring and Feedback. In M. Shermis & J. Burstein (Eds.), *Handbook of Automated Essay Evaluation: Current Applications and New Directions* (p. 251-266). New York: Routledge. doi: http://dx.doi.org/10.4324/9780203122761.ch15

Gamon, M., Gao, J., Brockett, C., Klementiev, A., Dolan, W. B., Belenko, D., & Vanderwende, L. (2008). Using Contextual Speller Techniques and Language Modeling for ESL Error Correction. In *Proceedings of the Third International Joint Conference on Natural Language Processing: Volume-I.*

Gao, Y., Driban, A., Xavier McManus, B., Musi, E., Davies, P., Muresan, S., & Passonneau, R. (2019). Rubric Reliability and Annotation of Content and Argument in Source-Based Argument Essays. In *Proceedings of the Workshop on Innovative Use of NLP for Building Educational Applications (BEA)* (pp. 507–518). doi: http://dx.doi.org/10.18653/v1/w19-4452

Gardner, J., Brooks, C., & Baker, R. (2019). Evaluating the Fairness of Predictive Student Models through Slicing Analysis. In *Proceedings of the International Conference on Learning Analytics & Knowledge (LAK)* (p. 225–234). doi: http://dx.doi.org/10.1145/3303772.3303791

Gaspard, H., Dicke, A.-L., Flunger, B., Brisson, B. M., Häfner, I., Nagengast, B., & Trautwein, U. (2015). Fostering Adolescents' Value Beliefs for Mathematics with a Relevance Intervention in the Classroom. *Developmental Psychology*, *51*(9), 1226. doi: http://dx.doi.org/10.1037/dev0000028

Geertzen, J., Alexopoulou, T., Korhonen, A., et al. (2013). Automatic Linguistic Annotation of Large Scale L2 Databases: the EF-Cambridge Open Language Database (EFCAMDAT). In *Proceedings of the Second Language Research Forum. Somerville, MA: Cascadilla Proceedings Project* (pp. 240–254).

Ghosh, D., Khanam, A., Han, Y., & Muresan, S. (2016). Coarse-Grained Argumentation Features for Scoring Persuasive Essays. In *Proceedings of the Annual Meeting of the Association for Computational Linguistics (ACL)* (pp. 549–554). doi: http://dx.doi.org/10.18653/v1/p16-2089

Gibson, A., Aitken, A., Sándor, Á., Buckingham Shum, S., Tsingos-Lucas, C., & Knight, S. (2017). Reflective Writing Analytics for Actionable Feedback. In *Proceedings of the Seventh International Learning Analytics & Knowledge Conference* (pp. 153–162). doi: http://dx.doi.org/10.1145/3027385.3027436

Gillam, S. L., Gillam, R. B., Fargo, J. D., Olszewski, A., & Segura, H. (2017). Monitoring Indicators of Scholarly Language: a Progress-Monitoring Instrument for Measuring Narrative Discourse Skills. *Communication Disorders Quarterly*, *38*(2), 96-106. doi: http://dx.doi.org/10.1177/1525740116651442

Godfrey, J. J., Holliman, E. C., & McDaniel, J. (1992). SWITCHBOARD: Telephone Speech Corpus for Research and Development. In *Proceedings of the IEEE International Conference on Acoustics, Speech, and Signal Processing* (Vol. 1, pp. 517–520). doi: http://dx.doi.org/10.1109/icassp.1992.225858

Goldberg, Y. (2017). Neural Network Methods for Natural Language Processing. *Synthesis Lectures on Human Language Technologies*, *10*(1), 1–309. doi: http://dx.doi.org/10.2200/s00762ed1v01y201703hlt037

Golding, A. R., & Roth, D. (1999). A Winnow-Based Approach to Context-Sensitive Spelling Correction. *Machine Learning*, *34*(1-3), 107–130.

Goldwater, S., & Griffiths, T. (2007). A Fully Bayesian Approach to Unsupervised Part-of-Speech Tagging. In *Proceedings of the Annual Meeting of the Association of Computational Linguistics (ACL)* (pp. 744–751).

Gonen, H., & Goldberg, Y. (2019). Lipstick on a Pig: Debiasing Methods Cover Up Systematic Gender Biases in Word Embeddings But Do Not Remove Them. In *Proceedings of the Conference of the North American Chapter of the Association for Computational Linguistics: Human Language Technologies (NAACL-HLT)* (pp. 609–614).

Gong, J., Chen, X., Qiu, X., & Huang, X. (2016). End-to-End Neural Sentence Ordering Using Pointer Network. *Arxiv Preprint Arxiv:1611.04953*.

Goyal, A., Riloff, E., & Daumé, H. (2010). Automatically Producing Plot Unit Representations for Narrative Text. In *Proceedings of the Conference on Empirical Methods in Natural Language Processing (EMNLP)* (p. 77–86).

Graesser, A., McNamara, D., & Kulikowich, J. (2011). Coh-Metrix: Providing Multilevel Analyses of Text Characteristics. *Educational Researcher*, *40*(5), 223-234. doi: `http://dx.doi.org/10.3102/0013189x11413260`

Graesser, A., McNamara, D., Louwerse, M., & Cai, Z. (2004). Coh-Metrix: Analysis of Text on Cohesion and Language. *Behavior Research Methods*, *36*(2), 193–202. doi: `http://dx.doi.org/10.3758/bf03195564`

Graham, S., & Hebert, M. (2011). Writing to Read: a Meta-Analysis of the Impact of Writing and Writing Instruction on Reading. *Harvard Educational Review*, *81*(4), 710–744. doi: `http://dx.doi.org/10.17763/haer.81.4.t2k0m13756113566`

Graham, S., & Perin, D. (2007a). A Meta-Analysis of Writing Instruction for Adolescent Students. *Journal of Educational Psychology*, *99*(3), 445. doi: `http://dx.doi.org/10.1037/0022-0663.99.3.445`

Graham, S., & Perin, D. (2007b). *Writing Next: Effective Strategies to Improve Writing of Adolescents in Middle and High Schools – a Report to Carnegie Corporation of New York*. Washington, DC:Alliance for Excellent Education.

Granger, S. (2003). The International Corpus of Learner English: a New Resource for Foreign Language Learning and Teaching and Second Language Acquisition Research. *TESOL Quarterly*, *37*(3), 538–546. doi: `http://dx.doi.org/10.2307/3588404`

Granger, S., & Bestgen, Y. (2014). The Use of Collocations by Intermediate Vs. Advanced Non-Native Writers: a Bigram-Based Study. *International Review of Applied Linguistics in Language Teaching*, *52*(3), 229–252. doi: `http://dx.doi.org/10.1515/iral-2014-0011`

Graves, A., Mohamed, A.-r., & Hinton, G. (2013). Speech Recognition with Deep Recurrent Neural Networks. In *Proceedings of the IEEE International Conference on Acoustics, Speech and Signal Processing (ICASSP)* (pp. 6645–6649). doi: `http://dx.doi.org/10.1109/icassp.2013.6638947`

Gretz, S., Friedman, R., Cohen-Karlik, E., Toledo, A., Lahav, D., Aharonov, R., & Slonim, N. (2019). *A Large-Scale Dataset for Argument Quality Ranking: Construction and Analysis*. doi: `http://dx.doi.org/10.1609/aaai.v34i05.6285`

Grimes, D., & Warschauer, M. (2010). Utility in a Fallible Tool: a Multi-Site Case Study of Automated Writing Evaluation. *The Journal of Technology, Learning and Assessment*, *8*(6).

Grosz, B. J., Weinstein, S., & Joshi, A. K. (1995). Centering: a Framework for Modeling the Local Coherence of Discourse. *Computational Linguistics*, *21*(2), 203–225.

Guinaudeau, C., & Strube, M. (2013). Graph-Based Local Coherence Modeling. In *Proceedings of the Annual Meeting of the Association for Computational Linguistics (ACL)* (pp. 93–103).

Gutierrez, E. D., Cecchi, G. A., Corcoran, C., & Corlett, P. (2017). Using Automated Metaphor Identification to Aid in Detection and Prediction of First-Episode Schizophrenia. In *Proceedings of the Conference on Empirical Methods in Natural Language Processing (EMNLP)* (pp. 2923–2930). doi: `http://dx.doi.org/10.18653/v1/d17-1316`

Haberman, S. J. (2004). STATISTICAL AND MEASUREMENT PROPERTIES OF FEATURES USED IN ESSAY ASSESSMENT. *ETS Research Report Series*, *2004*(1), i-58. doi: `http://dx.doi.org/10.1002/j.2333-8504.2004.tb01948.x`

Haberman, S. J. (2019). Measures of Agreement Versus Measures of Prediction Accuracy. *ETS Research Report Series*, *2019*(1), 1-23. doi: `http://dx.doi.org/10.1002/ets2.12258`

Habermehl, K., Nagarajan, A., & Dooley, S. (2020). A Seamless Integration of Human and Automated Scoring. In *Handbook of Automated Scoring: Theory Into Practice* (pp. 263–280). Taylor & Francis Group. doi: `http://dx.doi.org/10.1201/9781351264808-14`

Hajian, S., & Domingo-Ferrer, J. (2013). A Methodology for Direct and Indirect Discrimination Prevention in Data Mining. *IEEE Transactions on Knowledge and Data Engineering*, *25*(7), 1445 – 1459. doi: `http://dx.doi.org/10.1109/tkde.2012.72`

Hall, L., & Saerchinger, C. (Eds.). (1915). *A Narrative History of Music, Book II: Classicism and Romanticism.* New York: the National Society of Music.

Han, W.-B., Chen, J.-J., Yang, C., & Chang, J. (2019). Level-Up: Learning to Improve Proficiency Level of Essays. In *Proceedings of the Annual Meeting of the Association for Computational Linguistics (ACL)* (pp. 207–212). doi: `http://dx.doi.org/10.18653/v1/p19-3033`

Harackiewicz, J., Canning, E., Tibbetts, Y., Priniski, S., & Hyde, J. (2016). Closing Achievement Gaps with a Utility-Value Intervention: Disentangling Race and Social Class. *Journal of Personality and Social Psychology*, *111*(5), 745. doi: `http://dx.doi.org/10.1037/pspp0000075`

Heilman, M., Cahill, A., Madnani, N., Lopez, M., Mulholland, M., & Tetreault, J. (2014). Predicting Grammaticality on an Ordinal Scale. In *Proceedings of the Annual Meeting of the Association for Computational Linguistics (ACL)* (pp. 174–180). doi: `http://dx.doi.org/10.3115/v1/p14-2029`

Heilman, M., & Madnani, N. (2015). The Impact of Training Data on Automated Short Answer Scoring Performance. In *Proceedings of the Workshop on Innovative Use of NLP for Building Educational Applications (BEA)* (pp. 81–85). doi: `http://dx.doi.org/10.3115/v1/w15-0610`

Hidey, C., Musi, E., Hwang, A., Muresan, S., & McKeown, K. (2017). Analyzing the Semantic Types of Claims and Premises in an Online Persuasive Forum. In *Proceedings of the Workshop on Argument Mining* (pp. 11–21). doi: `http://dx.doi.org/10.18653/v1/w17-5102`

Higgins, D., Burstein, J., & Attali, Y. (2006). Identifying Off-Topic Student Essays Without Topic-Specific Training Data. *Natural Language Engineering*, *12*(2), 145–159. doi: http://dx.doi.org/10.1017/s1351324906004189

Higgins, D., & Heilman, M. (2014). Managing What We Can Measure: Quantifying the Susceptibility of Automated Scoring Systems to Gaming Behavior. *Educational Measurement: Issues and Practice*, *33*(3), 36–46. doi: http://dx.doi.org/10.1111/emip.12036

Hirst, G., & Budanitsky, A. (2005). Correcting Real-Word Spelling Errors by Restoring Lexical Cohesion. *Natural Language Engineering*, *11*(1), 87–111. doi: http://dx.doi.org/10.1017/s1351324904003560

Hochreiter, S., & Schmidhuber, J. (1997). Long Short-Term Memory. *Neural Computation*, *9*(8), 1735–1780. doi: http://dx.doi.org/10.1162/neco.1997.9.8.1735

Hoerl, A. E., & Kennard, R. W. (1970). Ridge Regression: Biased Estimation for Nonorthogonal Problems. *Technometrics*, *12*(1), 55–67. doi: http://dx.doi.org/10.1080/00401706.1970.10488634

Hofmann, T. (2001). Unsupervised Learning by Probabilistic Latent Semantic Analysis. *Machine Learning*, *42*(1-2), 177–196.

Horbach, A., Palmer, A., & Pinkal, M. (2013). Using the Text to Evaluate Short Answers for Reading Comprehension Exercises. In *Proceedings of the Second Joint Conference on Lexical and Computational Semantics (* SEM)* (pp. 286–295).

Horbach, A., Scholten-Akoun, D., Ding, Y., & Zesch, T. (2017). Fine-Grained Essay Scoring of a Complex Writing Task for Native Speakers. In *Proceedings of the Workshop on Innovative Use of NLP for Building Educational Applications (BEA)* (pp. 357–366). doi: http://dx.doi.org/10.18653/v1/w17-5040

Hornik, K. (1991). Approximation Capabilities of Multilayer Feedforward Networks. *Neural Networks*, *4*(2), 251 - 257. doi: http://dx.doi.org/10.1016/0893-6080(91)90009-t

Hovy, D., & Spruit, S. L. (2016). The Social Impact of Natural Language Processing. In *Proceedings of the Annual Meeting of the Association for Computational Linguistics (ACL)* (pp. 591–598). doi: http://dx.doi.org/10.18653/v1/p16-2096

Hovy, E., Lin, C.-Y., & Zhou, L. (2005). Evaluating Duc 2005 Using Basic Elements. In *Proceedings of Document Understanding Conference (DUC)* (Vol. 2005).

Hsieh, C.-N., Zechner, K., & Xi, X. (2020). FEATURES MEASURING FLUENCY AND PRONUNCIATION. In K. Zechner & K. Evanini (Eds.), *Automated Speaking Assessment: Using Language Technologies to Score Spontaneous Speech* (pp. 101–122). Routledge. doi: http://dx.doi.org/10.4324/9781315165103-7

Huang, Y., Murakami, A., Alexopoulou, T., & Korhonen, A. (2018). Dependency Parsing of Learner English. *International Journal of Corpus Linguistics*, *23*(1), 28–54. doi: http://dx.doi.org/10.1075/ijcl.16080.hua

Hulleman, C., Godes, O., Hendricks, B., & Harackiewicz, J. (2010). Enhancing Interest and Performance with a Utility Value Intervention. *Journal of Educational Psychology*, *102*(4), 880. doi: http://dx.doi.org/10.1037/a0019506

Hulleman, C., & Harackiewicz, J. (2009). Promoting Interest and Performance in High School Science Classes. *Science*, *326*(5958), 1410–1412. doi: http://dx.doi.org/10.1126/science.1177067

Hulsman, R., Harmsen, A., & Fabriek, M. (2009). Reflective Teaching of Medical Communication Skills with Dividu: Assessing the Level of Student Reflection on Recorded Consultations with Simulated Patients. *Patient Education and Counseling*, *74*(2), 142 - 149. doi: http://dx.doi.org/10.1016/j.pec.2008.10.009

Hutchinson, B., & Mitchell, M. (2019). 50 Years of Test (Un)Fairness: Lessons for Machine Learning. In *Proceedings of FAT**. doi: http://dx.doi.org/10.1145/3287560.3287600

Hutto, C., & Gilbert, E. (2014). Vader: a Parsimonious Rule-Based Model for Sentiment Analysis of Social Media Text. In *Proceedings of the International AAAI Conference on Weblogs and Social Media (ICWSM)* (p. 1-10).

Hyland, K., & Hyland, F. (2006). Feedback on Second Language Students' Writing. *Language Teaching*, *39*(2), 83–101. doi: http://dx.doi.org/10.1017/s0261444806003399

Ishioka, T., & Kameda, M. (2006). Automated Japanese Essay Scoring System Based on Articles Written by Experts. In *Proceedings of the International Conference on Computational Linguistics and the Annual Meeting of the Association for Computational Linguistics (COLING-ACL)* (pp. 233–240). doi: http://dx.doi.org/10.3115/1220175.1220205

Islam, A., & Inkpen, D. (2009). Real-Word Spelling Correction Using Google Web 1T 3-Grams. In *Proceedings of the Conference on Empirical Methods in Natural Language Processing (EMNLP)* (pp. 1241–1249). doi: http://dx.doi.org/10.3115/1699648.1699670

Israel, R., Dickinson, M., & Lee, S.-H. (2013). Detecting and Correcting Learner Korean Particle Omission Errors. In *Proceedings of the Sixth International Joint Conference on Natural Language Processing* (pp. 1419–1427).

Israel, R., Tetreault, J., & Chodorow, M. (2012). Correcting Comma Errors in Learner Essays, and Restoring Commas in Newswire Text. In *Proceedings of the Conference of the North American Chapter of the Association for Computational Linguistics: Human Language Technologies (NAACL-HLT)* (pp. 284–294).

Jabbari, F., Falakmasir, M., & Ashley, K. (2016). Identifying Thesis Statements in Student Essays: the Class Imbalance Challenge and Resolution. In *Proceedings of the Florida Artificial Intelligence Research Society Conference.*

Janda, H., Pawar, A., Du, S., & Mago, V. (2019). Syntactic, Semantic and Sentiment Analysis: the Joint Effect on Automated Essay Evaluation. *IEEE Access*, 7, 108486-108503. doi: `http://dx.doi.org/10.1109/access.2019.2933354`

Jin, C., He, B., Hui, K., & Sun, L. (2018). TDNN: a Two-Stage Deep Neural Network for Prompt-Independent Automated Essay Scoring. In *Proceedings of the Annual Meeting of the Association for Computational Linguistics (ACL)* (pp. 1088–1097). doi: `http://dx.doi.org/10.18653/v1/p18-1100`

Joachims, T. (2002). Optimizing Search Engines Using Clickthrough Data. In *Proceedings of the ACM SIGKDD International Conference on Knowledge Discovery and Data Mining (KDD)* (pp. 133–142). doi: `http://dx.doi.org/10.1145/775047.775067`

Jones, S., Fox, C., Gillam, S., & Gillam, R. B. (2019). An Exploration of Automated Narrative Analysis Via Machine Learning. *PLOS ONE*, *14*(10), 1-14. doi: `http://dx.doi.org/10.1371/journal.pone.0224634`

Jorge-Botana, G., Luzón, J., Gómez-Veiga, I., & Cordero, M. (2015). Automated LSA Assessment of Summaries in Distance Education. *Journal of Educational Computing Research*, *52*(3), 341-264. doi: `http://dx.doi.org/10.1177/0735633115571930`

Jorge-Botana, G., Olmos, R., & Luzón, J. (2019). Could LSA Become a "Bifactor" Model? Towards a Model with General and Group Factors. *Expert Systems with Applications*, *131*. doi: `http://dx.doi.org/10.1016/j.eswa.2019.04.055`

Junczys-Dowmunt, M., & Grundkiewicz, R. (2014). The AMU System in the Conll-2014 Shared Task: Grammatical Error Correction by Data-Intensive and Feature-Rich Statistical Machine Translation. In *Proceedings of the Conference on Computational Natural Language Learning: Shared Task* (pp. 25–33). doi: `http://dx.doi.org/10.3115/v1/w14-1703`

Kakkonen, T., & Mozgovoy, M. (2010). Hermetic and Web Plagiarism Detection Systems for Student Essays—an Evaluation of the State-of-the-Art. *Journal of Educational Computing Research*, *42*(2), 135-159. doi: `http://dx.doi.org/10.2190/ec.42.2.a`

Kakkonen, T., Myller, N., & Sutinen, E. (2006). Applying Latent Dirichlet Allocation to Automatic Essay Grading. In *International Conference on Natural Language Processing (in Finland)* (pp. 110–120). doi: `http://dx.doi.org/10.1007/11816508_13`

Kakkonen, T., Myller, N., Sutinen, E., & Timonen, J. (2008). Comparison of Dimension Reduction Methods for Automated Essay Grading. *Journal of Educational Technology & Society*, *11*(3), 275–288.

Kakkonen, T., Myller, N., Timonen, J., & Sutinen, E. (2005). Automatic Essay Grading with Probabilistic Latent Semantic Analysis. In *Proceedings of the Second Workshop on Building Educational Applications Using NLP* (pp. 29–36). doi: http://dx.doi.org/10.3115/1609829.1609835

Kakkonen, T., & Sutinen, E. (2004). Automatic Assessment of the Content of Essays Based on Course Materials. In *Proceedings of the International Conference on Information Technology: Research and Education* (pp. 126–130). doi: http://dx.doi.org/10.1109/itre.2004.1393660

Kamiran, F., & Calders, T. (2009). Classifying Without Discriminating. In *Proceedings of the IEEE International Conference on Computer, Control and Communication* (pp. 1–6). doi: http://dx.doi.org/10.1109/ic4.2009.4909197

Kamiran, F., & Calders, T. (2012). Data Preprocessing Techniques for Classification Without Discrimination. *Knowledge and Information Systems, 33*(1), 1 – 33. doi: http://dx.doi.org/10.1007/s10115-011-0463-8

Kamiran, F., Karim, A., & Zhang, X. (2012). Decision Theory for Discrimination-Aware Classification. In *International Conference on Data Mining (ICDM)*. doi: http://dx.doi.org/10.1109/icdm.2012.45

Kamishima, T., Akaho, S., Asoh, H., & Sakuma, J. (2012). Fairness-Aware Classifier with Prejudice Remover Regularizer. *Machine Learning and Knowledge Discovery in Databases*, 35-50. doi: http://dx.doi.org/10.1007/978-3-642-33486-3_3

Kaneko, M., & Bollegala, D. (2019). Gender-Preserving Debiasing for Pre-Trained Word Embeddings. In *Proceedings of the Annual Meeting of the Association for Computational Linguistics (ACL)* (pp. 1641–1650). doi: http://dx.doi.org/10.18653/v1/p19-1160

Kang, D., Ammar, W., Dalvi, B., van Zuylen, M., Kohlmeier, S., Hovy, E., & Schwartz, R. (2018). A Dataset of Peer Reviews (Peerread): Collection, Insights and NLP Applications. In *Proceedings of the Conference of the North American Chapter of the Association for Computational Linguistics: Human Language Technologies (NAACL-HLT)* (pp. 1647–1661). doi: http://dx.doi.org/10.18653/v1/n18-1149

Karlgren, J., & Sahlgren, M. (2001). From Words to Understanding. In Y. Uesaka, P. Kanerva, & H. Asoh (Eds.), *Foundations of Real-World Intelligence* (p. 294-308). CSLI Publications.

Kasewa, S., Stenetorp, P., & Riedel, S. (n.d.). Wronging a Right: Generating Better Errors to Improve Grammatical Error Detection. In *Proceedings of the Conference on Empirical Methods in Natural Language Processing (EMNLP)* (pp. 4977–4983). doi: http://dx.doi.org/10.18653/v1/d18-1541

Kassim, N. L. A. (2011). Judging Behaviour and Rater Errors: an Application of the Many-Facet Rasch Model. *GEMA Online®Journal of Language Studies*, *11*(3).

Kaufer, D., & Butler, B. (2000). *Principles of Writing as Representational Composition*. Mahwah, NJ: Lawrence Erlbaum Associates. doi: http://dx.doi.org/10.4324/9781410606037

Kaufer, D., Ishizaki, S., Butler, B., & Collins, J. (2004). *The Power of Words: Unveiling the Speaker and Writer's Hidden Craft*. Routledge. doi: http://dx.doi.org/10.4324/9781410609748

Ke, Z., Inamdar, H., Lin, H., & Ng, V. (2019). Give Me More Feedback II: Annotating Thesis Strength and Related Attributes in Student Essays. In *Proceedings of the Annual Meeting of the Association for Computational Linguistics (ACL)* (pp. 3994–4004). doi: http://dx.doi.org/10.18653/v1/p19-1390

Kearns, M., Neel, S., Roth, A., & Wu, Z. S. (2018). Preventing Fairness Gerrymandering: Auditing and Learning for Subgroup Fairness. In *International Conference on Machine Learning* (pp. 2564–2572).

Kim, M., Reingold, O., & Rothblum, G. (2018). Fairness through Computationally-Bounded Awareness. In S. Bengio, H. Wallach, H. Larochelle, K. Grauman, N. Cesa-Bianchi, & R. Garnett (Eds.), *Advances in Neural Information Processing Systems 31* (pp. 4842–4852).

Klein, D., & Manning, C. (2003). Accurate Unlexicalized Parsing. In *Proceedings of the Annual Meeting of the Association for Computational Linguistics (ACL)* (pp. 423–430). doi: http://dx.doi.org/10.3115/1075096.1075150

Klein, D., & Milgram, J. (2000). *The Role of Long Division in the K–12 Curriculum*. https://www.csun.edu/~vcmth00m/longdivision.pdf.

Kluyver, T., Ragan-Kelley, B., Pérez, F., Granger, B., Bussonnier, M., Frederic, J., … Team, J. D. (2016). Jupyter Notebooks — a Publishing Format for Reproducible Computational Workflows. In *Proceedings of the International Conference on Electronic Publishing*.

Kochmar, E., & Briscoe, T. (2014). Detecting Learner Errors in the Choice of Content Words Using Compositional Distributional Semantics. In *Proceedings of the International Conference on Computational Linguistics (COLING)* (pp. 1740–1751).

Koh, P. W., & Liang, P. (2017). Understanding Black-Box Predictions Via Influence Functions. In *Proceedings of the International Conference on Machine Learning (ICML)* (pp. 1885–1894).

Kovanović, V., Joksimović, S., Mirriahi, N., Blaine, E., Gašević, D., Siemens, G., & Dawson, S. (2018). Understand Students' Self-Reflections through Learning Analytics. In *Proceedings of the International Conference on Learning Analytics and Knowledge (LAK)* (p. 389–398). doi: http://dx.doi.org/10.1145/3170358.3170374

Krizhevsky, A., Sutskever, I., & Hinton, G. E. (2012). Imagenet Classification with Deep Convolutional Neural Networks. In *Advances in Neural Information Processing Systems* (pp. 1097–1105). doi: http://dx.doi.org/10.1145/3065386

Kryscinski, W., Keskar, N. S., McCann, B., Xiong, C., & Socher, R. (2019). Neural Text Summarization: a Critical Evaluation. In *Proceedings of the Conference on Empirical Methods in Natural Language Processing and the International Joint Conference on Natural Language Processing (EMNLP-IJCNLP)* (pp. 540–551). doi: http://dx.doi.org/10.18653/v1/d19-1051

Kuhn, H. (1955). The Hungarian Method for the Assignment Problem. *Naval Research Logistics Quarterly*, *2*(1-2), 83–97. doi: http://dx.doi.org/10.1002/nav.3800020109

Kumar, S., Chakrabarti, S., & Roy, S. (2017). Earth Mover'S Distance Pooling Over Siamese Lstms for Automatic Short Answer Grading. In *Proceedings of the International Joint Conference on Artificial Intelligence (IJCAI)* (pp. 2046–2052). doi: http://dx.doi.org/10.24963/ijcai.2017/284

Kuribayashi, T., Ouchi, H., Inoue, N., Reisert, P., Miyoshi, T., Suzuki, J., & Inui, K. (2019). An Empirical Study of Span Representations in Argumentation Structure Parsing. In *Proceedings of the Annual Meeting of the Association for Computational Linguistics (ACL)* (pp. 4691–4698). doi: http://dx.doi.org/10.18653/v1/p19-1464

Kuzi, S., Cope, W., Ferguson, D., Geigle, C., & Zhai, C. (2019). Automatic Assessment of Complex Assignments Using Topic Models. In *Proceedings of the ACM Conference on Learning @ Scale (L@S)*.

Lafferty, J., McCallum, A., & Pereira, F. (2001). Conditional Random Fields: Probabilistic Models for Segmenting and Labeling Sequence Data. In *Proceedings of the International Conference on Machine Learning (ICML)*.

Lai, A., & Tetreault, J. (2018). Discourse Coherence in the Wild: a Dataset, Evaluation and Methods. In *Proceedings of the Annual Meeting on Discourse and Dialogue (SIGDIAL)* (pp. 214–223). doi: http://dx.doi.org/10.18653/v1/w18-5023

Lakoff, G. (1991). Metaphor and War: the Metaphor System Used to Justify War in the Gulf. *Peace Research*, *23*, 25–32.

Landauer, T., Laham, D., & Foltz, P. (2003). Automated Scoring and Annotation of Essays with the Intelligent Essay Assessor. *Automated Essay Scoring: a Cross-Disciplinary Perspective*, 87–112.

Landauer, T. K., Foltz, P. W., & Laham, D. (1998). An Introduction to Latent Semantic Analysis. *Discourse Processes*, *25*(2-3), 259–284. doi: http://dx.doi.org/10.1080/01638539809545028

Larkey, L. S. (1998). Automatic Essay Grading Using Text Categorization Techniques. In *Proceedings of the Annual International ACM Conference on Research and Development in Information Retrieval (SIGIR)* (pp. 90–95). doi: http://dx.doi.org/10.1145/290941.290965

Lau, J. H., Clark, A., & Lappin, S. (2015). Unsupervised Prediction of Acceptability Judgements. In *Proceedings of the Annual Meeting of the Association for Computational Linguistics and the International Joint Conference on Natural Language Processing (ACL-IJCNLP)* (pp. 1618–1628). doi: http://dx.doi.org/10.3115/v1/p15-1156

Lau, J. H., Clark, A., & Lappin, S. (2017). Grammaticality, Acceptability, and Probability: a Probabilistic View of Linguistic Knowledge. *Cognitive Science, 41*(5), 1202–1241. doi: http://dx.doi.org/10.1111/cogs.12414

Lawson, C. L., & Hanson, R. J. (1981). *Solving Least Squares Problems*. Prentice-Hall. doi: http://dx.doi.org/10.1137/1.9781611971217

Le, Q., & Mikolov, T. (2014). Distributed Representations of Sentences and Documents. In *Proceedings of the International Conference on Machine Learning (ICML)* (pp. 1188–1196).

Leacock, C., Chodorow, M., Gamon, M., & Tetreault, J. (2014). Automated Grammatical Error Detection for Language Learners. *Synthesis Lectures on Human Language Technologies, 7*(1), 1–170. doi: http://dx.doi.org/10.2200/s00562ed1v01y201401hlt025

Lebanon, G., Mao, Y., & Dillon, J. (2007). The Locally Weighted Bag of Words Framework for Document Representation. *Journal of Machine Learning Research, 8*(Oct), 2405–2441.

LeCun, Y., Boser, B., Denker, J. S., Henderson, D., Howard, R. E., Hubbard, W., & Jackel, L. D. (1989). Backpropagation Applied to Handwritten Zip Code Recognition. *Neural Computation, 1*(4), 541–-551. doi: http://dx.doi.org/10.1162/neco.1989.1.4.541

Lee, J., & Seneff, S. (2006). Automatic Grammar Correction for Second-Language Learners. In *Proceedings of the International Conference on Spoken Language Processing (ICSLP)*.

Lee, J., & Seneff, S. (2008). Correcting Misuse of Verb Forms. In *Proceedings of the Annual Meeting of the Association for Computational Linguistics: Human Language Technologies (ACL-HLT)* (pp. 174–182).

Lee, J., Yeung, C. Y., & Chodorow, M. (2014). Automatic Detection of Comma Splices. In *Proceedings of the Pacific Asia Conference on Language, Information and Computing (PACLIC)* (pp. 551–560).

Lee, Y.-H., & von Davier, A. (n.d.). Monitoring Scale Scores Over Time Via Quality Control Charts, Model-Based Approaches, and Time Series Techniques. *Psychometrika*. doi: http://dx.doi.org/10.1007/s11336-013-9317-5

Lee, Y.-W., Gentile, C., & Kantor, R. (2008). Analytic Scoring Of TOEFL® CBT Essays: Scores From Humans and E-rater®. *ETS Research Report Series*, *2008*(1), i-71. doi: `http://dx.doi.org/10.1002/j.2333-8504.2008.tb02087.x`

Lemaire, B., & Dessus, P. (2001). A System to Assess the Semantic Content of Student Essays. *Journal of Educational Computing Research*, *24*, 305–320. doi: `http://dx.doi.org/10.2190/g649-0r9c-c021-p6x3`

Lemaire, B., Mandin, S., Dessus, P., & Denhiere, G. (2005). Computational Cognitive Models of Summarization Assessment Skills. In *Proceedings of the Annual Meeting of the Cognitive Science Society (Cogsci)* (p. 1266-1271).

Leng, Y., Yu, L., & Xiong, J. (2019). Deepreviewer: Collaborative Grammar and Innovation Neural Network for Automatic Paper Review. In *Proceedings of the International Conference on Multimodal Interaction (ICMI)* (p. 395–403). doi: `http://dx.doi.org/10.1145/3340555.3353766`

Lennon, P. (2000). The Lexical Element in Spoken Second Language Fluency. In H. Riggenbach (Ed.), *Perspectives on Fluency* (pp. 25–42). University of Michigan Press.

Levy, R., Gretz, S., Sznajder, B., Hummel, S., Aharonov, R., & Slonim, N. (2017). Unsupervised Corpus–Wide Claim Detection. In *Proceedings of the Workshop on Argument Mining* (pp. 79–84). doi: `http://dx.doi.org/10.18653/v1/w17-5110`

Lewis, M. L., & Frank, M. C. (2016). The Length of Words Reflects Their Conceptual Complexity. *Cognition*, *153*, 182 - 195. doi: `http://dx.doi.org/10.1016/j.cognition.2016.04.003`

Li, B., Lee-Urban, S., Johnston, G., & Riedl, M. (2013). Story Generation with Crowdsourced Plot Graphs. In *Proceedings of the AAAI Conference on Artificial Intelligence*.

Li, H., Cai, Z., & Graesser, A. (2018). Computerized Summary Scoring: Crowdsourcing-Based Latent Semantic Analysis. *Behavior Research Methods*, *50*(5), 2144–2161. doi: `http://dx.doi.org/10.3758/s13428-017-0982-7`

Li, J., & Hovy, E. (2014). A Model of Coherence Based on Distributed Sentence Representation. In *Proceedings of the Conference on Empirical Methods in Natural Language Processing (EMNLP)* (pp. 2039–2048). doi: `http://dx.doi.org/10.3115/v1/d14-1218`

Li, J., & Jurafsky, D. (2017). Neural Net Models of Open-Domain Discourse Coherence. In *Proceedings of the Conference on Empirical Methods in Natural Language Processing (EMNLP)* (pp. 198–209). doi: `http://dx.doi.org/10.18653/v1/d17-1019`

Li, J., & Nenkova, A. (2015). Fast and Accurate Prediction of Sentence Specificity. In *Proceedings of the AAAI Conference on Artificial Intelligence*.

Li, Z., Ding, X., & Liu, T. (2019). Story Ending Prediction by Transferable BERT. In *Proceedings of the Twenty-Eighth International Joint Conference on Artificial Intelligence, IJCAI–19* (pp. 1800–1806). doi: http://dx.doi.org/10.24963/ijcai.2019/249

Lilja, M. (2018). *Automatic Essay Scoring of Swedish Essays Using Neural Networks.* Student Thesis.

Lin, C.-Y. (2004). ROUGE: a Package for Automatic Evaluation of Summaries. In *Text Summarization Branches Out* (pp. 74–81).

Lin, C.-Y., & Hovy, E. (2000). The Automated Acquisition of Topic Signatures for Text Summarization. In *Proceedings of the International Conference on Computational Linguistics (COLING)* (pp. 495–501). doi: http://dx.doi.org/10.3115/990820.990892

Lin, C.-Y., & Hovy, E. (2003). Automatic Evaluation of Summaries Using N-Gram Co-Occurrence Statistics. In *Proceedings of the Annual Conference of the North American Chapter of the Association for Computational Linguistics: Human Language Technologies (HLT-NAACL)* (pp. 71–78). doi: http://dx.doi.org/10.3115/1073445.1073465

Lin, Z., Ng, H., & Kan, M.-Y. (2014). A PDTB-Styled End-to-End Discourse Parser. *Natural Language Engineering*, *20*(2), 151–184. doi: http://dx.doi.org/10.1017/s1351324912000307

Lin, Z., Ng, H. T., & Kan, M.-Y. (2011). Automatically Evaluating Text Coherence Using Discourse Relations. In *Proceedings of the Annual Meeting of the Association for Computational Linguistics: Human Language Technologies (ACL-HLT)* (pp. 997–1006).

Lindsay, G., Kell, L., Ouellette, J., & Westall, H. (2010). Using 'I' in Scholarly Writing: How Does Reflecting on Experience Matter? *Reflective Practice*, *11*(3), 271-283. doi: http://dx.doi.org/10.1080/14623943.2010.487372

Ling, G., Mollaun, P., & Xi, X. (2014). A Study on the Impact of Fatigue on Human Raters When Scoring Speaking Responses. *Language Testing*, *31*, 479–499. doi: http://dx.doi.org/10.1177/0265532214530699

Lipnevich, A., & Smith, J. (2008). Response to Assessment Feedback: the Effect of Grades, Praise, and Source of Information. *ETS Research Report No. RR-08-30.*

Lippi, M., & Torroni, P. (2015). Context-Independent Claim Detection for Argument Mining. In *Proceedings of the International Joint Conference on Artificial Intelligence (IJCAI)* (pp. 185–191).

Lipton, Z. C. (2016). The Mythos of Model Interpretability. In *Proceedings of the ICML Workshop on Human Interpretability in Machine Learning.*

Liu, J., & Dorans, N. J. (2016). Fairness in Score Interpretation. In N. J. Dorans & L. L. Cook (Eds.), *Fairness in Educational Assessment and Measurement* (pp. 77–96). Routledge.

Liu, N. F., Gardner, M., Belinkov, Y., Peters, M. E., & Smith, N. A. (2019). Linguistic Knowledge and Transferability of Contextual Representations. In *Proceedings of the Conference of the North American Chapter of the Association for Computational Linguistics: Human Language Technologies (HLT-NAACL)* (pp. 1073–1094). doi: `http://dx.doi.org/10.18653/v1/n19-1112`

Liu, O. L., Brew, C., Blackmore, J., Gerard, L., Madhok, J., & Linn, M. C. (2014). Automated Scoring of Constructed-Response Science Items: Prospects and Obstacles. *Educational Measurement: Issues and Practice*, *33*(2), 19–28. doi: `http://dx.doi.org/10.1111/emip.12028`

Liu, Y., Pang, B., & Liu, B. (2019). Neural-Based Chinese Idiom Recommendation for Enhancing Elegance in Essay Writing. In *Proceedings of the Annual Meeting of the Association for Computational Linguistics (ACL)* (pp. 5522–5526). doi: `http://dx.doi.org/10.18653/v1/p19-1552`

Lloret, E., Plaza, L., & Aker, A. (2018). The Challenging Task of Summary Evaluation: an Overview. *Language Resources and Evaluation*, *52*(1), 101–148. doi: `http://dx.doi.org/10.1007/s10579-017-9399-2`

Logeswaran, L., Lee, H., & Radev, D. (2018). Sentence Ordering and Coherence Modeling Using Recurrent Neural Networks. In *Proceedings of the AAAI Conference on Artificial Intelligence*.

Loraksa, C., & Peachavanish, R. (2007). Automatic Thai-Language Essay Scoring Using Neural Network and Latent Semantic Analysis. In *Proceedings of the First Asia International Conference on Modelling Simulation (AMS'07)* (p. 400-402). doi: `http://dx.doi.org/10.1109/ams.2007.19`

Lorenzen, S., Hjuler, N., & Alstrup, S. (2019). Investigating Writing Style Development in High School. *Corr, abs/1906.03072*.

Lotteridge, S., & Hoefer, N. (2020). System Architecture Design for Scoring and Delivery. In *Handbook of Automated Scoring: Theory Into Practice* (pp. 195–214). Taylor & Francis Group. doi: `http://dx.doi.org/10.1201/9781351264808-11`

Louis, A., & Higgins, D. (2010). Off-Topic Essay Detection Using Short Prompt Texts. In *Proceedings of the Workshop on Innovative Use of NLP for Building Educational Applications (BEA)* (pp. 92–95).

Louis, A., & Nenkova, A. (2009). Automatically Evaluating Content Selection in Summarization Without Human Models. In *Proceedings of the Conference on Empirical Methods in*

Natural Language Processing (EMNLP) (pp. 306–314). doi: http://dx.doi.org/10.3115/1699510.1699550

Louis, A., & Nenkova, A. (2012). A Coherence Model Based on Syntactic Patterns. In *Proceedings of the Joint Conference on Empirical Methods in Natural Language Processing and Computational Natural Language Learning (EMNLP-Conll)* (pp. 1157–1168).

Louis, A., & Nenkova, A. (2013). What Makes Writing Great? First Experiments on Article Quality Prediction in the Science Journalism Domain. *Transactions of the Association for Computational Linguistics, 1,* 341-352. doi: http://dx.doi.org/10.1162/tacl_a_00232

Loukina, A., Beigman Klebanov, B., Lange, P., Gyawali, B., & Qian, Y. (2017). Developing Speech Processing Technologies for Shared Book Reading with a Computer. In *Proceedings of the International Workshop on Child Computer Interaction (WOCCI)* (pp. 46–51). doi: http://dx.doi.org/10.21437/wocci.2017-8

Loukina, A., Madnani, N., Cahill, A., Yao, L., Johnson, M. S., Riordan, B., & McCaffrey, D. F. (2020). Using PRMSE to Evaluate Automated Scoring Systems in the Presence of Label Noise. In *Proceedings of the Workshop on Innovative Use of NLP for Building Educational Applications (BEA)* (pp. 18–29). doi: http://dx.doi.org/10.18653/v1/2020.bea-1.2

Loukina, A., Madnani, N., & Zechner, K. (2019). The Many Dimensions of Algorithmic Fairness in Educational Applications. In *Proceedings of the Workshop on Innovative Use of NLP for Building Educational Applications (BEA)* (pp. 1–10). doi: http://dx.doi.org/10.18653/v1/w19-4401

Loukina, A., Zechner, K., Bruno, J., & Beigman Klebanov, B. (2018). Using Exemplar Responses for Training and Evaluating Automated Speech Scoring Systems. In *Proceedings of the Workshop on Innovative Use of NLP for Building Educational Applications (BEA)* (pp. 1–12). doi: http://dx.doi.org/10.18653/v1/w18-0501

Loukina, A., Zechner, K., Chen, L., & Heilman, M. (2015). Feature Selection for Automated Speech Scoring. In *Proceedings of the Workshop on Innovative Use of NLP for Building Educational Applications (BEA)* (pp. 12–19). doi: http://dx.doi.org/10.3115/v1/w15-0602

Loukina, A., Zechner, K., Yoon, S.-Y., Zhang, M., Tao, J., Wang, X., ... Mulholland, M. (2017). Performance of Automated Speech Scoring on Different Low-to Medium-Entropy Item Types for Low-Proficiency English Learners. *ETS Research Report Series, 2017*(1), 1–17. doi: http://dx.doi.org/10.1002/ets2.12139

Lu, X. (2010). Automatic Analysis of Syntactic Complexity in Second Language Writing. *International Journal of Corpus Linguistics, 15*(4), 474–496. doi: http://dx.doi.org/10.1075/ijcl.15.4.02lu

Ludwig, O., Do, Q. N. T., Smith, C., Cavazza, M., & Moens, M. (2018). Learning to Extract Action Descriptions from Narrative Text. *IEEE Transactions on Games, 10*(1), 15-28. doi: http://dx.doi.org/10.1109/tciaig.2017.2657690

Lundberg, S. M., & Lee, S.-I. (2017). A Unified Approach to Interpreting Model Predictions. In *Advances in Neural Information Processing Systems 30* (pp. 4765–4774).

Luo, W., & Litman, D. (2016). Determining the Quality of a Student Reflective Response. In *Proceedings of the International FLAIRS Conference.*

Luong, B. T., Ruggieri, S., & Turini, F. (2011). K-NN as an Implementation of Situation Testing for Discrimination Discovery and Prevention. In *Proceedings of the ACM SIGKDD International Conference on Knowledge Discovery and Data Mining (KDD)* (pp. 502–510). doi: http://dx.doi.org/10.1145/2020408.2020488

Lynn, V., Goodman, A., Niederhoffer, K., Loveys, K., Resnik, P., & Schwartz, H. A. (2018). Clpsych 2018 Shared Task: Predicting Current and Future Psychological Health from Childhood Essays. In *Proceedings of the Workshop on Computational Linguistics and Clinical Psychology: from Keyboard to Clinic* (pp. 37–46). doi: http://dx.doi.org/10.18653/v1/w18-0604

Madnani, N., Burstein, J., Elliot, N., Beigman Klebanov, B., Napolitano, D., Andreyev, S., & Schwartz, M. (2018). Writing Mentor: Self-Regulated Writing Feedback for Struggling Writers. In *Proceedings of the International Conference on Computational Linguistics (COLING)* (pp. 113–117).

Madnani, N., Burstein, J., Sabatini, J., Biggers, K., & Andreyev, S. (2016). Language Muse: Automated Linguistic Activity Generation for English Language Learners. In *Proceedings of ACL-2016 System Demonstrations* (pp. 79–84). doi: http://dx.doi.org/10.18653/v1/p16-4014

Madnani, N., Burstein, J., Sabatini, J., & O'Reilly, T. (2013). Automated Scoring of a Summary-Writing Task Designed to Measure Reading Comprehension. In *Proceedings of the Workshop on Innovative Use of NLP for Building Educational Applications (BEA)* (pp. 163–168).

Madnani, N., & Cahill, A. (2018). Automated Scoring: Beyond Natural Language Processing. In *Proceedings of the International Conference on Computational Linguistics (COLING)* (pp. 1099–1109).

Madnani, N., Cahill, A., Blanchard, D., Andreyev, S., Napolitano, D., Gyawali, B., ... Riordan, B. (2018). A Robust Microservice Architecture for Scaling Automated Scoring Applications. *ETS Research Report Series, 2018*(1). doi: http://dx.doi.org/10.1002/ets2.12202

Madnani, N., Cahill, A., & Riordan, B. (2016). Automatically Scoring Tests of Proficiency in Music Instruction. In *Proceedings of the Workshop on Innovative Use of NLP for Building Educational Applications (BEA)* (pp. 217–222). doi: http://dx.doi.org/10.18653/v1/w16-0524

Madnani, N., Heilman, M., & Cahill, A. (2016). Model Combination for Correcting Preposition Selection Errors. In *Proceedings of the Workshop on Innovative Use of NLP for Building Educational Applications (BEA)* (pp. 136–141). doi: http://dx.doi.org/10.18653/v1/w16-0515

Madnani, N., Heilman, M., Tetreault, J., & Chodorow, M. (2012). Identifying High-Level Organizational Elements in Argumentative Discourse. In *Proceeding of the Annual Conference of the North American Chapter of the Association for Computational Linguistics: Human Language Technologies (NAACL-HLT)* (pp. 20–28).

Madnani, N., Loukina, A., & Cahill, A. (2017). A Large Scale Quantitative Exploration of Modeling Strategies for Content Scoring. In *Proceedings of the Workshop on Innovative Use of NLP for Building Educational Applications (BEA)* (pp. 457–467). doi: http://dx.doi.org/10.18653/v1/w17-5052

Madnani, N., Loukina, A., von Davier, A., Burstein, J., & Cahill, A. (2017). Building Better Open-Source Tools to Support Fairness in Automated Scoring. In *Proceedings of the Workshop on Ethics in Natural Language Processing* (pp. 41–52). doi: http://dx.doi.org/10.18653/v1/w17-1605

Mahmoud El-Haj, Rayson, P., Young, S., Bouamor, H., & Ferradans, S. (Eds.). (2019). *Proceedings of the Second Financial Narrative Processing Workshop (FNP 2019)*. LinkÖPing University Electronic Press.

Mancuhan, K., & Clifton, C. (2014). Combating Discrimination Using Bayesian Networks. *Artif. Intell. Law*, *22*(2), 211–238. doi: http://dx.doi.org/10.1007/s10506-014-9156-4

Mani, I. (2012). Computational Modeling of Narrative. *Synthesis Lectures on Human Language Technologies*, *5*(3), 1–142. doi: http://dx.doi.org/10.2200/s00459ed1v01y201212hlt018

Mann, K., Gordon, J., & MacLeod, A. (2009). Reflection and Reflective Practice in Health Professions Education: a Systematic Review. *Advances in Health Sciences Education*, *14*(4), 595. doi: http://dx.doi.org/10.1007/s10459-007-9090-2

Mann, W. C., & Thompson, S. A. (1988). Rhetorical Structure Theory: Toward a Functional Theory of Text Organization. *Text*, *8*(3), 243–281. doi: http://dx.doi.org/10.1515/text.1.1988.8.3.243

Mao, L., Liu, O. L., Roohr, K., Belur, V., Mulholland, M., Lee, H.-S., & Pallant, A. (2018). Validation of Automated Scoring for a Formative Assessment That Employs Scientific Argumentation. *Educational Assessment*, *23*(2), 121-138. doi: `http://dx.doi.org/10.1080/10627197.2018.1427570`

Marcu, D. (2000). *The Theory and Practice of Discourse Parsing and Summarization*. MIT Press. doi: `http://dx.doi.org/10.7551/mitpress/6754.001.0001`

Martin, L. J., Ammanabrolu, P., Wang, X., Hancock, W., Singh, S., Harrison, B., & Riedl, M. O. (2018). Event Representations for Automated Story Generation with Deep Neural Nets. In *Proceedings of the Thirty-Second AAAI Conference on Artificial Intelligence*.

Marvaniya, S., Saha, S., Dhamecha, T. I., Foltz, P., Sindhgatta, R., & Sengupta, B. (2018). Creating Scoring Rubric from Representative Student Answers for Improved Short Answer Grading. In *Proceedings of the ACM International Conference on Information and Knowledge Management (CIKM)* (pp. 993–1002). doi: `http://dx.doi.org/10.1145/3269206.3271755`

Mathias, S., & Bhattacharyya, P. (2018). ASAP++: Enriching the ASAP Automated Essay Grading Dataset with Essay Attribute Scores. In *Proceedings of the Eleventh International Conference on Language Resources and Evaluation (LREC)*.

Mathias, S., & Bhattacharyya, P. (2020). Can Neural Networks Automatically Score Essay Traits? In *Proceedings of the Workshop on Innovative Use of NLP for Building Educational Applications (BEA)* (pp. 85–91). doi: `http://dx.doi.org/10.18653/v1/2020.bea-1.8`

Mathias, S., Kanojia, D., Patel, K., Agrawal, S., Mishra, A., & Bhattacharyya, P. (2018). Eyes are the Windows to the Soul: Predicting the Rating of Text Quality Using Gaze Behaviour. In *Proceedings of the Annual Meeting of the Association for Computational Linguistics (ACL)* (pp. 2352–2362). doi: `http://dx.doi.org/10.18653/v1/p18-1219`

Matthews, B. W. (1975). Comparison of the Predicted and Observed Secondary Structure of T4 Phage Lysozyme. *Biochimica Et Biophysica Acta (BBA)-Protein Structure*, *405*(2), 442–451. doi: `http://dx.doi.org/10.1016/0005-2795(75)90109-9`

Mayfield, E., & Black, A. W. (2020). Should You Fine-Tune BERT for Automated Essay Scoring? In *Proceedings of the Workshop on Innovative Use of NLP for Building Educational Applications (BEA)* (pp. 151–162). doi: `http://dx.doi.org/10.18653/v1/2020.bea-1.15`

Mayfield, E., Madaio, M., Prabhumoye, S., Gerritsen, D., McLaughlin, B., Dixon-Román, E., & Black, A. W. (2019). Equity Beyond Bias in Language Technologies for Education. In *Proceedings of the Workshop on Innovative Use of NLP for Building Educational Applications (BEA)* (pp. 444–460). doi: `http://dx.doi.org/10.18653/v1/w19-4446`

Mays, E., Damerau, F. J., & Mercer, R. L. (1991). Context Based Spelling Correction. *Information Processing & Management*, *27*(5), 517–522. doi: http://dx.doi.org/10.1016/0306-4573(91)90066-u

McIntyre, N., & Lapata, M. (2009). Learning to Tell Tales: a Data-Driven Approach to Story Generation. In *Proceedings of the Joint Conference of the 47th Annual Meeting of the ACL and the 4th International Joint Conference on Natural Language Processing of the AFNLP* (pp. 217–225). doi: http://dx.doi.org/10.3115/1687878.1687910

McNamara, D., Crossley, S., & Roscoe, R. (2013, 01). Natural Language Processing in an Intelligent Writing Strategy Tutoring System. *Behavior Research Methods*, *45*(2), 499–515. doi: http://dx.doi.org/10.3758/s13428-012-0258-1

McNamara, T., & Lumley, B. (1997). A Generalizability Theory Study of Ratings and Test Design in the Oral Interaction and Writing Modules. In G. Brindley & G. Wigglesworth (Eds.), *Access: Issues in Language Test Design and Delivery*. Macquarie University: National Center for English Language.

Menekse, M., Stump, G., Krause, S., & Chi, M. (2011). The Effectiveness of Students' Daily Reflections on Learning in Engineering Context. In *Proceedings of the ASEE Annual Conference and Exposition*. doi: http://dx.doi.org/10.18260/1-2--19002

Mensonides, J.-C., Harispe, S., Montmain, J., & Thireau, V. (2019). Automatic Detection and Classification of Argument Components Using Multi-Task Deep Neural Network. In *Proceedings of the International Conference on Natural Language and Speech Processing* (pp. 25–33).

Merriam, T. V., & Matthews, R. A. (1994). Neural Computation in Stylometry II: an Application to the Works of Shakespeare and Marlowe. *Literary and Linguistic Computing*, *9*(1), 1–6. doi: http://dx.doi.org/10.1093/llc/9.1.1

Mesgar, M., & Strube, M. (2018). A Neural Local Coherence Model for Text Quality Assessment. In *Proceedings of the Conference on Empirical Methods in Natural Language Processing (EMNLP)* (pp. 4328–4339). doi: http://dx.doi.org/10.18653/v1/d18-1464

Meurers, D., Ziai, R., Ott, N., & Kopp, J. (2011). Evaluating Answers to Reading Comprehension Questions in Context: Results for German and the Role of Information Structure. In *Proceedings of the Textinfer 2011 Workshop on Textual Entailment* (pp. 1–9).

Mezher, R., & Omar, N. (2016). A Hybrid Method of Syntactic Feature and Latent Semantic Analysis for Automatic Arabic Essay Scoring. *Journal of Applied Sciences*, *16*(5), 209. doi: http://dx.doi.org/10.3923/jas.2016.209.215

Mezler, D. (2014). *Assignments Across the Curriculum: a National Study of College Writing.* Logan, UT: Utah State University Press. doi: http://dx.doi.org/10.7330/9780874219401

Mihalcea, R., & Tarau, P. (2004). Textrank: Bringing Order Into Text. In *Proceedings of the Conference on Empirical Methods in Natural Language Processing (EMNLP)* (pp. 404–411).

Mikolov, T., Chen, K., Corrado, G., & Dean, J. (2013). Efficient Estimation of Word Representations in Vector Space. *Arxiv Preprint Arxiv:1301.3781.*

Mikolov, T., et al. (2012). Statistical Language Models Based on Neural Networks. *Presentation At Google, Mountain View, 2nd April*, *80*, 26.

Mikolov, T., Sutskever, I., Chen, K., Corrado, G. S., & Dean, J. (2013). Distributed Representations of Words and Phrases and Their Compositionality. In *Advances in Neural Information Processing Systems 26* (pp. 3111–3119).

Milne, D., & Witten, I. H. (2008). An Effective, Low-Cost Measure of Semantic Relatedness Obtained from Wikipedia Links. In *Proceedings of the AAAI Workshop on Wikipedia and Artificial Intelligence: an Evolving Synergy* (pp. 25–30).

Miltsakaki, E., & Kukich, K. (2000). The Role of Centering Theory's Rough-Shift in the Teaching and Evaluation of Writing Skills. In *Proceedings of the Annual Meeting of the Association for Computational Linguistics (ACL)* (pp. 408–415). doi: http://dx.doi.org/10.3115/1075218.1075270

Minsky, M., & Papert, S. A. (1969). *Perceptrons.* MIT Press.

Mizumoto, T., Hayashibe, Y., Komachi, M., Nagata, M., & Matsumoto, Y. (2012). The Effect of Learner Corpus Size in Grammatical Error Correction of ESL Writings. In *Proceedings of the International Conference on Computational Linguistics (COLING)* (pp. 863–872).

Mochales-Palau, R., & Moens, M.-F. (2009). Argumentation Mining: the Detection, Classification and Structure of Arguments in Text. In *Proceedings of the International Conference on Artificial Intelligence and Law* (pp. 98–107). doi: http://dx.doi.org/10.1145/1568234.1568246

Mohit, B., Rozovskaya, A., Habash, N., Zaghouani, W., & Obeid, O. (2014). The First QALB Shared Task on Automatic Text Correction for Arabic. In *Proceedings of the EMNLP 2014 Workshop on Arabic Natural Language Processing (ANLP)* (pp. 39–47). doi: http://dx.doi.org/10.3115/v1/w14-3605

Mohler, M., Bunescu, R., & Mihalcea, R. (2011). Learning to Grade Short Answer Questions Using Semantic Similarity Measures and Dependency Graph Alignments. In *Proceedings of ACL: HLT* (pp. 752–762).

Molnar, C. (2019). *Interpretable Machine Learning*. (https://christophm.github.io/interpretable-ml-book/) doi: http://dx.doi.org/10.21105/joss.00786

Mostafazadeh, N., Chambers, N., He, X., Parikh, D., Batra, D., Vanderwende, L., ... Allen, J. (2016). A Corpus and Cloze Evaluation for Deeper Understanding of Commonsense Stories. In *Proceedings of the Conference of the North American Chapter of the Association for Computational Linguistics: Human Language Technologies* (pp. 839–849). doi: http://dx.doi.org/10.18653/v1/n16-1098

Mostafazadeh, N., Roth, M., Louis, A., Chambers, N., & Allen, J. (2017). Lsdsem 2017 Shared Task: the Story Cloze Test. In *Proceedings of the Workshop on Linking Models of Lexical, Sentential and Discourse-Level Semantics* (pp. 46–51). doi: http://dx.doi.org/10.18653/v1/w17-0906

Mosteller, F., & Wallace, D. L. (1963). Inference in an Authorship Problem: a Comparative Study of Discrimination Methods Applied to the Authorship of the Disputed Federalist Papers. *Journal of the American Statistical Association*, *58*(302), 275–309. doi: http://dx.doi.org/10.1080/01621459.1963.10500849

Musi, E., Ghosh, D., & Muresan, S. (2016). Towards Feasible Guidelines for the Annotation of Argument Schemes. In *Proceedings of the Third Workshop on Argument Mining (Argmining2016)* (pp. 82–93). doi: http://dx.doi.org/10.18653/v1/w16-2810

Nadeem, F., Nguyen, H., Liu, Y., & Ostendorf, M. (2019). Automated Essay Scoring with Discourse-Aware Neural Models. In *Proceedings of the Workshop on Innovative Use of NLP for Building Educational Applications (BEA)* (pp. 484–493). doi: http://dx.doi.org/10.18653/v1/w19-4450

Napoles, C., Gormley, M., & Van Durme, B. (2012). Annotated Gigaword. In *Proceedings of the Joint Workshop on Automatic Knowledge Base Construction and Web-Scale Knowledge Extraction* (pp. 95–100).

National Assessment Governing Board, U. D. o. E. (2007). *Writing Framework and Specifications for the 2007 National Assessment of Educational Progress*. Washington, DC:Government Printing Office.

National Assessment Governing Board, U. D. o. E. (2011). *Writing Framework for the 2011 National Assessment of Educational Progress*. Washington, DC:Government Printing Office.

National Assessment Governing Board, U. D. o. E. (2017). *Writing Framework for the 2011 National Assessment of Educational Progress*. Washington, DC:Government Printing Office.

Needels, M., & Knapp, M. (1994). Teaching Writing to Children Who are Underserved. *Journal of Educational Psychology*, *86*, 339-349. doi: http://dx.doi.org/10.1037/0022-0663.86.3.339

Nenkova, A., & McKeown, K. (2011). Automatic Summarization. *Foundations and Trends®in Information Retrieval*, 5(2–3), 103–233. doi: http://dx.doi.org/10.1561/1500000015

Nenkova, A., & Passonneau, R. (2004). Evaluating Content Selection in Summarization: the Pyramid Method. In *Proceedings of Human Language Technologies: the Conference of the North American Chapter of the Association for Computational Linguistics (HLT-NAACL)* (pp. 145–152).

Ng, H. T., Wu, S. M., Briscoe, T., Hadiwinoto, C., Susanto, R. H., & Bryant, C. (2014). The Conll-2014 Shared Task on Grammatical Error Correction. In *Proceedings of the Conference on Computational Natural Language Learning: Shared Task* (pp. 1–14). doi: http://dx.doi.org/10.3115/v1/w14-1701

Nguyen, H., & Litman, D. (2015). Extracting Argument and Domain Words for Identifying Argument Components in Texts. In *Proceedings of the Workshop on Argumentation Mining* (pp. 22–28). doi: http://dx.doi.org/10.3115/v1/w15-0503

Nguyen, H., & Litman, D. (2016a). Context-Aware Argumentative Relation Mining. In *Proceedings of the Annual Meeting of the Association for Computational Linguistics (ACL)* (pp. 1127–1137). doi: http://dx.doi.org/10.18653/v1/p16-1107

Nguyen, H., & Litman, D. (2016b). Improving Argument Mining in Student Essays by Learning and Exploiting Argument Indicators Versus Essay Topics. In *Proceedings of the Florida Artificial Intelligence Research Society Conference (FLAIRS)* (pp. 485–490).

Nguyen, H., & Litman, D. J. (2018). Argument Mining for Improving the Automated Scoring of Persuasive Essays. In *Proceedings of the Thirty-Second AAAI Conference on Artificial Intelligence*.

Nguyen, H., Xiong, W., & Litman, D. (2016). Instant Feedback for Increasing the Presence of Solutions in Peer Reviews. In *Proceedings of the Conference of the North American Chapter of the Association for Computational Linguistics: Human Language Technologies (NAACL-HLT)* (pp. 6–10). doi: http://dx.doi.org/10.18653/v1/n16-3002

Nicholls, D. (2003). The Cambridge Learner Corpus: Error Coding and Analysis for Lexicography and ELT. In *Proceedings of the Corpus Linguistics 2003 Conference* (Vol. 16, pp. 572–581).

Niculae, V., Park, J., & Cardie, C. (2017). Argument Mining with Structured Svms and Rnns. In *Proceedings of the Annual Meeting of the Association for Computational Linguistics (ACL)* (pp. 985–995). doi: http://dx.doi.org/10.18653/v1/p17-1091

Nielsen, R. D., Ward, W. H., & Martin, J. H. (2008). Learning to Assess Low-Level Conceptual Understanding. In *Proceedings of the FLAIRS Conference* (pp. 427–432).

Oliveri, M. E., & von Davier, A. (2016). Psychometrics in Support of a Valid Assessment of Linguistic Minorities: Implications for the Test and Sampling Designs. *International Journal of Testing*, *16*(3), 220-239. doi: http://dx.doi.org/10.1080/15305058.2015.1069743

Olmos, R., Jorge-Botana, G., Luzón, J., Cordero, M., & León, J. (2016). Transforming LSA Space Dimensions Into a Rubric for an Automatic Assessment and Feedback System. *Information Processing and Management*, *52*, 359–373. doi: http://dx.doi.org/10.1016/j.ipm.2015.12.002

Ong, N., Litman, D., & Brusilovsky, A. (2014). Ontology-Based Argument Mining and Automatic Essay Scoring. In *Proceedings of the First Workshop on Argumentation Mining* (pp. 24–28). doi: http://dx.doi.org/10.3115/v1/w14-2104

Opitz, J., & Frank, A. (2019). Dissecting Content and Context in Argumentative Relation Analysis. In *Proceedings of the Workshop on Argument Mining* (pp. 25–34). doi: http://dx.doi.org/10.18653/v1/w19-4503

O'Rourke, S. T., Calvo, R. A., & McNamara, D. S. (2011). Visualizing Topic Flow in Students' Essays. *Journal of Educational Technology & Society*, *14*(3).

Oyama, H., & Matsumoto, Y. (2010). Automatic Error Detection Method for Japanese Particles. *Ritsumeikan Asia Pacific University Polyglossia*, *18*, 55–63.

Pado, U., & Kiefer, C. (2015). Short Answer Grading: When Sorting Helps and When It Doesn'T. In *Proceedings of the Workshop on NLP for Computer Assisted Language Learning At NODALIDA* (pp. 42–50).

Page, E. B. (1966). The Imminence of Grading Essays by Computer. *The Phi Delta Kappan*, *47*(5), 238–243.

Papineni, K., Roukos, S., Ward, T., & Zhu, W.-J. (2002). BLEU: a Method for Automatic Evaluation of Machine Translation. In *Proceedings of the Annual Meeting of the Association for Computational Linguistics (ACL)* (pp. 311–318). doi: http://dx.doi.org/10.3115/1073083.1073135

Parker, R., Graff, D., Kong, J., Chen, K., & Maeda, K. (2011). *English Gigaword Fifth Edition LDC2011T07*. Web Download. Philadelphia: Linguistic Data Consortium.

Passonneau, R., Chen, E., Guo, W., & Perin, D. (2013). Automated Pyramid Scoring of Summaries Using Distributional Semantics. In *Proceedings of the Annual Meeting of the Association for Computational Linguistics (ACL)* (pp. 143–147).

Passonneau, R., Goodkind, A., & Levy, E. (2007). Annotation of Children's Oral Narrations: Modeling Emergent Narrative Skills for Computational Applications. In *Proceedings of the International FLAIRS Conference* (pp. 253–258).

Passonneau, R., Poddar, A., Gite, G., Krivokapic, A., Yang, Q., & Perin, D. (2018, 01). Wise Crowd Content Assessment and Educational Rubrics. *International Journal of Artificial Intelligence in Education*, *28*(1), 29–55. doi: http://dx.doi.org/10.1007/s40593-016-0128-6

Paul, M., Zhai, C., & Girju, R. (2010). Summarizing Contrastive Viewpoints in Opinionated Text. In *Proceedings of the Conference on Empirical Methods in Natural Language Processing (EMNLP)* (pp. 66–76).

Pedersen, T., Patwardhan, S., & Michelizzi, J. (2004). Wordnet::Similarity: Measuring the Relatedness of Concepts. In *Proceeding of the Annual Conference of the North American Chapter of the Association for Computational Linguistics: Human Language Technologies (HLT-NAACL)* (pp. 38–41). doi: http://dx.doi.org/10.3115/1614025.1614037

Pedregosa, F., Varoquaux, G., Gramfort, A., Michel, V., Thirion, B., Grisel, O., ... Duchesnay, E. (2011). Scikit-Learn: Machine Learning in Python. *Journal of Machine Learning Research*, *12*, 2825–2830. doi: http://dx.doi.org/10.1145/2786984.2786995

Peldszus, A., & Stede, M. (2013). From Argument Diagrams to Argumentation Mining in Texts: a Survey. *Int. J. Cogn. Inform. Nat. Intell.*, *7*(1), 1–31. doi: http://dx.doi.org/10.4018/jcini.2013010101

Penfield, R. D. (2016). Fairness in Test Scoring. In N. J. Dorans & L. L. Cook (Eds.), *Fairness in Educational Assessment and Measurement* (pp. 55–76). Routledge.

Pennington, J., Socher, R., & Manning, C. D. (2014). Glove: Global Vectors for Word Representation. In *Proceedings of the Conference on Empirical Methods in Natural Language Processing (EMNLP)* (pp. 1532–1543). doi: http://dx.doi.org/10.3115/v1/d14-1162

Perelman, C., & Olbrechts-Tyteca, L. (1969). *The New Rhetoric: a Treatise on Argumentation*. Wilkinson, J. doi: http://dx.doi.org/10.2307/j.ctvpj74xx

Perelman, L. (2014). When "the State of the Art" is Counting Words. *Assessing Writing*, *21*, 104–111. doi: http://dx.doi.org/10.1016/j.asw.2014.05.001

Persing, I., & Ng, V. (2013). Modeling Thesis Clarity in Student Essays. In *Proceedings of the Annual Meeting of the Association for Computational Linguistics (ACL)* (pp. 260–269).

Persing, I., & Ng, V. (2014). Modeling Prompt Adherence in Student Essays. In *Proceedings of the Annual Meeting of the Association for Computational Linguistics (ACL)* (pp. 1534–1543). doi: http://dx.doi.org/10.3115/v1/p14-1144

Persing, I., & Ng, V. (2015). Modeling Argument Strength in Student Essays. In *Proceedings of the Annual Meeting of the Association for Computational Linguistics and the International Joint Conference on Natural Language Processing (ACL-IJCNLP)* (pp. 543–552). doi: http://dx.doi.org/10.3115/v1/p15-1053

Persing, I., & Ng, V. (2016a). End-to-End Argumentation Mining in Student Essays. In *Proceedings of the Conference of the North American Chapter of the Association for Computational Linguistics: Human Language Technologies (NAACL-HLT)* (pp. 1384–1394). doi: http://dx.doi.org/10.18653/v1/n16-1164

Persing, I., & Ng, V. (2016b). Modeling Stance in Student Essays. In *Proceedings of the Annual Meeting of the Association for Computational Linguistics (ACL)* (pp. 2174–2184). doi: http://dx.doi.org/10.18653/v1/p16-1205

Persky, H., Daane, M., & Jin, Y. (2003). *The Nation'S Report Card: Writing 2002. National Center for Education Statistics NCES 2003-529*. Washington, DC: Government Printing Office.

Petasis, G., & Karkaletsis, V. (2016). Identifying Argument Components through Textrank. In *Proceedings of the Third Workshop on Argument Mining (Argmining2016)* (pp. 94–102). doi: http://dx.doi.org/10.18653/v1/w16-2811

Peters, M. E., Neumann, M., Iyyer, M., Gardner, M., Clark, C., Lee, K., & Zettlemoyer, L. (2018). Deep Contextualized Word Representations. In *Proceeding of the Annual Conference of the North American Chapter of the Association for Computational Linguistics: Human Language Technologies (HLT-NAACL)* (pp. 2227–2237). doi: http://dx.doi.org/10.18653/v1/n18-1202

Petersen, D. (2011). A Systematic Review of Narrative-Based Language Intervention with Children Who Have Language Impairment. *Communication Disorders Quarterly*, *32*(4), 207–220. doi: http://dx.doi.org/10.1177/1525740109353937

Petersen, D., Gillam, S. L., & Gillam, R. (2008). Emerging Procedures in Narrative Assessment: the Index of Narrative Complexity. *Topics in Language Disorders*, *28*(2), 115–130. doi: http://dx.doi.org/10.1097/01.tld.0000318933.46925.86

Phandi, P., Chai, K. M. A., & Ng, H. T. (2015). Flexible Domain Adaptation for Automated Essay Scoring Using Correlated Linear Regression. In *Proceedings of the Conference on Empirical Methods in Natural Language Processing (EMNLP)* (pp. 431–439). doi: http://dx.doi.org/10.18653/v1/d15-1049

Pitler, E., & Nenkova, A. (2009). Using Syntax to Disambiguate Explicit Discourse Connectives in Text. In *Proceedings of the ACL-IJCNLP 2009 Conference Short Papers* (pp. 13–16). doi: http://dx.doi.org/10.3115/1667583.1667589

Pleiss, G., Raghavan, M., Wu, F., Kleinberg, J., & Weinberger, K. Q. (2017). On Fairness and Calibration. In *Advances in Neural Information Processing Systems* (pp. 5680–5689).

Popham, W. J. (1997). What's Wrong – and What's Right – with Rubrics. *Educational Leadership*, *55*, 72–75.

Potash, P., Romanov, A., & Rumshisky, A. (2017). Here's My Point: Joint Pointer Architecture for Argument Mining. In *Proceedings of the Conference on Empirical Methods in Natural Language Processing (EMNLP)* (pp. 1364–1373). doi: `http://dx.doi.org/10.18653/v1/d17-1143`

Potthast, M., Hagen, M., Gollub, T., Tippmann, M., Kiesel, J., Rosso, P., … Stein, B. (2014). Overview of the 6th International Competition on Plagiarism Detection. In *Proceedings of the CLEF Conference on Multilingual and Multimodal Information Access Evaluation*.

Powers, D., Burstein, J., Chodorow, M., Fowles, M., & Kukich, K. (2001). Stumping E-Rater: Challenging the Validity of Automated Essay Scoring. *ETS Research Report Series*, *2001*(1), i–44. doi: `http://dx.doi.org/10.1002/j.2333-8504.2001.tb01845.x`

Pragglejaz, G. (2007). MIP: a Method for Identifying Metaphorically Used Words in Discourse. *Metaphor and Symbol*, *22*(1), 1–39.

Prasad, R., Dinesh, N., Lee, A., Miltsakaki, E., Robaldo, L., Joshi, A. K., & Webber, B. L. (2008). The Penn Discourse Treebank 2.0. In *Proceedings of the International Conference on Language Resources and Evaluation*. doi: `http://dx.doi.org/10.1007/978-94-024-0881-2_45`

Prince, E. (1981). Toward a Taxonomy of Given-New Information. In P. Cole (Ed.), *Radical Pragmatics* (pp. 223–255). Academic Press.

Qian, Y., Lange, P., & Evanini, K. (2020). Automatic Speech Recognition for Automated Speech Scoring. *Automated Speaking Assessment: Using Language Technologies to Score Spontaneous Speech*, 61–74. doi: `http://dx.doi.org/10.4324/9781315165103-4`

Qian, Y., Ubale, R., Mulholland, M., Evanini, K., & Wang, X. (2018). A Prompt-Aware Neural Network Approach to Content-Based Scoring of Non-Native Spontaneous Speech. In *Proceedings of the IEEE Spoken Language Technology Workshop (SLT)* (pp. 979–986). doi: `http://dx.doi.org/10.1109/slt.2018.8639697`

Quinlan, J. R. (1993). *C4.5: Programs for Machine Learning*. Morgan Kaufmann Publishers.

Radford, A., Wu, J., Child, R., Luan, D., Amodei, D., & Sutskever, I. (2019). Language Models are Unsupervised Multitask Learners. *Openai Blog*, *1*(8).

Rahimi, Z., Litman, D., Correnti, R., Wang, E., & Matsumura, L. C. (2017). Assessing Students' Use of Evidence and Organization in Response-to-Text Writing: Using Natural Language Processing for Rubric-Based Automated Scoring. *International Journal of Artificial Intelligence in Education*, *27*(4), 694–728. doi: `http://dx.doi.org/10.1007/s40593-017-0143-2`

Rahimi, Z., Litman, D., Wang, E., & Correnti, R. (2015). Incorporating Coherence of Topics as a Criterion in Automatic Response-to-Text Assessment of the Organization of Writing. In *Proceedings of the Workshop on Innovative Use of NLP for Building Educational Applications (BEA)* (pp. 20–30). doi: http://dx.doi.org/10.3115/v1/w15-0603

Rahimi, Z., Litman, D. J., Correnti, R., Matsumura, L. C., Wang, E., & Kisa, Z. (2014). Automatic Scoring of an Analytical Response-to-Text Assessment. In *12th International Conference on Intelligent Tutoring Systems-Volume 8474* (pp. 601–610). doi: http://dx.doi.org/10.1007/978-3-319-07221-0_76

Ramachandran, L., Cheng, J., & Foltz, P. (2015). Identifying Patterns for Short Answer Scoring Using Graph-Based Lexico-Semantic Text Matching. In *Proceedings of the Workshop on Innovative Use of NLP for Building Educational Applications* (pp. 97–106). doi: http://dx.doi.org/10.3115/v1/w15-0612

Ramineni, C., Trapani, C. S., & Williamson, D. M. (2015). Evaluation of E-Rater®for the Praxis I®Writing Test. *ETS Research Report Series, 2015*(1), 1–28.

Ramineni, C., & Williamson, D. (2018). Understanding Mean Score Differences Between the E-Rater® Automated Scoring Engine and Humans for Demographically Based Groups in the GRE® General Test. *ETS Research Report Series, 2018*(1), 1–31. doi: http://dx.doi.org/10.1002/ets2.12192

Ramineni, C., & Williamson, D. M. (2013). Automated Essay Scoring: Psychometric Guidelines and Practices. *Assessing Writing, 18*(1), 25–39. doi: http://dx.doi.org/10.1016/j.asw.2012.10.004

Ranalli, J., Link, S., & Chukharev-Hudilainen, E. (2017). Automated Writing Evaluation for Formative Assessment of Second Language Writing: Investigating the Accuracy and Usefulness of Feedback as Part of Argument-Based Validation. *Educational Psychology, 37*(1), 8-25. doi: http://dx.doi.org/10.1080/01443410.2015.1136407

Rao, G., Gong, Q., Zhang, B., & Xun, E. (2018). Overview of NLPTEA-2018 Share Task Chinese Grammatical Error Diagnosis. In *Proceedings of the Workshop on Natural Language Processing Techniques for Educational Applications* (pp. 42–51). doi: http://dx.doi.org/10.18653/v1/w18-3706

Rao, G., Zhang, B., Xun, E., & Lee, L.-H. (2017). IJCNLP-2017 Task 1: Chinese Grammatical Error Diagnosis. In *Proceedings of the IJCNLP 2017, Shared Tasks* (pp. 1–8).

Rao, S., & Tetreault, J. (2018). Dear Sir or Madam, May I Introduce the GYAFC Dataset: Corpus, Benchmarks and Metrics for Formality Style Transfer. In *Proceedings of the Conference of the North American Chapter of the Association for Computational Linguistics: Human Language*

Technologies (NAACL-HLT) (pp. 129–140). doi: http://dx.doi.org/10.18653/v1/n18-1012

Regneri, M., & King, D. (2016). Automated Discourse Analysis of Narrations by Adolescents with Autistic Spectrum Disorder. In *Proceedings of the Workshop on Cognitive Aspects of Computational Language Learning* (pp. 1–9). doi: http://dx.doi.org/10.18653/v1/w16-1901

Rei, M. (2017). Semi-Supervised Multitask Learning for Sequence Labeling. In *Proceedings of the Annual Meeting of the Association for Computational Linguistics (ACL)* (pp. 2121–2130). doi: http://dx.doi.org/10.18653/v1/p17-1194

Rei, M., & Cummins, R. (2016). Sentence Similarity Measures for Fine-Grained Estimation of Topical Relevance in Learner Essays. In *Proceedings of the Workshop on Innovative Use of NLP for Building Educational Applications (BEA)* (pp. 283–288). doi: http://dx.doi.org/10.18653/v1/w16-0533

Rei, M., Felice, M., Yuan, Z., & Briscoe, T. (2017). Artificial Error Generation with Machine Translation and Syntactic Patterns. In *Proceedings of the Workshop on Innovative Use of NLP for Building Educational Applications (BEA)* (pp. 287–292). doi: http://dx.doi.org/10.18653/v1/w17-5032

Rei, M., & Søgaard, A. (2019). Jointly Learning to Label Sentences and Tokens. In *Proceedings of the AAAI Conference on Artificial Intelligence* (Vol. 33, pp. 6916–6923). doi: http://dx.doi.org/10.1609/aaai.v33i01.33016916

Rei, M., & Yannakoudakis, H. (2016). Compositional Sequence Labeling Models for Error Detection in Learner Writing. In *Proceedings of the Annual Meeting of the Association for Computational Linguistics (ACL)* (pp. 1181–1191). doi: http://dx.doi.org/10.18653/v1/p16-1112

Rei, M., & Yannakoudakis, H. (2017). Auxiliary Objectives for Neural Error Detection Models. In *Proceedings of the Workshop on Innovative Use of NLP for Building Educational Applications (BEA)* (pp. 33–43). doi: http://dx.doi.org/10.18653/v1/w17-5004

Resnik, P., Garron, A., & Resnik, R. (2013). Using Topic Modeling to Improve Prediction of Neuroticism and Depression in College Students. In *Proceedings of the Conference on Empirical Methods in Natural Language Processing (EMNLP)* (pp. 1348–1353).

Reynaert, M. (2004). Text Induced Spelling Correction. In *Proceedings of the International Conference on Computational Linguistics (COLING)* (pp. 834–840). doi: http://dx.doi.org/10.3115/1220355.1220475

Ribeiro, M. T., Singh, S., & Guestrin, C. (2016). "Why Should I Trust You?": Explaining the Predictions of Any Classifier. In *Proceedings of the ACM SIGKDD International Conference on*

Knowledge Discovery and Data Mining (KDD) (pp. 1135–1144). doi: http://dx.doi.org/10.1145/2939672.2939778

Ribeiro, M. T., Singh, S., & Guestrin, C. (2018). Anchors: High-Precision Model-Agnostic Explanations. In *Proceedings of the AAAI Conference on Artificial Intelligence.*

Riegl, S., & Veale, T. (2018). Live, Die, Evaluate, Repeat: Do-Over Simulation in the Generation of Coherent Episodic Stories. In *Proceedings of the Ninth International Conference on Computational Creativity* (pp. 80–87).

Rinott, R., Dankin, L., Alzate Perez, C., Khapra, M. M., Aharoni, E., & Slonim, N. (2015). Show Me Your Evidence - an Automatic Method for Context Dependent Evidence Detection. In *Proceedings of the Conference on Empirical Methods in Natural Language Processing (EMNLP)* (pp. 440–450). doi: http://dx.doi.org/10.18653/v1/d15-1050

Riordan, B., Bichler, S., Bradford, A., King Chen, J., Wiley, K., Gerard, L., & C. Linn, M. (2020). An Empirical Investigation of Neural Methods for Content Scoring of Science Explanations. In *Proceedings of the Workshop on Innovative Use of NLP for Building Educational Applications (BEA)* (pp. 135–144). doi: http://dx.doi.org/10.18653/v1/2020.bea-1.13

Riordan, B., Flor, M., & Pugh, R. (2019). How to Account for Mispellings: Quantifying the Benefit of Character Representations in Neural Content Scoring Models. In *Proceedings of the Workshop on Innovative Use of NLP for Building Educational Applications (BEA)* (pp. 116–126). doi: http://dx.doi.org/10.18653/v1/w19-4411

Riordan, B., Horbach, A., Cahill, A., Zesch, T., & Lee, C. M. (2017). Investigating Neural Architectures for Short Answer Scoring. In *Proceedings of the Workshop on Innovative Use of NLP for Building Educational Applications (BEA)* (pp. 159–168). doi: http://dx.doi.org/10.18653/v1/w17-5017

Roark, B., Mitchell, M., Hosom, J.-P., Hollingshead, K., & Kaye, J. (2011). Spoken Language Derived Measures for Detecting Mild Cognitive Impairment. *IEEE Transactions on Audio, Speech, and Language Processing, 19*(7), 2081–2090. doi: http://dx.doi.org/10.1109/tasl.2011.2112351

Rock, J. L. (2007). THE IMPACT OF SHORT-TERM USE OF CRITERIONSM ON WRITING SKILLS IN NINTH GRADE. *ETS Research Report Series, 2007*(1), i–24. doi: http://dx.doi.org/10.1002/j.2333-8504.2007.tb02049.x

Roemmele, M., Mardo, P., & Gordon, A. (2017). Natural-Language Interactive Narratives in Imaginal Exposure Therapy for Obsessive-Compulsive Disorder. In *Proceedings of the Fourth Workshop on Computational Linguistics and Clinical Psychology — from Linguistic Signal to Clinical Reality* (pp. 48–57). doi: http://dx.doi.org/10.18653/v1/w17-3106

Romei, A., & Ruggieri, S. (n.d.). Discrimination Data Analysis: a Multi-Disciplinary Bibliography. In B. Custers, T. Calders, B. Schermer, & T. Zarsky (Eds.), *Discrimination and Privacy in the Information Society: Data Mining and Profiling in Large Databases* (pp. 109–135). doi: `http://dx.doi.org/10.1007/978-3-642-30487-3_6`

Romei, A., & Ruggieri, S. (2013). A Multidisciplinary Survey on Discrimination Analysis. *The Knowledge Engineering Review*, 1–57. doi: `http://dx.doi.org/10.1017/s0269888913000039`

Roscoe, R. D., & McNamara, D. S. (2013). Writing Pal: Feasibility of an Intelligent Writing Strategy Tutor in the High School Classroom. *Journal of Educational Psychology*, *105*(4), 1010. doi: `http://dx.doi.org/10.1037/a0032340`

Rosenblatt, F. (1957). *The Perceptron – a Perceiving and Recognizing Automaton*. Report 85-460-1, Cornell Aeronautical Laboratory.

Rosenblatt, F. (1958). The Perceptron: a Probabilistic Model for Information Storage and Organization in the Brain. *Psychological Review*, *65*(6), 386. doi: `http://dx.doi.org/10.1037/h0042519`

Rouhizadeh, M., Prud'hommeaux, E., Roark, B., & van Santen, J. (2013). Distributional Semantic Models for the Evaluation of Disordered Language. In *Proceedings of the Conference of the North American Chapter of the Association for Computational Linguistics: Human Language Technologies (NAACL-HLT)* (pp. 709–714).

Rozovskaya, A., Bouamor, H., Habash, N., Zaghouani, W., Obeid, O., & Mohit, B. (2015). The Second QALB Shared Task on Automatic Text Correction for Arabic. In *Proceedings of the Second Workshop on Arabic Natural Language Processing* (pp. 26–35). doi: `http://dx.doi.org/10.18653/v1/w15-3204`

Rozovskaya, A., & Roth, D. (2010a). Generating Confusion Sets for Context-Sensitive Error Correction. In *Proceedings of the Conference on Empirical Methods in Natural Language Processing (EMNLP)* (pp. 961–970).

Rozovskaya, A., & Roth, D. (2010b). Training Paradigms for Correcting Errors in Grammar and Usage. In *Proceedings of the Conference of the North American Chapter of the Association for Computational Linguistics: Human Language Technologies (NAACL-HLT)* (pp. 154–162).

Rozovskaya, A., & Roth, D. (2011). Algorithm Selection and Model Adaptation for ESL Correction Tasks. In *Proceedings of the Annual Meeting of the Association for Computational Linguistics: Human Language Technologies (ACL-HLT)* (pp. 924–933).

Rozovskaya, A., & Roth, D. (2016). Grammatical Error Correction: Machine Translation and Classifiers. In *Proceedings of the Annual Meeting of the Association for Computational Linguistics (ACL)* (pp. 2205–2215). doi: `http://dx.doi.org/10.18653/v1/p16-1208`

Rozovskaya, A., & Roth, D. (2019). Grammar Error Correction in Morphologically Rich Languages: the Case of Russian. *Transactions of the Association for Computational Linguistics*, 7, 1-17. doi: http://dx.doi.org/10.1162/tacl_a_00251

Rozovskaya, A., Roth, D., & Sammons, M. (2017). Adapting to Learner Errors with Minimal Supervision. *Computational Linguistics*, *43*(4), 723–760. doi: http://dx.doi.org/10.1162/coli_a_00299

Rozovskaya, A., Sammons, M., & Roth, D. (2012). The UI System in the HOO 2012 Shared Task on Error Correction. In *Proceedings of the Seventh Workshop on Building Educational Applications Using NLP* (pp. 272–280).

Rudin, C. (2019). Stop Explaining Black Box Machine Learning Models for High Stakes Decisions and Use Interpretable Models Instead. *Nature Machine Intelligence*, *1*(5), 206–215. doi: http://dx.doi.org/10.1038/s42256-019-0048-x

Rumelhart, D. E., Hinton, G. E., & Williams, R. J. (1986). Learning Representations by Back-Propagating Errors. *Nature*, *323*(6088), 533–536. doi: http://dx.doi.org/10.1038/323533a0

Rupp, A. A., Casabianca, J. M., Krüger, M., Keller, S., & Köller, O. (2019). Automated Essay Scoring At Scale: a Case Study in Switzerland and Germany. *ETS Research Report Series*, *2019*(1), 1-23. doi: http://dx.doi.org/10.1002/ets2.12249

Ryan, M. (2011). Improving Reflective Writing in Higher Education: a Social Semiotic Perspective. *Teaching in Higher Education*, *16*(1), 99–111. doi: http://dx.doi.org/10.1080/13562517.2010.507311

Saal, F. E., Downey, R. G., & Lahey, M. A. (1980). Rating the Ratings: Assessing the Psychometric Quality of Rating Data. *Psychological Bulletin*, *88*(2), 413. doi: http://dx.doi.org/10.1037/0033-2909.88.2.413

Saha, S., Dhamecha, T. I., Marvaniya, S., Sindhgatta, R., & Sengupta, B. (2018). Sentence Level or Token Level Features for Automatic Short Answer Grading?: Use Both. In *Proceedings of the International Conference on Artificial Intelligence in Education* (pp. 503–517). doi: http://dx.doi.org/10.1007/978-3-319-93843-1_37

Sainath, T. N., Mohamed, A.-r., Kingsbury, B., & Ramabhadran, B. (2013). Deep Convolutional Neural Networks for LVCSR. In *Proceedings of the IEEE International Conference on Acoustics, Speech and Signal Processing (ICASSP)* (pp. 8614–8618). doi: http://dx.doi.org/10.1109/icassp.2013.6639347

Sakaguchi, K., Heilman, M., & Madnani, N. (2015). Effective Feature Integration for Automated Short Answer Scoring. In *Proceeding of the Annual Conference of the North American*

Chapter of the Association for Computational Linguistics: Human Language Technologies (HLT-NAACL) (pp. 1049–1054). doi: http://dx.doi.org/10.3115/v1/n15-1111

Sakai, S., Togasaki, M., & Yamazaki, K. (2003). A Note on Greedy Algorithms for the Maximum Weighted Independent Set Problem. *Discrete Applied Mathematics*, *126*(2-3), 313–322. doi: http://dx.doi.org/10.1016/s0166-218x(02)00205-6

Samuel, A. L. (1959). Some Studies in Machine Learning Using the Game of Checkers. *IBM Journal of Research and Development*, *3*(3), 210-229. doi: http://dx.doi.org/10.1147/rd.33.0210

Saon, G., Kurata, G., Sercu, T., Audhkhasi, K., Thomas, S., Dimitriadis, D., ... others (2017). English Conversational Telephone Speech Recognition by Humans and Machines. *Arxiv Preprint Arxiv:1703.02136*. doi: http://dx.doi.org/10.21437/interspeech.2017-405

Sap, M., Card, D., Gabriel, S., Choi, Y., & Smith, N. A. (2019). The Risk of Racial Bias in Hate Speech Detection. In *Proceedings of the Annual Meeting of the Association for Computational Linguistics (ACL)* (pp. 1668–1678). doi: http://dx.doi.org/10.18653/v1/p19-1163

Scarselli, F., Gori, M., Tsoi, A. C., Hagenbuchner, M., & Monfardini, G. (2008). The Graph Neural Network Model. *IEEE Transactions on Neural Networks*, *20*(1), 61–80. doi: http://dx.doi.org/10.1109/tnn.2008.2005605

Schmaltz, A., Kim, Y., Rush, A. M., & Shieber, S. (2016). Sentence-Level Grammatical Error Identification as Sequence-to-Sequence Correction. In *Proceedings of the Workshop on Innovative Use of NLP for Building Educational Applications (BEA)* (pp. 242–251). doi: http://dx.doi.org/10.18653/v1/w16-0528

Schneider, D., & McCoy, K. F. (1998). Recognizing Syntactic Errors in the Writing of Second Language Learners. In *Proceedings of the Annual Meeting of the Association for Computational Linguistics and the International Conference on Computational Linguistics (ACL-COLING)* (pp. 1198–1204). doi: http://dx.doi.org/10.3115/980432.980765

Shen, A., Salehi, B., Baldwin, T., & Qi, J. (2019). A Joint Model for Multimodal Document Quality Assessment. In *Proceedings of the ACM/IEEE Joint Conference on Digital Libraries (JCDL)* (pp. 107–110). doi: http://dx.doi.org/10.1109/jcdl.2019.00024

Shermis, M. (2014). The Challenges of Emulating Human Behavior in Writing Assessment. *Assessing Writing*, *22*, 91–99. doi: http://dx.doi.org/10.1016/j.asw.2014.07.002

Shermis, M. (2015). Contrasting State-of-the-Art in the Machine Scoring of Short-Form Constructed Responses. *Educational Assessment*, *20*(1), 46-65. doi: http://dx.doi.org/10.1080/10627197.2015.997617

Shermis, M., Burstein, J., & Apel Bursky, S. (2013). Introduction to Automated Essay Evaluation. In M. Shermis & J. Burstein (Eds.), *Handbook for Automated Essay Evaluation.* New York: Taylor. doi: `http://dx.doi.org/10.4324/9780203122761.ch1`

Shermis, M., Garvan, C., & Diao, Y. (2008). The Impact of Automated Essay Scoring on Writing Outcomes. *Online Submission, ERIC.*

Shiue, Y.-T., Huang, H.-H., & Chen, H.-H. (2017). Detection of Chinese Word Usage Errors for Non-Native Chinese Learners with Bidirectional LSTM. In *Proceedings of the Annual Meeting of the Association for Computational Linguistics (ACL)* (pp. 404–410). doi: `http://dx.doi.org/10.18653/v1/p17-2064`

Simpson, E. H. (1949). Measurement of Diversity. *Nature, 163,* 168. doi: `http://dx.doi.org/10.1038/163688a0`

Sinharay, S., Zhang, M., & Deane, P. (2019). Prediction of Essay Scores from Writing Process and Product Features Using Data Mining Methods. *Applied Measurement in Education, 32*(2), 116-137. doi: `http://dx.doi.org/10.1080/08957347.2019.1577245`

Slack, D., Hilgard, S., Jia, E., Singh, S., & Lakkaraju, H. (2020). Nothing to See Here: Hiding Model Biases by Fooling Post-Hoc Explanation Methods. In *AAAI/ACM Conference on Artificial Intelligence, Ethics, and Society (AIES).*

Sladoljev-Agejev, T., & Šnajder, J. (2017). Using Analytic Scoring Rubrics in the Automatic Assessment of College-Level Summary Writing Tasks in L2. In *Proceedings of the Eighth International Joint Conference on Natural Language Processing (Volume 2: Short Papers)* (pp. 181–186).

Šnajder, J., Sladoljev-Agejev, T., & Kolić Vehovec, S. (2019). Analysing Rhetorical Structure as a Key Feature of Summary Coherence. In *Proceedings of the Workshop on Innovative Use of NLP for Building Educational Applications (BEA)* (pp. 46–51). doi: `http://dx.doi.org/10.18653/v1/w19-4405`

Sobel, L., Beckman, M., Jiang, D., & Perelman, L. (2014). *BABEL Generator.* `http://babel-generator.herokuapp.com`.

Socher, R., Perelygin, A., Wu, J., Chuang, J., Manning, C. D., Ng, A., & Potts, C. (2013). Recursive Deep Models for Semantic Compositionality Over a Sentiment Treebank. In *Proceedings of the Conference on Empirical Methods in Natural Language Processing (EMNLP)* (pp. 1631–1642).

Somasundaran, S., Burstein, J., & Chodorow, M. (2014). Lexical Chaining for Measuring Discourse Coherence Quality in Test-Taker Essays. In *Proceedings of COLING 2014, the 25th International Conference on Computational Linguistics: Technical Papers* (pp. 950–961).

Somasundaran, S., Flor, M., Chodorow, M., Molloy, H., Gyawali, B., & McCulla, L. (2018). Towards Evaluating Narrative Quality in Student Writing. *Transactions of the Association for Computational Linguistics*, *6*, 91-106. doi: http://dx.doi.org/10.1162/tacl_a_00007

Somasundaran, S., Lee, C. M., Chodorow, M., & Wang, X. (2015). Automated Scoring of Picture-Based Story Narration. In *Proceedings of the Workshop on Innovative Use of NLP for Building Educational Applications (BEA)* (pp. 42–48). doi: http://dx.doi.org/10.3115/v1/w15-0605

Somasundaran, S., Riordan, B., Gyawali, B., & Yoon, S.-Y. (2016). Evaluating Argumentative and Narrative Essays Using Graphs. In *Proceedings of the International Conference on Computational Linguistics (COLING)* (pp. 1568–1578).

Song, W., Liu, T., Fu, R., Liu, L., Wang, H., & Liu, T. (2016). Learning to Identify Sentence Parallelism in Student Essays. In *Proceedings of the International Conference on Computational Linguistics (COLING)* (pp. 794–803).

Song, W., Wang, D., Fu, R., Liu, L., Liu, T., & Hu, G. (2017). Discourse Mode Identification in Essays. In *Proceedings of the Annual Meeting of the Association for Computational Linguistics (ACL)* (pp. 112–122). doi: http://dx.doi.org/10.18653/v1/p17-1011

Song, Y., Deane, P., & Beigman Klebanov, B. (2017). *Toward the Automated Scoring of Written Arguments: Developing an Innovative Approach to Annotation* (Vol. 17-11; Tech. Rep.). Educational Testing Service. doi: http://dx.doi.org/10.1002/ets2.12138

Song, Y., & Ferretti, R. (2013). Teaching Critical Questions About Argumentation through the Revising Process: Effects of Strategy Instruction on College Students' Argumentative Essays. *Reading and Writing*, *26*(1), 67–90. doi: http://dx.doi.org/10.1007/s11145-012-9381-8

Song, Y., Heilman, M., Beigman Klebanov, B., & Deane, P. (2014). Applying Argumentation Schemes for Essay Scoring. In *Proceedings of the First Workshop on Argumentation Mining* (pp. 69–78). doi: http://dx.doi.org/10.3115/v1/w14-2110

Soricut, R., & Marcu, D. (2006). Discourse Generation Using Utility-Trained Coherence Models. In *Proceedings of the COLING/ACL 2006 Main Conference Poster Sessions* (pp. 803–810). doi: http://dx.doi.org/10.3115/1273073.1273176

Speicher, T., Heidari, H., Grgic-Hlaca, N., Gummadi, K. P., Singla, A., Weller, A., & Zafar, M. B. (2018). A Unified Approach to Quantifying Algorithmic Unfairness: Measuring Individual & Group Unfairness Via Inequality Indices. In *Proceedings of the ACM SIGKDD International Conference on Knowledge Discovery & Data Mining (KDD)* (pp. 2239–2248). doi: http://dx.doi.org/10.1145/3219819.3220046

Srihari, S., Collins, J., Srihari, R., Srinivasan, H., Shetty, S., & Brutt-Griffler, J. (2008). Automatic Scoring of Short Handwritten Essays in Reading Comprehension Tests. *Artificial Intelligence*, *172*(2-3), 300–324. doi: http://dx.doi.org/10.1016/j.artint.2007.06.005

Stab, C., & Gurevych, I. (2014). Annotating Argument Components and Relations in Persuasive Essays. In *Proceedings of the International Conference on Computational Linguistics (COLING)* (pp. 1501–1510).

Stab, C., & Gurevych, I. (2016). Recognizing the Absence of Opposing Arguments in Persuasive Essays. In *Proceedings of the Third Workshop on Argument Mining (Argmining2016)* (pp. 113–118). doi: http://dx.doi.org/10.18653/v1/w16-2813

Stab, C., & Gurevych, I. (2017a). Parsing Argumentation Structures in Persuasive Essays. *Computational Linguistics*, *43*(3), 619–659. doi: http://dx.doi.org/10.1162/coli_a_00295

Stab, C., & Gurevych, I. (2017b). Recognizing Insufficiently Supported Arguments in Argumentative Essays. In *Proceedings of the Conference of the European Chapter of the Association for Computational Linguistics (EACL)* (pp. 980–990). doi: http://dx.doi.org/10.18653/v1/e17-1092

Stamatatos, E. (2009). A Survey of Modern Authorship Attribution Methods. *Journal of the American Society for Information Science and Technology*, *60*(3), 538–556. doi: http://dx.doi.org/10.1002/asi.21001

Stonebraker, M., Çetintemel, U., & Zdonik, S. (2005). The 8 Requirements of Real-Time Stream Processing. *SIGMOD Rec.*, *34*(4), 42–47. doi: http://dx.doi.org/10.1145/1107499.1107504

Strubell, E., Ganesh, A., & McCallum, A. (2019). Energy and Policy Considerations for Deep Learning in NLP. In *Proceedings of the Annual Meeting of the Association for Computational Linguistics (ACL)* (pp. 3645–3650). doi: http://dx.doi.org/10.18653/v1/p19-1355

Stymne, S., Pettersson, E., Megyesi, B., & Palmér, A. (2017). Annotating Errors in Student Texts: First Experiences and Experiments. In *Proceedings of the Joint 6th NLP4CALL and 2nd NLP4LA Nodalida Workshop* (pp. 47–60).

Sukkarieh, J. Z., Mohammad-Djafari, A., Bercher, J.-F., & Bessiére, P. (2011). Using a Maxent Classifier for the Automatic Content Scoring of Free-Text Responses. In *Proceedings of the Conference on American Institute of Physics* (Vol. 1305, p. 41). doi: http://dx.doi.org/10.1063/1.3573647

Sun, T., Gaut, A., Tang, S., Huang, Y., ElSherief, M., Zhao, J., ... Wang, W. Y. (2019). Mitigating Gender Bias in Natural Language Processing: Literature Review. In *Proceedings of the Annual Meeting of the Association for Computational Linguistics (ACL)* (pp. 1630–1640). doi: http://dx.doi.org/10.18653/v1/p19-1159

Surowiecki, J. (2005). *The Wisdom of Crowds*. New York: Anchor.

Sweeney, C., & Najafian, M. (2019). A Transparent Framework for Evaluating Unintended Demographic Bias in Word Embeddings. In *Proceedings of the Annual Meeting of the Association for Computational Linguistics (ACL)* (pp. 1662–1667). doi: http://dx.doi.org/10.18653/v1/p19-1162

Szegedy, C., Ioffe, S., Vanhoucke, V., & Alemi, A. (2016). Inception-V4, Inception-Resnet and the Impact of Residual Connections on Learning. *Arxiv Preprint Arxiv:1602.07261*.

Szegedy, C., Vanhoucke, V., Ioffe, S., Shlens, J., & Wojna, Z. (2016). Rethinking the Inception Architecture for Computer Vision. In *Proceedings of the IEEE Conference on Computer Vision and Pattern Recognition* (pp. 2818–2826). doi: http://dx.doi.org/10.1109/cvpr.2016.308

Taghipour, K., & Ng, H. T. (2016). A Neural Approach to Automated Essay Scoring. In *Proceedings of the Conference on Empirical Methods in Natural Language Processing (EMNLP)* (pp. 1882–1891). doi: http://dx.doi.org/10.18653/v1/d16-1193

Tajiri, T., Komachi, M., & Matsumoto, Y. (2012). Tense and Aspect Error Correction for ESL Learners Using Global Context. In *Proceedings of the Annual Meeting of the Association for Computational Linguistics (ACL)* (pp. 198–202).

Tan, J., Wan, X., Liu, H., & Xiao, J. (2018). Quoterec: Toward Quote Recommendation for Writing. *ACM Trans. Inf. Syst.*, *36*(3). doi: http://dx.doi.org/10.1145/3183370

Tao, J., Chen, L., & Lee, C. M. (2016). DNN Online with Ivectors Acoustic Modeling and Doc2Vec Distributed Representations for Improving Automated Speech Scoring. In *Proceedings of Interspeech* (pp. 3117–3121). doi: http://dx.doi.org/10.21437/interspeech.2016-1457

Tarp, S., Fisker, K., & Sepstrup, P. (2017). L2 Writing Assistants and Context-Aware Dictionaries: New Challenges to Lexicography. *Lexikos*, *27*(1), 494–521. doi: http://dx.doi.org/10.5788/27-1-1412

Tausczik, Y. R., & Pennebaker, J. W. (2010). The Psychological Meaning of Words: LIWC and Computerized Text Analysis Methods. *Journal of Language and Social Psychology*, *29*(1), 24-54. doi: http://dx.doi.org/10.1177/0261927x09351676

Tay, Y., Phan, M. C., Tuan, L. A., & Hui, S. C. (2018). Skipflow: Incorporating Neural Coherence Features for End-to-End Automatic Text Scoring. In *Proceedings of the Thirty-Second AAAI Conference on Artificial Intelligence*.

Tetreault, J. R., & Chodorow, M. (2008). The Ups and Downs of Preposition Error Detection in ESL Writing. In *Proceedings of the International Conference on Computational Linguistics (COLING)* (pp. 865–872). doi: http://dx.doi.org/10.3115/1599081.1599190

Tetreault, J. R., & Chodorow, M. (2009). Examining the Use of Region Web Counts for ESL Error Detection. In *Web as Corpus Workshop (WAC5)* (p. 71).

Thibodeau, P., & Boroditsky, L. (2011). Metaphors We Think with: the Role of Metaphor in Reasoning. *Plos ONE*, *6*(2), e16782. doi: http://dx.doi.org/10.1371/journal.pone.0016782

Tibshirani, R. (1996). Regression Shrinkage and Selection Via the Lasso. *Journal of the Royal Statistical Society: Series B (Methodological)*, *58*(1), 267–288. doi: http://dx.doi.org/10.1111/j.2517-6161.1996.tb02080.x

Tien Nguyen, D., & Joty, S. (2017). A Neural Local Coherence Model. In *Proceedings of the Annual Meeting of the Association for Computational Linguistics (ACL)* (pp. 1320–1330). doi: http://dx.doi.org/10.18653/v1/p17-1121

Toulmin, S. E. (2003). *The Uses of Argument: Updated Edition*. Cambridge University Press.

Tsai, C.-T., Chen, J.-J., Yang, C.-Y., & Chang, J. S. (2020). Lingglewrite: a Coaching System for Essay Writing. In *Proceedings of the Annual Meeting of the Association for Computational Linguistics (ACL)* (pp. 127–133). doi: http://dx.doi.org/10.18653/v1/2020.acl-demos.17

Turner, J., & Charniak, E. (2007). Language Modeling for Determiner Selection. In *Proceedings of the Conference of the North American Chapter of the Association for Computational Linguistics: Human Language Technologies (NAACL-HLT)* (pp. 177–180). doi: http://dx.doi.org/10.3115/1614108.1614153

Ullmann, T. (2019). Automated Analysis of Reflection in Writing: Validating Machine Learning Approaches. *International Journal of Artificial Intelligence in Education*, *29*(2), 217–257. doi: http://dx.doi.org/10.1007/s40593-019-00174-2

Uto, M., & Okano, M. (2020). Robust Neural Automated Essay Scoring Using Item Response Theory. In *Proceedings of the International Conference on Artificial Intelligence in Education (AIED)* (pp. 549–561). doi: http://dx.doi.org/10.1007/978-3-030-52237-7_44

Uto, M., & Ueno, M. (2018). Item Response Theory Without Restriction of Equal Iinterval Scale for Rater'S Score. In *Proceedings of the International Conference on Artificial Intelligence in Education (AIED)* (pp. 363–368).

Veale, T. (2018). A Massive Sarcastic Robot: What a Great Idea! Two Approaches to the Computational Generation of Irony. In *Proceedings of the Ninth International Conference on Computational Creativity*.

Veale, T., Chen, H., & Li, G. (2017). I Read the News Today, Oh Boy - Making Metaphors Topical, Timely and Humorously Personal. In N. Streitz & P. Markopoulos (Eds.), *Proceedings of the International Conference on Distributed, Ambient and Pervasive Interactions* (pp. 696–709). doi: http://dx.doi.org/10.1007/978-3-319-58697-7_52

Veale, T., Shutova, E., & Beigman Klebanov, B. (2016). Metaphor: a Computational Perspective. *Synthesis Lectures on Human Language Technologies*, *9*(1), 1–160. doi: http://dx.doi.org/10.2200/s00694ed1v01y201601hlt031

Villalón, J., Kearney, P., Calvo, R. A., & Reimann, P. (2008). Glosser: Enhanced Feedback for Student Writing Tasks. In *Proceedings of the Eighth IEEE International Conference on Advanced Learning Technologies* (pp. 454–458). doi: http://dx.doi.org/10.1109/icalt.2008.78

Vincze, V., Zsibrita, J., Durst, P., & Szabó, M. K. (2014). Automatic Error Detection Concerning the Definite and Indefinite Conjugation in the Hunlearner Corpus.

Vinyals, O., Fortunato, M., & Jaitly, N. (2015). Pointer Networks. In C. Cortes, N. Lawrence, D. Lee, M. Sugiyama, & R. Garnett (Eds.), *Advances in Neural Information Processing Systems* (Vol. 28).

von Davier, A. (n.d.). *Fairness Concerns in Computational Psychometrics*. Presented at the panel on Fairness and Machine Learning for Educational Practice, Annual Meeting of the National Council on Measurement in Education, Washington DC.

Wachsmuth, H., Da San Martino, G., Kiesel, D., & Stein, B. (2017). The Impact of Modeling Overall Argumentation with Tree Kernels. In *Proceedings of the Conference on Empirical Methods in Natural Language Processing (EMNLP)* (pp. 2379–2389). doi: http://dx.doi.org/10.18653/v1/d17-1253

Wade-Stein, D., & Kintsch, E. (2004). Summary Street: Interactive Computer Support for Writing. *Cognition and Instruction*, *22*(3), 333–362. doi: http://dx.doi.org/10.1207/s1532690xci2203_3

Wagner, J., Foster, J., & van Genabith, J. (2007). A Comparative Evaluation of Deep and Shallow Approaches to the Automatic Detection of Common Grammatical Errors. In *Proceedings of the Joint Conference on Empirical Methods in Natural Language Processing and Computational Natural Language Learning (EMNLP-Conll)* (pp. 112–121).

Walchuk, K. (2016). *An Examination of the Efficacy of the Plagiarism Detection Software Program Turnitin* (Unpublished master's thesis). University of Ontario Institute of Technology.

Walton, D. (1992). *The Place of Emotion in Argument.* University Park, PA: the Pennsylvania State University Press.

Walton, D. (1996). *Argumentation Schemes for Presumptive Reasoning.* Mahwah, NJ: Lawrence Erlbaum. doi: http://dx.doi.org/10.4324/9780203811160

Walton, D., & Macagno, F. (2015). A Classification System for Argumentation Schemes. *Argument & Computation*, *6*(3), 219–245. doi: http://dx.doi.org/10.1080/19462166.2015.1123772

Wambsganss, T., Niklaus, C., Cetto, M., Söllner, M., Handschuh, S., & Leimeister, J. M. (2020). AL: an Adaptive Learning Support System for Argumentation Skills. In *Proceedings of the Conference on Human Factors in Computing Systems (CHI)* (pp. 1–14). doi: http://dx.doi.org/10.1145/3313831.3376732

Wang, A., Singh, A., Michael, J., Hill, F., Levy, O., & Bowman, S. (2018). GLUE: a Multi-Task Benchmark and Analysis Platform for Natural Language Understanding. , 353–355. doi: http://dx.doi.org/10.18653/v1/w18-5446

Wang, E. L., Matsumura, L. C., Correnti, R., Litman, D., Zhang, H., Howe, E., … Quintana, R. (2020). Erevis(Ing): Students' Revision of Text Evidence Use in an Automated Writing Evaluation System. *Assessing Writing*, *44*, 100449. doi: http://dx.doi.org/10.1016/j.asw.2020.100449

Wang, T., Inoue, N., Ouchi, H., Mizumoto, T., & Inui, K. (2019). Inject Rubrics Into Short Answer Grading System. In *Proceedings of the Workshop on Deep Learning Approaches for Low-Resource NLP* (pp. 175–182). doi: http://dx.doi.org/10.18653/v1/d19-6119

Wang, T., & Wan, X. (2019). Hierarchical Attention Networks for Sentence Ordering. In *Proceedings of the AAAI Conference on Artificial Intelligence* (Vol. 33, pp. 7184–7191). doi: http://dx.doi.org/10.1609/aaai.v33i01.33017184

Wang, X., Bruno, J., Molloy, H., Evanini, K., & Zechner, K. (2017). Discourse Annotation of Non-Native Spontaneous Spoken Responses Using the Rhetorical Structure Theory Framework. In *Proceedings of the Annual Meeting of the Association for Computational Linguistics (ACL)* (pp. 263–268). doi: http://dx.doi.org/10.18653/v1/p17-2041

Wang, X., & Evanini, K. (2020). Features Measuring Content and Discourse Coherence. *Automated Speaking Assessment: Using Language Technologies to Score Spontaneous Speech*, 138–156. doi: http://dx.doi.org/10.4324/9781315165103-9

Wang, X., Evanini, K., Mulholland, M., Qian, Y., & Bruno, J. V. (2019). Application of an Automatic Plagiarism Detection System in a Large-Scale Assessment of English Speaking Proficiency. In *Proceedings of the Workshop on Innovative Use of NLP for Building Educational Applications (BEA)* (pp. 435–443). doi: http://dx.doi.org/10.18653/v1/w19-4445

Wang, X., Evanini, K., & Zechner, K. (2013). Coherence Modeling for the Automated Assessment of Spontaneous Spoken Responses. In *Proceedings of the Conference of the North American Chapter of the Association for Computational Linguistics: Human Language Technologies (NAACL-HLT)* (pp. 814–819).

Wang, X., Evanini, K., Zechner, K., & Mulholland, M. (2017). Modeling Discourse Coherence for the Automated Scoring of Spontaneous Spoken Responses. In *Proceedings of the Speech and Language Technology in Education (Slate)* (pp. 132–137). doi: `http://dx.doi.org/10.21437/slate.2017-23`

Wang, X., Gyawali, B., Bruno, J. V., Molloy, H. R., Evanini, K., & Zechner, K. (2019). Using Rhetorical Structure Theory to Assess Discourse Coherence for Non-Native Spontaneous Speech. In *Proceedings of the Workshop on Discourse Relation Parsing and Treebanking 2019* (pp. 153–162). doi: `http://dx.doi.org/10.18653/v1/w19-2719`

Wang, X., Yoon, S.-Y., Evanini, K., Zechner, K., & Qian, Y. (2019). Automatic Detection of Off-Topic Spoken Responses Using Very Deep Convolutional Neural Networks. In *Proceedings of Interspeech* (pp. 4200–4204). doi: `http://dx.doi.org/10.21437/interspeech.2019-1848`

Wang, Y., Wang, Y., Liu, J., & Liu, Z. (2020). A Comprehensive Survey of Grammar Error Correction. *Arxiv Preprint Arxiv:2005.06600*.

Wang, Y., Wei, Z., Zhou, Y., & Huang, X. (2018). Automatic Essay Scoring Incorporating Rating Schema Via Reinforcement Learning. In *Proceedings of the Conference on Empirical Methods in Natural Language Processing (EMNLP)* (pp. 791–797). doi: `http://dx.doi.org/10.18653/v1/d18-1090`

Wang, Y., & Zhao, H. (2015). A Light Rule-Based Approach to English Subject-Verb Agreement Errors on the Third Person Singular Forms. In *Proceedings of the Pacific Asia Conference on Language, Information and Computation (PACLIC)* (pp. 345–353).

Wang, Z., & von Davier, A. (2014). Monitoring of Scoring Using the E-Rater® Automated Scoring System and Human Raters on a Writing Test. *ETS Research Report Series, 2014*(1), 1–21. doi: `http://dx.doi.org/10.1002/ets2.12005`

Wang, Z., Zechner, K., & Sun, Y. (2016). Monitoring the Performance of Human and Automated Scores for Spoken Responses. *Language Testing*, 1-20. doi: `http://dx.doi.org/10.1177/0265532216679451`

Wanner, L., Verlinde, S., & Alonso Ramos, M. (2013). Writing Assistants and Automatic Lexical Error Correction: Word Combinatorics. *Electronic Lexicography in the 21st Century: Thinking Outside the Paper.*, 472–487.

Warstadt, A., Singh, A., & Bowman, S. R. (2019). Neural Network Acceptability Judgments. *Transactions of the Association for Computational Linguistics*, 7, 625-641. doi: `http://dx.doi.org/10.1162/tacl_a_00290`

Weber, N., Balasubramanian, N., & Chambers, N. (2018). Event Representations with Tensor-Based Compositions. In *Proceedings of the Thirty-Second AAAI Conference on Artificial Intelligence.*

Weiss, Z., & Meurers, D. (2019). Analyzing Linguistic Complexity and Accuracy in Academic Language Development of German Across Elementary and Secondary School. In *Proceedings of the Workshop on Innovative Use of NLP for Building Educational Applications (BEA)* (pp. 380–393). doi: `http://dx.doi.org/10.18653/v1/w19-4440`

Wilcox-O'Hearn, A., Hirst, G., & Budanitsky, A. (2008). Real-Word Spelling Correction with Trigrams: a Reconsideration of the Mays, Damerau, and Mercer Model. In *International Conference on Intelligent Text Processing and Computational Linguistics* (pp. 605–616). doi: `http://dx.doi.org/10.1007/978-3-540-78135-6_52`

Williams, R. J., & Zipser, D. (1989). A Learning Algorithm for Continually Running Fully Recurrent Neural Networks. *Neural Computation*, 1(2), 270-280. doi: `http://dx.doi.org/10.1162/neco.1989.1.2.270`

Williamson, D. M., Xi, X., & Breyer, F. J. (2012). A Framework for Evaluation and Use of Automated Scoring. *Educational Measurement: Issues and Practice*, 31(1), 2–13. doi: `http://dx.doi.org/10.1111/j.1745-3992.2011.00223.x`

Wilson, J. (2017, 01). Associated Effects of Automated Essay Evaluation Software on Growth in Writing Quality for Students with and Without Disabilities. *Reading and Writing*, 30(4), 691–718. doi: `http://dx.doi.org/10.1007/s11145-016-9695-z`

Wilson, J., & Czik, A. (2016). Automated Essay Evaluation Software in English Language Arts Classrooms: Effects on Teacher Feedback, Student Motivation, and Writing Quality. *Computers & Education*, 100(94-109). doi: `http://dx.doi.org/10.1016/j.compedu.2016.05.004`

Wilson, J., & Roscoe, R. (2020). Automated Writing Evaluation and Feedback: Multiple Metrics of Efficacy. *Journal of Educational Computing Research*, 58(1), 87-125. doi: `http://dx.doi.org/10.1177/0735633119830764`

Wilson, T., Wiebe, J., & Hoffmann, P. (2005). Recognizing Contextual Polarity in Phrase-Level Sentiment Analysis. In *Proceedings of the Conference on Human Language Technology and Empirical Methods in Natural Language Processing* (pp. 347–354). doi: `http://dx.doi.org/10.3115/1220575.1220619`

Wolpert, D. H. (1992). Stacked Generalization. *Neural Networks*, *5*, 241–259. doi: `http://dx.doi.org/10.1016/s0893-6080(05)80023-1`

Wu, Y., & Ng, H. T. (2013). Grammatical Error Correction Using Integer Linear Programming. In *Proceedings of the Annual Meeting of the Association for Computational Linguistics (ACL)* (pp. 1456–1465).

Xia, M., Kochmar, E., & Briscoe, T. (2019). Automatic Learner Summary Assessment for Reading Comprehension. In *Proceedings of the Conference of the North American Chapter of the Association for Computational Linguistics: Human Language Technologies (NAACL-HLT)* (pp. 2532–2542). doi: `http://dx.doi.org/10.18653/v1/n19-1261`

Xie, S., Evanini, K., & Zechner, K. (2012). Exploring Content Features for Automated Speech Scoring. In *Proceedings of the Conference of the North American Chapter of the Association for Computational Linguistics: Human Language Technologies (NAACL-HLT)* (pp. 103–111).

Xiong, W., Droppo, J., Huang, X., Seide, F., Seltzer, M. L., Stolcke, A., … Zweig, G. (2017). Toward Human Parity in Conversational Speech Recognition. *IEEE/ACM Transactions on Audio, Speech, and Language Processing*, *25*(12), 2410–2423. doi: `http://dx.doi.org/10.1109/taslp.2017.2756440`

Yan, D., & Bridgeman, B. (2020). Validation of Automated Scoring Systems. In *Handbook of Automated Scoring: Theory Into Practice* (pp. 297–318). Taylor & Francis Group. doi: `http://dx.doi.org/10.1201/9781351264808-16`

Yang, P., Sun, X., Li, W., & Ma, S. (2018). Automatic Academic Paper Rating Based on Modularized Hierarchical Convolutional Neural Network. In *Proceedings of the Annual Meeting of the Association for Computational Linguistics (ACL)* (pp. 496–502). doi: `http://dx.doi.org/10.18653/v1/p18-2079`

Yang, Q., Passonneau, R., & De Melo, G. (2016). PEAK: Pyramid Evaluation Via Automated Knowledge Extraction. In *Proceedings of the Thirtieth AAAI Conference on Artificial Intelligence*.

Yannakoudakis, H., & Briscoe, T. (2012). Modeling Coherence in ESOL Learner Texts. In *Proceedings of the Seventh Workshop on Building Educational Applications Using NLP* (p. 33–43).

Yannakoudakis, H., Briscoe, T., & Medlock, B. (2011). A New Dataset and Method for Automatically Grading ESOL Texts. In *Proceedings of the Annual Meeting of the Association for Computational Linguistics (ACL)* (p. 180–189).

Yannakoudakis, H., Øistein E Andersen, Geranpayeh, A., Briscoe, T., & Nicholls, D. (2018). Developing an Automated Writing Placement System for ESL Learners. *Applied Measurement in Education*, *31*(3), 251-267. doi: `http://dx.doi.org/10.1080/08957347.2018.1464447`

Yao, L., Haberman, S. J., & Zhang, M. (2019). Penalized Best Linear Prediction of True Test Scores. *Psychometrika*, *84*(1), 186–211. doi: http://dx.doi.org/10.1007/s11336-018-9636-7

Yenaeng, S., Saelee, S., & Samai, W. (2014). Automatic Medical Case Study Essay Scoring by Support Vector Machine and Genetic Algorithms. *International Journal of Information and Education Technology*, *4*(2), 132. doi: http://dx.doi.org/10.7763/ijiet.2014.v4.384

Yeung, C. Y., & Lee, J. (2015). Automatic Detection of Sentence Fragments. In *Proceedings of the Annual Meeting of the Association for Computational Linguistics and the International Joint Conference on Natural Language Processing (ACL-IJCNLP)* (pp. 599–603). doi: http://dx.doi.org/10.3115/v1/p15-2099

Yi, X., Gao, J., & Dolan, W. B. (2008). A Web-Based English Proofing System for English as a Second Language Users. In *Proceedings of the Third International Joint Conference on Natural Language Processing: Volume-II.*

Yim, W.-w., Mills, A., Chun, H., Hashiguchi, T., Yew, J., & Lu, B. (2019). Automatic Rubric-Based Content Grading for Clinical Notes. In *Proceedings of the Tenth International Workshop on Health Text Mining and Information Analysis* (pp. 126–135). doi: http://dx.doi.org/10.18653/v1/d19-6216

Yin, Y., Song, L., Su, J., Zeng, J., Zhou, C., & Luo, J. (2019). Graph-Based Neural Sentence Ordering. In *Proceedings of the International Joint Conference on Artificial Intelligence (IJCAI)* (pp. 5387–5393). doi: http://dx.doi.org/10.24963/ijcai.2019/748

Yoon, S.-Y., Cahill, A., Loukina, A., Zechner, K., Riordan, B., & Madnani, N. (2018). Atypical Inputs in Educational Applications. In *Proceedings of the Conference of the North American Chapter of the Association for Computational Linguistics: Human Language Technologies (NAACL-HLT)* (pp. 60–67). doi: http://dx.doi.org/10.18653/v1/n18-3008

Yoon, S.-Y., Lu, X., & Zechner, K. (2020). Features Measuring Vocabulary and Grammar. , 123–137. doi: http://dx.doi.org/10.4324/9781315165103-8

Yuan, Z., & Felice, M. (2013). Constrained Grammatical Error Correction Using Statistical Machine Translation. In *Proceedings of the Seventeenth Conference on Computational Natural Language Learning: Shared Task* (pp. 52–61).

Zechner, K. (2009). What Did They Actually Say? Agreement and Disagreement Among Transcribers of Non-Native Spontaneous Speech Responses in an English Proficiency Test. In *Proceedings of the International Workshop on Speech and Language Technology in Education (Slate)* (p. 25-28).

Zechner, K., & Evanini, K. (Eds.). (2020). *Automated Speaking Assessment: Using Language Technologies to Score Spontaneous Speech*. Routledge.

Zechner, K., Higgins, D., Xi, X., & Williamson, D. M. (2009). Automatic Scoring of Non-Native Spontaneous Speech in Tests of Spoken English. *Speech Communication*, *51*(10), 883–895. doi: http://dx.doi.org/10.1016/j.specom.2009.04.009

Zemel, R. S., Wu, Y., Swersky, K., Pitassi, T., & Dwork, C. (2013). Learning Fair Representations. In *Proceedings of ICML* (pp. 325–333). doi: http://dx.doi.org/10.1145/3442381.3450015

Zesch, T., Heilman, M., & Cahill, A. (2015). Reducing Annotation Efforts in Supervised Short Answer Scoring. In *Proceedings of the Workshop on Innovative Use of NLP for Building Educational Applications* (pp. 124–132). doi: http://dx.doi.org/10.3115/v1/w15-0615

Zesch, T., Wojatzki, M., & Scholten-Akoun, D. (2015). Task-Independent Features for Automated Essay Grading. In *Proceedings of the Workshop on Innovative Use of NLP for Building Educational Applications (BEA)* (pp. 224–232). doi: http://dx.doi.org/10.3115/v1/w15-0626

Zhang, F., Hwa, R., Litman, D., & Hashemi, H. B. (2016). Argrewrite: a Web-Based Revision Assistant for Argumentative Writings. In *Proceedings of the Conference of the North American Chapter of the Association for Computational Linguistics: Human Language Technologies (NAACL-HLT)* (pp. 37–41). doi: http://dx.doi.org/10.18653/v1/n16-3008

Zhang, H., & Litman, D. (2017). Word Embedding for Response-to-Text Assessment of Evidence. In *Proceedings of the 55th Annual Meeting of the Association for Computational Linguistics: Student Research Workshop* (pp. 75–81). doi: http://dx.doi.org/10.18653/v1/p17-3013

Zhang, H., & Litman, D. (2018). Co-Attention Based Neural Network for Source-Dependent Essay Scoring. In *Proceedings of the Workshop on Innovative Use of NLP for Building Educational Applications (BEA)* (pp. 399–409). doi: http://dx.doi.org/10.18653/v1/w18-0549

Zhang, J., & Bareinboim, E. (2018). Fairness in Decision-Making – the Causal Explanation Formula. In *Thirty-Second AAAI Conference on Artificial Intelligence*.

Zhang, M., Breyer, F. J., & Lorenz, F. (2013). Investigating the Suitability of Implementing the E-Rater®Scoring Engine in a Large-Scale English Language Testing Program. *ETS Research Report Series*, *2013*(2), i–60.

Zhang, M., Chen, J., & Ruan, C. (2016). Evaluating the Advisory Flags and Machine Scoring Difficulty in the E-Rater®Automated Scoring Engine. *ETS Research Report Series*, *2016*(2), 1–14.

Zhang, M., Dorans, N. J., Li, C., & Rupp, A. A. (2017). Differential Feature Functioning in Automated Essay Scoring. In H. Jiao & R. Lissitz (Eds.), *Test Fairness in the New Generation of Large-Scale Assessment.*

Zhang, Y., & Clark, S. (2011). Syntactic Processing Using the Generalized Perceptron and Beam Search. *Computational Linguistics*, *37*(1), 105–151. doi: `http://dx.doi.org/10.1162/coli_a_00037`

Zhu, M., Liu, O. L., Mao, L., & Pallant, A. (2016). Use of Automated Scoring and Feedback in Online Interactive Earth Science Tasks. In *Proceedings of the IEEE Integrated STEM Education Conference.* doi: `http://dx.doi.org/10.1109/isecon.2016.7457538`

Zieky, M. J. (2016). Fairness in Test Design and Development. In N. J. Dorans & L. L. Cook (Eds.), *Fairness in Educational Assessment and Measurement* (pp. 9–32). Routledge.

Zipf, G. (1936). *The Psychobiology of Language.* London: Routledge. doi: `http://dx.doi.org/10.4324/9781315009421`

Zou, H., & Hastie, T. (2005). Regularization and Variable Selection Via the Elastic Net. *Journal of the Royal Statistical Society: Series B (Statistical Methodology)*, *67*(2), 301–320. doi: `http://dx.doi.org/10.1111/j.1467-9868.2005.00503.x`

Authors' Biographies

BEATA BEIGMAN KLEBANOV

Beata Beigman Klebanov is a Senior Research Scientist at Educational Testing Service, Princeton, NJ. She specializes in development of language technology for education in the subfields of reading and writing. She has led projects on developing automated methods for assessing quality of arguments, topic development, use of figurative language, as well as worked on methods for estimating text complexity and predicting the rate of oral reading of a given text. She has also worked on the effect of noise in language data on the performance of statistical models, as well as on characteristics of class vs test performance. She is the principal investigator behind Relay Reader™—innovative technology to support development of reading fluency.

Dr. Beigman Klebanov's research appeared in leading journals, such as *Computational Linguistics*, *Transactions of the ACL*, *ACM Transactions on Speech and Language Processing*, *Journal of AI in Education*, *Language Testing*, *Journal of Educational Psychology*, as well as in proceedings of top-tier conferences such as Association for Computational Linguistics' annual meetings (*ACL*), Learning Analytics and Knowledge conferences (*LAK*), and the annual meetings of the National Council on Measurement in Education (*NCME*). She has co-organized a series of ACL workshops and shared tasks on processing of metaphor and other types of figurative language. Beata is currently serving as an action editor for the *Transactions of the ACL* journal and has served as an area chair or senior area chair for the NAACL/ACL conferences in 2019–2022.

NITIN MADNANI

Nitin Madnani is a Distinguished Research Engineer in the AI Research Labs at the Educational Testing Service (ETS) in Princeton. His NLP adventures began with an elective course on computational linguistics he took while studying computer architecture at the University of Maryland, College Park. As a Ph.D. student at the *Institute of Advanced Computer Studies (UMIACS)*, he worked on automated document summarization, statistical machine translation, and paraphrase generation. After earning his Ph.D. in 2010, he joined the NLP & Speech research group at ETS where he led—and continues to lead—a wide variety of projects that use NLP to build useful educational applications and technologies. Examples include mining Wikipedia revision history to correct grammatical errors, automatically detecting organizational elements in argumentative discourse, creating a service-based, polyglot framework for implementing robust, high-performance automated scoring & feedback systems, and building the first-ever, fully open-source, comprehensive evaluation toolkit for automated scoring.

Dr. Madnani's work has appeared in leading journals such as *Computational Linguistics*, *Transactions of the ACL*, *ACM Transactions on Speech and Language Processing*, *ACM Transactions on Intelligent Systems and Technology*, *Machine Translation*, *Journal of Writing Analytics*, and the *Journal of Open Source Software*. His research has also appeared in the proceedings of top-tier conferences such as *Association for Computational Linguistics'* annual meeting series (*ACL*, *NAACL*, *EACL*, *EMNLP*), *Learning Analytics and Knowledge*, *Learning @ Scale*, and the annual meetings of the *American Educational Research Association (AERA)* and the *National Council on Measurement in Education* (NCME). Nitin is currently serving as an action editor for the *Transactions of the ACL (TACL)* journal, an executive board member of the *ACL Special Interest Group on Building Educational Applications (SIGEDU)*, and the Chief Information Officer for ACL. He has served as senior area chair, area chair, or a member of the organizing committee for the NAACL/ACL/EMNLP series of conferences since 2017.

Printed in the United States
by Baker & Taylor Publisher Services